THOMAS MORE

THOMAS MORE

by

R. W. CHAMBERS

ANN ARBOR PAPERBACKS
THE UNIVERSITY OF MICHIGAN PRESS

Fifth printing 1973
First edition as an Ann Arbor Paperback 1958
All rights reserved
ISBN 0-472-06018-x
Reprinted by special arrangement with Jonathan Cape, Ltd.
Published in the United States of America by
The University of Michigan Press
Manufactured in the United States of America

TO

J. E. NEALE AND C. H. WILLIAMS

CONTENTS

PREFACE

My thanks are due to Messrs. Sheed and Ward for permitting me to repeat some paragraphs which I contributed to a small volume published by them in 1929, on 'The Fame of Sir Thomas More'; and to the British Academy for allowing me to use portions of a lecture which I delivered on 5 November, 1926. I have also included in this book the substance of an unprinted lecture which I first delivered in 1902 in University College, arguing the complete consistency of More's life and death. More's early biographers brooded for twenty or thirty years before writing the life of their hero; and in this, at least, I have striven to imitate them.

During these thirty-three years the task of every biographer of More has been lightened in many ways. The magnificent edition of the letters of Erasmus, upon which, when the first volume appeared in 1906, Dr. P. S. Allen had been already labouring for thirteen years, 'under the gloom of Indian summers and in high valleys in Cashmere', is now nearing completion under the care of Mrs. Allen. Professor A. F. Pollard has provided, in his *Life of Wolsey*, a background indispensable to every biographer of More. Dr. E. V. Hitchcock has toiled to supply correct texts of those early lives of More upon which all later biographies must be based. I have had the advantage of using the proofs of her 'Roper', and the manuscript of her forthcoming edition of the Life by 'Ro. Ba.' Dr. Hitchcock has read my proofs and made the Index. More himself knew the labour of 'sorting out and placing principal matters' contained in a book. I also thank my colleagues, Mrs. F. Blackman, Dr. E. C. Batho, and Miss H. W. Husbands for reading the proofs and for helpful criticisms.

It is a pleasure to express gratitude for the encouragement which my work on More has received, from its earliest stages, at the hands of Prof. A. F. Pollard, and to remember the many acts of kindness I have received from him and his. I owe much also to the encouragement of two younger scholars who are helping to carry on the great historical tradition which Prof. Pollard has established in London. To them this book is in friendship dedicated.

R. W. CHAMBERS

UNIVERSITY COLLEGE
LONDON
6 February 1935

I have made some small corrections and additions at the suggestion of friends — Prof. P. Geyl, Prof. G. R. Potter, and Dr. G. G. Coulton, all of whom I wish to thank.
6 July 1936

THOMAS MORE

PROLOGUE: THE SOURCES

§ I. CONCERNING PROLOGUES

WHEN Fielding prefixed to each of the eighteen books of *Tom Jones* a prefatory, or, as he called it, a 'prolegomenous' chapter, he claimed to have conferred upon the reader the same benefit that a prologue confers upon the playgoer. Since no one is obliged either to see the prologue, or to read the prolegomenous chapter, the playgoer has a quarter of an hour longer allowed him to sit at dinner, and the reader has the advantage of beginning to read each book of *Tom Jones* at the fourth or fifth page instead of the first.

Nevertheless, I trust that the gentle reader will not skip this chapter, and begin More's life on page 48. To tell the life of Thomas More is no easy task. Erasmus said that he was not competent to portray More's many-sided character; and where that subtle, mighty intellect felt abashed, a modern biographer may well fear to tread.

By a brief survey of the path, before we begin to tread it, reader and writer may alike be helped.

In a few weeks, throughout the English-speaking world and beyond it, those of the faith for which he suffered will be commemorating the four hundredth anniversary of the death of St. Thomas More. To them, the meaning of More's life and death is clear. What is the meaning of More's life and death to those who are not of that fold?

This book attempts to answer the question, and to depict More not only as a martyr (which he was) but also as a great European statesman; More's far-sighted outlook was neglected amid the selfish despotisms of his age; yet his words, his acts, and his sufferings were consistently, throughout life, based upon principles which have survived him. More was killed, but these principles must, in the end, triumph. If they do not, the civilization of Europe is doomed.

The great English historians who have dealt with More

have maintained the very opposite of this. They have reverenced the heroism of his death and the beauty of his home life,
but have almost always denied the consistency of his political
thinking. Yet from the verdict of Froude and Acton and
Creighton and Lindsay and Sidney Lee (not to mention living
historians) an appeal can be made to the writings of More himself and to the records of those who knew him.

This Prologue aims at giving an account of those records,
and weighing their biographical value.

§ 2. THOMAS MORE AND SOCRATES

More's first formal biographer, Nicholas Harpsfield, described his hero as 'our noble new Christian Socrates'. The
parallel is obvious. Three years after More's death, Reginald
Pole, the future Cardinal-Archbishop, had drawn the comparison; it is three years since one of our leading classical
scholars spoke of Socrates as 'the man of all men in ancient
times likest More in disposition, as in destiny'.[1] And those who,
in the years between, have emphasized one or other point of
resemblance between More and Socrates, are too many to
record here.

But one vital difference there is, which makes the compiling
of a life of More the less impossible task. More, unlike Socrates,
was a writer, and though some important things have been
lost, there still remains to us a great mass of his works. An
elaborate life of More could be put together, even though we
had nothing to guide us save the words he has written.

Our second source of information about More comes from
the fact that people who knew him felt, as those felt who knew
Socrates, or as those felt who knew St. Francis of Assisi, that
they must record what they could remember of the words and
acts and character of their hero. Socrates and More were
friends of the young; and the young passed on the story of their
friend. Here again much has been lost; accident and neglect
have combined to destroy the remembrances of the one young
man who probably entered most closely into More's life and
thoughts. Nevertheless, so much remains that a life of More

---

[1] J. A. K. THOMSON, *Erasmus in England*; *Bibliothek Warburg*, *Vorträge*,
1930-1, p. 79.

could be written, if we had no writings of his own, but merely the recollections of his friends.

Possessing both kinds of information, we should be able to get very near the truth. We have only to study the life of St. Francis of Assisi to realize how vital to our understanding of a man may be the survival of anything, however short, which is beyond dispute written by him. The writings of St. Francis, though they fill only a few pages, offer a criterion by which we can judge the rather conflicting accounts which his friends and their disciples have left behind. What a flash of insight into the saint's mind is given by the brief *Canticle of Brother Sun*. And when the writings are so abundant and so intimate as are those of More, the help afforded is proportionately great. Over and over again we are able to compare something which a friend has remembered with some words which More himself has written; and we are startled at the light which the two records throw upon each other.

And it is here that the contrast between More and Socrates is most marked. Whilst we cannot be sure to what extent the ideas of his *Republic* were ever put forward by the historic Socrates, *Utopia* is More's own. We may doubt how much of the *Apology*, as Plato gives it to us, was ever really spoken by Socrates before his judges; but in the *Apology of Sir Thomas More* the Englishman gives us his own thoughts on the matters nearest to his heart. Persons present at More's trial have left reports of what he said to his judges. We can compare these reports with the actual words written by More during his long imprisonment – words which were unknown to many, and probably to all of these persons, at least at the time they made their reports. More's own words, written in the Tower, agree so closely with the accounts of his speech before his judges that there can be no doubt as to the truth of those accounts.

The most remarkable parallel between More and Socrates, both in its resemblance and in its difference, is that between the *Crito* of Plato, and the dialogue between More and his daughter, in which More, like Socrates, gives the reasons why he may not avoid death. Every reader of the *Crito* must have wondered how much the historic Socrates really spoke of the marvellous argument which opens in the prison at Athens just upon the dawn of the second day before his death; we may even doubt if Crito did really come to Socrates with the announcement that the preparations for stealing him out of prison had been made. But in the dialogue between More and his daughter we have something almost without parallel in literature. Their debate was written down immediately after it took place, by one or other of them – perhaps by both in collaboration. We have from his own mouth the reasons why More would not save his life, as he could have done, by a few words.

Our material for the life of More is therefore peculiarly weighty and peculiarly certain. Yet historians are perplexed as to the meaning and the consistency of his life. They debate the first and deny the second. Here, before we leave that puzzling subject for the moment, to resume it from time to time as our tale proceeds, we may note that a partial explanation (though only a very partial one) lies in a characteristic common to More and to Socrates – their irony.

More and Socrates are two of the greatest masters of irony who ever lived. (Small wonder that both were admired by that great ironist Jonathan Swift, a man not given to excessive admiration.) More had a habit of uttering his deepest convictions in a humorous way, and his wildest jokes with a solemn countenance. That was the *festivitas* which his friends noted as his most marked characteristic. He gives his own account of it when he makes a friend say to him, 'Ye use to look so sadly when ye mean merrily, that many times men doubt whether ye speak in sport, when ye mean good earnest.'[1]

From this common characteristic comes the likeness in the last words recorded as having been spoken by these two men. Both had been discoursing earnestly with their friends of the things that really mattered – Socrates talking in his prison, More writing and speaking in prison, and speaking on the scaffold. Then, having settled these problems, they took leave of this world without any excessive solemnity. Socrates (accused of impiety towards the old gods) had drunk the hemlock, and his face had been covered up. But he drew the covering aside to make a last, conventionally pious, request: 'Crito, we owe a cock to Aesculapius; pay it, and neglect it not.' It was

[1] *Works*, 1557, p. 127.

in vain that Crito and the rest waited for something more illuminating. Socrates would say no more.

More (accused of treason) 'laying his head upon the block, bade the executioner stay until he had removed aside his beard, saying that *that* had never committed any treason'.[1] Thus, says the unsympathetic contemporary chronicler, More ended his life with a mock. It was not seemly, some of More's fellow Englishmen thought, that a wise man should mingle his wit, and even his death, with so much 'taunting and mocking', as they, rather stupidly, called it. Much in the same way did his slower-witted contemporaries find themselves puzzled by Socrates. And, great as is our advantage in possessing so much of More's written work, that work may sometimes mislead us, unless we are on the look out for his ever-present irony.

§ 3. MORE'S WRITINGS

The most important guide to the man who would write a life of More is to be found in the letters written to and by him, in Latin or in English. These number about two hundred – the exact figure will vary according to our conception of what constitutes a letter. The Latin collection begins with a few precious epistles from or to his learned friends, which give us a picture of the young scholar at the very beginning of the Sixteenth Century.[2] Later, but probably before More was thirty, his first extant English letter was written: the dedication of his *Life of John Picus* to Joyeuce Leigh, a Poor Clare of the House of the Minoresses at Aldgate, sister of his friend Edward Leigh or Lee, afterwards Archbishop of York. During and after his first mission to Bruges – the embassy with which the opening pages of *Utopia* are connected – More's epistles first begin to survive in some bulk. We have English letters to Henry VIII, Wolsey, and Cromwell, on business of state, and Latin letters to foreign scholars, especially to Erasmus. Finally we have the group of twelve English letters and one Latin letter, written by More to his friends when he was prisoner in the

[1] CRESACRE MORE, 1726, p. 275; cf. HALL's *Chronicle*, ed. WHIBLEY, II, 266.
[2] In translating More's Latin letters I use quite modern English, often colloquial English; the reader will find no difficulty in distinguishing them from More's English letters. More's correspondence with Erasmus is all, of course, in Latin; Erasmus had no literary command of any modern language.

Tower; these have all the more value because they were
evidently written with no idea that they would be printed, or
read save among a very small band of friends.

Though, all his life, More wrote fluently both in Latin and
English, the Latin works are more bulky during his early and
middle life. The great mass of his English work was written
during his last seven years.

More's Latin Epigrams were printed when he was about
forty; but we gather from Erasmus that many of them had been
written when he was a young man.[1] We can learn a great deal
from them about More as a young enthusiast for letters.
Utopia gives us a much deeper insight. Something can be
gleaned from the early translations from Lucian, and a little
even from the Latin controversy with Luther, in which More
showed his extraordinary power of 'calling bad names in good
Latin'.

The English works have very largely been preserved to us
by the pious care of William Rastell, More's sister's son, who,
of all those young people who had not actually dwelt in More's
house, shared his thoughts most deeply. Of the voluminous
works in English prose composed by More and printed during
his lifetime, William Rastell had printed all, amounting
approximately to a million words.[2] More's resignation of the
Chancellorship did not put any stop either to his own work as
an author or his nephew's work as a printer; but four months
after that resignation William Rastell secured a second string
to his bow; he was specially admitted at Lincoln's Inn, More's
own Inn. For more than a year the controversy with heretics
went on busily, with More as author and Rastell as printer, and
Rastell also found time for important law printing. But the task
of printer was growing perilous, and Rastell definitely abandoned typography for law, about the time that his uncle was
imprisoned in the Tower. Yet Rastell did not abandon his
interest in his uncle's books. Better days might come. The

---

[1] Cf. STAPLETON, I, p. 158.

[2] More's short story in verse, *How a sergeaunt wolde lerne to be a frere*, was printed
by Julian Notary about 1516; and the translation of the *Life of John Picus, Earl
of Mirandola*, printed by William's father, John Rastell, was apparently pirated by
W. de Worde (REED, *Early Tudor Drama*, p. 8). Otherwise, William Rastell
seems to have had a monopoly as printer of More's English works during More's
lifetime.

account of his stewardship which he subsequently gave to Queen
Mary, begins rather breathlessly:

> When I considered with myself, most gracious sovereign,
> what great eloquence, excellent learning, and moral virtues
> were and be contained in the works and books that the wise
> and godly man, Sir Thos. More, Kt., sometime Lord Chan-
> cellor of England, (my dear uncle) wrote in the English
> tongue, so many and so well as no one Englishman (I sup-
> pose) ever wrote the like; whereby his works be worthy to
> be had and read of every Englishman that is studious or
> desirous to know and learn not only the eloquence and
> property of the English tongue, but also the true doctrine
> of Christ's Catholic Faith –

To cut Rastell's eloquence to his 'gracious liege lady' short, he
'further considered' how his uncle's works, being either un-
published or published only in odd volumes, might 'in time
percase perish and utterly vanish away, to the great loss and
detriment of many'. So he collected as many of More's letters
and books, printed and unprinted, in the English tongue, as he
could come by,

> and the same (certain years in the evil world past, keeping
> in my hands very surely and safely) now lately have caused
> to be imprinted in this one volume . . . finished the last day of
> April 1557.

This magnificent folio (which will be quoted below from
time to time as *Works*, 1557) preserves to us a great deal which
we should otherwise have lost. Firstly, a number of English
poems written by More when a youth; then a correct text of
the *History of Richard III* from a copy in More's own handwriting (for the version which had found its way into the
Chronicles printed by Grafton was, as Rastell complained,
'corrupt and altered in words and whole sentences'); then the
fragmentary treatise on the *Four Last Things*. The controversial
works against the heretics have survived in Rastell's fine first
editions, printed by him when his uncle wrote them. Yet even
here, those who do not find the body of controversy printed at
the time sufficient for their needs, may turn to the volume of
1557 for a fragmentary Ninth Book of the *Confutation of Tyndale*,
which had never been before in print. But it is when we come

to that portion of all More's writings which (together with
Utopia) is most important to us who would try to understand
him, that our debt to William Rastell passes all measure. He
preserved the books and letters written by his uncle in the
Tower. It is true that, even without Rastell, some of these might
have come down to us. For example, the book on the blank
spaces of which More wrote prayers in prison has survived;
it is now in the possession of the Earl of Denbigh. But just after
More's death it was a dangerous thing to have any of his books
in keeping, if they were unprinted, and if they touched in any
way upon the King's matters. And everything that More wrote
in the Tower, by implication (sometimes by very obvious
implication), did touch upon the King's matters. His daughter
Margaret was called before the Council to answer the charge of
keeping unprinted papers of her father, and of meaning to set
them in print, and also of keeping his head as a relic. She
answered that she had saved her father's head from being food
for fishes, in order to bury it, and that she had hardly any
unprinted papers of her father's, except some intimate letters —
and these she begged to be allowed to keep for her consolation.
Even in those evil days, women were treated less harshly than
men. The letters were preserved, and Margaret Roper returned
home, either at once or after a short imprisonment.[1] But the
dangerous documents were pretty evidently handed over to
William Rastell, and in time taken abroad by him. For our
knowledge of More as a Catholic martyr we are therefore,
above everything else, indebted to Margaret Roper and to
William Rastell.

We have, then, an abundant supply of More's own writing.
Yet this very wealth of material is in itself a difficulty. That
difficulty is only a particular form of the problem which beset
the study of sixteenth-century English history generally; our
greatest living student of the period has written: 'The materials
for sixteenth-century history are so vast that no one can hope to
master them all in the allotted span of human life.'[2]

Coming even to so comparatively small and specialized a

---

[1] STAPLETON, XX, p. 359; CRESACRE MORE, 1726, p. 281. Stapleton does not
mention any imprisonment; Cresacre More does.
[2] A. F. POLLARD, *Cranmer*, p. v.

section as the writings of More, the difficulty is that none of us can know them all equally well, or read them all with equal sympathy. A great Socialist has concentrated upon *Utopia*, and can see in the devotional works of More's last days nothing but 'fanatical' and 'ecstatic' writings, which 'for us, have only a pathological interest'.[1] Others, in contemplating the figure of More the martyr, dismiss *Utopia* too lightly, as if it were merely a happy fantasy written by More for the amusement of his fellow humanists. Yet surely the whole meaning of More's life lies in the fact that the martyr is also the happy scholar who wrote *Utopia* when the sound of joy was in the air. We may call *Utopia* a fantasy; but a man may be known by his fantasies as well as by his more solemn utterances. In estimating More's character, *Utopia* has to be taken into account in a different way from the *Treatise upon the Passion*. But neither can be neglected. And, of the two books, *Utopia* has, so far, had an influence upon the world which is beyond measure greater. Written in the universal language, Latin, *Utopia* had been translated, within twenty years of More's death, into German, Italian, French, and Dutch; the British Museum collection, very incomplete as it is, possesses eighty-four editions and translations. On the other hand, although More's devotional works are coming every day to have a wider and wider circulation, the fact remains that the *Treatise upon the Passion* was printed for the first time in 1557 and has never yet been reprinted.

More's biographers can be classified by observing the portions of his work to which they instinctively turn to illustrate his character.

§ 4. *LETTERS AND PAPERS*

But before passing to the biographers of More, mention must be made of the series of summaries of documents known as the *Letters and Papers, Foreign and Domestic, of the Reign of Henry VIII*[2] published by the Record Office, under the editorship, first of Mr. Brewer, and then of Dr. James Gairdner. For the life of anybody who lived during that reign, these extra-

---

[1] KARL KAUTSKY, *Thomas More*, 1890, p. 156.

[2] Quoted below as *L.P.* They must be distinguished from the *State Papers of Henry VIII*, published 1830-52. These *State Papers* were select documents printed in full; *L.P.* are summaries.

ordinary collections are of the first importance. They 'constitute the most magnificent body of materials for the history of any reign, ancient or modern, English or foreign'.[1] When Mr. Brewer was editor, he prefaced these volumes with introductions which were elaborate histories of the period covered by the documents. Dr. Gairdner was instructed to keep his prefaces within more moderate limits. But his *Lollardy and the Reformation* gives the result of a patient investigation extending over more than fifty years. No biographer of More, not even Roper or Harpsfield or Stapleton or Bridgett, has shown a deeper devotion to the memory of More than Dr. James Gairdner.

§5. MORE'S BIOGRAPHERS

The first two biographies of More were written during his lifetime. *Utopia* had excited curiosity as to its author among foreign scholars, and Erasmus wrote to Ulrich von Hutten an account of the life and character of his friend. At the time of writing (1519) Erasmus had known More for twenty years. This account was printed in the same year. It is so intimate that we might have expected More to dislike its publication; but he does not seem to have done so. This very intimacy renders it of extraordinary value to us.

The second brief biography is the epitaph written by More himself for the tomb in Chelsea Church where his bones were not destined to rest. It has the same value that, for example, an entry in *Who's Who* might have for a modern biographer; it shows at any rate what the writer thought were the things about himself which the public might know.

§6. WILLIAM ROPER

Roper's *Life of More* gives us, in some seventy octavo pages, what is probably the most perfect little biography in the English language. How Roper came to write it he has himself explained:

> For as much as Sir Thomas More, Knight, sometime Lord Chancellor of England, a man of singular virtue and of a clear unspotted conscience, as witnesseth Erasmus, more pure

[1] A. F. POLLARD, *Henry VIII*, p. vii.

and white than the whitest snow, and of such an angelical wit as England, he saith, never had the like before nor never shall again, universally, as well in the laws of our own Realm (a study in effect able to occupy the whole life of a man) as in all other sciences right well studied, was in his days accounted a man worthy perpetual famous memory: I, William Roper, though most unworthy, his son-in-law by marriage of his eldest daughter, knowing, at this day, no one man living that of him and his doings understood so much as myself, for that I was continually resident in his house by the space of sixteen years and more, thought it therefore my part to set forth such matters touching his life as I could at this present call to remembrance; amongst which things, very many notable things not meet to have been forgotten, through negligence and long continuance of time are slipped out of my mind.

The historical value of Roper's work has been somewhat overestimated; its value as a work of art has been enormously underrated. People have forgotten that it was written some twenty years after the latest of the events which it records, and that of many of these events Roper was not himself an eye-witness. Roper's dialogues are so cleverly worded that his characters live as do those of Shakespeare. More's wife, Dame Alice, is not less vivid than Mistress Quickly, and indeed uses the same expletives – *Tilly vally, What the good year*. According to Roper, Mistress Alice obtained licence to visit her husband after he had been some time prisoner in the Tower, and 'bluntly saluted him' thus:

'What the good year, Master More,' quoth she, 'I marvel that you, that have been always hitherto taken for so wise a man, will now so play the fool to lie here in this close filthy prison, and be content thus to be shut up amongst mice and rats, when you might be abroad at your liberty, and with the favour and goodwill both of the King and his Council, if you would but do as all the bishops and best learned of this realm have done. And seeing you have at Chelsea a right fair house, your library, your books, your gallery, your garden, your orchard, and all other necessaries so handsome about you, where you might in the company of me your wife, your children, and household, be merry, I muse what a God's name you mean here still thus fondly to tarry.'

After he had a while quietly heard her, with a cheerful

countenance he said unto her: 'I pray thee, good Mistress Alice, tell me one thing.'

'What is that?' quoth she.

'Is not this house,' quoth he, 'as nigh heaven as mine own?'

To whom she, after her accustomed homely fashion, not liking such talk, answered, 'Tilly vally, Tilly vally.'

'How say you, Mistress Alice,' quoth he, 'is it not so?'

'Bone deus, Bone deus, man, will this gear never be left?' quoth she.

'Well then, Mistress Alice, if it be so,' quoth he, 'it is very well: for I see no great cause why I should much joy, either of my gay house or of anything belonging thereunto, when, if I should but seven years lie buried under the ground, and then arise and come thither again, I should not fail to find some therein that would bid me get me out of doors, and tell me it were none of mine. What cause have I then to like such an house, as would so soon forget his master?'[1]

Now, why do surveys of English literature not think dialogue like this worth notice? Probably because it is dismissed as historical, as something which has nothing to do with the literature of the imagination. Yet surely it is highly imaginative. I do not mean that the interview did not take place; Roper's word proves that it did. But, in the days of Henry VIII, the Tower was not furnished with that 'King's Lugg' within which Sir Walter Scott (in *The Fortunes of Nigel*) represents King James I as hiding, in order to overhear the conversations of prisoners. Whatever James might do, Roper could not, by permission of the Lieutenant, lurk unseen to take notes of the interview between Sir Thomas More and his lady. Roper must presumably have written his account of that interview from memories of the very confused narrative which Mistress Alice brought home with her, more than twenty years before, to the sad house at Chelsea. Now, let anyone try to put down on paper a conversation reported to him, at second hand, twenty years ago, by a woman too worried and too angry to know what she was saying. Further, it would be a grave injustice to Mistress Alice to suppose the conversation to be verbatim. *She* was not the woman, after so brave an opening, to have tamely

---

[1] ROPER, pp. 82-4.

allowed her batteries to be silenced. But Roper had lived in the same house as his step-mother-in-law 'for sixteen years and more'. The dialogue has its origin, as Wordsworth held that good imaginative writing should have, in emotion recollected in tranquillity.

After More's death there was trouble between Dame Alice and Roper. Dame Alice even accused Roper of having 'gotten away part of her living'.[1] They came at last to an agreement, and we need not suspect malice in Roper's picture of Lady More. More's own writings confirm the picture in every detail. If Roper had learnt how to imitate his mother-in-law, I suspect he learnt it from his father-in-law. Anyway, in More's writings we meet with a certain anonymous lady who is very unmistakably Dame Alice. For example, when More is writing his devotional works in prison, he gives us scraps of the conversation of a certain great lady who, of her charity, visits a certain poor prisoner:

> Whom she found in a chamber (to say the truth) meetly fair, and at the leastwise it was strong enough; but with mats of straw the prisoner had made it so warm, both under the foot and round about the walls, that in these things for the keeping of his health, she was on his behalf glad and very well comforted. But among many other displeasures that for his sake she was sorry for, one she lamented much in her mind, that he should have the chamber door upon him by night made fast by the jailer, that should shut him in. 'For by my troth,' quoth she, 'if the door should be shut upon me, I would ween it would stop up my breath.' At that word of hers the prisoner laughed in his mind (but he durst not laugh aloud, nor say nothing to her, for somewhat indeed he stood in awe of her, and had his finding there, much part, of her charity for alms). But he could not but laugh inwardly. Why, he wist well enough, that she used on the inside to shut every night full surely her own chamber to her, both door and windows too, and used not to open them of all the long night.[2]

The prisoner, we may note, had his maintenance, his 'finding', of her charity. In a letter to Cromwell, Dame Alice tells of the

---

[1] Depositions in Chancery, C. 24/52, Roper v. Royden; Pleadings in Chancery, C. 3. 153/1. I owe these references to Prof. C. J. Sisson.
[2] *Works,* 1557, p. 1247.

sums she has every week to pay 'for the board-wages of my poor
husband and his servant; for the maintaining whereof I have
been compelled, of very necessity, to sell part of mine apparel,
for lack of other substance to make money of'.[1]

Roper's picture, then, is confirmed by More's own words, in
a way which enforces the importance of More's writings both
as a check upon his earlier biographers, and as a source for his
later ones. This source was scarcely used by Roper, who found
sufficient materials for his little book in his own knowledge.
Yet, intimate as this knowledge was, Roper depicts himself as
holding rather aloof, not quite understanding the man whose
memory he later grew to revere. Perhaps this is why, although
he draws More as without a fault, he never arouses that dislike
which we usually cherish towards the faultless, and those who
ask us to revere them. Roper disarms us, by the innocent
humility with which he unconsciously shows his own character.
Before the trouble over the King's marriage began, Roper
congratulated More on England having so Catholic a prince as
Henry, and subjects all in one faith agreeing together. All this
More admitted, yet he foretold evil to come. Roper protested.
More stuck to his prophecy, but would not give his reasons
(probably he was not free to give his reasons, even to Roper).
Roper, not unnaturally, got flurried and annoyed, and at last
turned on his father-in-law:

> I said, 'By my troth, Sir, it is very desperately spoken.' That
> vile term, I cry God mercy, did I give him. Who, by these
> words perceiving me in a fume, said merrily unto me, 'Well,
> well, Son Roper, it shall not be so, it shall not be so.' Whom
> in sixteen years and more, being in his house conversant with
> him, I could never perceive as much as once in a fume.

And a certain slowness to follow More's thought persists to the
end. In the boat on the way to Lambeth, where (as Roper knew)
the oath was to be demanded from More, More sat silent a
while, and at last suddenly whispered, 'Son Roper, I thank our
Lord the field is won.' 'What he meant thereby,' says Roper, 'I
then wist not; yet loath to seem ignorant I answered, "Sir, I am
thereof very glad".' These are their last recorded words. For

---

[1] HOWARD, L., *Collection of Letters*, i. 272 (1756); compare the copy of the petition
from Lady More to the King, MS. Arundel 152, fol. 300b.

here Roper drops out of the story, and it is Roper's wife who by word and by letter comforted her father during the fifteen months of his imprisonment.

There is something very admirable in the rectitude of memory by which Roper, writing more than ten years after the death of his wife, never claims for himself a share in the peculiar intimacy of More and his daughter Margaret, never forgets the distinction between 'Son Roper' and 'Meg'. This honesty entitles us to believe in the real truth of Roper's dialogues, even where the actual wording must often be his own reconstruction.

We have, then, four main characters – More and his wife, Roper and his wife – acting upon each other. Behind them we have the background of the world, the flesh, and Henry VIII. The world: represented by the Duke of Norfolk, scandalized, when he came to dine with More at Chelsea, to find him in church, singing in the choir, with a surplice on his back. Norfolk protested, as he went arm in arm with his host to the Great House, 'God's body, God's body, my Lord Chancellor, a parish clerk, a parish clerk! You dishonour the King and his office.' More replied, and certainly with truth, that King Henry would not consider the service of God a dishonour to his office. The flesh: Queen Anne Boleyn, More's bitterest enemy, exasperating the king against him by her importunate clamour, yet all the time pitied by her victim, because he realizes 'into what misery, poor soul, she shall shortly come'. King Henry: shown not so much in proper person, as in the reflected light which these anecdotes throw on *him*. Roper refrains from uttering any very direct censure upon his late king, the father of his queen. We have only one glimpse of Henry himself, as he walks after dinner in the garden at Chelsea, holding his arm about More's neck. And the point lies in More's comment afterwards: 'If my head could win him a castle in France, it should not fail to go.'

Amongst the proofs of More's sanctity, his biographers did not forget to place his peculiar gift of prophecy.

We have every reason to believe that Roper preserves truly the atmosphere of the Great House at Chelsea, and this is the important thing for us. But we cannot use Roper's *Life* as a document giving us absolutely reliable evidence of names, places, and dates. Memory plays strange tricks after twenty or thirty years, and Roper was neither a Boswell making systematic notes, nor a historian using documents to check his recollections. We must always keep in mind the apology for lapses of memory with which Roper begins his little book; not only has Roper forgotten much which we should have wished him to record, but among the things he records we can trace the confusion, and especially the confusion of chronology, which must ensue if a man trusts entirely to his memory over a space of nearly a generation. Two or three of Roper's mistakes are remarkable. He tells us of More's advancement at Court:

> Then died one Master Weston, Treasurer of the Exchequer whose office, after his death, the king, of his own offer, without any asking, freely gave unto Sir Thomas More.

The office was that of Under-Treasurer, not Treasurer. More was never Treasurer; that post was held at the time by the Duke of Norfolk and was soon to be held by his son. This is a sufficiently careless blunder for an important official, such as Roper, to have committed. But, what is more noteworthy, Sir Richard Weston did not precede More as Under-Treasurer; he followed him (though not immediately), and lived twenty-one years after the date at which he is alleged by Roper to have died, surviving More himself by seven years. Sir Richard Weston lived to stand godfather to another Thomas More, a grandson of Sir Thomas, born three years after his grandfather's execution. For a quarter of a century Weston had been one of the most prominent figures about the Court; there was hardly an official ceremony from which he was absent; and even the violent death of his only son Sir Francis, who was beheaded on the charge of adultery with Queen Anne Boleyn, did not interrupt the even tenor of Sir Richard's attendance upon his King. Roper, one would have thought, must have known Weston well. But Roper is writing more than a dozen years after Weston's death, and time has foreshortened everything. Roper remembers Weston occupying the same office which More occupied, and so he puts his name in place of that of Sir John Cutte, the Under-Treasurer whom More really succeeded. Roper had probably no clear recollection of Sir John Cutte acting as Under-Treasurer. Other similar inaccuracies of Roper will have to be noted in the course of our story. But there is nothing to shake our confidence in his complete honesty.

§ 7. NICHOLAS HARPSFIELD

Roper probably wrote, as gentlemen wrote in Tudor days, intending his notes to be merely passed round in manuscript among friends; and, in fact, it was not till nearly a century after More's death that Roper's life was printed. In Mary's reign the task of writing the formal life of More was given by Roper himself, together with his notes, to a young friend, Nicholas Harpsfield. This life clearly *was* intended for the printer; it is as much a manifesto as, later, was Foxe's *Book of Martyrs* on the other side. But the death of Mary stopped its printing, and the first edition, from a collation of the eight known manuscripts, was made by Dr. Elsie Hitchcock only three years ago. It is nearly sixty years since Lord Acton complained that not one of More's fifteen biographers had worked from manuscripts. The tireless labours of Dr. Hitchcock upon the manuscripts of More's *Lives* ought to be recorded here.

Harpsfield had not deserved to be so neglected. He was a scholar and an enthusiast; he had already suffered exile for his faith during the reign of Edward VI; under Elizabeth he was to suffer at least twelve years' imprisonment in the Fleet before he and his brother were released on bail, late in August, 1574, 'in respect of their infirmities and diseases' to 'go and remain at the Baths in Somersetshire'. But his health was broken, and he died at the end of the following year.

The two Harpsfields, Archdeacon John and Archdeacon Nicholas, are interesting figures. They were mainstays of the Catholic restoration under Mary. John was the better classical scholar: he had been the first Regius Professor of Greek at Oxford. Nicholas was a canonist, a theologian, and a historian; he solaced the weary years of his captivity by writing a history of the English Church in Latin prose, whilst his brother wrote a shorter history in Latin verse. Nicholas Harpsfield's *Life of More* is an achievement. It is the first formal biography in the English language. Cavendish's *Life of Wolsey* may have been written a few months earlier; but that, like Roper's *Life of More*, is nothing but the personal memoir of a man with a genius for narrative. Harpsfield is the first to compile a complete biography in English; he ransacks More's writings for autobiographical fragments similar to those which I have just quoted; he translates and incorporates the description of More which he found in the Letters of Erasmus, and the account of More's trial which was circulated at the time on the Continent. Harpsfield's *Life* has a finished design and a power of arranging material which is noteworthy. Most of his material is still extant elsewhere, so that it is rather as a literary document than as a historical source that Harpsfield's *Life* interests us. Yet Harpsfield has his own contributions to make to the story. I will quote two of these, for the further light they throw on facts which Roper mentions.

Roper tells us that, after More's resignation of the Chancellorship, the bishops and abbots of England, knowing him to be no rich man, collected a great sum as a recompense for his writings in defence of the Church, and that More would not take a penny. How great More's poverty then was, we learn from Harpsfield:

> He . . . was enforced and compelled, for lack of other fuel, every night before he went to bed to cause a great burden of fern to be brought into his own chamber, and with the blaze thereof to warm himself, his wife, and his children, and so without any other fires to go to their beds.

We can imagine Mistress Alice More, shivering over the embers of a fire of Chelsea bracken, and reflecting that her husband had refused a sum which would have placed them all in luxury.

The other story for which we are indebted to Harpsfield is startling. It will be told more at length below. For the moment it is enough to say that William Roper, about the time of his marriage to Margaret, had reduced himself by immoderate prayer and fasting to such a state of mind, that he 'thought there could be no truth but that which was come forth out of Germany'. So he became a Lutheran. He must have been an awkward inmate of More's house, for in addition to other absurdities, 'of all the world he did, during that time, most abhor' Sir Thomas More. After much vain dispute, More abandoned argument, and took to prayer. Prayer proved effective.

Not content with telling the tale in the most unsparing fashion in the body of his work, Harpsfield alludes to it again in the *Epistle Dedicatorie* to Roper, recording how More saved Roper's soul 'overwhelmed and full deep drowned in the deadly dreadful depth of horrible heresies'. With greater tact Harpsfield expresses his debt to Roper for so much of his material: 'Ye shall receive', he says, 'I will not say a pig of your own sow (it were too homely and swinish a term) but rather a comely and goodly garland, picked and gathered even out of your own garden.' Still, Harpsfield claims, he has 'paid some part of the shot', and has 'with poor Ruth leased (i.e. gleaned) some good corn'.

The story which Harpsfield gives of Roper's lapse into heresy throws a new light upon the whole of Roper's memoir. It shows us Roper as a man of more independence of judgment than perhaps we should have gathered from his own account; he was not a colourless person whose orthodoxy was due to his never having investigated what could be said on the other side. Roper and Pole were apparently, after Sir Thomas More, the men to whom Harpsfield was most deeply attached, and it is evidence of his honesty that he tells the truth about them both unsparingly in his historical work, even with regard to matters which they themselves would perhaps have wished forgotten.

But if the story of Roper's heresy adds to our knowledge of his character, it adds even more to our knowledge of More's. For sixteen years this sometimes very difficult young man had lived with More, and Roper had never known him 'in a fume'.

'Harpsfield', says Lord Acton, 'relates nearly everything that is in Roper's *Life of More* without his mistakes.' That is too high praise. Harpsfield follows many of Roper's errors, though he corrects him frequently. With more reason Acton praises Harpsfield for the candour and moderation of his numerous historical works. 'He is one of the earliest ecclesiastical writers whose mind fell naturally into an historical attitude, and with whom religious controversy resolves itself into the discussion of fact.' Harpsfield even tries to be just to Henry VIII; the worst thing he says about him[1] is that he 'cutt off St Peter's head,

---

[1] In the *Pretended Divorce* Harpsfield is somewhat more violent against Henry than in the *Life of More*; but he always keeps within certain bounds.

and put it, an uggly sight to beholde, upon his owne shoulders'. Harpsfield is bitter enough, but neither during his Marian triumph, nor during his weary imprisonment, does he show that extreme bitterness which characterizes some of the Elizabethan refugees.

§ 8. WILLIAM RASTELL AND THE REFUGEES

The same claim cannot be made for the writer of the next *Life of More* which we have to record – More's nephew, William Rastell. William Rastell's career has been traced above, very briefly, up to the year 1557, when, a distinguished lawyer of nearly fifty, he issued the collected edition of his uncle's English works. In the very last weeks of Mary's reign he was raised to the bench. Elizabeth had been ruling a little more than four years when Judge Rastell went overseas to Louvain, accompanied by other old friends of More. The Queen's views on religion had become so clear that there could be no hope of any reaction. From this, their second exile, these refugees were never to return. The flight of a Justice of the Queen's Bench was a misdemeanour which rendered his belongings forfeit to the Crown; and the special commission which sat at the Guildhall to take an inventory of the recusant's goods and chattels provides us with one of those documents which Professor A. W. Reed has used so excellently in reconstructing the figure of Mr. Justice Rastell.

Before his first exile Rastell had married Winifred, the daughter of two members of More's household who had been not less dear to the martyr than his own children, John Clement and Margaret Gigs. Winifred had died of fever abroad. One of Rastell's last acts before returning to England from exile, upon the accession of Queen Mary, had been to lay his wife to rest in St. Peter's Church in Louvain; one of his earliest acts as a Bencher of Lincoln's Inn under Mary had been to redecorate the altar of the Chapel of the Inn, and to procure from the Council of the Inn a promise of prayer at every mass for the souls of Winifred, her kin and friends; and now, after two and a half years of renewed exile in Louvain, Rastell too died of fever, and was buried beside her.[1] Sixteen years after

[1] See A. W. REED, *Early Tudor Drama*, pp. 85-93.

his death the Council of Lincoln's Inn solemnly cancelled the promise of prayer for Winifred's soul, as an act of foolish 'abomination and superstition'.

Rastell's *Life of More* found no printer, and even among the refugees its existence was known to few. It was a very elaborate work – what we should nowadays call a 'Life and Times' of More. It must count against Rastell that he seems to have repeated a tale, disgusting and chronologically impossible, which represented Henry as the father of Anne Boleyn. This scandal had apparently been current abroad since the time of Henry's marriage with Anne, but Rastell should have been too well informed to take it seriously. We must admit that Rastell, unlike Roper or Harpsfield, had a contempt for Henry which passed all bounds. And the truth was bad enough, for there is no doubt that Anne's sister Mary had been Henry's mistress; Henry did not deny it. He *did* deny having ever had illicit relations with Anne's mother, when that charge was repeated to him to his face.[1] Still, bad as the truth was, one cannot help feeling that it tends to diminish Rastell's credit that he should have repeated this scandal. It should serve to warn us of his bitterness and prejudice whenever Henry is concerned. When relating the death of Fisher, Rastell says, 'I think in this point King Henry passed all the Turks or Tyrants that ever was read or heard of.'

Rastell's *Life* has been lost – but not entirely. Considerable fragments, chiefly relating to Fisher, but also containing a good deal about the trial and execution of the Carthusians, and some scanty but exceedingly valuable information about More himself, are preserved in the British Museum.[2] They were copied from Rastell's *Life of More*, and sent across from Belgium to England, to help in the compilation of a *Life of Fisher* which was being carried on in Catholic circles in England during the early years of Elizabeth.

We might turn to these fragments, expecting to find in them little but the outpourings of an exile; a specimen of that Refugee literature which became so active just about the time

[1] By Sir George Throgmorton, who reminded Henry of the details in a letter which is extant in the Record Office. See Brewer's Preface to *L.P.*, IV, p. cccxxix (footnote). See also ibid., p. ccxxxiii (footnote).
[2] MS. Arundel, 152.

of Rastell's death.[1] But, on the contrary, we find them to be part of what must have been an amazing work. There is a power of passionate narrative and of reconstructed dialogue which is not inferior to that of Roper, or of Cavendish in his *Life of Wolsey.* But whereas Roper and Cavendish never give us dates, and often state facts which are hard to reconcile with the dates we know, we find in these fragments of Rastell's *Life* something unparalleled in any biography which till now had been written in English.[2] The Rastell fragments bristle with names and dates. And though much of Rastell's narrative deals with matter which is not recorded elsewhere, when we come to the enumeration of dates and names we can control him, because the official records of the trials of the Carthusians, of Fisher, and of More, have been preserved. Though these official documents do not give us what would most interest us, the pleadings, they do at any rate supply the framework of dry fact. It is just in these names and dates that we might expect to find Rastell, writing after a quarter of a century, to be confused and inaccurate. Instead, we find that Rastell's names and dates are proved correct from the official records.

The most obvious explanation seems to be that Rastell is using the notes which he made at the time. When Fisher and More were being tried, Rastell was a student of law at Lincoln's Inn, with every opportunity and motive for making the fullest record, for his own use, of such epoch-making trials, an understanding of which would be so important for any student of the law. He was probably present at the trials. He tells us himself that he was present at Fisher's execution.

As we realize the value of the scanty fragments of Rastell's *Life of More* which have survived, we are appalled at the loss we have suffered by the disappearance of all the rest. Some idea of the size of this biography we can gather from the fact that it was in the Seventy-seventh Chapter of the Third Book of his *Life* that Rastell told how More's head was placed upon London Bridge. It is true that Rastell, closely as he had co-operated with More, had not lived in the Great House with

---

[1] In 1565 sixteen books by English Catholics were printed abroad—thirteen in Antwerp.

[2] The nearest parallel is to be found in More's *Richard III*: a space is there left for dates which More hoped subsequently to learn, but which he never filled in.

him; we think of Rastell as a rather more independent figure
than Roper. But Margaret and John Clement, who had gone
into exile with Rastell, had shared More's home as intimately
as Margaret and William Roper had. So Rastell's opportunities
for gathering information about his uncle were almost un-
limited. His *Life of More* must have been, as a biography,
unrivalled in English till, more than half a century later, we
come to the *Henry VII* of Francis Bacon and the *Henry VIII* of
Lord Herbert of Cherbury. And it had authority as a primary
source such as neither of those two works can claim. [1]

Roper's amazing power of reconstructing dialogue would
have enabled him to write a book which might have equalled
some of the great French memoirs; he has been content to
leave us just a few pages which show what he could have done.
Rastell wrote at length, and his work is lost. It is deplorable.
Yet at least we can be sure that More would have wished that,
if only a few fragments were to survive of the *Life* to which his
nephew devoted so much care, they should be those which
commemorate his fellow-sufferers rather than himself.

But the recollections of the refugees in the Low Countries
were not to be entirely lost. One by one these faithful young
friends of More had grown old and died in exile, waiting for
the day which never came, the day which was to have enabled
them to enjoy at once the land they loved, and the religion
they loved even more. William Rastell was the first to pass
away, followed by both the Clements and by Harris, who had
long been More's secretary. Later still died John Heywood,
dramatist and wit, who had married More's niece, William
Rastell's sister Joan. Heywood had been condemned among
the little group of sufferers in 1544, one of whom was John
Larke, the rector of More's parish church of Chelsea. But
Heywood, after condemnation, had at the last moment decided
that the martyr's crown was not for him, and had been pardoned by Henry. Early in Elizabeth's reign, he left England
for ever; at the age of eighty-one he again narrowly escaped
martyrdom for the faith (this time without recantation), and at

[1] The Rastell Fragments have now been made generally accessible in the
Appendix to the Early English Text Society's edition of Harpsfield's *Life of More*,
edited by Dr. E. V. Hitchcock.

last, more than forty years after More's death, he was making his dying confession. The confessor sought to console his penitent for his faults, chief among which, we may be sure, was his failure to die 'when time was'; the kindly ecclesiastic kept on murmuring 'the flesh is weak, the flesh is weak'. 'Verily, you seem to reproach God for not making me a fish' was the last recorded remark of the author of the 'many mad plays'. If he could not imitate his hero in martyrdom, he could at least be cheerful on his deathbed, which More had asserted to be no small evidence of a proper state of mind. And now not one of the group of intimates was left, save only Dorothy Colly. She had been maid to Margaret Roper, and wife to Harris, More's secretary. Fifty-three years ago she had been carrying comforts to More in prison. 'I like special well Dorothy Colly: I pray you be good unto her', More had written in his last letter. She had been one of the three faithful women who had seen to the burial of his body.

And now this old lady, living in exile in Douai, was the last repository of the More tradition. She would tell her tales of him again and again.[1] And from her husband she had inherited many of More's letters and papers, now falling to pieces from age, and, we may believe, from loving handling as relics. It must have meant some self-sacrifice for her to hand them over, as she did, to the great scholar and controversialist, Thomas Stapleton.

§9. THOMAS STAPLETON

According to Thomas Fuller, Roman Catholics observed that Thomas Stapleton was born in the same year and month wherein Thomas More was beheaded, 'as if divine providence had purposely dropped from heaven an acorn in place of the oak that was felled'. Stapleton records that, among the friends of his boyhood, More's fame and his martyrdom were the constant and inspiring subjects of talk.[2] He became prebendary of Chichester in Mary's reign, but, more fortunate than the Harpsfields, he managed to escape to the Low Countries early in the reign of Elizabeth. Here he took up from Harpsfield the work of controversy with the Protestants in Latin and English,

[1] STAPLETON, XX, p. 358.   [2] The same, p. 360.

as Harpsfield had taken it up from More; Stapleton had such success that, Fuller tells us, many wondered that it was not he, but Allen, who was chosen for the Cardinal's cap. Yet such consider not, says Fuller, that Stapleton's ability was drowned with Allen's activity, one grain of the statesman being too heavy for a pound of the student, practical policy, in all ages, beating pen-pains out of distance in the race of preferment.[1]

Stapleton was master of a beautiful English style, as his translation of Bede's *Ecclesiastical History* shows. It is to be regretted that his boyish enthusiasm did not lead him to compile his *Life of More* earlier, and in English, when he was in constant communication with the friends of More who have just been mentioned. Unfortunately, he did not write till the great Elizabethan quarrel was at its hottest, and his book appeared in Latin, in 1588, the Armada year. By then his memories of what his older fellow-exiles had told him had become a good deal blurred. Still, we must be grateful that he did, at last, write these recollections down – foreseeing, as he says, that with old age death must be approaching, and that these remembrances might die with him.

The *Life* which Stapleton wrote had, then, two distinct sources: the documents which Dorothy Colly had given him, and the anecdotes he had heard during nearly half a century. In both cases we have to thank Stapleton for having preserved what, but for him, would almost certainly have perished. To help him in his task, Stapleton had also Harpsfield's *Life* as a background.

Stapleton's forty years' labour has been strangely neglected by his countrymen, and this neglect extends to his *Life of More*. This most important life was printed in Douai, Paris, Cologne, Frankfort, Leipzig, Graz, and in more recent times has been published in French and Spanish translations; it has never been printed in England, and the first English translation was made by Mgr. Hallett only seven years ago.

§ 10. 'RO. BA.' AND CRESACRE MORE

To some extent, this neglect has been made good by the later biographers, who have used the material supplied them

[1] FULLER's *Worthies* (1811), II, p. 398 (Sussex).

by Stapleton. At least three such composite English biographies existed. One is lost, except for an odd leaf preserved in the Bodleian.[1] The second, which was written by a certain 'Ro. Ba.' about 1599, is extant in at least eight MSS.[2] The description of More's life, says 'Ro. Ba.', has 'wearied painful Stapleton, gravelled learned Harpsfield, made silent eloquent Pole'. His own biography gives the story of More in its most complete form; it contains little that is new, but is a careful combination of the Roper-Harpsfield tradition with the tradition of the refugees as preserved by Stapleton. It follows that in some ways it is the best *Life of More*. The writer is more than a mere translator and compiler. He can tell a tale well; and he turns Stapleton's anecdotes from their rather jejune Latin into masterly Elizabethan English. Even in Stapleton's Latin the story of the Winchester man who spoke with More, as More passed on his way to execution, is a noble and touching one. But in the Tudor English of the *Life of More* by 'Ro. Ba.' it becomes one of the great stories of the world:

Afterwards, as he passed, there came to him a citizen of Winchester, who had been once with Sir Thomas before, and it was upon this occasion.

This poor man was grievously vexed with very vehement and grievous tentations of desperation, and could never be rid of it, either by counsel or prayer of his own or of his friends. At last a good friend of his brought him to Sir Thomas, then Chancellor. Who, taking compassion of the poor man's misery, gave him the best counsel and advice he could. But it would not serve. Then fell he to his prayers for him, earnestly beseeching Almighty God to rid the poor man of his trouble of mind. He obtained it; for, after that, the Hampshire man was never troubled with it any more, so long as he would come to Sir Thomas More; but after he was imprisoned and could have no access unto him, his tentation began again more vehement and troublesome than ever before. So he spent his days with a heavy heart, and without all hope of remedy.

But when he heard that Sir Thomas was condemned, he

---

[1] MS. Rawl. D. 923, fol. 261.
[2] A critical edition of the life of More by 'Ro. Ba.' is being edited for the Early English Text Society by Dr. E. V. Hitchcock from a collation of all eight MSS., but based upon the Lambeth MS. The Lambeth MS. was the one used in the reprint in Wordsworth's *Ecclesiastical Biography*, vol. II.

posted from Winchester, hoping at least to see him as he should go to execution, and so determined to speak with him, come what would of it. And for that cause he placed himself in the way. And at his coming by, he thrust through the throng, and with a loud voice said, 'Mr. More, do you know me? I pray you for our Lord's sake, help me: I am as ill troubled as ever I was.' Sir Thomas answered, 'I remember thee full well. Go thy ways in peace, and pray for me: and I will not fail to pray for thee.'

And from that time after, so long as he lived, he was never troubled with that manner of tentation.

The third of these composite lives was compiled by More's great-grandson, Cresacre More.

Stapleton and Cresacre More, unlike the matter-of-fact Roper, sometimes tell stories which have an air of miracle. Sometimes the story is pathetic. On the day of More's death, Margaret Roper went from shrine to shrine, praying and distributing alms for the good of her father's soul. When she came to the Tower to bury his body, there was no money for a shroud. So her maid, Dorothy Colly, 'went to the next draper's shop, and, agreeing upon the price, made as though she would look for some money in her purse, and then try whether they would trust her or no. And she found in her purse the same sum for which they agreed.' Dorothy Colly believed, and assured Stapleton during their common exile at Douai, that the money could only have come there by a miracle.[1]

Sometimes the story has a touch of humour which would have pleased More. John Heywood left to his sons, Jasper and Ellis, one of More's teeth. Each son desired to have the relic for himself. The tooth, suddenly, 'to the admiration of both, parted in two'.[2]

By various accretions the life of More in the hands of his great-grandson Cresacre had expanded to an octavo volume of some three hundred pages, which has been not infrequently reprinted. Naturally, therefore, historians and biographers have often quoted Cresacre More, in preference to other early sources, generally less accessible. Yet, owing to the fact that Henry VIII had confiscated the family papers, 'seized all our

---

[1] STAPLETON, xx, p. 358.   [2] CRESACRE MORE, *Life*, 1726, p. 304.

evidences', as Cresacre puts it, there was little new which Cresacre could add to what Roper, Harpsfield, and Stapleton had recorded in an earlier age. Cresacre's life is a compilation for Stuart times, just as Harpsfield's is for Tudor days; but it is less well done. Cresacre sometimes tries to improve his sources, with unfortunate results.

§ 11. DOUBTFUL DEVELOPMENT OF ANECDOTE

More's foresight was remarkable enough, and sufficient to gain him the reputation of a prophet. But such a reputation is dangerous. As tales pass from mouth to mouth, the temptation to make the prophecy a little more pointed is one which few can overcome. And here not only Cresacre More, but Stapleton also, is apt to err. With no personal knowledge of More, with no survivor who had known More to guide him at the time he was writing, save only the aged Dorothy Colly, Stapleton cannot fairly be expected always to select the best form of an anecdote.

And, just as the prophecies are made more pointed, so we shall meet with instances when an authentic jest is elaborated in the later version of Cresacre More, till it becomes buffoonery. And other jests were fathered on More without any foundation at all. Stapleton speaks of his doubt as to some of these humorous anecdotes,[1] which he therefore omits. But of those which he records, and which Cresacre More and others repeat, some seem doubtful; for example the tale of the cut-purse.[2]

A fellow magistrate, we are told, was in the habit of chiding those who had had their purses cut, saying that it was due to their negligence that so many cut-purses came before the bench. More arranged over-night with one of the chief cut-purses in Newgate that next day he was to pretend that he had some private information to give to this magistrate, and was to cut his purse during the interview. The culprit succeeded, returned to his place, and made a sign to More. More thereupon suggested a collection for some charitable object. The

---

[1] Cap. xiii, p. 286.
[2] STAPLETON, xiii, pp. 286-8 [numbered erroneously 246]; CRESACRE MORE, *Life*, 1726, p. 87.

censorious magistrate discovered that his purse was missing, though he was sure he had had it when he took his place on the bench. More made the thief return the purse, and, we are to understand, secured his pardon in exchange for the joke.

Neither Stapleton nor Cresacre seems to feel the horror of tempting a man by way of a jest to commit a capital crime, and then rewarding the jester by relieving him of the penalty of earlier crimes. The same tale is dramatized, with much sense of humour, in the play of *Sir Thomas More*, written at the end of Elizabeth's reign, and therefore falling in date between Stapleton and Cresacre. The playwright does not blame More for his fun, but he *does* realize the fear and terror of the cut-purse. When More has suggested to Lifter the cut-purse that, if he will pick or cut the justice's purse, he will procure his pardon for the jest, Lifter replies:

> Good Mr. Sheriff, seek not my overthrow.
> You know, Sir, I have many heavy friends
> And more indictments like to come upon me;
> You are too deep for me to deal withal.
> You are known to be one of the wisest men
> That is in England. I pray you, Mr. Sheriff,
> Go not about to undermine my life.[1]

The story is very well told in the *Life* by Ro. Ba.; the writer is translating from Stapleton, but he modifies the tale in a way which shows that he felt the cruelty of it. We are told, 'Cut-purse art was not then so frequent, nor yet so heinous as now.' More gives the cut-purse a cautionary lecture, and, 'after he had thoroughly chidden him, said unto him, "I have good hope thou wilt do better hereafter – and see it prove so. For this time I will stand your friend, but you must show me a trick of your cunning".'[2]

Now we cannot impute our own feelings to an earlier age; and it would be no argument against the truth of this story that it revolts us to-day. I find the reason for doubting it in More's own works. In the treatise of *The Four Last Things*, written about four years after More had given up his post of Under-Sheriff, he says:

---

[1] *Sir Thomas More*, ed. W. W. GREG, lines 169-75.
[2] *Ecclesiastical Biography*, II, pp. 98-9.

I remember me of a thief once cast at Newgate, that cut a purse at the bar, when he should be hanged on the morrow. And when he was asked why he did so, knowing that he should die so shortly, the desperate wretch said, that it did his heart good, to be lord of that purse one night yet. And in good faith, methinketh, as much as we wonder at him, yet see we many that do much like, of whom we nothing wonder at all.[1]

And More goes on to speak of those who, with one foot in the grave already, pursue dishonest gain as energetically as if they had still seven score years to live.

Is it likely that More would have spoken with such real horror of this act, if he himself had prompted it, or another quite like it, as a jest? Everyone must judge for himself, but it seems to me improbable, although the tale appears to have been current, by the end of the sixteenth century, both in London and among the recusant refugees abroad.

We can see how easily the story may have arisen. For what seemed to More horrible would strike others as a jest; and it appears from More's own words that he was present when the incident occurred. It may have been he who cross-questioned the thief as to his motives. As the tale passed from mouth to mouth, we can understand More being made to play a larger and larger part in the story – his reputation as a jester would inevitably lead to this.

But the fact that Stapleton's *Life* contains many doubtful, and some clearly fictitious, stories does not mean that his anecdotes are not of great value. Very often Stapleton names his authority, and sometimes we can get independent confirmation. I think we are justified in believing in the story of the citizen of Winchester and his appeal to More on the way to the scaffold, for two reasons. The first is that More used words on the scaffold which might well have been suggested to him by this incident. The second, and weightier, reason, is that the heroic Margaret Clement was present at More's execution, and we have reason to believe that Stapleton's account of what passed, so far as it is not drawn from Hall's *Chronicle*, is the account of Margaret Clement.

[1] *Works*, 1557, col. 93.

At another time it is More's devoted secretary, John Harris, who is Stapleton's informant; at another the faithful Dorothy Colly. Stapleton is very good in the way he quotes his authorities. But when we cannot be sure of his authority, when he seems to be merely quoting from the flotsam of pious or humorous anecdotes about More current among the refugees, it is better to be entirely sceptical. It is not enough to say, 'Stapleton tells us'. The question is, who told Stapleton?

The scattered anecdotes of More which we meet with first in the seventeenth century have passed through too many mouths to carry authority. At best they can only show us what people in the seventeenth century believed More to have been like – though this also is a useful thing to know. But the anecdotes first told by Francis Bacon, or by Henry Peacham, or by John Aubrey, can in some cases be demonstrated to be untrue. For example, we read in Bacon's *Apophthegms*:

Sir Thomas More had only daughters at the first, and his wife did ever pray for a boy. At last she had a boy, which being come to man's estate proved but simple. Sir Thomas said to his wife, 'Thou prayedst so long for a boy, that he will be a boy as long as he lives'.

As John's mother died within some three years of his birth, she could hardly have been reproached because her boy remained a boy too long. But the anecdote has probably helped to encourage a tradition that John was backward and stupid as a youth, a tradition for which there is no sufficient evidence.

§ 12. THE ELIZABETHAN PLAY OF *SIR THOMAS MORE*

The History Play of *Sir Thomas More* is the work of a group of Elizabethan dramatists of whom I think it may be said with certainty that Shakespeare was one. For biographical detail the play is of little value. There is no fact in it which, unless confirmed by some outside source, can be held authoritative. The references to More in Hall's *Chronicle* provided the most important source of fact; although at least one error of fact, made by Hall, is corrected by the playwrights. Beyond this, it is difficult to say how far the play draws upon recollections of

what Roper or Stapleton had written, and how far it is dependent upon London tradition.

But, much more essential than any additional facts could be
to us, is the general picture which it gives of More's character;
and in this the play certainly reflects current London opinion.
Although London has become a predominantly Protestant city,
More is still its hero; at the end of the sixteenth century he is
still remembered as being what the City in 1521 said he was,
'a special lover and friend in the businesses and causes of this
city'.

Shakespeare's historical plays are enough to show us that
we cannot turn to the Elizabethan stage for impartial history.
The Shakespearean plays dealing with the period of the Wars
of the Roses are drawn from sources which are coloured, now
by Yorkist, now by Lancastrian, now by Tudor, and now by
Burgundian prejudice. But where a play gives us, as does the
play of *Sir Thomas More*, a view of its hero which contradicts the
contemporary propaganda, then it must be founded on a very
strongly based and obstinate tradition. During two generations
(save only for the five years of Mary's reign) the memory of
More had been consistently and vigorously attacked. But
Foxe's tales of cruelty, and Hall's sneers, repeated in edition
after edition, have not made the London playwrights revere
More the less. It is the English ideal – which is alive to-day as
much as ever – of a statesman fearless, bluff, honest, sympathetic, full of humour. The humorous side is a little over-
done, but then it is the business of the playwright to amuse his
audience.

Perhaps the most noteworthy feature of this play is More's
tenderness. The playwrights take Hall's *Chronicle* as their
source, but they deliberately reject the picture of the cynical
mocker, as, with a good deal of partisan bitterness, it had been
drawn by the chronicler. Hall tells us how, as More was even
going to his death, at the Tower Gate,

> a poor woman called unto him, and besought him to declare
> that he had certain evidences of hers in the time that he was
> in office (which after he was apprehended she could not come
> by) and that he would intreat she might have them again,
> or else she was undone.

More, according to Hall, 'thought nothing to be well spoken except he had ministered some mock in the communication', so he made answer:

> Good woman, have patience a little while, for the King is good unto me, that even within this half hour he will discharge me of all business, and help thee himself.[1]

In this Hall sees nothing but a heartless jibe; to him, More is still the same old mocking More, even a few minutes before execution.

This is how the playwright depicts the scene:

> WOMAN Now, good Sir Thomas More, for Christ's dear sake,
> Deliver me my writings back again
> That do concern my title.
> MORE What, my old client, art thou got hither too?
> Poor silly wretch, I must confess indeed,
> I had such writings as concern thee near,
> But the King has ta'en the matter into his own hand,
> He has all I had. Then, woman, sue to him.
> I cannot help thee. Thou must bear with me.
> WOMAN Ah, gentle heart, my soul for thee is sad,
> Farewell, the best friend that the poor e'er had.[2]

When we find Elizabethan playwrights deliberately altering their source in this way, it is significant. This, then, is the Londoners' idea of More. They care nothing about his European outlook, little about his religious views – to them he is the just judge. His honesty, his shrewdness, his rapidity of mind and his humour made him the ideal man for settling difficult cases in record time. Thus he was a godsend to a litigious generation. And, to the London playwrights, he is

> . . . the best friend that the poor e'er had.

So, despite its amazing confusion of facts and dates, the old play is one of the most important of all documents concerning Thomas More. It shows what his own city thought of him, more than half a century after his death. It is in the place where a man's folk live that the truth is known about him:

> He might ha' been that, or he might ha' been this,
> But they love and they hate him for what he is.[3]

---

[1] Ed. WHIBLEY, II, p. 265.   [2] ll. 1638-48.
[3] RUDYARD KIPLING, *Puck of Pook's Hill*.

THE YOUNG LAWYER OF LINCOLN'S INN

(1478–1509)

§ I. FATHER AND SON

OUR story begins with a fifteenth-century Londoner, who has just lived through what must be, to most men who have experienced it, the most satisfactory event of a lifetime. He is a methodical man, whose habits will, in course of time, lead him to a place of eminence in a great profession. So he duly notes the event, in the Latin which (though steadily yielding place to English) is still the current language of the London business man.

We may render his Latin thus:

Memorandum, that on the Friday next after the Feast of the Purification of the Blessed Virgin Mary, between two and three in the morning, was born Thomas More, son of John More, gentleman, in the seventeenth year of King Edward, the Fourth after the Conquest of England.

An entirely competent statement. But unfortunately John More did not leave it at that. Feeling that his wording lacked precision, he added between the lines, at some subsequent but quite uncertain period, 'to wit, the seventh day of February'.

But the Friday next after the Purification in the seventeenth year of Edward IV was the sixth of February, not the seventh.

It was nearly seventy years ago that this entry was discovered, and the discovery was important, because Thomas More, on the strength of a mistaken statement made by his great-grandson, Cresacre More, had always been supposed to have been born in 1480, and that date gave a quite unintelligible precocity to some of the records of his youth. But unfortunately, when John More's memorandum was published, nearly four centuries after it was made, in *Notes and Queries*,[1] his original statement, and his interlined afterthought, were printed continuously, as if both carried equal authority. We were consequently left uncertain whether it was the year, or the day of the month, or of the week which John More had got wrong. Pages and pages of learned publications have been filled with discussions as to whether Thomas More was born on 7 Feb. 1477, or 6 Feb. 1478, or 7 Feb. 1478. Yet all this ink (which the present writer has helped in spilling) might have been spared, if only someone had done earlier what A. W. Reed, that unwearied searcher into everything concerning Thomas More and his circle, has now insisted should be done. He has driven me to Cambridge and we have together inspected the manuscript.

I am writing these words in Wren's beautiful library in Trinity College, where John More's memorandum has found its permanent home.[2] John More's statement is clear: his son was born on 6 Feb. 1478. It was only later that he made his addition. By that time his recollection of the day of the month may well have grown hazy, and he may, by a natural mistake, have written 7 Feb. But it would seem improbable that, at a time when events were dated by the year of the reigning monarch, a man of affairs should have stated inaccurately the year of King Edward in which he was dating an important event. Perhaps in the first few days of the year he might have done so. But the regnal year was now many months old.

Unless some more conclusive evidence should be discovered, it would, then, seem that we can accept as More's birthday, with fair certainty, 6 Feb. 1478.

This seventeenth year of King Edward IV has a second link which connects it with the printed page now lying under the reader's eye. It was the year in which the first book printed in England was published. Whatever books John More possessed when he set up housekeeping, they were all in manuscript, and it was in the manuscript which is now lying before me that John More made his memoranda. It is a neatly written copy of the *History of the Kings of Britain* by Geoffrey of Monmouth –

---

[1] 17 Oct., 31 Oct., 7 Nov. 1868, FOURTH SERIES, II, pp. 365, 422, 449.
[2] MS. O. 2, 21.

that most unveracious history of Lear and Cordelia, of Arthur and Merlin and Mordred and Guinevere, which had been a best seller in the twelfth century, and which was still maintaining its popularity in the fifteenth. The manuscript contains other things – medical hints, information concerning the journey of the soul after death, and so on. It is on the blank leaves at the end that John More has entered his family history.

As we look down the row of memoranda, they bring before us the annals of a fifteenth-century London household. The first runs:

> Memorandum that on Sunday in the Vigil of St. Mark the Evangelist in the fourteenth year of the reign of King Edward the Fourth after the Conquest, John More, Gentleman, was married to Agnes, daughter of Thomas Graunger, in the parish of St. Giles, outside Cripplegate, London.

The date is 24 April 1474. The church is the same church of St. Giles Cripplegate in which Oliver Cromwell was married, and Milton was buried – but hardly the same building. For although St. Giles Cripplegate was one of the few London churches which survived the Great Fire, the building in which John More was married had succumbed to an earlier conflagration.

Thomas Granger, the maternal grandfather of Thomas More, from whom possibly he derived his Christian name, lived to be a prosperous London citizen, and was elected Sheriff on 11 Nov. 1503. In the *Dictionary of National Biography* Sir Sidney Lee tells us that he died, two days later, at the Sergeants' feast held on the occasion when John More, by that time a prosperous lawyer of over fifty, was made a Sergeant. Sir Sidney quotes Stowe's *Chronicle* as his authority. Thomas More was then a young man who had passed his twenty-fifth year, had been called to the Bar, and for some time had been Reader in Law at Furnivall's Inn. 'Young More', as he was coming to be named, was no doubt present at this banquet. The sudden death of Thomas More's grandfather, at the feast held to celebrate the attainment by his father of high rank in the hierarchy of the law, would be a *memento mori* for father and son very much in the spirit of More's *Four Last Things*, or of the *Rueful Lamentation* which he was about that time writing.

But, gentle reader, albeit there are many tragic events in More's career, this is not one of them. What is recorded in Stowe's *Chronicle* is not that Thomas Granger *died* on 13 November 1503, but that he *dined*. It was the day on which, as newly-elected Sheriff, he should have been host at a City feast – but since dates clashed, he was instead a guest at the even more important and, in fact, royal feast provided by the ten new Sergeants, of whom his son-in-law was one. That is all which Stowe records; it would appear that a vagrant 'n' must at some date have wandered out of Sir Sidney's narrative. The statement runs:

> The xiii of November was holden within the palace of the Archbishop of Canterbury, at Lambeth, the Sergeants' feast, where dined the King and all his nobles, and upon the same day, Thomas Granger, newly chosen Sheriff of London, was presented before the Barons of the King's Exchequer, there to take his oath, and after went with the Mayor unto the same feast, which saved him money in his purse, for if that day that feast had not been kept, he must have feasted the Mayor, Aldermen, and others Worshipful of the City. This feast was kept at the charge of ten learned men, newly admitted to be Sergeants to the King's law, whose names were ... John More ...[1]

No doubt careful search of City records could, and will, reveal more details of Thomas Granger, but we will take leave of him here, as he congratulates his son-in-law on his well-deserved honour, and himself on having secured a good dinner and saved his expenses. We will pass from the ancestor who (perhaps) gave Thomas More his Christian name to those from whom he derived his surname.

We seem to see in them a prosperous London family – entitled to call themselves gentle, but with no distinguished history behind them. Thomas More, in the brief biography which he placed upon the tomb that he built for himself in Chelsea church, but which he was not spared to occupy, described himself as born of no famous family, but of honest stock. After More's execution, the French scholar, Nicholas Bourbon, in an invective against him, reviled More as being of obscure origin;[2] another way of putting the same thing, for if

---

[1] *Chronicles of England*, 1580, p. 876.
[2] *Nugarum Lib. V*, Carmen cxiii, Lugduni, 1538.

the stock had not been honest, Bourbon would have said so. Bourbon was a courtier of Henry VIII – Holbein's sketch of his rather unprepossessing face is preserved at Windsor with those of other English courtiers. The invective, in mingled Latin and Greek verses, is a piece of propaganda, intended to counter the indignation which More's death had raised in all the humanist circles of Europe. It is noteworthy that Bourbon can find nothing worse with which to attack More's memory than the obscure birth of his father. Modern research, peering into that obscurity, has discovered in the 'Black Books' of Lincoln's Inn the dim figure of an earlier John More, the grandfather of Thomas More. This John More was raised from the post of butler to that of seneschal or steward of the Inn: that is to say, he was the officer at the head of the servants of the house, and keeper of the accounts, in which connection his name occurs from time to time. It was during the temporary restoration of Henry VI, in 1470, that this John More the elder was rewarded for his faithful services as butler and steward (offices which he is stated to have held for a long time) by being admitted a member of the Society. In 1489 and in 1495 he held the office of Reader.[1]

His son, John More, junior, father of Thomas More, followed in his father's steps as butler to the Society. We can trace his different children in the memoranda of the book before us.

First came a daughter Joan (11 March 1475). She married one Richard Staverton, and later we find John More, now 'one of the King's justices', and Mr. Thomas More, together pressing the fortunes of Richard Staverton in the City.[2] The Mores are a united family in spite of some trouble with the versatile, eccentric and difficult John Rastell, who will be mentioned presently. When Joan dies, long after the beheading of her famous brother, at the age of 67, her executor is one of the most faithful of Thomas More's friends, John Heywood the dramatist, who had wedded Joan Rastell, More's niece.[3]

Next on the list of John More's children comes his son

---

[1] Details of the careers of the two John Mores are given in Foss, *Judges of England*, v (1857), pp. 191-203.
[2] Repertory of the Court of Aldermen, 18 Aug. 1519 (IV, fol. 18b; v, fol. 142); 13 Sept. 1520 (IV, fol. 63b).
[3] A. W. REED, *Early Tudor Drama*, pp. 84, 202, etc.

Thomas, the hero of our story, born, as we have seen, on 6 February 1478. Then comes Agatha, born on 31 January 1479. We hear no more of Agatha – probably she died young. Tudor families were usually large, but were thinned out by an enormous death-rate. On 6 June 1480 John More was born; he lived to be over thirty, and became a skilled scribe, perhaps acting as secretary to his brother. Erasmus writes from Cambridge complaining of the bad handwriting in that University; there is no one who can transcribe for him the work he is sending; he suggests that his correspondent might do so, or, if that is inconvenient, might arrange with Thomas More for his brother to copy it.[1] That is the last we know of this John More. On 3 September 1481 an Edward was born, of whom nothing further is known; and finally, on 22 September 1482, a daughter Elizabeth. She married the John Rastell above mentioned,that extraordinary Tudor figure: printer, lawyer, venturer, dramatist, military engineer, and would-be colonizer of North America. Their son was William Rastell, the printer, lawyer and judge, More's biographer, and editor of his collected works.

It is not very easy for us to picture the young butler of Lincoln's Inn who made these entries concerning his growing family. To us, John More must always be the grandfather, seated by Thomas More's side as Holbein sketched him half a century later, in all probability in the early spring of 1527. On Holbein's drawing, John More the grandfather is stated to be in his seventy-sixth year. He was therefore probably born in 1451. This would make him about twenty-three when he married, and about twenty-seven when he became father of Thomas More. But the man we know is the aged judge who faces us in Holbein's drawing, with his shrewd, humorous and kindly face. He seems to have become a Judge of the Common Pleas about the age of sixty-six, and a Judge of the King's Bench about the age of seventy-two. It is not clear when he was knighted. Thomas More, in the epitaph which he drew up for himself, took occasion to celebrate his father's virtues; and an early biographer, basing his account on More's filial words, has described the old judge in a way which agrees very well with Holbein's portrait:

[1] 27 Nov. 1511, ALLEN, I, No. 246.

A man very virtuous, and of a very upright and sincere conscience, both in giving of counsel and judgement; a very
merciful and pitiful man; and among other his good qualities
and properties, a companionable, a merry, and pleasantly
conceited man.[1]

(We shall meet the word 'conceit' more than once, and it is to
be noted that it is still quite free from the bad sense which it has
acquired by being used in place of the correct 'self-conceit'.)

Judge John More possessed a book of good precedents
(though not of his collection) which was one of the sources of
the *Book of Entries* compiled by his grandson Judge William
Rastell, which in its turn was for long a leading legal work of
reference. Yet Judge John is not remembered for any epoch-
making legal decisions, but rather for two *obiter dicta* concerning
matrimony, which were duly placed on record by his illustrious
son. He ruled that matrimony was a 'perilous choice', as if 'ye
should put your hand into a blind bag full of snakes and eels
together, seven snakes for one eel'.[2] Since Judge More married
four times, and must have been nearly seventy when he put his
hand into the bag for the last dip, we might assume that he had
drawn an eel at least three times, were it not for his second
dictum: 'When he heard folk blame their wives and say that
they be so many of them shrews, he would merrily say that they
diffame them falsely, for he would say plainly that there was
but one shrewd wife in the world; but he said indeed that every
man weeneth that he hath her.'[3]

Names are recorded of Agnes Granger's successors as wife
to John More; but we cannot be sure of the order in which they
succeeded, nor do we hear of More having had any half-
brothers or sisters. Erasmus tells us, in a letter of 1519, that
Thomas behaved as a model son to his two stepmothers. When
Erasmus republished this letter two years later, Judge More
had married for the fourth time, and the virtuous Thomas was
enthusiastically applauding the choice, 'he had never seen a
better woman'.[4] It might have tried the temper of a less
equable man, for the last stepmother survived him some nine

---

[1] HARPSFIELD, *Life of More*, p. 9.   [2] *Works*, 1557, p. 165.
[3] HARPSFIELD, *Life of More*, pp. 9-10, following MORE, *Works*, 1557, p. 233.
[4] ALLEN, IV, No. 999, p. 19. Compare *Farrago*, 1519, p. 333, with *Epistolae ad
diversos*, 1521, p. 435.

years, and kept him out of much of his paternal inheritance. After his retirement from public life More boasted of his honourable poverty 'while my mother-in-law (i.e. stepmother) liveth, whose life and good health I pray God long keep and continue'.[1] At the time of More's attainder his stepmother was in possession of John More's estate of More Place, at North Mimms in Hertfordshire. Thomas More's great-grandson, Cresacre More, tells us that she was a little before her death thrust out of all by King Henry's fury. Yet Cresacre in due course inherited the estate, for Queen Mary restored it.

But all these troubles were in the very distant future when young John More was bringing up his family in Cripplegate ward; perhaps he lived in Milk Street, in Cripplegate Within, perhaps in the parish of St. Giles Cripplegate, outside the walls.

One vivid recollection of these early years Thomas More retained:

> The self night in which King Edward died, one Mistlebrook, long ere morning, came in great haste to the house of one Pottier, dwelling in Redcross Street without Cripplegate; and when he was with hasty rapping quickly letten in, he showed unto Pottier that King Edward was departed. 'By my troth, man,' quoth Pottier, 'then will my master the Duke of Gloucester be king.' What cause he had so to think, hard it is to say; whether he, being toward him,[2] anything knew that he such thing purposed, or otherwise had any inkling thereof; but he was not likely to speak it of naught.[3]

So the story is recorded in the *History of Richard III*, in the English version. But in the Latin version there is a significant addition, to the effect that the writer remembers this speech having been repeated, by one who had overheard it, to his father, at a time when no suspicion of treason toward the young princes was as yet entertained. As there is no doubt whatever that both the Latin and the English version of *Richard III* were written by More himself, we can form a picture of a bright boy of five years and two months, suddenly startled by the horror which his father shows at a mysterious speech, and keeping it in his memory till the time comes when he understands its full significance.

[1] *Apology: Works*, 1557, p. 867.   [2] i.e. in personal attendance upon him.
[3] *Works*, 1557, pp. 37-8.

Father and son remained associated through life. When Chancellor, More was accustomed, on his knees, to seek his father's blessing in the law-courts at Westminster.[1] Judge John fortunately did not live to see his son's troubles, and when he died,[2] More felt that the time had come to write his own epitaph.

§ 2. A FIFTEENTH-CENTURY CITY SCHOOLBOY

More was 'brought up in the Latin tongue at St. Antony's in London'. St. Antony's was the leading London school; its rival in the City was the school of St. Thomas of Acre (St. Thomas à Becket), already connected with the Mercers Company. Later, Colet's foundation, St. Paul's School, was to rival both. The school of St. Antony in Threadneedle Street had already two and a half centuries of history behind it; it had been endowed by Henry VI, and again by Edward IV; and, though it was destined to decay in the near future, it was still to produce two archbishops. In More's day the schoolmaster was Nicholas Holt – to be distinguished from John Holt, a friend of More's of whom we shall hear further.

The most vivid account of these schools belongs to a period later than that of More's schooldays.

Education in Fifteenth and early Sixteenth Century London meant the habit of disputation, of course in Latin; the love of debate which we see everywhere in More's writings was implanted in him early. When John Stowe published his *Survey of London* in the year of the accession of James I, the practice was remembered:

> The arguing of the schoolboys about the principles of Grammar hath been continued even till our time. For I myself in my youth have yearly seen, on the eve of St. Bartholomew the Apostle, the scholars of divers Grammar schools repair unto the churchyard of St. Bartholomew, the Priory, in Smithfield, where, upon a bank boarded about under a tree, some one scholar hath stepped up, and there hath apposed and answered, till he were by some better scholar overcome and put down.

Stowe mentions St. Antony's School as the one which commonly

---

[1] STAPLETON, I, p. 156.
[2] John More's will was proved 5th December, 1530 (Somerset House, Jankyn, f. 24). It is an interesting document, and leaves instructions for prayer for the soul of Edward IV (cf. p. 117, below).

presented the best scholars and had the prize. The competition
of St. Paul's School was probably not serious, for Colet in his
Statutes had discouraged it: 'I will they use no cockfighting,
nor riding about of victory, nor disputing at St. Bartholomew's,
which is but foolish babbling and loss of time.'

After the dissolution of the monasteries these disputations
at St. Bartholomew's ceased – but not the disputatiousness of
the schoolboys:

> Howsoever the encouragement failed, the scholars of Paul's
> meeting with them of St. Antony's would call them 'Antony
> pigs', and they again would call the other 'pigeons of
> Paul's', because many pigeons were bred in Paul's Church,
> and St. Antony was always figured with a pig following him.

So, despite the cessation of official disputing, the boys of both
schools, 'mindful of the former usage, did for a long season
disorderly in the open street provoke one another' with a
challenge to disputation,

> and so proceeding from this to questions in grammar, they
> usually fall from words to blows, with their satchels full of
> books, many times in great heaps, that they troubled the
> streets and passengers, so that finally they were restrained
> with the decay of St. Antony's school.

Schoolboys remain much the same; but in one respect the
schoolboy scuffles which Stowe noted must have differed from
those in which More took part. The satchels full of books are
the product of the printing press. If we could see the school-
room of St. Antony's when More was being taught, it would be
the scarcity of books which would surprise us, and the largeness
of the classes. 'On the title pages of early schoolbooks are
sometimes found woodcuts which represent the children
sitting, like the Indian schoolboy of to-day, in crowds about
their master, taking only the barest amount of space, and content with the steps of his desk, or even the floor.' Twenty years
later, and in Germany, which was far ahead of England in
printing, we hear of classes in which only the preceptor had a
printed book. The teacher dictated the passage, then pointed
it, then construed it, and finally explained it: 'It was a weari-
some business for all concerned. The reading of a few lines of
text, the punctuation, the elaborate glosses full of well-nigh

incomprehensible abbreviations; all dictated slowly enough for a class of a hundred or more to take down every word.'[1]

Yet the shortage of books may not have been entirely a disadvantage. Boys had to trust their memories, and to train their memories so that they could trust them, to a degree that might astonish the modern schoolboy. And they were not distracted by the variety of the curriculum. Their aim was to read Latin, write Latin, and dispute in Latin. Not long ago an old-fashioned master, bored by an educational conference discussing optional subjects, at length burst out – 'It doesn't matter what you teach a boy, provided he doesn't like it.' The Fifteenth Century schoolboy never lacked the discipline of having to learn what he certainly cannot much have liked.

There is one passage, written by More in the Tower, which brings the London schoolboy vividly before us. More is speaking of those spiritual advisers who will not warn great men that they are courting destruction by persisting in their obstinate ways. He is thinking, there can be little doubt, of King Henry VIII, and his subservient clergy, who are leaving the duty of withstanding the King to him, Thomas More, a mere layman. It is a painful subject, but even then More's irony bursts forth:

> And in such wise deal they with him as the mother doth sometime with her child; which when the little boy will not rise in time for her, but lie still abed and slugg, and when he is up, weepeth because he hath lien so long, fearing to be beaten at school for his late coming thither, she telleth him then that it is but early days, and he shall come time enough, and biddeth him 'Go, good son, I warrant thee, I have sent to thy master myself, take thy bread and butter with thee, thou shalt not be beaten at all'. And thus, so she may send him merry forth at the door that he weep not in her sight at home, she studieth not much upon the matter, though he be taken tardy and beaten when he cometh to school.[2]

§ 3.   THE CHILD SERVING THE CHANCELLOR

More's next experience was to be more exciting. He must have left St. Antony's about the age of twelve, and

---

[1] P. S. ALLEN, *The Age of Erasmus*, 1914, pp. 35-6.
[2] *Dialogue of Comfort: Works*, 1557, p. 1156.

was by his father's procurement received into the house of
the right reverend, wise, and learned prelate Cardinal
Morton; where, though he was young of years, yet would he
at Christmas tide suddenly sometimes step in among the
players, and never studying for the matter, make a part of
his own there presently among them, which made the lookers
on more sport than all the players beside. In whose wit and
towardness the Cardinal much delighting, would often say
of him unto the nobles that divers times dined with him:
'This child here waiting at the table, whosoever shall live
to see it, will prove a marvellous man.'[1]

This practice of putting out children into the household of
others, was a survival of the old chivalrous custom by which
a youth of good birth was trained as a page in the household
of a great man. It seems to have been, at this time, more
prevalent in England than abroad, and it aroused the hostile
comment of foreigners:

> The want of affection in the English is strongly manifested
> towards their children; for after having kept them at home
> till they arrive at the age of seven or nine years at the utmost,
> they put them out, both males and females, to hard service
> in the houses of other people . . . And few are born who are
> exempted from this fate, for every one, however rich he may
> be, sends away his children into the houses of others, whilst
> he, in return, receives those of strangers into his own.

So we are informed by an Italian diplomat, who transmitted to
Venice (and so to us) a most valuable account of English
customs about the year 1500. He disapproves of this treatment
of the young:

> And on enquiring their reason for this severity, they answered
> that they did it in order that their children might learn
> better manners. But I, for my part, believe that they do it
> because they like to enjoy all their comforts themselves, and
> that they are better served by strangers than they would be
> by their own children. Besides which the English being
> great epicures, and very avaricious by nature, indulge in the
> most delicate fare themselves, and give their household the
> coarsest bread, and beer, and cold meat baked on Sunday
> for the week, which, however, they allow them in great

[1] ROPER, p. 5.

abundance. If they had their own children at home, they would be obliged to give them the same food they make use of for themselves.[1]

But, as Sir Walter Scott says in his *Essay on Chivalry*, the *theory* of the gentleman page, serving in a great house, was uniformly excellent. 'The noble youth was required to do the work which, in some respects, belonged to a menial; but not as a menial.' The practice deteriorated. Unless the magnate took very seriously his duty to his pages, the pages might pick up bad habits from less gentle fellow-servants. Readers of Ben Jonson may remember the discussion in which one of the characters declares this kind of service to be

> . . . the noblest way
> Of breeding up our youth in letters, arms,
> Fair mien, discourses, civil exercise
> And all the blazon of a gentleman.

But the other character protests that he would rather hang his boy with his own hand

> Than damn him to that desperate course of life.[2]

There can be no doubt as to the very great advantages More derived. It would be his business to master the elaborate rules of etiquette which are explained to us in Fifteenth Century Books of Courtesy; and in the household of Morton he would have a chance of watching the demeanour of all the greatest men of the realm. Morton was already Archbishop of Canterbury, and Lord Chancellor, though not yet Cardinal. That he kept a watchful eye upon the boy entrusted to him by John More, we gather from Roper's words just quoted, and from More's own words as well.

In *Utopia*, sixteen years after Morton's death, More paid his tribute to his old master. Raphael Hythlodaye, the traveller, is depicted as telling Peter Giles of Antwerp and Thomas More of London about his travels, and among other things about his visit to the house of Archbishop Morton:

a man, Master Peter (for Master More knoweth already that I will say) not more honourable for his authority, than for

---

[1] *A Relation of the Island of England*, trans. by C. A. SNEYD, London, 1847 (Camden Society), pp. 24-5.
[2] *The New Inn*, Act I, Sc. 1.

his prudence and virtue. He was of a mean [i.e. medium]
stature, and though stricken in age, yet bare he his body
upright. His looks begot reverence rather than fear. Gentle
in communication, yet earnest, and sage. He had great
delight many times with rough speech to his suitors, to prove,
but without harm, what prompt wit, and what bold spirit
were in every man. In the which, as in a virtue much agreeing with his nature, so that therewith were not joined im-
pudency, he took great delectation. And the same person, as
apt and meet to have an administration in the weal public,
he did lovingly embrace. In his speech he was fine, eloquent,
and pithy. In the law he had profound knowledge, in wit he
was incomparable, and in memory wonderful excellent . . .
And so by many and great dangers he learned the experience
of the world, which so being learned can not easily be forgotten.[1]

A recent discovery has thrown new light upon the description of More 'stepping in among the players' at the Archbishop's
Christmas feasts and 'making a part of his own'.

Sixteen years ago the unique copy of the earliest secular
play in English turned up, from a country mansion in Flint,[2]
where it had only once caught a scholar's eye, and then only
for a moment, to be immediately forgotten. It was purchased
at a record figure for the magnificent Huntington Library in
California. With praiseworthy public spirit, the American
millionaire at once made it accessible to scholars in facsimile.
The play, *Fulgens and Lucrece*, was printed by More's brother-in-
law, John Rastell. It was written by Henry Medwall, chaplain
to Cardinal Morton, and pioneer of the English drama. It was
probably written to be acted as a Christmas play, some half-
dozen years after More was serving Morton as a page. The
most noteworthy thing is that the play begins by the speeches
of two youths, A and B. A bids the guests welcome; B says that
there is going to be a play, and tells the plot. The play begins –
it deals with the rivalry between the worthless Patrician
Publius Cornelius, and the virtuous Plebeian Gaius Flaminius,
for the hand of Lucrece. B steps in among the players, and
takes service with Cornelius; A is scandalized at this intrusion,

---

[1] *Utopia*, ed. LUPTON, pp. 41-3.
[2] Mostyn Hall. Sold at Sotheby's, March 1919.

when B at first suggests it – 'By god, thou wilt destroy all the play'; but, later, A follows suit, and takes service with Flaminius. While the masters woo the mistress, the pages woo the maid. A and B are clearly professional actors, and have their parts written for them by the dramatist. But it looks as if the 'stepping in among the players' had become a popular feature, and, since there was no one like young More capable of doing it impromptu, the parts of the 'steppers-in' had to be written by the dramatist. Anyway, the connection of More with the beginnings of the English drama in the household of Cardinal Morton is established. And so is the intertwining of main plot and comic underplot, which became a convention of the English drama, and received its finished form at the hands of Shakespeare.

It was probably to the training under Morton that More owed his manners. More's manners, though good, were not those of the age of chivalry. It is indeed remarkable how the early Sixteenth Century has lost the chivalrous ideals which were still powerful in the Fourteenth. More's warmest admirers could not pretend that he was a man like Chaucer's Knight, who had never spoken any evil word

In all his life, unto no manner wight.

There is no Englishman in the reign of Henry VIII who comes up to the standard of manners which inspires the best of the good knights of whose deeds Froissart tells us, and which an anonymous contemporary of Chaucer drew with unsurpassable skill and subtlety in the character of Sir Gawayne in the romance of *Sir Gawayne and the Green Knight*. To Langland, as to Chaucer, chivalry was still a great ideal. But by the Sixteenth Century the age of chivalry was dead; though Henry VIII would have been shocked had he been told so, for he and his courtiers loved to deck themselves in its outworn trappings. But the spirit of chivalry was gone out of English life for the moment – for the moment only, because the spirit is immortal.

We shall find in More nothing of that knightly bearing which casts a glamour of romance over many a man of earlier and of later ages who in regard to prosaic, substantial virtues cannot be compared with him. More must have turned over the leaves of his father's book on King Arthur – the *History* of Geoffrey of

Monmouth. Books would not be so plentiful in More's home
that he could afford to neglect any he found there. But Arthur
made no impression: Table Round and Twelve Peers meant
nothing to Thomas More. He could never, like Spenser, have
thought of the men he met at court as knights riding and
conversing with Prince Arthur. Still less could he, like St.
Francis, have counted Charlemagne and his paladins, Roland
and Ogier the Dane, amongst the saints and martyrs of God.
But though without any touch of the 'fair mien' of chivalry,
More is always well bred and self-possessed. The ease with
which he moves among the *parvenu* world of the early Tudors is
remarkable. When he walks at Chelsea, discussing matters,
with the King's arm about his neck, or arm in arm with
the Duke of Norfolk, he can hold his own, proof against
either intimidation or flattery. More had been early initiated
into the ways of the great; like Swift, who, when a mere lad,
was sent by Sir William Temple to try and get complicated
ideas of the British Constitution into the Dutch head of William
III. The writings of both Swift and More show how they had
been struck by the vastness of the issues placed upon the
shoulders of those who, after all, are mere men. But there had
been no ambiguity about the position of young More; he had
not been embittered, like young Swift, by being half servant
and half friend. He was the child, waiting at the table. In later
life Thomas More had a dispute with Mr. Secretary Cromwell –
as Swift had with Mr. Secretary St. John. More told of it in a
letter to his daughter Margaret, as Swift told of it in a letter to
Stella. But we cannot imagine More using to Margaret words
parallel to those which Swift uses to Stella: 'I think what I
said to Mr. Secretary was right. Don't you remember how I
used to be in pain when Sir William Temple would look out of
humour? He spoiled a fine gentleman.' When Morton looked
out of humour, More had learnt how to reply with prompt
wit and bold spirit. More is always sure of himself; on the
scaffold he knows exactly what is due to everybody; a cheery
jest to Mr. Lieutenant, encouragement to the executioner
('Pluck up thy spirits, man'), respect to himself, service to the
King, higher service to God. There is no trace in More of the
alternate hectoring and cringing which marks most con-

temporary Englishmen – even those of noblest birth. The poise of Thomas More is something beyond that of any of the great English nobles of the blood royal. For, despite the systematic slaughter, there was plenty of the blood royal about. (Henry VIII chose his wives from a wide circle, yet all were descended from Edward I, and so, says the genealogist, 'stood in the relation of cousins, in various degrees, to their arbitrary lord'.)[1] Royal blood, however, might often be an embarrassment; and sometimes it might be a capital crime; the head of a great aristocrat stood tickle on his shoulders; an indiscreet word might shake it off. But More's birth was too humble to arouse suspicion, and, if he was to end on the scaffold, it would be by his own deliberate act. Yet he had been brought up as well as any of them – he must have heard conversations at the Archbishop's table, in Latin and in English, which made him as well informed as any boy of his age in the realm.

More's good manners did not mean that he was incapable of flattery; and in those vulgar days the butter was laid on thick. But it must be the best butter[2] – flattery expressed in good English, or better still in good Latin.

§ 4. A STUDENT AT OXFORD

So, 'for his better furtherance in learning', Morton placed More, about the age of fourteen, at Oxford. The beauty of the buildings of Fifteenth-Century Oxford must have been amazing. But life at Oxford was democratic and austere, as it had been through the Middle Ages. Chaucer's Clerk of Oxenford was typical:

> As lene was his hors as is a rake
> And he nas nat right fat, I undertake.
> Ful thredbar was his overest courtepy.

Poor students were licensed to beg, under the Chancellor's seal; one of More's biographers speaks of poor scholars of Oxford, with bags and wallets, singing at rich men's doors.[3] The routine of the really industrious Oxford student in More's

---

[1] GEORGE FISHER, *Key to the History of England*, 1832, Table XVII.

[2] 'The taste of that age liked the butter spread thick, and Erasmus' was the best butter.' P. S. ALLEN, *The Age of Erasmus*, 1914, p. 132.

[3] HARPSFIELD, p. 144. Harpsfield was an Oxford man, and 'poor scholars of Oxford' is *his* addition to his source. See p. 67 below.

youth was probably not very different from that of 'divers'
diligent Cantabs some fifteen years after his death: Chapel from
five to six in the morning; work from six to ten; then dinner,
consisting of a penny piece of beef amongst four, with broth and
oatmeal, and nothing else; then work again until five, 'when
they have a supper not much better than their dinner'; then
work till nine or ten, when the scholars 'being without fire, are
fain to walk or run up and down half an hour, to get a heat on
their feet when they go to bed'.[1] And More's father did nothing
to alleviate this austerity. More had not money to get his shoes
mended, without asking his father. In later life he used often
to talk about his father's strictness, and to say it was quite right,
too. 'That', he would say, 'was why in his youth he did not
know the meaning of extravagance or luxury, could not put
money to evil uses, seeing that he had no money to put to any
uses at all, and, in short, had nothing to think about except his
studies.'[2] It must be remembered that the undergraduate who
was subjected to this rigorous treatment was between fourteen
and sixteen.

There has been dispute as to which was More's College or
Hall at Oxford. But a reputable authority[3] says Canterbury
College; and since it was the Archbishop of Canterbury who
'placed' More at Oxford, it would be natural for him to go
there. The name of Canterbury College is still preserved by
the Canterbury Quad of Christ Church, which occupies its site.
It was a home of the Benedictines. It was also a home of Greek
studies. Nearly a generation before More's time, a monk of
Canterbury, William Selling, sent to finish his studies at
Canterbury College, had been given leave to make the
Italian tour, and had brought Greek manuscripts back to
England. More's biographers tell us that at Oxford 'he was
both in the Greek and Latin tongue sufficiently instructed'.[4]
More's Latin by this time would be fluent; but it is not certain
that the boy learnt any Greek at Oxford, although he no doubt
acquired 'a firm conviction that there was such a language'.
Grocyn had returned to Oxford from Italy, where he had per-

---

[1] LEVER, *Sermon preached at Pauls Cross, 1550*, ed. ARBER, 1870, p. 122.
[2] STAPLETON, I, p. 156.   [3] CRESACRE MORE, 1726, p. 9.
[4] ROPER, p. 5; cf. STAPLETON, I, p. 155.

fected his Greek, not long before More went to the University, and it is possible that More may have learnt a little from him there; but it was not till about seven years after he had left Oxford, when he was a law student in London, that More first spoke of himself as making a serious study of Greek. Grocyn, Linacre and Colet have been christened 'the Oxford Reformers', and a pretty and quite imaginary picture has been drawn of these dons all studying Greek together with young Thomas More, aged fifteen.[1] But it was later, in London, that they all became close and intimate friends, and 'London Reformers' would be a better name for the group than 'Oxford Reformers'.

§ 5 .   NEW INN AND LINCOLN'S INN

After less than two years[2] at Oxford More was 'for the study of the law of the realm put to an Inn of Chancery called New Inn, where for his time he very well prospered; and from thence was admitted to Lincoln's Inn, with very small allowance, continuing there his study, until he was made and accounted a worthy utter barrister'.[3] But we must not think of More as an undergraduate whose career has been interrupted by a stern father, and who has been withdrawn from the joys of

> The measured pulse of racing oars
> Among the willows

to the

> brawling courts
> And dusty purlieus of the law.

London, and not Oxford, was the place where a young man of birth and ambition might at this date best be brought up. Erasmus speaks of 'London, the famous city where, among the English, it is held an honour to be born *and educated*'.[4] Oxford and Cambridge provided an education for those who meant to take Holy Orders. But the object of an ambitious father was to place his son at one of the Inns of Court. So much was this the case, that only six or eight of the Commons of Henry's great Reformation Parliament are known to have received what would now be called a university education. One of these was Edward Hall the Chronicler, who, like More,

---

[1] SEEBOHM, *The Oxford Reformers*, p. 25.   [2] HARPSFIELD, p. 12.
[3] ROPER, p. 5.   [4] *Epist. Opus*, Basel, 1538, p. 1071.

had been to a university before becoming a student of the law.[1]
But most young men ambitious of distinction in civil life went
straight to one of the Inns of Court. 'It was not then a metaphor
to call them an university: they had professors of law; they
conferred the characters of barrister and serjeant, analogous
to the degrees of bachelor, master and doctor, bestowed by
universities; and every man, before he became a barrister,
was subjected to examination, and obliged to defend a thesis.'[2]

From the material point of view, the change from Oxford
to London was a change from democratic penury to aristocratic comfort. After he had resigned his offices at Court, More
traced to his children his gradual growth in prosperity, and
suggested that the progress might now take place in the
opposite direction:

'I have been brought up', quoth he, 'at Oxford, at an Inn
of Chancery, at Lincoln's Inn, and also in the King's Court,
and so forth from the lowest degree to the highest, and yet
have I in yearly revenues at this present left me little above
an hundred pounds by the year. So that now must we hereafter, if we like to live together, be contented to become con-
tributaries together. But, by my counsel, it shall not be best
for us to fall to the lowest fare first: we will not therefore
descend to Oxford fare, nor to the fare of New Inn. But we
will begin with Lincoln's Inn diet, where many right wor-
shipful and of good years do live full well; which, if we find
not ourselves the first year able to maintain, then will we the
next year go one step down to New Inn fare, wherewith
many an honest man is well contented. If that exceed our
ability too, then will we the next year after descend to Oxford
fare, where many grave, learned, and ancient fathers be continually conversant.'[3]

But More cannot contemplate a lower stage than Oxford fare,
except begging. If their power does not stretch to maintain
Oxford fare,

then may we yet, with bags and wallets, go a begging together, and hoping that for pity some good folk will give us
their charity, at every man's door to sing *Salve Regina*, and
so still keep company and be merry together.

[1] A. F. POLLARD in *The Times*, 1 Oct. 1932.
[2] MACKINTOSH, *Life of Sir Thomas More*, p. 19.   [3] ROPER. pp. 53-4.

New Inn will be remembered by the older generation of Londoners. It was swept away to make room for the modern Aldwych; but the buildings then destroyed were much later than More's time.

Just after his eighteenth birthday More had reached sufficient standing to be admitted to Lincoln's Inn. At the instance of his father he was 'pardoned four vacations'.[1] At the same time, also at the instance of John More, and on the same terms, Richard Staverton was admitted; he has been already mentioned above as the future husband of More's elder sister, Joan. With one noteworthy exception, nothing stands in Lincoln's Inn to-day that was standing when More entered. That exception is the Hall, which had been completed four years before. It has since suffered many vicissitudes; but now, having just undergone a drastic but archaeologically careful restoration, it shows us an early Tudor building in all its freshness of red and blue-black brick and white stone, almost exactly as it must have struck the eye of young Thomas More.

In Lincoln's Inn Thomas was under the paternal eye; but a little more than three years after his entry occurred an event tending to encourage those distracting rival studies which John More feared. Erasmus paid his first visit to England, in the summer of 1499.

§ 6.   ERASMUS FINDS ENGLAND AND HIMSELF

The genius of Holbein has impressed upon the minds of us all a picture of Erasmus, which makes it more difficult in his case than in that of old Judge More to imagine him as a young man. For no one can look at Holbein's Judge More without seeing that he remembers that he has once been young. Erasmus looks as if he had forgotten it: 'The dainty hands, and the general primness of his appearance', a historian has said,[2] 'suggest a descent from a long line of maiden aunts.' The portrait suggests much more than that: a combination of discretion and resolution which will allow Erasmus to be made neither the tool nor the victim of any tyrant or of any extremist. Holbein's Erasmus shows us a man who for over a quarter of a

[1] 12 Feb. 1496; *The Black Books of Lincoln's Inn*, Book II, pt. I, fol. 34.
[2] LINDSAY, *Reformation*, I, p. 177.

century has been struggling against the bigotries of mankind. He will struggle on for many years more – but he is not a little weary.

The Erasmus however who came to England at the end of the Fifteenth Century was pretty certainly not yet thirty-three, perhaps not yet thirty. These uncertainties as to the date of his birth are due to the first of the many misfortunes against which Erasmus had to fight throughout life. He was an illegitimate child, and, to make matters worse, his father was probably already a priest when he was born. Opinions nowadays differ as to how strictly the clergy of the Sixteenth Century observed their vows; indeed opinions differed at the time. More's *Dialogue* shows that it was believed in London (wrongly, of course) that in Wales priests were allowed to have wives. More contradicts the rumour: 'But truth it is', he says, 'that incontinence is there in some place little looked unto, whereof much harm groweth in the country'.[1] In the more out of the way parts of the Low Countries things would seem to have been much the same. Rudolf Agricola, the great scholar of the generation before Erasmus, whom Erasmus prided himself on having as a schoolboy once met, was the son of a priest. The priest had just been elected Warden of a College of nuns, when a messenger came running to him from his home, to tell him of the birth of his son Rudolf. 'This is an auspicious day', exclaimed the new Warden, 'for it has twice made me father.'[2]

Whilst still a youth, Erasmus lost both his father and mother. His guardians badgered the unwilling boy into choosing a monastic life. He had no vocation for it. These personal misfortunes dogged Erasmus till well on in middle life. By an odd coincidence, the Papal dispensation which helped him out of all his early troubles came in the same year which saw the outburst of the great Lutheran quarrel that was to embitter all his later years, to wreck much of his work, and all his hopes. Erasmus was born to trouble as the sparks fly upward.

After uneasy years spent in the Priory of Augustinian Canons at Steyn, near Gouda, Erasmus gained a precarious freedom as Secretary to the Bishop of Cambrai. He then got leave to study in the University of Paris, where he maintained himself

[1] *Works*, 1557, p. 231.   [2] P. S. ALLEN, *The Age of Erasmus*, p. 14.

as a tutor. But the dread of being recalled to residence in the Dutch Priory hung over him during all these early years.

An English lord, Mountjoy, later tutor to Prince Henry, was among Erasmus' pupils, and remained throughout life, so far as his means allowed, one of his best patrons. Mountjoy, though young, was married, but his child-wife had been living with her father, Sir William Say, whilst her husband had been finishing his education in Paris. In the summer of 1499 Mountjoy brought Erasmus back to England with him, and they stayed together, probably at the house of Sir William Say at Bedwell in Hertfordshire. [1]

Sir William Say was a family friend of the Mores, and it may have been through him that More met Erasmus. There is an old story that Erasmus and More, neither of them knowing the other, met at the Lord Mayor's table, and were so struck with each other's wit as to exclaim, 'You must be More or no one', 'You must be Erasmus or the Devil'. The story is probably untrue. But the first authentic record of their friendship is even more striking. With the help of Mountjoy, More contrived suddenly to bring the rather timid foreign scholar face to face with the boy who was later to be Henry VIII. He may have wished to provide Erasmus with a future patron; he perhaps took a mischievous pleasure in watching the demeanour of his friend, who had not, like himself, had the advantage of an education in etiquette in the household of the greatest statesman of a great realm. How would Erasmus behave? This is how Erasmus himself tells the story, twenty years and more later:

Thomas More, who had visited me when I was staying in Mountjoy's country house, [2] had taken me out for a walk as far as the next village. [3] For there all the royal children were being educated, Arthur alone excepted, the eldest son. When we came to the hall, all the retinue was assembled; not only that of the palace, but Mountjoy's as well. In the midst stood Henry, aged nine, already with a certain royal demeanour; I mean a dignity of mind combined with a re-

[1] ALLEN, I, No. 103.
[2] Mountjoy was probably staying near Greenwich. See NICHOLS, I, p. 200.
[3] Eltham. The great hall, where the meeting took place, is still standing with its magnificent timber roof.

markable courtesy. On his right was Margaret, about eleven years old,[1] who afterwards married James, King of Scots. On the left Mary was playing, a child of four. Edmund was an infant in arms. More with his companion Arnold saluted Henry (the present King of England) and presented to him something in writing. I, who was expecting nothing of the sort, had nothing to offer; but I promised that somehow, at some other time, I would show my duty towards him. Meantime, I was a bit annoyed with More for having given me no warning, especially because the boy, during dinner, sent me a note inviting something from my pen. I went home, and though the Muses, from whom I had long been divorced, were unwilling, I finished the poem in three days.

It was a poem in praise of Henry VII, his children, and his kingdom.[2]

Erasmus was thoroughly enjoying himself at English country houses. He writes to Faustus Andrelinus, a flippant humanist poet-friend whom he had left behind him in Paris: 'We have made some progress in England. The Erasmus you once knew has now almost become a sportsman, not the worst possible rider, a fairly skilful courtier; he can make a polite bow, smile gracefully, and all this in spite of himself. You, too, will fly over here if you are wise. As for your gout stopping you, why, if you knew the charms of Britain you would wish for the wings of Daedalus.' And Erasmus goes on to refer to an English custom which is recorded by many other foreign visitors, that of greeting with a kiss:

To mention only one attraction out of many; there are girls here with divine features, gentle and kind; you may well prefer them to your Muses. And, moreover, there is a custom which cannot be sufficiently praised. Wherever you go, you are received with kisses from everybody; when you leave you are dismissed with kisses. You go back, and your kisses are returned to you. People arrive: kisses; they depart: kisses; wherever people foregather, there are lots of kisses; in fact, whatever way you turn, everything is full of kisses. Oh, Faustus, if you had once tasted how soft, how fragrant those kisses are, you would wish to exile yourself, not, as Solon did, for ten years, but all your life, in England.[3]

[1] Actually, Henry was a little over eight, and Margaret a little under ten.
[2] ALLEN, I, No. 1, p. 6.   [3] ALLEN, I, No. 103.

But Erasmus was already a very serious person, and this visit to England was not a frivolous pleasure trip, to be divided between the town and the country houses of his aristocratic patrons. A good deal of his time was spent at Oxford. Modern scholars have not been able to find any justification for the jibe to which Gibbon gave currency, that Erasmus learned at Oxford the Greek which he subsequently taught at Cambridge.[1] There were English scholars who could have improved the little Greek Erasmus brought with him, but there is no evidence that they were in Oxford at the time of his visit. Erasmus' own words show that his serious study of Greek came after his first English tour.[2] But in Oxford he came under the influence of John Colet.

Colet, the son of Sir Henry Colet, more than once Lord Mayor of London, had not been held back by the poverty which had depressed Erasmus. He had already accomplished Erasmus' yet unfulfilled ambition, and had spent years of travel and study in Italy. There is little trace of Erasmus having at this date influenced Colet. But the influence of Colet upon Erasmus was enormous. One biographer after another, writing the life of the great humanist, has felt that it was this friendship with Colet which 'definitely decided the bent of Erasmus' many-sided mind'.[3]

And as we run through the early correspondence of Erasmus we can hardly fail to be impressed by the change wrought in him through this visit to England, and his friendship with Colet and with More. Although Erasmus was destined to be one of the great figures of history, his growth till now had been slow. For the first time in his life, he made the friendship of men of his own calibre. Colet was about his own age, More much younger, but both had been developing much more quickly than he. Erasmus never formed two more fruitful friendships, although he was lucky throughout life in having many faithful and unselfish friends, and as we go over the list of his correspondents, we encounter the names of all the greatest men of his age.

But, till he met More and Colet, the letters of Erasmus are

<hr />

[1] *Decline and Fall*, Chap. LXVI, footnote.   [2] ALLEN, I, No. I, p. 8.
[3] HUIZINGA, *Erasmus*, 1924, p. 37.

those of an amiable but aimless young scholar, not too well friended. The most illustrious name we meet among his correspondents before this English visit is that of Hector Boyse,[1] a Scotsman from Dundee who was afterwards the first Principal of King's College, Aberdeen. And you may take it, reader, on the word of one who is being compelled, as a duty, to read through Boyse's *History of Scotland*, that, though an interesting man, Boyse was not the peer of the Erasmus of Rotterdam whose name he placed in the forefront of his *History*.

But in Colet Erasmus made a friend who was to help him to discover his life work; and with More he made the longest of all his friendships. When Erasmus had gone to Oxford, he still continued to write to More; it is with a letter from Erasmus that More's extant correspondence opens.[2] Erasmus had written other letters, which have been lost. More, busy no doubt with his law studies, had not replied – or, as Erasmus tactfully put it, the carelessness or perfidy of the letter-carrier had somehow made away with a letter which he could not suppose he had failed to receive through any fault of More's. Accordingly, Erasmus writes to demand, not a mere letter, but the packet which is due to him from More, 'the most good-natured of men, and one who, I am persuaded, loves me very dearly'. And never for a moment was that persuasion shaken by any shadow of unkindness, albeit their tempers were different, and that of Erasmus was not an easy one. When, nearly thirty-six years later, the news of More's execution reached Basel, Erasmus, worn out by work, disease, and disappointment, ran over the roll-call of the friends he had lost, in the preface of the book he was just publishing: 'First William Warham, Archbishop of Canterbury, then of late Mountjoy, and Fisher of Rochester, and Thomas More, Lord Chancellor of England, whose soul was more pure than any snow, whose genius was such as England never had – yea, and never shall have again, mother of good wits though England be.'[3] A few days later he writes to a friend, 'In More's death I seem to have died myself; we had but one soul between us.'[4]

---

[1] See ALLEN, I, No. 47 (8 Nov. 1495).   [2] 28 Oct. 1499, ALLEN, I, No. 114.
[3] The *De ratione concionandi* or *Ecclesiastes*, Basel, 1535.   [4] 31 Aug. 1535.

Still Erasmus, often bedridden, toils on, and it was a year before he himself got release from what he calls 'this raving world'.

But in 1499 the life work of Erasmus lay all before him, and it is proof of his greatness that he realized that he needed more preparation before he could even begin it. Colet was lecturing on St. Paul's Epistles at Oxford, and he had hoped that Erasmus would settle down there with him, and lecture either on Latin poetry, or on the Old Testament. In the letters of Erasmus to Colet there is, not infrequently, that touch of annoyance which is so conspicuously absent from all his relations with More. Erasmus replies to Colet's invitation by praising his work in restoring theology to its ancient brightness and dignity. Erasmus hopes that he also may some time take a hand in that work. But he is not qualified yet. If Colet says that he expected it, and complains that he has been disappointed, Erasmus tells him bluntly that he must blame himself: 'It was not I that disappointed you, for I neither promised nor hinted anything of the kind. You have disappointed yourself, because you would not believe me when I told you the truth about myself.' Erasmus says that he is returning before long to Paris.[1]

The meaning of it all, though Erasmus does not say so bluntly, is that, before he can do the work which Colet wishes him to do, and which he himself wishes to do, he must learn more Greek than either he or Colet at that moment possessed.

We find Erasmus back in London before the year is out, writing to an old pupil, Robert Fisher, a kinsman of John Fisher afterwards Bishop of Rochester and More's fellow sufferer. Robert Fisher was taking a Doctorate of Laws in Italy – the country, says Erasmus, where the very walls are more learned and eloquent than men are in our regions; so that England will expect Fisher to return not only learned in the law, but chattering Greek as well as Latin. Erasmus says that he would have been in Italy too, by now, had not Mountjoy, a young man so amiable that none can resist him, carried him off to England:

> Yes, you will say, but how do you like our England? If you have any confidence in me, Robert, I ask you to believe me, that nothing in my life has ever pleased me so much. I have

[1] ALLEN, I, No. 108.

found the climate both pleasant and healthy. And I have met with so much kindness and so much learning, not hackneyed and trivial, but deep, exact, ancient, Latin and Greek, that I am not hankering so much after Italy, except just for the sake of seeing it. When I hear my Colet, I seem to be listening to Plato himself. In Grocyn, who does not wonder at that perfect compass of all knowledge? What is more acute, more profound, more keen than the judgement of Linacre? What did nature ever create milder, sweeter or happier than the genius of Thomas More? But why should I run through the whole list? It is marvellous how widespread and how abundant is the harvest of ancient learning which is flourishing in this country. All the more reason for your returning to it quickly. From London, in haste.[1]

It is significant that More, not yet twenty-two, should be classed with men so much his seniors. Also we must not forget that it is to an Englishman that Erasmus is writing this praise of England; yet it shows that he had had a warm welcome. But Erasmus was reckoning without his host – in this case the parsimonious Henry VII. There was an old law of Edward IV forbidding temporarily the export of gold or silver coin, English or foreign, from England, and this had been re-enacted by Henry VII. More and Mountjoy, however, assured Erasmus that all would be well, provided his money were not in English currency. Erasmus was prepared to assert, moreover, that the money had neither been earned nor given in England, but that he had brought it with him into the country. Yet the custom-house officials were adamant. Of the £20 which Erasmus had with him, all but six angels (£2) was confiscated.

We must multiply these figures by at least fifteen to get a reasonable basis of comparison. But the blow to Erasmus cannot be reckoned in terms of cash. He was beginning to see his life-work clear. And before he could set to work to restore true theology to its dignity, he must secure leisure for study. His hopes were shattered, and he never ceased to resent the injury.

So much, he wrote many years later, did it cost me to learn one English law.[2]

[1] 5 Dec. 1499, ALLEN, I, No. 118.
[2] 30 Jan. 1523, *Catalogue of Lucubrations*, ALLEN, I, No. 1, p. 16.

It is odd that Erasmus had been so poorly advised by his lawyer-friend. For More was quite wrong: the Act, as anyone can verify for himself,[1] applies to 'money of the coin of any other realms, lands, or lordships'. Old John More might have said that such mistakes came from his son reading Greek, when he should have been reading Law. And in any case it was unwise of Erasmus to attempt to travel with so much coin. According to his own account, he had a narrow escape from being murdered, even for the little he had left, on the way to Paris.[2] In the early Sixteenth Century it was safer to transmit money by letter of credit than on the person; and Erasmus with proper care could probably have escaped more lightly than a foreign visiting scholar does nowadays, when he finds the Income Tax officials of perfidious Albion extracting four and sixpence in the pound from the fees earned by his lectures.

Henceforward, if ever Erasmus feels that he is being unfairly treated by England or an Englishman, bitterness is apt to peep out. It is all the more noteworthy that, irritable as Erasmus was, he never reproached More. He let his English friends and patrons know what had happened, and he clearly hoped that they would somehow make it good. But he took care to say, in quarters where he knew that it would be repeated, that the friends he had made in England were worth much more to him than the money he had lost. A tactful correspondent duly reports to Mountjoy the eloquence with which Erasmus had spoken of the learning of Colet and the sweetness of More, 'whilst as for you, most excellent Mountjoy, he drew such a picture of *you*, that now I love you as much as he does, and he loves you more than his own eyes'.[3]

Erasmus was attacked by fever when he got back to Paris, and amused his convalescence by compiling a collection of Adages, or familiar quotations from the classics. It was the first great success of his life. He kept on adding to the *Adages* and issuing enlarged collections. The book ran through sixty editions in his lifetime. He was not quite sure at first to whom he should dedicate it, but finally decided upon Mountjoy, in

---

[1] 4 Henry VII, cap. 23. See *Statutes of the Realm*, II, p. 543.
[2] ALLEN, I, No. 119. Compare NICHOLS, I, p. 277.
[3] Feb. 1500, James Batt to Mountjoy, ALLEN, I, No. 120.

order to show that he bore no grudge against his English friends. For the same reason he added to this book the poem in praise of Henry VII and his children which he had made after his visit with More to the royal nursery at Eltham.

He then turned to his preparation for what he had decided was the business of his life – the Restoration of Theology. But to do that he must master Greek. 'Greek is almost too much for me', he writes, 'I have no time, I have nothing with which to buy books or pay a teacher. And amidst all this trouble, I can scarcely get the wherewithal to sustain life. That is what it is to be a scholar.'[1] And there, struggling in Paris, we must leave Erasmus. He is out of the story for the moment, and will not be back among his London friends for some five years.

§ 7 . THE CHURCH OR THE LAW?

At any rate Erasmus had found his life-work. More, the younger man, was still hesitating. He continued his law studies at Lincoln's Inn, and was Reader in Law at Furnivall's Inn 'three years and more'. Furnivall's Inn has been swept off the map within the lifetime of those now living; but the building which some of us remember was only of the early Nineteenth Century. It was there that Dickens wrote *Pickwick*. And even the predecessor of that building was not the Inn of More's day.

But More was hesitating between Law and Holy Orders, not settling down to Law as his father wished. For about four years 'he gave himself to devotion and prayer in the Charterhouse of London'. He lived there, Roper says,[2] 'religiously'; that is, sharing, so far as a busy young law-student could, the religious life of the monks; but 'without vow'. Nowadays, of course, such a combination is impossible; but, as a modern Carthusian reminds us, 'in those days the rule which limits visits and retreats to ten days was not in force'.[3] More had also thoughts, we are told, of becoming a Franciscan friar.[4]

The Charterhouses and the Observant Franciscans of Greenwich were the two bodies which, thirty-five years later, were associated with More and Fisher, in their resistance to Henry's claims. More watched the Charterhouse priors, in

---

[1] March 1500, ALLEN, I, No. 123.　　　[2] ROPER, p. 6.
[3] HENDRIKS, *The London Charterhouse*, p. 65.　　　[4] STAPLETON, II, p. 161.

1535, 'as cheerfully going to their deaths as bridegrooms to their marriage', when they were bound on hurdles for their terrible journey from the Tower to Tyburn. But most of the Carthusians who then suffered were younger men, and cannot have worshipped with More in the chapel of the London Charterhouse at the beginning of the century.

We must not, as many biographers have done, consider More's 'faith in humanism' and his 'religious zeal' to have been two conflicting emotions. They were rather aspects of one and the same aspiration, easily reconcilable with each other, but not so easily reconcilable with the legal career which More's father planned for him. For law, as Bacon found later, 'drinks too much time'. More's learned friends, Colet, Grocyn, Linacre, Erasmus, were all in Orders. It was with a fifth friend, William Lily, as they studied Greek together, that More was weighing the question of the lay as against the clerical life. Lily, some ten years older than More, had had all the advantages for which the scholar of those days pined. After graduating at Oxford, he had made the pilgrimage to Jerusalem. He stayed at Rhodes, the outpost of Christendom against the Turk, and learnt Greek there from the refugees who had sought shelter under the strong arm of the Knights of St. John. On his way back, he was able to perfect this knowledge by studying at Rome. The study of Greek and the ideal of the priesthood go hand in hand in More's friendship with Lily. They are both parts of one aim: the restoration of Theology.

What did More, Erasmus and their friends mean by the restoration of Theology? We have seen Erasmus writing to Colet on this subject in connection with Colet's lectures at Oxford on St. Paul's *Epistles*. The manuscripts of Colet's Oxford discourses upon *Romans* and *I Corinthians*, after remaining unprinted nearly four centuries in the libraries (oddly enough) not of Oxford but of Cambridge, have been printed in our own day. They are not easy reading, but they are important as showing how thoroughly Colet had broken with the spirit of the Middle Ages.

The scholars of the Middle Ages had lived in the midst of an allegory. To them the Four Cardinal Virtues, and, still more, the Seven Deadly Sins, were as familiar as the acquaintances whom they met every day in the streets. Go where we will in medieval literature, we are beset by the Seven Deadly Sins, in Chaucer or in *Piers Plowman*, in a manual of devotion or in a scoffing poem.

So accustomed was the medieval man to allegory that he lost the ability to understand the plain statement of some of the books he studied, in the attempt to deduce from it some subtle moral. Biblical exposition, of course, offered wide opportunities. When an Anglo-Saxon preacher discoursed on the visit of the Queen of Sheba to King Solomon, he saw in the two monarchs representatives of the Church and of Christ. The Queen was the Church; she brought gold, gems, and spices; by gold true belief was signified, by spices the breath of prayer, and by gems the shining of good actions and holy virtues. These treasures were borne by camels; the camels must be the heathen who, humpbacked by avarice and deformed by crime, may nevertheless be converted by the Church and led to Jerusalem. Allegorizing earnestness frequently made men blind to the plain meaning of the Biblical text, and the preacher who interpreted 'the oxen were plowing and the asses feeding beside them' as referring to the labouring clergy, and the laity pasturing by their side, had no intention of writing his congregation down as asses. Strange physical facts were invented as bases for argument. The manner in which God hides his mysteries from man's gaze might be compared to the habit of the lion, who, knowing that the hunter will follow his foot-tracks in the sand, obliterates them by wagging his tail backwards and forwards. Or arguments could be drawn from the fictitious elasticity of the human skin after death. The saying of Thomas More, as a boy, was remembered years after he had grown to be a man: that this sort of thing was about as useful as if you should try to milk a he-goat into a sieve.[1]

Now Colet's commentaries mark a break with the allegorizing tradition. To him the *Epistles* of St. Paul are not a string of riddles, but the real letters of a real man, and he wants to get at what that man means. Colet is willing to admit that a non-literal interpretation may often be applicable to the Old Testament. Indeed, in dealing with certain passages, the

---

[1] PACE, *De fructu qui ex doctrina percipitur*, Basel, 1517, p. 83.

account of the Creation, for example, Colet displays a remarkably broad and open mind in insisting that the interpretation is *not* literal. In the days of Queen Victoria, few clerics would have dared to proclaim from the pulpit ideas as to the interpretation of the opening chapter of *Genesis* as liberal as those which Colet puts forward in the despised Fifteenth Century.

But, in the *New Testament*, Colet asserts that, except where a parable is avowedly being uttered, 'all the rest has the sense that appears on the surface, nor is one thing said and another meant, but the very thing is meant which is said, and the sense is wholly literal'.[1]

Colet helped Erasmus on a path where the Dutch scholar was destined far to outstrip him. Colet has no patience with a good deal of medieval learning: 'that filthiness and all such abusion, which the later blind world brought in, which more rather may be called blotterature than literature'. All such learning he wishes utterly to 'abanish and exclude', and to return to the works of the fathers of the early Christian Church, St. Jerome and St. Ambrose and St. Augustine, and to a close study of the text of the Bible itself. But Erasmus saw, much more clearly than Colet did, that for this realistic study the first essential was to get accurate texts, and in the original language.

And so Erasmus, using the printing press as his tool, in a way of which Colet could never have dreamed, toiled to place correct texts of the early Fathers in as many hands as possible. And, above all, his ambition was to print the *New Testament* in the original Greek, and to make a new Latin paraphrase which should free men from slavish service to the letter of the old Vulgate translation.

Nearly seventeen years after Erasmus had told Colet that he could not join him in his work at Oxford, because he was not yet qualified, he was able to present Colet with the final triumph of his studies: his Greek *New Testament*. Colet had the magnanimity to give Erasmus best. His feelings, he said, were divided; he grieved at not having learnt Greek himself, '*for without it we are nothing*'; but this was balanced by joy at the way in which Erasmus was spreading the light.[2]

---

[1] *Treatises on the Hierarchies*, ed. and trans. J. H. LUPTON, 1869, p. 107.
[2] ALLEN, II, No. 423.

Greek was the key of the new religious teaching, just as it was of the new scientific teaching. And so we find More, in the midst of his years of austere devotion among the fathers of the London Charterhouse, plunging deep into the study of Greek. To this period belongs his first extant letter,[1] addressed to a John Holt, who is probably the same as the John Holt who some years before had published a grammar, called *Lac Puerorum*. The grammar contains prefatory and concluding epigrams by More in its praise, and it must have been published before 1500, because it is dedicated to Cardinal Morton. The extant editions are later; but it is no uncommon thing for early editions of school books to be thumbed quite out of existence. The editions of Holt's book which have survived have themselves narrowly escaped destruction; they are extant in extremely rare, if not unique, copies. The book was probably published in 1497, so that it seems likely that More made his first appearance in print at the age of nineteen – a feat not usual in the Fifteenth Century.

The letter to John Holt we can date very closely. Among other things, More describes the entry of Catherine of Aragon into London as the bride of Prince Arthur (12 Nov. 1501). More gives a very scornful account of her Spanish escort: 'You would have burst with laughing if you had seen them. They looked like devils out of Hell.' But as to Catherine herself, 'Everyone', he says, 'is singing her praises. There is nothing wanting in her that the most beautiful girl should have.' 'May this most famous marriage be fortunate and of good omen to England.' More never wavered in his devotion to Catherine. Thirty-three years later he told his judges that it was because of his adherence to her that they sought his blood. In this, as in so many other things, More remains unchanged in a changing world.

'You will ask me,' More continues in the same letter, 'how I am getting on with my studies. Excellently; nothing could be better. I am giving up Latin, and taking to Greek. Grocyn is my teacher.' Grocyn and More were now together in London. Grocyn had been appointed vicar of St. Lawrence Jewry, near the London Guildhall, and he was now in residence.

[1] British Museum MS. Arundel 249, fol. 85b, printed (rather inaccurately) in *Anglia*, xiv, 1891-2, pp. 498-9,

Grocyn has left little written record of a long life of study and teaching. He stands as a silent reproach to us in these days, when a man's scholarship is estimated by the number of printed pages he has covered. All that remains of his writing is a one-page Latin letter, and a Latin epigram on a lady who threw a snowball at him. So at least it has always been stated (you will find it, for example, repeated by Sir Sidney Lee in the *Dictionary of National Biography*). The Latin epigram may be rendered thus:

> Julia flung snow at me, and now I know
> When Julia throws it, fire can be in snow.

Critics have said that the lady would not have taken such an unseemly liberty with a priest, unless both she and Grocyn had been no better than they ought to have been. So Fuller implies, not obscurely, in his *Worthies of England*. I am glad therefore to be able to announce that this epigram was included in a manuscript collection formerly at Beauvais, that this collection was compiled either in the Ninth or Tenth Century, and that therefore Grocyn cannot have composed in the Fifteenth Century a little poem which was already current five or six centuries earlier.[1] I regret that, in order to vindicate the character of the saintly and austere Grocyn from such touch of scandal as may be incurred by having a snowball thrown at him by a minx, I am compelled to deprive him of one half of his extant works. But Grocyn cannot complain, for he, in his day, had deprived people of works wrongly attributed to them.

More, in the same letter in which he tells us of his own studies under Grocyn, tells also how Grocyn has been lecturing at St. Paul's on the *Celestial Hierarchies* of Dionysius. This is a book which the Middle Ages firmly believed to have been written by that Dionysius the Areopagite who is mentioned in the *Acts of the Apostles*. Grocyn, in the course of his studies, became convinced that it was not, and said so. It was an epoch-making piece of 'Higher Criticism', for the work of Dionysius carried hardly less authority than Holy Writ itself.

About the same time, Grocyn invited More to lecture, in his church of St. Lawrence Jewry, on Augustine's *City of God*. The

---

[1] *Anthologia Latina*, I, ii (1906), ed. A. RIESE; No. 706, ex codice Isidor Bellovacensi, saec. IX, nunc deperdito.

lectures, we are told, were rather historical and philosophical than theological – they may have embodied some of the criticism of social evils which More later put into *Utopia.* Anyway, they drew bigger crowds than Grocyn's theological lectures in St. Paul's. It was a bold venture for a man of twenty-three to lecture to the mature ecclesiastics who, Erasmus tells us, flocked to hear him. With praiseworthy toleration of lay intrusion, More's biographer, Archdeacon Harpsfield, applauds the young lawyer's lectures on this difficult book,

> which though it be a book very hard for a well learned man to understand, and cannot be profoundly and exactly under-standed, and especially cannot be with commendation openly read, of any man that is not well and substantially furnished as well with divinity as profane knowledge; yet did Master More, being so young, being so distracted also and occupied in the study of the common laws, openly read in the Church of St. Lawrence in London the books of the said St. Augustine *de Civitate Dei*, to his no small commendation, and to the great admiration of all his audience. His lesson was frequented and honoured with the presence and resort, as well of that well learned and great cunning man, Master Grocyn . . . as also with the chief and best learned men of the City of London.[1]

Meantime More was learning Greek not only from Grocyn, but also from Thomas Linacre. Nowadays, when so much is available in translation, and when in so many ways we have built further upon the knowledge which Ancient Greece has left us, it requires an effort to realize how in the early Sixteenth Century Greek was the key, not only to the New Testament and to all the greatest literature, but to science also. The interests of Linacre were medical and scientific, and the most lasting of all his works were destined to be the lectureships which he founded in medicine at Oxford and Cambridge, and his share in the foundation of the Royal College of Physicians. More himself tells us how he attended Linacre's course on the *Meteorologica* of Aristotle.[2] This must have been in London, where all these scholars were now gathered together.

When we call this group of men 'Humanists', or speak of

[1] HARPSFIELD, *Life of More*, pp. 13-4.
[2] Ad Dorpium, *Lucubrationes*, 1563, p. 417.

their studies by the Sixteenth Century name of 'The New Learning', we must beware of an ambiguity. 'Humanism' may mean the study of the Latin and Greek classics; it may also mean 'a system of thought or action which is concerned with merely human interests, as against divine'. Now there certainly were Sixteenth Century scholars who were 'Humanists' in both senses. It may be that Linacre was so absorbed in curing the woes of the body that he gave little thought to those of the soul. It was told of him (perhaps untruly) that late in life, he, a priest who had received much ecclesiastical preferment, opened for the first time his New Testament; at the Sermon on the Mount, as it happened. He read the three chapters of St. Matthew with amazement, and then exclaimed 'Either this is not the Gospel, or we are not Christians'. Refusing to contemplate the possibility of the latter alternative, he flung the book from him, and resumed his medical studies.[1] Most English humanists, however, were deeply concerned with Divinity; and therefore, when the word 'Humanism' is used in this book, it is used to denote the study of the classics, with no further implication as to the presence or absence of interests other than human.

'The New Learning' originally meant the study of the classics, especially of the newly-introduced Greek. But the phrase also came to be used to signify the new doctrines of the Reformation. Obviously there is no necessary connection; a man may be devoted to Greek literature, without therefore holding Lutheran or Calvinist doctrines, or wishing to smash statuary in churches. Yet there were bigoted theologians of the old school who distrusted Greek scholarship. Plato, they said, was a heathen, and the Greek church was schismatic; therefore these old fashioned obscurantists foolishly identified Greek learning with heresy and Protestant dogma. Oddly enough, modern critical historians have perpetuated their error by using the term 'New Learning', without making clear, either to their readers or themselves, in which of its two senses they were using it. For example, Sidney Lee sees fatal miscalculation and inconsistency in the fact that More sought to further both the old religion and the new learning. If by 'new learning' we

---

[1] CHEKE, *De pronuntiatione Graecae linguae*, Basel, 1555, p. 282.

mean Protestant dogma, More never sought to further it; if we mean Greek scholarship, only partizans will see incompatibility between Catholicism and Greek scholarship.

But, though there was no inconsistency, we may well wonder how More found time for it all – the Law, his devotions at the Charterhouse, the study of the Fathers, the study of Greek without a Liddell and Scott to help him. A partial explanation lies in his amazingly rapid brain, which enabled him to take in a sentence at a flash. A fellow-scholar records this power of More's. 'Everybody who has ever existed,' he says, 'has had to put his sentences together from words, except our Thomas More alone. He, on the contrary, possesses this super-grammatical art, and particularly in reading Greek.'[1] Besides, More could do with very little sleep. Robert Louis Stevenson tells us of a Samurai scholar of Old Japan who put mosquitoes up his sleeve to keep himself awake.[2] We are assured that by wearing a hair-shirt, and sleeping on planks with a log for a pillow, More managed to be awake for nineteen or twenty hours out of the twenty-four.[3]

More's father began to think it was time to intervene. Erasmus tells us that John More was an upright man, and in other respects a sensible one, but he did not hold with all this Greek and all this philosophy. Probably he hardly realized the astonishing power of work which his son possessed; and he grew anxious. So he checked More's studies by cutting off supplies. 'Being himself skilled in English law, he almost disowned his son, because he seemed to be deserting his father's profession. The study of English law is as far removed as can be from true learning' – it is Erasmus who is speaking; 'but in England those who succeed in it are highly thought of. And there is no better way to eminence there; for the nobility are mostly recruited from the law. And no man is considered an expert unless he has laboured at it for a great many years. Although More's mind, fitted for better things, naturally dreaded these studies, still, after making trial of the schools, he became so skilled in the law that no one of those who concentrated entirely on it had a better practice.'[4]

[1] Pace, *De fructu*, p. 82.   [2] Yoshida-Torajiro.   [3] Stapleton, ii, p. 161.
[4] Allen, iv, No. 999, p. 17.

Erasmus goes on to speak of the austerities with which More tested himself. He nearly became a priest, Erasmus says, but he could not put off his desire for the wedded state.

It is just because of this careful testing and self-examination, which Erasmus so heartily commends, that More can never show any patience with a man who, having once taken vows of celibacy, then renounces them. He feels for such a man the angry contempt which a good soldier might feel for one who volunteers for a dangerous post, and then deserts it.

More was a man of strong passions. Erasmus speaks of his early love-affairs, in language which would certainly be understood by his readers to mean that More's youth had not been altogether blameless.[1] More did not object to this being published through Europe in edition after edition. He himself proclaimed to all Europe his gusts of passionate wrath against the heretics. But his patience and courtesy towards heretics – towards Roper or Grinaeus – is revealed only to the careful student of his private life. It is characteristic that the hair-shirt with which More 'tamed his flesh' was a secret which he tried to confine to his confessor, and to the daughter who washed the hair-shirt. Dame Alice used to wonder where his washing went. The hair-shirt still exists, and we shall get a peep at this gruesome relic from time to time as our story progresses. We shall also find More sadly looking back upon the monastic ideal, which he had forgone for the sake of wife and children. In later life he protests more than once, that but for wife and children he would return to it.[2]

It was just when More was settling down as a married man, abandoning all thought of becoming monk or friar, that another young man, as earnest as he, startled his family and friends by becoming an Augustinian Eremite; he did so, he tells us, because he doubted of himself, because 'in his case the proverb was true, *Doubt makes a monk*'.[3] His name was Martin Luther. So, years before either had heard the other's name, these two great men are brought into opposition.

---

[1] ALLEN, IV, No. 999, p. 17.   [2] See below, pp. 183, 307.
[3] LINDSAY, *Reformation*, 1909, I, pp. 197-8.

§ 8. 'A BEARDLESS BOY' BURGESS OF PARLIAMENT

But More was to give his father more trouble before he settled down as a married man.

In 1504 a Parliament was called, and More was elected a burgess. We do not know his constituency. The wedding between Prince Arthur and Catherine of Aragon, which More had hailed so enthusiastically, had ended tragically with the death of the Prince. But the King was entitled, by ancient custom, as the *Rolls of Parliament* tell us, to 'two reasonable aids', the one for the making knight of Arthur, late Prince of Wales deceased, and the other for the marriage of his eldest daughter Margaret to the King of Scots. It is clear from the *Rolls* that Parliament raised difficulties; in the end the King had to be satisfied with a grant of £40,000, and thought well to meet his subjects by, 'of his ample grace and pity', remitting a quarter of that.[1] According to Roper, the aid which the grasping Henry had in the first instance thought reasonable had been three 'fifteenths' (say £90,000) for the marriage of his eldest daughter. And this disappointment of the King's purpose was largely due to Thomas More, who made,

> such arguments and reasons thereagainst, that the King's demands thereby were clean overthrown. So that one of the King's privy chamber, named Master Tyler, being present thereat, brought word to the King out of the Parliament house that a beardless boy had disappointed all his purpose. Whereupon the King, conceiving great indignation towards him, could not be satisfied until he had some way revenged it. And, forasmuch as he, nothing having, nothing could lose, his Grace devised a causeless quarrel against his father, keeping him in the Tower until he had made him pay to him a hundred pounds fine.[2]

I would barter some few of the pious meditations which More wrote in the Tower thirty years later, for a true report of John More's meditations upon his boy's follies, made in the same place, but unfortunately not extant in writing.

[1] *Rot. Parl.*, VI, pp. 532-42.   [2] ROPER, pp. 7-8.

§ 9. LATIN WRITINGS: EPISTLES AND EPIGRAMS

We have no information about this incident other than what Roper gives us half a century later, perhaps with some exaggeration. More's correspondence is still too scanty. There are only three or four letters which we can place in the first thirty years of his life, before the accession of Henry VIII. The third of these belongs almost certainly to the autumn[1] of the same year in which More was a burgess of Parliament. We cannot be absolutely certain, because (as so often at this period) the letter is dated only by the day of the month, leaving us to fit in the year as best we can. The letter is addressed to Colet, who seems to have been recently appointed Dean of St. Paul's, though he had not yet been installed.[2] Colet held other ecclesiastical appointments in different parts of the country, and was at the moment absent from London. More, walking in the law courts, had met Colet's servant, and writes to say how sorry he is to find that this does not mean that Colet himself is back in town. Town of course is a hateful place – devoted to the service of the World, the Flesh and the Devil: nothing but 'confectioners, fishmongers, butchers, cooks, carriers, fishermen, and fowlers'. He doesn't blame Colet for preferring the country; but why not come at least as near as Stepney, which also needs his ministrations? (Colet was vicar of All Saints, Stepney, and in that country village, 'amongst the snipe, and the orchards and ploughmen', there stood, near the parish church, Great Place, the home of his father, Sir Henry Colet.[3]) The object of More's letter is to welcome Colet to the pulpit of St. Paul's. All are eagerly looking forward to the return of the new dean. One gathers that the Londoners had already had experience of Colet as preacher. His predecessor had been absent for a long time as ambassador at Rome, and Colet may have supplied the gap.

The letter concludes, 'Meantime, I pass my time with Grocyn, who is, as you know, in your absence the guide of my life' (Colet and Grocyn are apparently More's confessors);

---

[1] 23 Oct. 1504. See STAPLETON, II, p. 163.
[2] LUPTON, *Colet*, 1909, pp. 120n, 141n, 145n, 229.   [3] The same, p. 118.

'with Linacre, the guide of my studies' (More is apparently still hard at Greek); 'and with our friend Lily, my dearest friend.'

William Lily was the godson of William Grocyn. Years later, when Colet formed his school of St. Paul's, he made Lily the first High Master. More and Lily were working together translating epigrams from the Greek anthology into Latin. More's epigrams were not printed till he was forty, but we know from Erasmus that they had for the most part been written long before, and some were the work of his early youth.[1] First in More's book of epigrams comes his joint work with Lily – the Greek epigram is given, followed by their rival renderings. In his own epigrams More expresses his passionate hatred of royal tyranny, in a way he never permitted to himself later, when he was a servant to the King. The tyrant whom Death will lay low is satirized; so is the ecclesiastic, who has been made a bishop, not hastily, but after careful search has revealed the most unsuitable person possible; and so are many private follies: the man who affects French fashions in everything except his French, which he speaks with a most Britannic accent. More's epigrams, it has been said, form the elements of an autobiography.[2] Quite the most charming of all is addressed to a certain Elizabeth, otherwise unknown, who had caught More's fancy when he was a boy of sixteen, and when she was two years younger. Not till a quarter of a century later did More meet the lady again; then he wrote the little poem to remind her of the interruption of their first love:

> Severed, our different fates we then pursued,
> Till this late day my raptures has renewed.
> Crimeless, my heart you stole in life's soft prime,
> And still possess that heart without a crime.
> Pure was the love which in my youth prevailed,
> And age would keep it pure, if honour failed.
> O may the gods, who, five long lustres passed,
> Have brought us to each other well at last,
> Grant, that when numbered five long lustres more,
> Healthful, I still may hail thee healthful as before![3]

[1] ALLEN, IV, No. 1093.   [2] MARSDEN, *Philomorus*, 1878, p. 28.

[3] More, if sixteen, presumably met the girl in 1494 and again, twenty-five years later, in 1519. It agrees with these dates that, as Prof. A. W. Reed points out to me, the epigram is *not* in the first edition of 1518, but was added in the edition of 1520. The translation given above is that of Archdeacon Wrangham.

But, long before the 'five lustres' had run their course for the
second time, More's head had fallen on the scaffold.

§ 10. 'FOUR THINGS FOR HIS PASTIME'

Erasmus tells us that in his youth More wrote and acted
some little plays; whether in English or Latin remains unknown,
for they are lost. But four 'Things' which he wrote in English
'in his youth for his pastime' have been preserved. The first is
'A merry jest how a Sergeant would learn to play the Friar.'
It is a boisterous piece of knock-about fun. The closing words,
'Now make good cheer, and welcome every one', show that it
was meant to be recited as welcome to some feast. Dr. Reed
suggests that it may have been composed for the Sergeants'
Feast of 1503, when John More was one of the newly-elected
Sergeants-at-law. It is a moral poem, the moral being that
men should stick to their business:

> When an hatter will go smatter
>   In philosophy,
> Or a pedlar wax a meddler
>   In theology,

no good will come of it. 'Already More recognized the danger
of the busy meddler in theology.' The story tells how a thrifty
man died, leaving his son 'an hundred pound of nobles round'.
But the young man wasted the money, borrowed more, wasted
that, and then took refuge from arrest in the house of a friend,
where he pretended to lie sick. The sergeant, in order to arrest
him, disguised himself as a *frere* (friar):

> So was he dight that no man might
>   Him for a frere deny,
> He dopped and dooked, he spake and looked
>   So religiously.
> Yet in a glass, or he would pass,
>   He toted and he peered,
> His heart for pride leaped in his side
>   To see how well he *frere'd*.

The Sergeant gets admission on the pretext of giving spiritual
counsel. But when he reveals his character by arresting his
victim, the women of the house fall on him, and eject him
contumeliously, with an 'Adieu, Commend us to the Mayor.'

The sergeant whose duty it was to arrest this debtor was, of course, an official of the Mayor and Sheriffs, before whom he would be sworn annually. The Mayor and Sheriffs, as we have seen, were present at the Sergeants' feast, and, though the Sergeant of the poem is a very different kind of person from John More and his fellow Sergeants-at-law, the misfortunes of any Sergeant would serve for the occasion.

The second poem shows us the interior of John More's house in London. More 'devised in his father's house a goodly hanging of fine painted cloth, with nine pageants, and verses over every of those nine pageants'. The verses of the first eight pageants are in Chaucerian stanzas. Childhood, whipping a top, comes first; he tells of his childish games:

> But would to God these hateful bookës all
> Were in a fire brent to powder small.

In the next pageant the boy is ridden down by 'Manhood'. In the third Cupid triumphs over Manhood:

> Now thou which erst despisedst children small
> Shalt wax a child again, and be my thrall.

In succeeding pageants Age, 'wise and discreet', triumphs over Cupid, Death over Age, Fame over Death, Time over Fame, and Eternity over Time. In the ninth and last pageant the poet is depicted, sitting in a chair drawing the moral in Latin verses.

More's third poem is a lamentation at the death of Queen Elizabeth, the eldest daughter of Edward IV, who, by her marriage with Henry VII, had joined the White Rose to the Red. She died in childbed, in February 1503; it was thought that grief for the death of her eldest son Arthur had broken down her health. The poem is a lamentation put into the mouth of the dying Queen; it is full of historical allusions – for example to Henry's building at Richmond, and the Chapel at Westminster which he was just beginning:

> Where are our castles? Now where are our towers?
> Goodly Richmond, soon art thou gone from me,
> At Westminster, that costly work of yours,
> Mine own dear Lord, now shall I never see.
> Almighty God vouchsafe to grant that ye
> For you and your children well may edify.
> My palace builded is; and lo! now here I lie.

The poem is written throughout in Chaucer's seven-lined stanza; but repeatedly, by lengthening the last line to twelve syllables, More anticipates something of the effect of the stanza of Spenser.[1]

Finally, there were the metres which More wrote to be placed at the beginning of the *Book of Fortune*. They were intended to add literary dignity to a parlour game. The *Book of Fortune* leads the inquirer through a maze of kings, philosophers, stars, spirits, and astronomers till the astronomer tells the inquirer his fortune. The help of the dice has, of course, to be called in.[2]

§ 11. *THE LIFE OF JOHN PICUS*

The tradition in More's family, recorded by his great-grandson Cresacre, was that when More determined to marry, 'he propounded to himself as a pattern of life a singular layman, John Picus, Earl of Mirandula'. It may have been some ten years after the death of Pico, some eight years after that scholar's life had been published by his nephew, John Francis, as an introduction to his works, that More began on his translation. The attraction is obvious. Pico had been a great scholar and a great layman; not long before his premature death, he had longed to withdraw from the world. Like More himself, he had thought of becoming a friar. In an orchard at Ferrara, he had suddenly broken out to John Francis, 'Nephew, this will I show thee, I warn thee keep it secret. The substance that I have left, after certain books of mine finished, I intend to give out to poor folk, and barefoot walking about the world, in every town and castle, I purpose to preach of Christ.'[3] Later Pico confided to the great Dominican preacher Savonarola his intention of becoming a Dominican. But before he could fulfil this purpose, Pico died, suddenly and very piously, at Florence, in his thirty-second year. Yet Savonarola was not quite satisfied with the piety of Pico's end. With that almost ferocious intensity which characterizes the piety of Southern Europeans (when they are pious), Savonarola declared from the pulpit in 'the

---

[1] Sidney Lee notes how More's 'metrical effects adumbrate the art of Spenser' (*Great Englishmen*, 1904, p. 59).
[2] It is all explained by A. W. Reed, Introduction to MORE's *Works*, 1931, I, p. 17.
[3] MORE, *Works*, 1557, p. 8.

chief church of all Florence' that Pico 'as he was a man of delicate complexion' had shrunk from the labour of becoming a preaching friar; that for two years together the preacher had warned him that he would be punished if he 'forslothed' that service, and that now he knew that Pico was adjudged to suffer for it in Purgatory. Privately, to his friends, Savonarola said 'that Picus had after his death appeared unto him all compassed in fire, and showed unto him that he was such wise in Purgatory punished for his negligence'.[1]

There is a touch of humour in the fact that More, deciding that the religious life was not for him, should have chosen this life of Pico, with a selection from his writings, as a New Year's present to a friend. For that friend was Joyeuce Leigh, a girl who had taken the veil in the convent of Poor Clares outside the walls of London, known as the Minories. The Leighs were old friends of More; they and their father worshipped at St. Stephen's Walbrook, which was More's parish church when he lived in Bucklersbury. Edward Leigh (or Lee, as he preferred to spell his name), the brother of Joyeuce Leigh, was ordained, served the King on embassies, and later became involved in a controversy with More. Erasmus seemed to Edward Lee too bold an innovator; accordingly Lee attacked him, and More stepped forward to defend his friend.[2] But the controversy was a quite friendly one, and in a tactful letter More undertook that, should Erasmus in the future attack any book that Lee wrote, he in turn would defend that against Erasmus. Later still, when More filled Wolsey's place as Chancellor, Lee filled his place as Archbishop of York. But Lee's orthodoxy was not proof against Henry; he yielded, though most unwillingly, to Henry's schemes, and even joined in the attempt to make More yield. But this was nearly thirty years later, and meanwhile Joyeuce had probably died. She had been joined by her mother in the Minories, and there her mother had died and been buried in the choir. We hear nothing of Joyeuce at the time of the Dissolution. It was perhaps as well that she did not live to see her mother's tomb desecrated, and the choir where she had worshipped made into an armoury.

But these things were little thought of when More, turning

[1] *Works*, 1557, p. 10.   [2] May 1519, *Epistolae aliquot Eruditorum*, Antwerp, 1520.

from the religious life, dedicated his first book to the friend who had entered that life, 'his right entirely beloved sister in Christ', Joyeuce Leigh:

> It is, and of long time ·hath been (my well beloved sister), a custom in the beginning of the New Year, friends to send between, presents or gifts, as the witnesses of their love and friendship, and also signifying that they desire each to other that year a good continuance and prosperous end of that lucky beginning.

Such presents, More goes on to say, are commonly in food or clothing. He does not need to say that, to one of the 'Sisters Minoresses enclosed' these gifts could not be made; he continues:

> But, forasmuch as the love and amity of Christian folk should be rather ghostly friendship than bodily . . . I therefore, mine heartily beloved sister, in good luck of this New Year, have sent you such a present as may bear witness of my tender love and zeal to the happy continuance and gracious increase of virtue in your soul. And whereas the gifts of other folk declare that they wish their friends to be worldly fortunate, mine testifieth that I desire to have you godly prosperous.[1]

The Life of Picus was printed by More's brother-in-law, John Rastell, and pirated by Wynkyn de Worde. Neither edition bears any date. Much later John Rastell's son, William, dated the translation about 1510; but this is probably the time when his father printed the book, and we may follow the family tradition[2] that it was written about five years earlier, when More, having given up all thoughts of Holy Orders, was wooing his wife.

§ 12. THE NEW HOME IN BUCKLERSBURY

Roper tells us of the wooing:

He resorted to the house of one Master Colt, a gentleman of Essex, that had oft invited him thither, having three daughters, whose honest conversation and virtuous education provoked him there specially to set his affection. And albeit his mind most served him to the second daughter, for that he thought her the fairest and best favoured, yet when he

---

[1] *Works,* 1557, p. 1.   [2] See also A. W. REED, *Early Tudor Drama,* pp. 2, 8, 73, 74.

considered that it would be both great grief and some shame also to the eldest to see her younger sister in marriage preferred before her, he then of a certain pity framed his fancy towards her, and soon after married her.

The person vaguely referred to by Roper as Master Colt of Essex was John Colt, of Netherhall, near Roydon.[1] The family tombs of the Colts are in Roydon parish church, covered with brasses. John Colt married twice, and More's wife was one of eighteen brothers and sisters. The ruins of Netherhall itself can still be seen, with moat and gateway tower, and fragments of dark red brick walls with their blue patterns and stone facings.

More, Roper tells us, 'placed himself and his wife at Bucklersbury in London'. It was just after More had brought home his girl-bride to his London house that Erasmus paid a visit of a year (or perhaps less) to England. He found his friends now all settled in London. He wrote to the prior of his former monastery that he had come to England, not for money, but for learning. 'In London there are five or six men who are such accurate scholars both in Latin and Greek that I do not think Italy itself now possesses their equals; and they all make much of me.'[2]

Many years later Erasmus told a story (without names) of a newly married couple. This story, because of some phrases in it which he elsewhere applies to More's young wife, we can be quite sure relates to her and her husband.[3] Erasmus tells us that a man, exceptionally clever and tactful, had married a girl of seventeen, who had lived all her life in her country home in complete idleness, talking to the servants, and quite uneducated. Her husband tried to interest her in books and music, and to educate her, 'getting her to repeat the substance of the sermons she heard'. The wife would do nothing but cry, and wish herself dead. At last the tactful husband, to her great delight, suggested a visit to her country home. The husband told his

---

[1] CRESACRE MORE's *Life*, by a mistake, gives 'New Hall' for 'Netherhall'. The matter was cleared up in a most valuable article by the late Dr. P. S. Allen in the *Times Literary Supplement*, 26 Dec. 1918, p. 654. Dr. Allen also showed the light which could be got from the *Colloquies* of Erasmus. See also G. R. F. COLT, *History and Genealogy of the Colts*, 1887.

[2] ALLEN, I, No. 185.

[3] Erasmus' account of how More taught his undeveloped country wife letters and music (ALLEN, IV, No. 999) agrees almost verbally with the story told in the *Colloquies* (The Uneasy Wife).

father-in-law of his trouble. 'Use your rights,' said the father-in-law, 'and give her a good beating.' 'I know what my rights are,' said the husband, 'but I would rather you used your authority.' The father-in-law, who was a clever actor, pretended to be so furiously angry with his daughter that she took refuge by falling at her husband's feet in a fit of penitence. They kissed each other, and were friends.

Dr. P. S. Allen tells the story:

Life was hard in that first year to the girl-bride of seventeen, pent up in narrow streets and courts and pining for green fields and the old home; hard, too, for the young husband, ten years the elder, who, with sense enough to shrink from the rough methods of the time, yet tried to play the schoolmaster to his wife before their hearts were open one to another and their desires known. How their spirits must have risen as they rode down into Essex on a summer morning – summer was then the hunting season – past the great church of Waltham; she behind him on a pillion, and straining her eyes over his shoulder to catch the first view of Netherhall, as the road wound round the little hills which were to bring peace. It is good to remember that happiness came before the end. To More, when he wrote his own epitaph, she was 'chara uxorcula', and the years that they spent together were green.[1]

There are other tales which Erasmus tells which almost certainly relate to More and his father-in-law – good actors both. They are tales of high-spirited practical joking, involving a good deal of histrionic talent, and they perhaps helped to persuade young Mistress More that her learned husband was not as terribly solemn a person as she had at first feared, when he made her repeat sermons.

Since they had parted some five years before, More and Erasmus had both mastered Greek, and Erasmus was preparing himself for his great work of publishing the Greek *New Testament* to the world. The plays of Euripides had just been published in Venice.[2] It must have been a revelation; and Erasmus translated one of them, the *Hecuba*, into Latin. When

---

[1] *Times Literary Supplement*, 26 Dec. 1918, p. 654.
[2] Aldus, 1503. This was the first edition of Euripides, though some individual plays had been published earlier.

he and Grocyn went to dine with Warham, Archbishop of Canterbury, at Lambeth, Erasmus took this translation with him and presented it, after dinner, to the Archbishop. The Archbishop gave him a reward, in private. As they were returning from Lambeth, on the river, Grocyn asked Erasmus, 'How much?' Erasmus admitted disappointment, and asked whether the Archbishop was mean, or poor, or didn't think the work good enough? Grocyn explained that the Archbishop had not understood that it was an individual honour; he had supposed that a wandering scholar like Erasmus was going round Europe presenting the translation in manuscript to one person after another. Erasmus was nettled; he printed later the *Hecuba* and the *Iphigeneia*, and dedicated both to the Archbishop, with a letter explaining that these translations were only practice for the greater effort he hoped later to make. The Archbishop understood, and became one of the most energetic of Erasmus' friends.

Meantime More and Erasmus were busy translating some of the works of Lucian. More dedicated his translation to Ruthall, secretary to Henry VII, 'most prudent of princes';[1] Erasmus dedicated his to Richard Whitford, one of the chaplains of Bishop Foxe of Winchester.[2] Whitford was a close friend of both More and Erasmus, whom he styled 'the twins'. But the happy party was soon broken up. Erasmus got his long-deferred chance of a tour to Italy, whither he was asked to accompany the sons of Henry's Italian physician, as tutor. More had the shock of discovering how bitterly his action in Parliament was still resented. He happened to visit Foxe, Bishop of Winchester, now, after Morton's death, the King's chief adviser. Foxe promised to restore More to favour 'if he would be ruled by him', meaning, it was afterwards conjectured, if he would confess his offence against the King. Roper tells the tale. More, after leaving the Bishop

> fell in communication with one Master Whitford, his familiar friend, then chaplain to that bishop, and after a Father of Sion, and shewed him what the bishop had said unto him, desiring to have his advice therein; who, for the passion of God, prayed him in no wise to follow his counsel: 'For my

---

[1] NICHOL, I, No. 190.   [2] ALLEN, I, No. 191.

lord, my master,' quoth he, 'to serve the King's turn, will not stick to agree to his own father's death.' So Sir Thomas More returned to the bishop no more. And had not the King soon after died, he was determined to have gone over the sea, thinking that being in the King's indignation he could not live in England without great danger.[1]

It may be that Whitford was exaggerating the danger. We may surely regard as exaggeration the later story that the notorious Empson and Dudley had so fanned the King's anger that More was in actual danger of death, and that, afterwards, Dudley, when himself going to execution, told More that, if he had acknowledged his fault to the King, he would almost certainly have lost his head.[2]

But it was an unpleasant situation for a young man 'clogged' with children, as his great-grandson put it. His daughter Margaret had probably been born in 1505, Elizabeth in 1506, Cecily in 1507, his only son John in 1508 or 1509. We know that in 1508 More was visiting the Universities of Paris and Louvain,[3] and this may have been preparatory to an intended sojourn abroad.

The extortions of Empson and Dudley had grown to be an incubus to the nation, as a contemporary historian, though favourable to Henry VII, admits:

> And at this unreasonable and extort doing, noble men grudged, mean men kicked, poor men lamented, preachers openly at Paul's Cross and other places exclaimed, rebuked and detested, but yet they would never amend.[4]

A heavy weight must have been lifted from More's mind when, on 22 April 1509, it was known that Henry VII lay dead, and when next day, to the blast of trumpets, Henry VIII was proclaimed King 'with much gladness and rejoicing of the people'.

---

[1] ROPER, p. 8.   [2] STAPLETON, III, p. 181.
[3] *Lucubrationes*, Basel, 1563, p. 376.
[4] HALL, *Kyng Henry the vii*, fol. lix, verso.

AN UNDER-SHERIFF SEEKS UTOPIA

(1509–1517)

§ I. 'HEAVEN LAUGHS AND THE EARTH REJOICES'

How present and crushing had been the fear of the tyranny under which More had lived, is shown by the verses of congratulation which he wrote for the coronation of Henry VIII. More's words read like those of a man awaking from an evil dream into the presence of a strong and noble young friend. Tyranny is dead: liberty and the rule of law have been restored by the young king. It is no flattery when More dwells upon the combination of athletic strength and almost feminine beauty which marked the boy-king, still in his eighteenth year. Foreign observers were struck by just the same thing. With his face at once of a man and of a delicate girl, Henry reminds More of the legend of Achilles in woman's disguise. And there is presage of a noble mind in this noble body. What, More asks, cannot be expected from a King who has been nourished by Philosophy and the Nine Muses, and whose ancestors have been marked by such virtues? He enumerates the virtues. The prudence of Henry VII. (Three years before, in dedicating his translation of a dialogue of Lucian to Ruthall, the secretary of the late King, More had spoken of the old King's prudence, and he still allows him that virtue.) The piety of the young King's grandmother, the Lady Margaret. The sweet kindliness of his mother, Elizabeth of York, whose death More had been lamenting six years before. The noble heart of his grandfather Edward IV, the warrior King, for whose memory More had great respect, and of whom, in his *History of Richard III*, he was soon to draw a favourable picture. And then he turns to Queen Catherine. He compares her to the most faithful wives of Greek story, to Alcestis and Penelope. And that valiant-hearted

99

woman deserved all the praises of the great man who was to be faithful to her cause till death. But a great man may be a poor prophet, and More concludes his poem by dwelling on the son whom Catherine is to bear to Henry, and whose son and grandson are in turn to perpetuate his dynasty. And so, in line after line of this joyous poem, More shoots his shafts of compliment, which reach a mark the archer never meant. We can read his verses to-day in a small, beautifully written manuscript at the British Museum,[1] adorned with a combination of the Red Rose and the White. It is almost certainly the presentation copy which More placed in Henry's hand.

All men were saying the same, though not all in such elegant verses. England was 'called then the golden world, such grace of plenty reigned then within this realm'.[2] Mountjoy sent off a letter to his old teacher Erasmus, to invite him back from Rome to England:

Heaven laughs and the earth rejoices; everything is full of milk and honey and nectar. Avarice has fled the country. Our King is not after gold, or gems, or precious metals, but virtue, glory, immortality. I will give you a taste of it. Just lately, he was saying that he wished he were more learned. 'That is not what we want from you,' I said, 'but that you should foster and encourage learned men.' 'Why, of course,' he said, 'for without them life would hardly be life.'

Mountjoy tells Erasmus, who had been sick and in low spirits, that the last day of his sorrow has dawned. 'You will come to a Prince who will say, "Accept our wealth and be our greatest sage".'[3]

The invitation was seconded by the former patron of Erasmus, Warham, Archbishop of Canterbury.[4]

Erasmus was now a very different person from the impecunious scholar who had come to England, and first met More ten years before. He had spent years in Italy, and had become a scholar with a world-reputation. He was now a man whom Cardinal Grimani treated as an equal, and urged to stay in Rome. 'But,' says Erasmus, 'when I told him I had been sent for by the King of England, he ceased to press me.'[5]

---

[1] MS. Cotton Titus D. iv.   [2] CAVENDISH, *Life of Wolsey*, ed. ELLIS, 1899, p. 13.
[3] ALLEN, I, No. 215.   [4] ALLEN, I, No. 214.
[5] *Opera Omnia* (Le Clerc), Leyden, 1703, Vol. III, cols. 1374, 1375.

So Erasmus set out for England. And as he was riding over the Alps into Switzerland, 'his Genius touched him' whilst he thought of his friend Thomas More, whose face he was so soon to see again, and whose name *Moros*, the Greek for 'fool', seemed to have fallen to him by such a strange irony. And, as he rode, Erasmus thought out a book, which was destined to be the most popular of all his writings, the *Moria*, or *Moriae Encomium*, the *Praise of Folly*. As soon as he reached England, he went to More's house. He was attacked by lumbago; his books had not arrived; he could do no serious work, so in seven days he completed this book; or so he says. In the dedication to More he tells how the first inspiration came to him on horseback. At a later date he said that it was More who made him write the book, and that to do so was like setting a camel to dance.

The *Praise of Folly* is the denunciation, on behalf of the humanists, of all the wickedness and folly of the age. Few read it nowadays. But it is a book which helped to make history. Yet, though the *Praise of Folly* was written in More's house, with More's encouragement, we must not make the mistake of identifying its spirit with the spirit of More. There were distinctions between More and Erasmus; and it is characteristic of More that he could give such entire friendship to a man so different from himself. There are temperamental differences, and there are differences due to their different history. In these days of care-free laughter, More and Erasmus might pour scorn upon an ignorant and immoral monk in language almost identical. Yet More, who had decided, after the most careful testing, that he was not fitted for a monastic life, and who yet yearned for it, never looks upon monasticism as an institution in the same way as does Erasmus, who, without any vocation, had been thrust into the cloister, and only with difficulty obtained dispensation from obedience. Again, Erasmus in the *Praise of Folly*, and More in *Utopia*, express their hatred of the bestiality of war in language which is almost word for word the same. Yet we need to distinguish carefully. Erasmus was a man without a country, a wandering scholar at home all over Europe. He is a pacifist, to whom patriotism is an unintelligible folly, and we shall see that inadvertently he was largely responsible for a quarrel between More and a French scholar, because he could not see how two humanists *could* quarrel out of love of their respective countries. But More has a warm English patriotism, which combines with a warm European patriotism. And his struggle to reconcile these two loyalties is a much more inspiring and helpful thing to us, as we look back on it to-day, than the mere negation of Erasmus. Whilst More hates the purposeless wars into which the restless ambition of Henry or of Wolsey was constantly plunging his country, he is the very reverse of a selfish 'isolationist'.

More protested against the attempt, which men made in his day as they have done since, to identify his views with those of Erasmus in the *Praise of Folly*. He defends his friend, but maintains his own individuality. Tyndale had instanced *Moria*, the *Praise of Folly*, as proof that More had changed from what he once was. More replies that he had never approved of irreverence:

> Nor if there were any such thing in *Moria*, that thing could not yet make any man see that I were myself of that mind, the book being made by another man, though he were 'my darling' never so dear. Howbeit, that book of *Moria* doth indeed but jest upon the abuses of such things, after the manner of the disour's [i.e. jester's] part in a play.[1]

Between the autumn of 1509, when he was writing the *Praise of Folly* in More's house in Bucklersbury, and April 1511, when he left that house, to take the book to Paris to print it, Erasmus entirely disappears from our view. He was presumably in England, but where, or what he was doing, we do not know. Not a single letter has been preserved from the man whose letters are numbered by the thousand. As Dr. P. S. Allen says, 'If it had been anyone else, we might almost conjecture that he was in prison'.[2] But the most disordered imagination cannot imagine the discreet Erasmus in prison. He probably stayed a great deal with More, but just when some account of More's life with his infant children and his first wife would have been so precious, Erasmus fails us. For More's biography we must fall back on the dry official record of the 'Black Books of Lincoln's Inn',[3] which tell us how, in Michaelmas term 1510,

---

[1] *Works*, 1557, p. 422.   [2] ALLEN, *The Age of Erasmus*, p. 143.
[3] Book III, fol. 36.

he was elected Autumn Reader (for 1511), and how he subsequently served as Lent Reader in 1515. The 'Black Books' are
supplemented by the equally dry official record of the 'Journal
of the Court of Common Council of the City of London',[1]
which tells us how, on 3 September 1510, More was appointed
one of the Under-Sheriffs of the City. Our young lawyer is
getting on,[2] and we may believe Roper when he tells us that by
this office

> and his learning together (as I have heard him say) he
> gained without grief not so little as four hundred pounds by
> the year; sith there was at that time, in none of the Prince's
> courts of the laws of this realm, any matter of importance in
> controversy, wherein he was not with the one part of counsel.[3]

The office of Under-Sheriff was important. The Mayor and
Sheriffs had not, as a rule, any legal experience, and the Under-
Sheriff was the legal permanent official who advised the Sheriff
in 'those numerous cases which came under his jurisdiction,
part of which have since been decided by a regularly con-
stituted judge of the Sheriff's Court'.[4] Erasmus at a later date
tells us that the office, though a very honourable one, did not
involve much work. The court sat only on Thursday in the
forenoon, he says.

> No one has settled more cases than has More, and no one
> has acted with greater integrity. He usually remits the fees
> due from the litigants – three shillings from the plaintiff
> and as much from the defendant; no more may be exacted.
> He has made himself very popular in the City by this.[5]

We have evidence that this popularity lasted nearly a century.

§ 2. HENRY'S ENGLAND

Whilst we are waiting for Erasmus to reappear and to give
us some intimate details about More and his household, a
question may be asked, the answer to which will better enable
us to understand those details when they do appear. We have

---

[1] II, fol. 118b.
[2] I have given a list of More's activities, as recorded in the 'Black Books' and the
City Records, in the notes to HARPSFIELD's *Life of More*, pp. 307, 312-14. For
examining the City Records I am much indebted to Miss Winifred Jay.
[3] ROPER, pp. 8-9.   [4] FOSS, *Judges of England*, v (1857), p. 209.
[5] ALLEN, IV, No. 999, p. 20.

seen More and his England, so far, through the eyes of Erasmus.
How did the England to which Henry VIII succeeded appear
to other educated foreigners?

Benvenuto Cellini, in his astounding autobiography, has
told us how he came near to visiting England. Torrigiani, who
was being employed by Henry VIII on adorning the 'costly
work' of Henry VII at Westminster, was back in Italy, 'talking
every day about his gallant feats among those beasts of Englishmen', and looking out for able young men whom he could take
back to England to help him. He would have taken Cellini;
but unfortunately Torrigiani had, in his youth, knocked down
Michelangelo, and dared to boast of it. Cellini drew the line at
associating with one who had marred the divine visage of
Michelangelo, and Torrigiani had to return to England without him. It is a pity: Cellini would have given us much
interesting gossip, and perhaps even some stories about
Thomas More, which might have dissipated that atmosphere
of blamelessness which is the greatest difficulty with which
More's biographer has to cope.

'Those beasts of Englishmen.' Michelangelo was some three
years older than More; those Venetian masters of colour, Titian
and Giorgione, were perhaps a year older, Raphael five years
younger. Contemporary England has nothing to set against
such names. Turning to poetry, Ariosto was perhaps four years
older than More. Again, contemporary England has nothing;
Chaucer had been laid to rest in Westminster a century before,
and no great new poet had arisen.

Nevertheless, when we gaze upon Torrigiani's work at
Westminster, and then gaze around at the masterpiece of Tudor
Gothic in which it is enshrined, we perceive that the Italian's
judgment, 'those beasts of Englishmen', was too sweeping.
England was a land of mighty craftsmen. Mr. Rudyard
Kipling has seized this aspect of history with the insight of
genius, contrasting the two men working on the Chapel at
Westminster, the Englishman Hal, and Benedetto, whom
Torrigiani had brought with him (in place, I suppose, of the
unwilling Cellini).

And at the same time college after college was being built
at Oxford and at Cambridge. No one can stand inside King's

College Chapel, and believe that the Englishmen who raised it
were beasts:

> They dreamt not of a perishable home
> Who thus could build. Be mine, in hours of fear
> Or grovelling thought, to seek a refuge here.

It is obvious that the England which could produce such
things must have been not only a civilized, but also a wealthy
land; and the wealth of England, and its beauty, are the two
things which most struck foreign visitors at the beginning of the
Sixteenth Century. To-day we are trying to preserve some poor
fragments of that beauty, before it is all gone. We go to Venice,
and the visit is, to an Englishman to-day, a revelation of the
possibilities of colour. Few people realize that the secretary of a
Venetian ambassador, coming to England about the year 1500,
was amazed, not only at the number and size of our churches,
scattered all over the land, but at the blaze of riches inside them.
The Venetian describes England as a land of pleasant undulat-
ing hills and beautiful valleys; nothing is to be seen but agreeable woods, extensive meadows, lands in cultivation, plentiful
water springing everywhere. The population is small, but in
proportion to that population the riches of England are greater
than those of any other country in Europe, owing to the fer-
tility of the soil, and the export of tin and wool. The Venetian
is struck with the abundance of silver plate in all the houses.
In London,

> In one single street leading to St. Pauls, there are fifty-two
> goldsmith's shops, so rich and full of silver vessels, great and
> small, that in all the shops in Milan, Rome, Venice, and
> Florence put together, I do not think there would be found
> so many of the magnificence that are to be seen in London.
> ... But above all, are their riches displayed in the church
> treasures; for there is not a parish church in the kingdom so
> mean as not to possess crucifixes, candlesticks, censers,
> pattens and cups of silver; nor is there a convent of mendicant
> friars so poor, as not to have all these same articles in silver.
> ... Your magnificence may therefore imagine what the
> decorations of those enormously rich Benedictine, Carthusian
> and Cistercian monasteries must be.

Nowhere in the world had this Venetian seen anything to equal the Shrine of the Confessor in Westminster Abbey: and this was surpassed, he reported, by the shrine of St. Thomas at Canterbury; wherever he went, even in the heart of the country, he met these wonderful monastic churches.[1]

So that we must discriminate. As against Italy and some other countries in Europe, England at the beginning of the reign of Henry VIII could not boast of either painting or poetry. But England had great schools of craftsmanship – there was stone carving, wood carving, stained glass, metal work. There were English-born scholars who could rival those of any foreign country. Of the three outstanding humanists born abroad, Erasmus, Vives, Budé, the two first were anxious to settle in England. More, Erasmus, and the young Vives, working together, might have repeated in the Sixteenth Century, on a vastly larger stage, some features of the Eighth Century, of the age of Bede and Boniface and Alcuin, when England became the centre of European scholarship, the city of its refuge, from which learning was spread abroad over a war-troubled Europe.

England, then, however inferior to some continental lands in painting or sculpture, had magnificent architecture, craftsmanship, and scholarship. Further, poetry was reviving. During the wars of the Fifteenth Century English poetry had somehow been banished from the royal presence, and had been kept alive only by ballad and song through the countryside. But it was soon to return to court, adorned with the Italian fashions of Wyatt and his pupil Surrey. English prose, which right through the Middle Ages, since the time of Alfred, had continued a rather precarious existence, was now entering into its own, thrusting aside the French and Latin substitutes, which had so long kept it out of its proper place in English life. Unlike Erasmus, who had complete command of no language save Latin, More, Tyndale, and Cranmer, to mention only the three most influential names, combined supreme mastery of English prose with enthusiastic scholarship.

It is difficult for us to realize now, how fair was the promise of the opening years of Henry's reign, so complete was the

---

[1] *A Relation of the Island of England*, trans. by C. A. SNEYD, London, 1847 (Camden Society). See especially pp. 29, 30, 41, 42.

frustration brought about in the second half. Before Henry died, he had hacked to pieces or melted down nearly all the treasures of art which amazed the Venetian diplomatist. Some few survived; but they were barren. Stand in the midst of what William Morris called the most romantic work of the late Middle Ages, the Chapel of Henry VII at Westminster, or of King's College Chapel at Cambridge, and ask: How long was it to be before England was again to produce their like? By the deliberate destruction of most of the works of art existing in England, all English arts and crafts were arrested; some (the beautiful art of coloured tiles, for example) were quite destroyed.

What a classical scholar has called the arrest of humanism ran a parallel course. Henry slew Reynolds, More, and Fisher – the most learned monk, the most learned layman, and the most saintly patron of learning to be found in England. He had already scared away the discreet Erasmus; he imprisoned and expelled Vives; he broke Wolsey. He imprisoned Wyatt, and would have slain him, had he not made a broken-spirited submission, a few months after which he died. Surrey's spirit would not be broken: he was executed. Cranmer honestly believed (and tried to persuade More) that, in a world where all was uncertain, the one certain duty was to say you believed whatever it might please the King to command. Cranmer survived, to hold in his grasp Henry's dying hand.

Think of the household of Thomas More, and the merry young scholars teaching and learning there, men and women like Margaret Roper, Margaret Gigs, John Clement, John Harris, William Gunnell, Nicholas Kratzer: a household exchanging letters with the greatest scholars in Europe, and from time to time visited by them. When was there to be anything like that in England again?

Henry VIII destroyed more things of beauty, and more things of promise, than any other man in European history. And many of his countrymen admire him for it. To the sporting Englishman, there is something admirable in having created any kind of a record. Had such destruction been wrought by an ignorant iconoclastic fanatic, it would have been intelligible. Yet Henry had taste for, and some skill in, architecture, learning, music, and poetry.

But here is Erasmus, reappearing to interrupt these melancholy meditations on what is to happen a quarter of a century later.

§3. 'THE HOOKED BEAK OF THE HARPY'

The future was mercifully hid from the eyes of Erasmus when, on 10 April 1511, he wrote from Dover (on his way to Paris, to get the *Praise of Folly* printed), 'Remind More to see that the books I left in my room are returned to Colet.'[1] Erasmus had been staying with More, and so had the correspondent to whom he writes, Andrew Ammonio. Ammonio, an Italian from Lucca, was pushing his fortunes in England, and in due course became the King's Latin Secretary. He seems at one time to have been in the service of Lord Mountjoy, and the enthusiastic letter with which that nobleman invited Erasmus to England was probably composed with the help of Ammonio. For the time, Ammonio becomes the most intimate correspondent of Erasmus, and through them we hear a good deal of More and his hospitable house. 'Our dear and beloved More, and his kind wife, who never thinks of you without a blessing upon you, are well, together with their children and the whole household.' So Ammonio writes to Erasmus.[2] A few months later the kind wife was dying. Erasmus, now in Cambridge, writes from his rooms at Queens' College, where he had gone (probably at the invitation of Bishop Fisher) to teach Greek, and excuses More's slackness in writing: 'I should be to blame, indeed, if I did not forgive More, considering how pressed he is just now.'[3] The pressure was probably anxiety over the illness of his first wife, Jane. Yet it may have been preparation for his marriage with his second wife, Alice. For, indeed, 'it followed hard upon', like the other wedding, which distressed Hamlet.

How hard, we learn in a letter from quite another source. After the execution of Fisher and More, a Carthusian, Father John Bouge, is writing to comfort a high-born lady 'in this time of tribulation and calamity'. He advises her to avoid offence, and to refuse to discuss these troubled affairs. He goes

---

[1] 10 April 1511, ALLEN, I, No. 218.   [2] 19 May 1511, ALLEN, I, No. 221.
[3] 16 Sept. 1511, ALLEN, I, No. 228.

on to speak of his friendship at Cambridge with Fisher as an undergraduate and graduate; and then of Sir Thomas More:

> He was my parishioner at London. I christened him two goodly children. I buried his first wife. And within a month after, he came to me on a Sunday, at night, late, and there he brought me a dispensation to be married the next Monday, without any banns asking: and as I understand, she is yet alive.
>
> This Mr. More was my ghostly child: in his confession to be so pure, so clean, with great study, deliberation, and devotion, I never heard many such: a gentleman of great learning, both in law, art, and divinity, having no man like him now alive of a layman. Item, a gentleman of great soberness and gravity, one chief of the King's Council. Item, a gentleman of little refection and marvellous diet.

Father Bouge proceeds to speak of More's devotion. He tells Dame Katherine Manne, the lady to whom he is writing ('keep you this privily to yourself'), how More used to wear a great hair-shirt next his skin, 'in so much that my mistress [Dame Alice, his second wife] marvelled where his shirts was washed'. Dame Alice even went to the length of going to More's father-confessor about it:

> Item, this mistress his wife desired me to counsel him to put off that hard and rough shirt of hair: and yet is very long, almost a twelvemonth, ere she knew of this habergeon of hair; it tamed his flesh till the blood was seen in his clothes.[1]

Many are the hard things that have been said about Mistress Alice Middleton, More's second wife. She was the widow of John Middleton, citizen and mercer of London, and merchant of the Staple of Calais, who had died some two years previously. She was not young, and bore More no children. Of the children by her first husband, one, Alice, was brought up in More's household. We shall hear of her later. It is clear, as Erasmus remarked, that More married to provide a mother for his children. More was wont ungallantly to say that Dame Alice was 'neither a pearl nor a girl'. But Erasmus allows her the credit of being a vigilant housewife.[2]

[1] Record Office. The whole letter is printed in the *English Historical Review*, VII, 1892, pp. 713-5. I have supplied two or three missing words.
[2] ALLEN, IV, No. 999, p. 19.

More's biographer, Nicholas Harpsfield,[1] gives an account of Dame Alice, based on the words of Erasmus and on tales told by More himself. Although she was 'aged, blunt and rude', More 'full entirely loved her'.

And yet such as she was, being also spareful and given to profit, he so framed and fashioned her by his dexterity that he lived a sweet and pleasant life with her, and brought her to that case, that she learned to play and sing at the lute and virginals, and every day at his returning home he took a reckoning and account of the task he enjoined her touching the said exercise.

This wife, on a time after shrift, bad Sir Thomas be merry. 'For I have,' saith she, 'this day left all my shrewdness, and will begin afresh.' Which merry-conceited talk, though now and then it proved true in very deed, Sir Thomas More could well digest and like in her, and in his children and other.

Neither was he in her debt for repaying home again often time such kind of talk. Among other things, when he divers times beheld his wife, what pain she took in strait binding up her hair to make her a fair large forehead, and with strait bracing in her body to make her middle small, both twain to her great pain, for the pride of a little foolish praise, he said to her: 'Forsooth, Madam, if God give you not hell, he shall do you great wrong, for it must needs be your own of very right, for you buy it very dear, and take very great pain therefore.'

With friends like Erasmus, Ammonio, and Linacre coming and going, More's household was a busy one, and needed a mistress. We get a glimpse of it, when Erasmus, from Cambridge, writes to Ammonio in London, regretting that he had not met him in passing through:

When I arrived, I had not the least idea that you were still in More's house: I was told you had moved to the College of St. Thomas. Next morning I knocked at the door of your room, but you were out. When I got back from church I heard horses outside, so I asked Linacre to look out, because I was busy writing. He told me you were just off. I had a lot to say, but another time will do.[2]

---

[1] HARPSFIELD, Life of More, pp. 93-4. Cf. Works, 1557, pp. 1184, 1203.
[2] Erasmus to Ammonio, 5 Oct. 1511, ALLEN, I, No. 232.

Later in the same month, we learn that Ammonio has moved out of More's house, and is staying in the College of St. Thomas. But he is not happy there – in fact he does not know how he is going to go on living in England at all: English ways don't suit him – he could lodge happily with an Italian merchant, but that would not be proper. (For Ammonio was engaged upon the King's confidential affairs.) Still, Ammonio says, it is a relief to have left More's house, because he no longer sees – and then follow five words in Greek, a language occasionally used by these scholars to conceal something too malicious to be entrusted to the more generally understood Latin. Erasmus doubtless understood, but the Greek (corrupted by printers) has puzzled subsequent scholars; one of the wisest of them writes: 'I cannot understand to what deficiency in the English houses of 1511 the more fastidious Italian alludes.' Dr. P. S. Allen has solved this, as he solved so many thousand Erasmian problems. What Ammonio no longer saw, now he had left More's house, was 'the hooked beak of the harpy', an ungallant allusion to the nose of Dame Alice.[1] The first wife, Jane, young and teachable, may have learnt enough colloquial Latin to be polite to her husband's guests; but Dame Alice was probably too old to learn much Latin, though More taught her so many other things.

§ 4. THE FORTUNATE ISLES HEAR THE JULIAN TRUMPET

About the same time as More's domestic loss, there fell the first of the great blows which were to defeat this circle of humanists; and Erasmus felt it in all its bitterness. 'I was dreaming,' he wrote later, 'of a Golden Age and of Isles that were truly Blessed – and then I woke up . . . That trumpet of Julius summoned all the world to war.'[2] Julius is the warlike Pope, Julius II; and England had joined the Holy League which the Pontiff had formed against France. Few of his English friends had now much time or thought to spare for Erasmus; Erasmus does not blame them, nor does he blame Henry, 'for, if the laws are silent amid arms, how much more must the maiden Muses be so'.

[1] 27 Oct. 1511, ALLEN, I, No. 236.   [2] 15 May 1515, ALLEN, II, No. 333.

We are face to face with the tragedy of the early Sixteenth Century, which was to bring More to his death.

The difficulty was no new one, although it was growing more urgent year by year. The Pope was the Head of the Universal Church. As such he was an important factor in the lives of everyone, from the monarch downward. The fact that a Papal Dispensation had been needed before Henry could marry Catherine of Aragon is only one example of the manifold ways in which the Papacy affected English life. But, at the same time, the Pope was himself a monarch; a ruler of one of the Italian states whose uneasy relations helped to keep Italy and Europe in ferment. The combination of supreme spiritual power with the duty of governing a small, but not negligible state, had led to abuses against which Dante had declaimed, two centuries before:

> Ah, Constantine, of how much ill was cause
> (Not thy conversion, but) those rich domains
> That the first wealthy pope received of thee.

(Medieval tradition, quite wrongly, attributed to Constantine the endowment of the Papacy with its temporal domains.)

Now, during the first twenty years of Henry's reign, English interests were recklessly sacrificed to the interests of the small and not very reputable Italian state ruled by the Pope. Henry was proud to be 'the Paladin of the Church'; Wolsey was fighting the battles of the principality of which he hoped in time, as Pope, to be elected prince. So England made peace, England made war, as it suited the papal interest; even when Englishmen were not fighting, vast subsidies of English money were paid abroad to foster what, from time to time, was the papal policy. The more we understand this,[1] the more intelligible becomes the overmastering rage which seized Henry when he found that, in the matter of his divorce from Catherine of Aragon, the Pope would not or could not help him. It accounts for Henry's passionate anger against old friends like Thomas More or Sebastian Newdigate who would not, at his bidding, renounce what he held to be the usurped authority of this foreign potentate who had played him false, after England had, for twenty years, fought the battles of the Papal See.

[1] It is made very clear in POLLARD's *Wolsey*, especially p. 122.

To Erasmus it was from the first an unspeakably horrible thing that the Pope should be instigating war. The sympathies of Erasmus were at least as much on the French as on the English side. To More, a loyal Englishman, things naturally did not appear in the same way as they did to the cosmopolitan Erasmus, and when the honour of his country was attacked by a French poet,[1] More answered in epigrams which are not wanting in bellicose ardour. But at a later date we shall find More warning Henry about the temporal power of the papacy: 'The Pope is a prince as you are. It may hereafter fall out that your Grace and he may vary.'[2] More did not like to see the whole policy of England subserving the temporal interests of the papacy, as Henry made it do during the first half of his reign; nor on the other hand could he approve of that rejection of the spiritual power which was the main concern of the second half of Henry's reign.

Scattered as they were in different lands, the humanists were rendered ineffective by this war to which Julius II had summoned Europe. Some, so far as they dared, protested. Warham opened Parliament in 1512 with a reminder that God only permitted war because of the sins of kings and peoples.[3] Colet was the regular Court preacher on Good Fridays, and on Good Friday 1513 preparations were being made for the invasion of France. Colet from the pulpit lamented the war, urging, like a later writer, that 'there are few die well that die in a battle, for how can they charitably dispose of anything when blood is their argument?'[4] Men ought to follow Christ, said Colet, rather than Julius or Alexander – an obvious play upon the names of the world-conquerors, and those of the Popes Julius II and Alexander VI. Colet had to make his peace with Henry afterwards, which he did with tact in a private conference, saying that he had only uttered a warning against unjust wars. As Henry could not persuade himself that anything he did was unjust, he was quite satisfied. He returned with Colet to the crowd of waiting courtiers, pledged him, embraced him, and dismissed him with the words 'Let every man favour his own doctor; this is the doctor for me.'

[1] See below, p. 190.   [2] ROPER, p. 68. See below, p. 194.
[3] POLLARD, *Wolsey*, p. 17.   [4] ALLEN, IV, No. 1211, pp. 525-6.

And so the battles of the Spurs and of Flodden were won; Thérouanne and Tournay were taken. But the fortunate isles had ceased to be fortunate to Erasmus. The royal support he had looked for was not forthcoming. Archbishop Warham did what he could. He sent Erasmus ten gold nobles, wishing they were ten legions of angels. Erasmus was suffering from stone, and the Archbishop makes the time-honoured joke about gold being a potent medicine. 'What is Erasmus doing with stones? An Archbishop has to collect stones for building. But Erasmus has no such excuse. Let him get rid of his superfluous burden.'[1] Warham also appointed Erasmus to a Kentish living; Erasmus could not perform the duties, and probably never visited his parish. Warham then replaced him by another rector, on condition that £20 (more than half the value of the living) was henceforward to be paid to Erasmus as pension. Warham hated charging livings with pensions, he said; but Erasmus' love of England and service to the Church justified this exceptional case. The pension was payable to Erasmus abroad, and it did not diminish his wish to leave England. 'The whole genius of the island is being altered by these preparations for war,' he writes in a letter which was one of his many peace manifestos.[2] Yet, even as he wrote, peace was coming near. The warlike Julius was dead; and Erasmus, in a very funny dialogue, depicted him at the gate of heaven, with the rabble of ghosts slain in his wars. St. Peter refuses admission, but Julius is not daunted. He regards St. Peter consistently as a great monarch might regard a fisherman, and he is left threatening to take Heaven by storm when the reinforcements have arrived, which the continued slaughter will send him. *Julius Excluded* got spread abroad, and in process of time was printed; though anonymous, it was recognized as Erasmus' work. Erasmus became alarmed, for he was dedicating his great work to the new Pope, and there were limits to the liberty he could take with the Pope's predecessor. He excused himself to the Cardinals, Campeggio and Wolsey, and to others. 'How malicious people are. His enemies are trying to father *Julius* upon him. They attribute everything to him, even More's *Utopia*. Five years ago he glanced through *Julius*. He doesn't quite know

[1] 5 Feb. 1514, ALLEN, I, No. 286.   [2] 14 March 1514, ALLEN, I, No. 288.

what to think, but he has suspicions who wrote it. Certainly the writer was very foolish. But to have published the book was even more unpardonable. His own books are in everyone's hands, so it is not strange that his style can be imitated.' And so on; all the statements are true; Erasmus avoids the lie direct. The equivocation is so skilful that some have even doubted whether Erasmus *was* really the author. But the question of authorship is settled by a letter of More's, which did not get published for nearly two centuries: Erasmus would have taken good care that it should not appear in his lifetime. Through the carelessness of an English friend, a copy of *Julius* had got abroad *in Erasmus' own handwriting*. More, the ever-ready friend, gets hold of the manuscript and writes to Erasmus for instructions as to what is to be done with it. This letter of More, like all his letters to Erasmus, is full of kindness, and concludes with greetings from Dame Alice, who thanks Erasmus for his wishes for her long life.[1] She wishes for it too, says More, in order that she may plague her husband the longer. She sometimes plagued Erasmus; towards the end of one of his visits he writes, 'I am tired of England, and More's wife is tired of me'.[2] (One is rather inclined to wonder at her toleration of a guest whose witty Latin conversation with her husband she must have found very boresome.) But, amid all these kindnesses, nothing save courtesies and promises came from the King. Linacre praised Erasmus at the King's supper-table, and the King agreed so enthusiastically that (More writes in glee to Erasmus) they are expecting something quite extraordinary in the way of preferment. But nothing came of it.[3]

In July 1514 Erasmus left England for a long stay abroad, where he found many things which he could not get in England: above all, the sympathetic printer he needed – John Froben of Basel. When Erasmus and More were next to meet, it was to be in Bruges, when More was meditating *Utopia*.

§ 5. MORE'S *RICHARD III*

The writing of *Utopia* interrupted More's writing of another book, the *History of Richard III*. This is a fragment, extant in

---

[1] 15 Dec. 1516, ALLEN, II, No. 502.   [2] 14 Aug. 1516, ALLEN, II, No. 451.
[3] 17 Feb. 1516, ALLEN, II, No. 388.

English for Englishmen, and in Latin for humanists abroad. It was planned as a complete history of his own time, coming up to the death of Henry VII some five years before: but More never had leisure to resume his task, and he may well have come to think it too dangerous. Erasmus confessed to More that in England he did not feel quite free.[1] More also may have been beginning to feel a need for greater caution. Henry was no longer the girl-faced boy of eighteen whom he had hailed as King. There is some very plain speaking in *Richard III* as to how the 'gathering of money' is 'the only thing that withdraweth the hearts of Englishmen from the Prince'. *Richard III* is as much an onslaught on tyranny as are some of More's epigrams. Such things might better be written and printed out of England: and so, whilst *Richard III* was left unfinished, *Utopia* was printed at Louvain, Paris, and Basel. *Utopia* is sometimes spoken of as if it had been a freak of More's youth. In fact, *Richard III* and *Utopia* belong to the period when More had just passed what Dante calls the middle point in the path of our life – the age of 35. More's nephew, Rastell, places *Richard III* about 1513: Thomas Howard (who later as Duke of Norfolk was to be More's colleague) is spoken of as Earl of Surrey; this allusion cannot be earlier than the spring of 1514 (New Style). The second book of *Utopia* seems to belong to 1515 or earlier; the first book (which is an introduction to the second) was written in 1516, in haste, which accounts, says Erasmus, for some unevenness in the style.

    Richard III and *Utopia* have much in common. Both show More's extraordinary narrative and dramatic art. In *Utopia* More looks back to the *Republic* and *Laws* of Plato, and initiates a long series of 'Ideal Commonwealths'. In *Richard III* he looks back to the Greek and Latin historians, and initiates modern English historical writing. *Richard III* remained the pattern for historians. Sixteenth-Century English authors from time to time give it that position, and confess that no later writer has been able to equal it. It is a remarkable example of the 'arrest of humanism' in England that we have to wait for any rival to *Richard III* or *Utopia* till Francis Bacon, more than a century later, produced *Henry VII* and the *New Atlantis*.

<hr />

[1] 8 July 1517, ALLEN, III, No. 597. See below, p. 147

With all its grim characterization of the last Yorkist king, *Richard III* is *not* (as is often asserted) Lancastrian. More does full justice, perhaps more than full justice, to Henry's Yorkist grandfather, Edward IV. *Richard III* is an attack on the non-moral statecraft of the early Sixteenth Century, exactly as *Utopia* is. There were Machiavellians before Machiavelli, and it is as true of *Richard III* as we shall find it to be of *Utopia*, that, if *The Prince* of Machiavelli had been published when it was written, we should have thought there was direct reference to that work. Shakespeare's Richard is More's Richard, and Shakespeare (scorning chronology) makes Richard say that he will

> set the murderous Machiavel to school.[1]

But Shakespeare owes other things to More than the Machiavellian character of Richard. It is important to remember that Shakespeare came under the influence of More early, when he was learning his work as a tragic poet. It is from More that Shakespeare takes something of the tragic idea in which his *Richard III* reminds us of Greek drama: the feeling of fate hanging over blind men who can see what is happening to others but are unconscious of their own danger. 'The vain surety of man's mind, so near his death' – that is the moral of More's *Richard III*. On the way to a Council in the Tower, where he is in fact to be slain, Hastings rejoices over the memory of his escape from former perils which, as a friend and he recall, had beset him in that same place long ago. He gloats over the impending destruction which he knows is to fall on his foes – 'nothing ware that the axe hang over his own head'. He says to his friend:

> I was never so sorry, nor never stood in so great dread in my life, as I did when thou and I met here. And lo! how the world is turned: now stand mine enemies in the danger . . . and I never in my life so merry, nor never in so great surety.

A comparison of Shakespeare's *Richard III* with More's leaves one astonished at the debt.

Obviously the long speeches in More's history are his own composition, like the speeches in his Latin or Greek models. They are masterpieces of eloquence.

[1] *III Henry VI*, Act iii, Sc. 2.

§ 6. MORE'S MISSION TO FLANDERS

On 8 May 1515 the Court of Aldermen permitted More to occupy his office of Under-Sheriff by deputy, whilst he went 'on the kinges ambasset into Flaunders'.[1] It is the embassy which More has made famous by the allusions at the beginning of *Utopia*. More there tells how he was sent ambassador with Cuthbert Tunstall – whose praises he takes the opportunity of singing – to Bruges; and how he then moved on to Antwerp, where he met Peter Giles, to whom also he gives a glowing testimonial. Peter Giles was town clerk of Antwerp. Erasmus (a close friend of Giles) was in the meantime paying a flying visit to England, to make some investigations necessary for his Greek *New Testament*. The same day (May 7) that More and his colleagues were appointed ambassadors, Erasmus had written from London to Peter Giles a letter of introduction for 'the two most learned men of all England, Cuthbert Tunstall, chancellor to the Archbishop of Canterbury, and Thomas More, to whom I dedicated my *Moria*: both my warmest friends. If by any chance you can do them any kindness, it will be a service extraordinarily well bestowed.'[2]

All Giles' friendliness was needed, for Wolsey had done his best to make the ambassadors unpopular. He had obtained the bishopric of the town of Tournay, which Henry had conquered from the French, and this intrusion was resented by French and Flemings alike. But there was also a French claimant to the bishopric, and Sampson, Wolsey's representative in Tournay, had been in a difficult position. So Wolsey added Sampson to the King's embassy and thus secured diplomatic immunity for him. Then he told him to act energetically in the matter of the bishopric: 'Handle the matter boldly, and fulminate the censures, not fearing for any excommunication of any man.' It was typical of Wolsey's aggressive acquisitiveness. He had already more Church preferment in England than he could attend to – he was Archbishop of York – and nevertheless he was compromising the position of More and Tunstall in order to help his commissary at Tournay. Yet More and Tunstall were on business of national importance, whilst Wolsey's

<hr />

[1] Repertory, iii, fol. 22. See also *L.P.*, ii, No. 422.   [2] ALLEN, II, No. 332.

Tournay bishopric was a mere abuse of power. More was having personal experience of some of the complications caused by the European warfare and the European diplomacy of which he complains in *Utopia*. Tunstall reports the ambassadors' troubles to Wolsey. Sampson has been excommunicated openly in all the churches. But for the protection of the King's commission, Sampson would find the secular arm invoked against him. Meantime, funds are running low: 'Master More, at this time, as being at a low ebb, desires by Your Grace to be set on float again.'[1]

It was poor compensation that Sampson, as Wolsey's representative in the bishopric of Tournay, offered Erasmus a canonry in the Cathedral there. This was an uncertain and troublesome piece of preferment – uncertain, because Tournay might be, and indeed was, soon ceded back to France: troublesome, because it would involve residence, if it was to be of any value. Erasmus was now on his way back to Basel. He traversed the road between London and Basel four times altogether in these thirteen months, always on the same horse, which the rector of Hackney had given him. Ulysses, says Erasmus, was wise, because he had visited many cities. What must this horse be, who has gone to so many universities. Erasmus stopped at Bruges, to see More. He placed the objections about the canonry at Tournay very frankly before his friend. Meantime Wolsey gave the canonry elsewhere; it then became More's duty to represent to Wolsey how seriously the interests of Erasmus would be damaged by the loss of this excellent preferment, unless something better could be provided.

More's letters to Erasmus about this time show him astutely looking after Erasmus' interests in many directions, with a good deal of *finesse*. For More, who would lay down his life rather than take a false oath on a matter of importance, does not shrink from a little misrepresentation when it will help a friend. He owes Erasmus three letters: 'If I say that I have answered them, I don't suppose you will believe me, however solemnly I lie; especially when you know that I am lazy at letter-writing, and not so superstitiously truthful as to shrink

<hr />

[1] 9 July, 1516. Tunstall's autograph (MS. Cotton Galba B. iii, fol. 293b).

from a little fib as if it were parricide.'[1] Erasmus had reason to know this: More explains to him the methods by which he is arranging for Erasmus' pension from the Kentish living to be properly paid abroad by the money broker; the manœuvres are complicated and difficult to follow; but it is clear that in More the broker had met his match.

No wonder that with the Tournay complications More found his embassy prolonged. When finally back in London, he wrote to Erasmus that he had expected it to last two months, and it had lasted six. Poor Tunstall, after barely ten days at home, not one of them spent as he would have wished, had been sent off again on a new embassy. Embassies are all very well, says More, for you clergy, who have no wives and children, or who can manage to find them wherever you may travel. But he has had to keep two households going, and, good husband and indulgent father though he is, his family won't fast all the time he is away. Besides, churchmen can be recompensed with church preferment – laymen are not so easily rewarded. The King, it is true, has offered him a good pension; but he has refused it, because it is incompatible, he thinks, with his post in the City, which he prefers to a higher office. There is always the possibility of a dispute between the King and the citizens as to their privileges, and the citizens would not like their official to be a pensioner.[2]

But, says More, the great joy of the embassy has been the comradeship with Tunstall, and Busleiden, and Peter Giles. Jerome Busleiden was the wealthy cleric of Brussels who founded the College of the Three Languages (Latin, Greek, and Hebrew) at Louvain. More celebrates in his *Epigrams* Busleiden's lovely house and his collection of coins, *Utopia* he addresses to Peter Giles, and Giles in turn passes on the compliment to Busleiden, in a letter worthy of More himself.

As iron sharpeneth iron, so doth the converse of a man his friends. Everywhere in *Utopia* we can trace the influence of these foreign scholars and foreign men of affairs, as well as of the civilization of the noble Flemish cities.

<hr />

[1] c. 17 Feb. 1516, ALLEN, II, No. 388; compare c. 21 June 1516, ALLEN, II, No. 424.
[2] c. 17 Feb. 1516, ALLEN, II, No. 388.

§ 7. THE WONDERFUL YEAR OF ERASMIAN
REFORM

The next year, 1516, was the year of triumph of the Eras-
mian reformers. In February[1] Erasmus dedicated his Greek
New Testament, the great work of his life, to Pope Leo X. In
March[2] he dedicated the *Institute of the Christian Prince* to the
sixteen year old King Charles of Castile and the Netherlands.
The book is a passionate plea for peace, arbitration, mercy to
the poor, the fostering of learning – but, above all, for peace.
In April[3] Erasmus had the first part of the great edition of
Jerome ready; he had been working at it intermittently for
sixteen years. So much of this work had been done in England
that it was rightly dedicated to the most generous and considerate of all Erasmus' English patrons, Archbishop Warham of
Canterbury. Erasmus praises the career of that statesman, as of
one who had sought peace and ensued it:

> Would that in all our princes were the same mind that is in
> you. Then these insane and wretched wars would end, and
> rulers would turn their minds to making their age illustrious
> by the arts of peace.

And Erasmus goes on to point out what the patronage of learning, such as Warham had shown, had done for England.

Finally, on 1 November of this year of wonders, we have
the introductory letter of *Utopia*, addressed by Peter Giles to
Jerome Busleiden. More presented a copy of *Utopia* to Warham,
together with a letter congratulating him on his resignation of
the burden of the Chancellorship, and upon the integrity with
which he had borne that burden.[4] The letter is strangely
applicable to More's own resignation, seventeen years after
Warham's. There was indeed much sympathy between the two
statesmen.

The triumph of the humanists was to be short. Just one year
later, 1 November 1517, Luther's theses were hanging upon the
church door at Wittenberg, and the Erasmian reformers were
to be rapidly thrust out of the way by figures more passionate

---

[1] ALLEN, II, No. 384.   [2] ALLEN, II, No. 393.   [3] ALLEN, II, No. 396.
[4] STAPLETON, VII, p. 236.

and more violent. Some would say, greater? It will be easier to estimate that, a few hundred years from now.

Meanwhile, in the lull before the storm, let us look once again at their aims.

Listen to the prefatory words of Erasmus' *New Testament*, or *New Instrument*, as he called it: the instrument which is to teach men how to order their lives aright:

> I would have the weakest woman read the Gospels and the Epistles of St. Paul . . . I would have those words translated into all languages, so that not only Scots and Irishmen, but Turks and Saracens might read them. I long for the plough-boy to sing them to himself as he follows the plough, the weaver to hum them to the tune of his shuttle, the traveller to beguile with them the dullness of his journey . . . Other studies we may regret having undertaken, but happy is the man upon whom death comes when he is engaged in these. These sacred words give you the very image of Christ speaking, healing, dying, rising again, and make him so present, that were he before your very eyes you would not more truly see him.

In contrast with this ideal, *Utopia* tells how men were ordering their lives in contemporary Europe:

> the endless wars, the faithless leagues, the military expenditure, the money and time wasted upon instruments and means of offence, to the neglect of all social improvements, trains of idle serving men, broken and disabled soldiers turning to theft, husbandry broken up, villages and hamlets depopulated to feed sheep, agricultural labourers turned adrift, justice proud of its executions, and wondering that theft multiplied faster than the gibbet.[1]

There was something wrong with Europe, judged, not even by the Christian ideal, but merely from that of poor unaided human reason.

During his stay in Antwerp, after service in the noble cathedral, then in the first freshness of its beauty, More had seen Giles talking to an aged, sunburnt, bearded stranger, with a cloak cast carelessly round his shoulder. Giles introduced them. The stranger was no mariner, as More had at first

[1] BREWER, *Reign of Henry VIII*, I, pp. 288-92.

thought, but a Portuguese philosopher with a passion for Greek, Raphael Hythlodaye. From a love of travel, he had given his patrimony to his brothers, and had accompanied Amerigo Vespucci on the last three of his four voyages. He had obtained leave to stay behind among the twenty-four men whom Vespucci had left as a settlement in 1504, on what we should call the coast of Brazil. After much travelling, he had reached Ceylon and Calicut, whence Portuguese vessels had carried him home.

The traveller's claim is startling, when we remember that the first circumnavigator of the globe, Sebastian del Cano, the lieutenant of Magellan, did not make his circuit till some six years after More published *Utopia*. But More's complete confidence in Raphael quells any doubts that may arise in our minds; we can understand how the Vicar of Croydon came to take *Utopia* seriously. More asks Hythlodaye and Giles back to his lodgings, and there, on a grassy seat in the garden, Raphael tells of the states and cities he has known, whose customs and laws are a reproof and example to those of Europe. Evils like those of Europe must exist, he says, wherever individual property is allowed. More objects that communism will not work. 'That,' retorts Hythlodaye, 'is because you have never seen it working, as I did for five years in Utopia.' Giles, with European complacency, refuses to believe that things can be better in the New World than they are in the Old.

But by that time the morning has passed, so they go to dinner, and in the afternoon return to the same garden seat, where Raphael gives a detailed account of Utopia. There the towns are well built, beautiful, and sanitary. A six hours' working day suffices for the wants of the community, and people have the rest of their time for attending lectures, or practising music. They despise gold, silver, and precious stones, which nevertheless the State accumulates, and uses if necessary to sow dissentions among its foolish and mercenary enemies. The Utopians aim at a life of true pleasure, and understand wherein it consists: not in cruel field sports, but in health, and above all in the pleasures of the mind, of which they think a clear conscience the greatest. Heinous offences are punished in the first instance with bondage, though the death penalty is kept in reserve for recalcitrant criminals. The Utopians mastered eagerly the Greek learning which Hythlodaye brought among them, and some were converted to Christianity. The different religions of Utopia, which once strove together, have been made to tolerate one another, and bondage is the penalty for any kind of violence in religious matters. The Utopians loathe warfare, and yet, for what they feel to be great national interests, both men and women are prepared in the last resort to fight. All religions meet for a solemn service on the first and last day of every month and year, in their large, beautiful, solemn, dark churches, lighted with many wax tapers; the service is of a kind which can offend no one. So soon as the priest in his gorgeous and mysterious apparel appears from the vestry, the white vested congregation prostrate themselves to the ground, and then follows a ritual with music and frankincense, ending with solemn prayer. The rest of the holy day is devoted to 'play and exercise of chivalry'.

And the Utopian who, after such a life, does not at the end depart merrily, and full of good hope, to God, is held to be disgraced.

More would have liked to question Raphael further. But Raphael is tired of talking, and More is not quite certain if he will bear patiently anything being said contrary to his mind; 'therefore I, praising both the institutions of the Utopians and his communication, took him by the hand, and led him in to supper, saying that we would choose another time to talk more at large'.

But the time never came. In his dedicatory letter to Peter Giles, More is a little troubled. His scholar-servant, young John Clement, had been present at the discussion – for More suffers him to be away from no talk where profit is to be got. (The woodcut of Ambrose Holbein, in the Basel edition of *Utopia*, shows Clement carrying much-needed refreshment to the discoursing Raphael.) More's recollection is that the bridge over the river Anyder at the town of Amaurot (the bridge of the Dim Town over the Waterless Stream) was 500 paces in length. But Clement says 300. Can Giles decide? If not, More will follow his own recollection. But perhaps Giles could consult Raphael: in fact he must do so, because they unfortunately had forgotten to ask where, in the New World, Utopia is to be found. And now a professor of Divinity is anxious to go out as bishop to Utopia. (Tradition has it that this would-be missionary was Rowland Phillips, the famous Vicar of Croydon, a notable preacher.) Could not Giles submit the manuscript of More's book to Raphael? Perhaps Raphael himself wants to publish an account of Utopia. More is not certain about publishing his own version, people are so critical. So he leaves it to the judgment of his friends, and especially of Raphael and Giles.

§ 8 . THE MEANING OF *UTOPIA*

An ex-Cabinet minister is still alive who dates his political career from the accidental purchase of a copy of *Utopia* at a second-hand bookstall. One of his colleagues in the Cabinet has written of *Utopia*, that no treatise is better calculated to nourish the heart of a Radical. *Utopia* has become a text-book of Socialist propaganda. It did more to make William Morris a Socialist than ever Karl Marx did. All this testifies to its abiding power; yet we must never think of More as writing it for Nineteenth-Century Radicals or Twentieth-Century Socialists. Even he could not do that.

The first step to an appreciation of *Utopia* is to understand how it must have struck a scholar in the early Sixteenth Century. That is a difficult task, yet not an impossible one; and if we would understand More himself, it is a task which we must undertake.

We shall then find, I think, that few books have been more misunderstood than *Utopia*. It has given the English language a word 'Utopian' to signify something visionary and unpractical. Yet the remarkable thing about *Utopia* is the extent to which it adumbrates social and political reforms which have either been actually carried into practice, or which have come to be regarded as very practical politics. Utopia is depicted as a sternly righteous and puritanical State, where few of us would feel quite happy; yet we go on using the word 'Utopia' to signify an easy-going paradise, whose only fault is that it is too happy and ideal to be realized. *Utopia* is the first of a series which we have christened 'Ideal Commonwealths'. Some of these, for example William Morris' *News from Nowhere*, really *are* ideal.

They are 'Utopian' in the current sense, that is to say, they are quite unpractical fancies of what this world might be like if the dreamer could shatter it to bits, and then remould it nearer to the heart's desire. For instance, in *News from Nowhere* we might be sure that the Divine Worship of the citizens would be Morris' ideal. If he gives them no Divine Worship, that also tells its tale. Now, More does not make his Utopians Christian. So modern scholars have argued: 'Utopia is an ideal commonwealth; *argal* More thought the vague deism of his Utopians more ideal than the popular religious beliefs of his time.'

Such argument might be reasonable if *Utopia* were a modern 'Ideal Commonwealth'. But we must never forget that More's education fell not in the Nineteenth but in the Fifteenth Century. To a man educated in that century, the distinction was obvious between the virtues which might be taught by human reason alone, and the further virtues taught by Catholic orthodoxy. It was part of the medieval system to divide the virtues into the Four Cardinal Virtues (to which the heathen might attain) and the Three Christian Virtues. The Four Cardinal Virtues – Wisdom, Fortitude, Temperance, and Justice – are the foundation of Plato's commonwealths, as outlined in the *Republic* and the *Laws*.[1] These virtues were taken into the medieval system – part of the immense debt it owes to Greek philosophy. The Three Christian Virtues – Faith, Hope, and Charity – come of course from St. Paul's *First Epistle to the Corinthians*. Four and Three make Seven – the Perfect Number, which was extremely comforting. The perfect Christian character must comprise all seven. But the four heathen virtues were sufficient to ensure that a man or a State might be a model of conduct in secular matters. In Dante's *Divine Comedy* Virgil represents Philosophy, Reason, Human Wisdom. He is able to rescue Dante from the dark wood (although he was one of those who had not the three sacred virtues) because he knew and followed the four other virtues without fault. So Virgil can guide Dante till he meets Beatrice, but can go no further.

For a pattern of a State, Dante turns to Heathen Rome or to Heathen Greece. And it is not because of his deep learning that Dante does this. Our great English medieval poet, William

---

[1] *Republic*, Book IV; *Laws*, Book XII.

Langland, the author of *Piers Plowman*, had but a commonplace
education, but his system is similar. *Do Well* is the virtue of
secular life, and the examples of it are the great non-Christian
philosophers and rulers: Aristotle, Solomon, Socrates, Trajan.
Do Better and *Do Best* represent forms of Christian virtues. And
so More's friend, Busleiden, in his introductory letter to *Utopia*,
tells us that the perfect commonwealth must unite 'Wisdom in
the ruler, Fortitude in the soldiers, Temperance in private
individuals, and Justice in all'.

In basing his *Utopia* upon these four heathen virtues, More
is following medieval tradition; further, he is following his
great examples, Plato's *Republic* and *Laws*; but, above all, he
makes his satire upon contemporary European abuses more
pointed. The virtues of Heathen Utopia show up by contrast
the vices of Christian Europe. But the Four Cardinal Virtues
are subsidiary to, not a substitute for, the Christian Virtues.
More has done his best to make this clear. It is not his fault if he
has been misunderstood, as the following example will show.

Most of us would agree with Dame Alice in deploring More's
extreme austerities. We have seen that, years before *Utopia* was
written, she had complained to More's confessor about that
shirt of hair. It was no good. It may have been some ten years
after *Utopia* was written that, as Roper tells us, More's daughter-
in-law, young Anne Cresacre, noticed it:

> My sister More, in the summer as he sat at supper, singly in
> his doublet and hose, wearing thereupon a plain shirt, with-
> out ruff or collar, chancing to spy, began to laugh at it. My
> wife [Margaret Roper] not ignorant of his manner, perceiving
> the same, privily told him of it; and he, being sorry that she
> saw it, presently amended it. He used also sometimes to
> punish his body with whips, the cords knotted, which was
> known only to my wife, whom for her secrecy above all other
> he specially trusted, causing her, as need required, to wash
> the same shirt of hair.[1]

Now, despite all this, we are told that the Utopians condemn
bodily austerities as 'a point of extreme madness, and a token of
a man cruelly minded toward himself'.

More's biographers and commentators have been puzzled.

[1] ROPER, p. 49.

Yet the very next sentence of *Utopia* explains the puzzle. The Utopians have only reason to guide them, and they believe that *by man's reason* nothing can be found truer than their view, '*unless any godlier be inspired into man from Heaven*'. The same point is made by More later. There *are* orders of ascetics in *Utopia*: if the ascetics grounded their action on reason the Utopians would mock them; but as they base it on religion, the Utopians honour them and regard them as holy.[1]

We find More, a dozen years later, urging against the Reformers this same doctrine which lies at the root of *Utopia*: 'That Reason is servant to Faith, not enemy.' More argues that Reason, Philosophy, and even Poetry have their part to play: zealots who, neglecting 'a good mother wit' would cast away all learning except the Bible are, says More, 'in a mad mind', and he quotes St. Jerome to prove that pagan Philosophy and Poetry have their use for Christians. By 'Poetry' More of course means any work of the imagination: his Protestant critics deride *Utopia* as 'poetry', and More himself as a 'poet'. When a Sixteenth-Century Catholic depicts a pagan state founded on Reason and Philosophy, he is not depicting his ultimate ideal. Erasmus tells us that More's object was 'to show whence spring the evils of States, with special reference to the English State, with which he was most familiar'. The underlying thought of *Utopia* always is, *With nothing save Reason to guide them, the Utopians do this; and yet we Christian Englishmen, we Christian Europeans . . . !*

Just as More scored a point against the wickedness of Christian Europe, by making his philosophers heathen, so Jonathan Swift scored a point against the wickedness of mankind by representing *his* philosophers, the Houyhnhnms, as having the bodies of horses. Yet we do not call Swift inconsistent, because he did not live on a diet of oats, or, like poor Gulliver, fall into the voice and manner of horses in speaking. Swift did not mean that all horses are better than all men. He meant that some men are worse than horses. More did not mean that Heathendom is better than Christianity. He meant that some Christians are worse than heathen.

Dante and Langland and innumerable medieval writers had

[1] *Utopia*, ed. LUPTON, pp. 210, 282.

said the same before him. The conviction that life might be nobly lived on the basis of the four heathen cardinal virtues was one which the Catholic Middle Ages had inherited from Greek philosophy.

So, naturally, More is interested in the problem which for half a lifetime tormented Dante and Langland; what will be the fate, in the next world, of the just heathen, who are an example to us in the affairs of this world? More's answer is tentative, but he quotes with approval the 'comfortable saying' of Master Nicholas de Lyra, the Franciscan, Dante's younger contemporary. Nicholas de Lyra argued that, though a much fuller faith is demanded from Christians, it suffices for the heathen to have believed 'that God is, and that He is the rewarder of them that seek Him'; these are, says de Lyra, 'two points such as every man may attain by natural reason, holpen forth with such grace as God keepeth from no man'.

And More quoted this,[1] not in his alleged 'emancipated' youth, but in his last book, the *Treatise upon the Passion*, written in the Tower, when he had dismissed all worldly affairs, and was awaiting martyrdom 'for the faith of the Catholic Church'.

What, then, is the attitude of *Utopia* as to these two articles, which represent, in More's view, the orthodoxy to which a heathen may attain? King Utopus tolerated all varieties of belief and disbelief, save on these two points: he forbade, 'earnestly and straitly' that any man should disbelieve in either (1) Divine Providence, or (2) a future life in which, as the Utopians believed, the just would be rewarded by God's presence.

So far was this simple creed from appearing lax to More's friends, that the marginal note (written either by Erasmus or by Peter Giles) contrasts the Utopian faith in immortality with the laxity and doubts of many Christians: '*The immortality of the soul, concerning which not a few, though Christians, to-day doubt or dispute.*' But in Utopia, the man who disbelieves either of these articles is not counted as a citizen, or even as a man; he is excluded from all office, and despised, as being necessarily of a base and vile nature. To suffer lifelong public contumely, in a land where all life is lived in public, and where, save as a

---

[1] *Works*, 1557, p. 1287-8.

citizen, a man has and is nothing, is a punishment which many would feel to be worse than death. Yet the sceptic may not, publicly, argue in his own defence. Then comes the sentence which has been so often quoted, out of its context. In the old translation it runs, 'Howbeit they put him to no punishment'. Of course, More did not write such nonsense. What he really says is, 'They do not put him to any bodily punishment' – so long, that is, as he humbly submits to the disgrace and to the silence which his heresies involve. The charge against More of inconsistency rests upon refusing to notice his distinction between liberty to hold an opinion, and liberty to preach that opinion; between a man being in More's phrase 'a heretic alone by himself', and being 'a seditious heretic'.

Bishop Creighton, to prove that More in later life 'put his principles aside', quotes the passage which tells how King Utopus, when settling the Utopian constitution, found many religions prevalent in the land, and ordained that they should all be tolerated. Creighton then omits the passage about Utopus disgracing and muzzling those who held the opinions he thought pernicious. But this passage is vital; for, in the light of it, we find that Utopus did *not* tolerate the preaching of all views, but only of those which he, in his wisdom, thought tolerable. Then Creighton begins to quote again. Even those who held most noxious opinions 'were put to no punishment'. They are put to no bodily punishment, so long as they will submit to being disfranchised, despised, and silenced.

But, as the watchman says to Dogberry, 'How if they will not?'

We can tell what would happen *then*, when we remember that, even in the discussion of such opinions as the State allows, any violent or seditious speech is punished in Utopia by banishment or bondage. And, in Utopia, if a man condemned to bondage jibs at his punishment, he is slain out of hand like a wild beast. Suppose that two sceptics, who did not believe the soul of man to be immortal, had discussed, in private, in Utopia, how they could get the law repealed which silenced and disfranchised them. They would have incurred the penalty imposed on those who plot against the fundamental laws of Utopia. And, even for the highest magistrats, that penalty is death.

Still, within these narrow limits, the Utopian has liberty of conscience. He may not spread among the common people a belief which the State thinks harmful, nor may he discuss the most innocent opinions in a way likely to cause sedition and dissension. He may not, in private, discuss any affair of State. But, if he submits to these restrictions, he is left alone; he is not to be terrorized into saying that he believes what he does not believe.

It may be a low ideal of liberty which allows, to a man who holds views disapproved by the authorities, freedom of thought only on condition that he does not claim freedom of speech. But that *is* the liberty Utopia allows. I shall try, later, to show how far More stuck to that ideal.

§9. *UTOPIA* AND THE PROBLEMS OF 1516

But we merely confuse the issues if we use our modern question-begging terminology, and contrast More's alleged 'emancipated youth' with his orthodox old age. If we try to judge it in relation to the early Sixteenth Century, we shall find that *Utopia* is by no means 'emancipated'; it is rather a protest against undue 'emancipation'.

Utopia is, in part, a protest against the New Statesmanship: against the new idea of the autocratic prince to whom everything is allowed. I do not say that it is an impartial protest. The evil counsellors, who are represented in the First Book of *Utopia* egging the prince to despotism, might have replied that their ideal was not necessarily base or sycophantic. Patriots have sometimes seen in tyranny the only force strong enough to make their country great; reformers have sometimes seen in it the only force strong enough to carry through the reformation they desire. But *Utopia* is hostile to it.

Again, *Utopia* is, in part, a protest against the New Economics: the enclosures of the great landowners, breaking down old law and custom, destroying the old common-field agriculture. Here again, we must not suppose that *Utopia* gives us the full story. There was much more in the problem of enclosures than the greed of the great landlord, 'the very plague of his native country'.[1] The up-to-date farmer was also in favour of sweep-

---

[1] *Utopia*, ed. LUPTON, p. 53.

ing away all traces of the older communal husbandry. Thomas
Tusser, a humble but practical agriculturist, says:

> Where all things in common do rest,
> Yet what doth it stand ye in stead?

Now, in contrast to this changing world, More depicts a
state where 'all things in common do rest', and where there is
no place for the grabbing superman. More's theoretical *Utopia*,
looking back to Plato's *Republic* and to corporate life in the
Middle Ages, probably seemed to some contemporaries the
reverse of 'progressive'. Cardinal Pole has told of a conversation he had in his youth with Thomas Cromwell. Cromwell
ridiculed the *Republic* of Plato, which, after so many centuries,
had led to nothing. *He* had a book on statesmanship in manuscript, by a practical modern writer, based on experience.
The book, which Cromwell offered to lend to Pole, was *The
Prince* of Nicholas Machiavelli. [1]

It is noteworthy that the two most potent books on the State
written in the Sixteenth Century were written within so few
years of each other. Parts of *Utopia* read like a commentary on
parts of *The Prince*, as Johnson's *Rasselas* reads like a commentary
on Voltaire's *Candide*, though we know that in neither case can
the English writer have read his continental predecessor. There
is a reason for the coincidence; before *The Prince* was written,
ideas used in *The Prince* had been gaining ground. They were
the 'progressive' ideas, and we may regard *Utopia* as a 'reaction'
against them. [2] Over and over again, in Book I of *Utopia*,
Raphael Hythlodaye imagines himself as counselling a prince,
telling him what he ought to do, against those who are telling
him what he *can* do; and always Raphael admits that these
ideas of justice which he has brought from Utopia are opposed
to all that the most up-to-date statesmen of Europe are thinking
and doing.

And so, from the point of view of the new age of Machiavellian statesmanship and commercial exploitation, *Utopia* is old-

---

[1] *Epistolarum*, Pars I, BRESCIA, 1744, pp. 135-7. An attempt has been made to argue
that Pole mistook the book, and that Cromwell really meant to lend him *The
Courtier* of CASTIGLIONE. (VAN DYKE, *Renascence Portraits*, p. 401.) The argument
is unconvincing.

[2] I had written this before reading Hermann Oncken's lecture on the *Utopia*
(1922), but I am glad to find that I have the support of his authority: *Sitzungsberichte
der Heidelberger Akademie, Phil.-Hist. Klasse* (1922), 2, p. 12.

fashioned. The King is to 'live of his own', in medieval wise, and to turn a deaf ear to the counsellors who would make him all-powerful. The big landlords are to have mercy on their tenants, and not to allow them to be sacrificed to economic progress, and the law of supply and demand in the wool market.

And the outlook of *Utopia* on the ecclesiastical problems of 1516 is also conservative and orthodox. Among the most pressing problems of church government was that of the immunity of the clergy; among the most pressing problems of doctrine, the immortality of the soul; beyond all these was the problem of monasticism.

Most urgent in England, at this date, was the question of clerical immunity. If a cleric committed felony, was he to be hanged like a mere layman, or was he to be left to the gentler reproof of the ecclesiastical courts? The question had been fought out between Henry II and Becket – a battle of giants: the murder of Becket had caused a revulsion of feeling which left the victory on the ecclesiastical side. But now the problem was being raised again: the first rumblings of a storm which was to burst in fury twenty years later. Whilst More was planning *Utopia*, London had been in a ferment over the question whether clerks in minor orders were to enjoy immunity. The problem, of course, was not limited to England. It had just been declared in the Lateran Council that laymen had no jurisdiction over the clergy,[1] but there were many reasons why discussion was peculiarly acute in London throughout the whole of 1515.

Very characteristically, More sticks to the medieval principle, whilst stripping it of its abuses. Priests in Utopia who commit any offence suffer no temporal punishment; they are left only to God and themselves: 'For they think it not lawful to touch him with man's hand, be he never so vicious, who after so singular a sort was dedicate and consecrate to God, as a holy offering.' But inconveniences do not result to the State, because in Utopia priests are so few, and so carefully chosen: 'of exceeding holiness, and therefore', More grimly says, 'very few'.

[1] 5 May 1514.

Now, if we read *Utopia* as a modern skit, we may think that
this discussion of clerical immunity was introduced merely as
an opening for the 'satirical observation' that priests of exceeding holiness are very few. That, for example, was how
Benjamin Jowett took More's words.[1] They seemed to him to
show More's 'detestation of priests', and therefore 'curiously
disagree' with More's life. There is no disagreement. A dozen
years later, in his defence of the Church, we find More insisting
on selecting priests carefully, and limiting the number. But
if, alike in England and in Utopia, the laymen fitted to be
made priests are few, that is a reflection, not on the clergy, but
on us, the laity: 'for of us', says More, 'they be made'. And he
quotes a saying he heard Colet make, many years before, that
the clergy will always be one degree better than the laity.[2]

The feeling in London had been embittered by the case of
Richard Hunne. Hunne was a prosperous Merchant Taylor of
high character, who had a quarrel with the clergy. He was
accused of heresy, and whilst in the bishop's prison, awaiting
trial, he was found hanged. Had he added the crime of suicide
to the crime of heresy? Or had the clergy added the crime of
murder to that of false-witness? More was certain that it was a
case of suicide. He discussed the matter at length many years
after. But popular feeling accused the bishop's officials of
murder. Bishop FitzJames of London declared that the
Londoners were so set in favour of heresy that a London jury
would condemn a clerk 'though he were as innocent as Abel'.
Bishop FitzJames was given to exaggerated language, but,
allowing for that, it is clear that there was a good deal of anti-
clerical feeling in London at the time. It is all the more noteworthy that so loyal a Londoner as our under-Sheriff should
represent the inviolability of the clergy as a sound principle,
prescribed by the law of reason which governs Utopia.

We must never forget then that in Utopia the despotic
supremacy of the State is balanced by the inviolability of a
priesthood entirely exempt from State control.

Another leading problem of controversy was the immortality
of the soul. Did philosophy and human reason, apart from
revelation, teach such immortality? There were philosophers

[1] *Dialogues of Plato*, 1875, III, p. 189.   [2] *Dialogue, Works*, 1557, pp. 225-8.

who said 'No'; and, three years before *Utopia* was published, this matter also had come before the Lateran Council.[1] Teachers of philosophy were enjoined to point out how Christian philosophy corrected the views of the heathen on immortality; they were to refute these heathen errors, and steps were taken to ensure that the student *in sacris ordinibus constitutus* should not spend more than five years upon philosophy and poetry, before diluting them with the safer studies of theology and pontifical law.

Now, let us try and look at *Utopia* from the point of view of 1516. Here is a heathen community, whose religion is founded on philosophy and natural reason. Yet, so far from doubting the immortality of the soul, they base their whole polity upon it. No disbeliever in immortality may be a citizen of Utopia. In life, and in death, every true Utopian has a firm trust in the communion of saints.

So that, in the eyes of More's friends, Erasmus or Peter Giles, *Utopia* is a striking defence of a vital tenet of the Christian faith. More will not tolerate the ambiguous formula: 'As an orthodox Catholic I believe in immortality; as a philosopher I doubt.' Reason and philosophy teach the Utopian to affirm that he is somehow in touch with the souls of the noble dead, mighty overseers whose presence encourages him to do his duty the more courageously.

Thus here we find More in *Utopia* opposing the scepticism of his age, precisely as we have seen him opposing its Machiavellian statecraft. And so thoroughly is *Utopia* a book of the hour, that here again More seems to be making a comment on a book which he had never seen. For it was in the very same November of 1516, in which Peter Giles was writing the dedicatory epistle of *Utopia*, that the professor of Philosophy at Bologna, Pomponazzi, published his famous treatise on the Immortality of the Soul. Pomponazzi submitted to the Church in all matters of faith, but, as a philosopher, he stubbornly upheld his doubt concerning the doctrine of immortality.[2]

Therefore More's *Utopia*, among other things, is a contribu-

---

[1] 19 Dec. 1513: *Concilium Lateranense V, Sessio viii*. See *Conciliorum Omnium tomus XXXIV*, Paris, 1644, pp. 333-5, 557.

[2] The *Tractatus de immortalitate animae* is dated Bologna, 6 Nov. 1516; *Utopia* is dated Antwerp, 1 Nov. 1516.

tion to this current controversy. More attacks the enemy in their philosophical camp, and makes his heathen Utopians into unexpected allies of the Catholic faith with regard to this great dogma – and, as we shall see later, with regard to other things as well.

But the imminent problem was monasticism. There was an incompatibility between the declining spirit of the monastic common life, and the rising commercialism of the grasping 'new rich'. Within a quarter of a century commercialism was to destroy monasticism in England. More stands, as it were, at the crossways, and asks, 'Why not destroy commercialism? Is not the spirit of the common life really better worth preserving?' It is significant that *the religious houses are the one European institution which the Utopians are said to approve.* And with reason, for in Utopia, though the rule of celibacy is necessarily absent, the monastic idea is at work. The Utopian State is as sumptuous as many a religious house was. But the Utopian, like the monk or friar, may possess nothing. Everyone in Utopia must wear the common habit (in a letter to Erasmus we shall find More calling it Franciscan).[1] There are four varieties, for men and women, married and unmarried. 'The cloaks of the Utopians are all of one colour, and that is the natural colour of the wool.' Their hours of work, of recreation, the very games they may play, are all regulated. There are no foolish and pernicious games like dice. Instead, the Utopians have two games, one of which is intended to teach mathematics, and the other to teach morals. The Utopians eat in refectories, beginning every dinner and supper by reading something pertaining to good manners and virtue. Talk at table is initiated and directed by the elders, who graciously encourage the younger married people to join in the discussion, by turning it into a kind of oral examination. As for the men below twenty-two and the girls below eighteen: they serve, or else stand by, in marvellous silence, watching their elders eat and talk.

In much of this, More is perhaps joking; it was his way to utter his jests with such a solemn face as to puzzle his own household.[2] But, underneath More's fun, was a creed as stern as that of Dante, just as, underneath his gold chain, was the

---

[1] ALLEN, II, No. 499.   [2] CRESACRE MORE, 1726, p. 179; cf. *Works,* 1557, p. 127.

shirt of hair. And, quite certainly, the ideal of *Utopia* is discipline, not liberty. It is influenced by some of the most severe disciplines the world has ever known. Through Plato's *Republic* it goes back to the barrack life of a Spartan warrior, through More's own experience to the life of a Charterhouse monk. And the discipline of Utopia is enforced rigidly, even ferociously. If the Utopian attempts to break the laws of his native land, there is the penalty of bondage, and, if that fails, of death. We have seen that even to speak of State affairs, except at the licensed place and hour, is punishable in Utopia with death, lest permission to discuss politics might lead to revolution. Has any State, at any time, carried terrorism quite so far?

Many framers of ideal commonwealths have shirked the question of compulsion, by imagining their citizens to have all become moral overnight. More does not choose this easy way. He recognizes that there will be a minority, to whom higher motives do not appeal. For them, there is penal servitude; if that fails, death.

But no great State can be founded on terrorism. For the mass of its citizens, Utopia is founded on religious enthusiasm. Faith in God, and in the immortal destiny of the human soul, supplies the driving power which is to quench human passion and human greed.[1] Based on religion, Utopia is supported by a belief in the dignity of manual labour. Even rulers and magistrates, although legally exempt, share in this work as an example to others.[2] So a six-hours' day suffices, and the rest of the time is free for those intellectual and artistic pursuits in which, to the Utopians, pleasure consists.[3] But religion is the basis of all.

Now a monk of to-day, Dom Ursmer Berlière, of the Abbey of Maredsous, has pointed out how at the beginning of the Middle Ages, monasticism, as St. Benedict shaped it, gave a pattern to the State. St. Benedict's monastery 'was a little State, which could serve as a model for the new Christian society which was arising from the fusion of the conquered and conquering races – a little State which had for its basis, religion; for its support, the honour given to work; for its crown a new

---

[1] pp. 274-5.   [2] p. 147.   [3] *passim*, especially pp. 152, 206.

intellectual and artistic culture'.[1] The writer was not thinking of *Utopia*. I do not know if he had ever read it. But, at the end of the Middle Ages, we find More depicting a State founded on just these things: the common life, based on religion; honour given to manual labour; intellectual and artistic culture. However far these things might sometimes be from monastic practice, the writer of *Utopia* could never have approved of the destruction of monasticism; he looked for its reform.

And, just as the customs of Utopia have their bearing on the urgent questions of the time, so has the framework of the book – the story of the travels and circumnavigation of Raphael Hythlodaye. We have only to look at a globe – a flat Mercator's map conceals the fact – to see how the destiny of England had been shaped by the discovery of the New World. England, till More's day remote from the centre of things, and unable to employ very profitably the skill of her mariners, was now found to be peculiarly well placed. The farther from the Equator, the shorter the way round the world. A similar favourable situation had enabled the Norsemen to discover America five centuries before, though they could not exploit their discovery. But now Englishmen were bound to seek for a north-west passage to Japan, China, and India. True, America blocked their way. But this only meant that they found something even better than they sought. And so, under an Italian captain, resident in Bristol, Bristol men in a Bristol ship first discovered the mainland of America, with authority to set up the royal banners of Henry VII in 'any village, town, castle, island or mainland of them newly found', and to import into England free of customs any merchandise they might get there. If every man had his due, America would be called Cabota; and Henry VII, rather than a modern peer, would be hailed as the first Crusader for Empire Free Trade. But Cabot had a bad press, or rather no press at all; the new art of printing spread the fame of a later explorer, Amerigo Vespucci; so Amerigo became godfather of the new continent, and, as we have seen, it was *his* travels, 'now in print and abroad in every man's hands', which inspired Thomas More.

[1] *L'ordre monastique des origines au XIIe. siècle*, 2ᵉ. edit., 1921, p. 45.

Yet recent research has shown that More had also domestic inspiration.

More was about nineteen when John Cabot discovered the mainland of America. During the rest of the reign of Henry VII transatlantic exploration was kept before men's eyes. The 'Company Adventurers into the New Found Lands' were busy at Bristol. About 1502, three specimen savages, clothed in skins and eating raw flesh, were presented to the King. Two years later, two of them were still to be seen about the Palace at Westminster, clothed and looking like Englishmen. More had probably seen them, and wondered what thoughts lay behind their inscrutable faces. In 1505 'wild cats and popinjays of the Newfound Island' were brought to the King at Richmond. In the last year of the reign of Henry VII, Sebastian Cabot went in search of the North-West Passage. It seems clear that he penetrated the strait later known by the name of Hudson, and found it opening into the immense expanse which we call Hudson Bay. Such an anticipation by Cabot, in 1509, of later Elizabethan and even Stuart exploration seems almost incredible. Yet 'if he was lying, he had the devil's own luck. For we know now that the facts are substantially as he represented them'.[1] Cabot naturally assumed that Hudson Bay was what we call the Pacific, and consequently that he had discovered the North-West Passage. He returned to England with the glorious secret to find Henry VII dead, and Henry VIII and Wolsey obsessed with their continental schemes. After three years of disappointment, Sebastian left England and entered the Spanish service. He lived nearly fifty years longer without ever having an opportunity of finding that his magnificent discovery was only a dead end. For him, perhaps it was as well that he was not destined to be numbered among the 'frozen pilots' upon whose funeral the Arctic stars have looked down. But the cessation of North American exploration meant that for England valuable experience was lost, the work of Henry VII was undone, and England was 'beaten back from the seas into the dusty vortex of European politics'.[2]

Yet there were still Englishmen who understood the

---

[1] J. A. WILLIAMSON, *The Voyages of the Cabots*, 1929, p. 241.
[2] CALLENDER, *The Naval side of British History*, p. 47.

importance of transatlantic adventure, and Professor A. W. Reed's research into the circle of Thomas More has brought to light the story of the first attempt at the colonization of North America by England. Six months after the publication of *Utopia*, More's brother-in-law, John Rastell, set off on the *Barbara* of Greenwich on a voyage of discovery to the New Found Lands. That not merely exploration, but the establishment of some kind of settlement was in his mind, follows from the fact that he took 'tools for masons and carpenters, and other engines that he had prepared for the New Lands'. John Rastell expected to be away for three years, during which he had arranged by prepayment that Judge John More should keep his wife and servants. Judge More seems to have taken a large share in guaranteeing the venture. The expedition turned back, owing to an organized mutiny, which apparently had the approval of the Earl of Surrey, the Lord High Admiral, who was opposed to sending any part of the fleet across the Atlantic when it might be needed in the Channel. Spirited interference in continental politics did not allow of valuable fighting ships being sent on voyages of exploration, likely to last three years.

Now every reader of *Utopia* must be struck by the weight there placed on colonization. The Utopians hate war: 'War they do detest and abhor; and contrary to the custom almost of all other nations, they count nothing so much against glory, as glory gotten in war.'[1] But to secure colonies for an overflowing population, they consider that even war is justified 'by the law of nature'. 'For they count this the most just cause of war, when any people holdeth a piece of ground void and vacant, to no good nor profitable use, keeping others from the use and possession of it.'[2]

All this sounds so imperialistic that some foreign critics have seen in Thomas More one further typical perfidious Englishman, who (with a Machiavellism more subtle than that of Machiavelli himself) propounded exactly such pretexts for expansion as would be useful to the British Empire of future centuries, and who yet, with characteristic English hypocrisy, pretended to be fighting for morality all the time.

But, when More emphasizes that the Utopians only go to

---

[1] *Utopia*, ed. LUPTON, p. 243.   [2] The same, p. 155.

war for reasons which concern the welfare of their citizens or of their allies, he is wishing to get in a side blow at the state of Europe in 1516, and to censure wars waged at the whim of, and for the personal aggrandizement of, autocrats like Francis I, or Henry, or Wolsey. I admit that the reasons for warfare approved by the Utopians, if made into a code, and applied to history from the Seventeenth Century to the present day, would load the dice heavily in favour of the British Empire; for they are adapted to a great colonizing island State, such as Utopia is supposed to be, and such as Britain later became. But could More, with all his foresight, have foreseen all this?

One recent German historian[1] has suggested that More, when he makes the Utopians claim the right as a populous nation to colonize empty spaces, may have been thinking of English settlements in North America. Another[2] argues that these theories of the natural right of colonization are no part of the original description of Utopia, already written in 1515; they do not harmonize with it, he thinks, but are a later addition made in 1516. And it must be admitted that this is acute criticism, for these German historians were quite unaware of Professor Reed's discovery; it had not been published when they wrote. And it is certain that John Rastell was not thinking merely of the North-West Passage to the Indies. He describes his object at some length. He wants *colonization*: that Englishmen should make 'first building and habitation' in the lands Cabot had discovered; that the king should have his 'dominion extending into so far a ground', that the heathen should be evangelized. The trade Rastell thinks of is not in oriental spices, gold or jewels, but in the products of the North American coast – timber, pitch, tar, and above all fish. But, he complains, the French are getting there before us: 'yearly of fish there they [the French] lade above an hundred sail'.[3]

The moment was favourable. Of course Englishmen could only at their peril trespass in the Spanish Indies; but there was nothing to hinder them from exploiting the claim which the

---

[1] HERMANN ONCKEN in *Sitzungsberichte der Heidelberger Akademie, Phil.-Hist. Klasse,* 1922.

[2] ERNST TRÖLTSCH, *Christian Thought, its history and application,* London, 1923, pp. 145 etc.

[3] See RASTELL's *New Interlude of the Four Elements.*

wise Henry VII had staked out in the North. The Spaniards had enough to do in the warm water, without venturing among the ice-floes. Charles V could not, and would not, quarrel with England over a claim which was of no use to him. Indeed he would not quarrel with England over much more important matters; for he had his life-long feud with Francis of France, and if Henry had sided with Francis they could together have closed the English Channel against him, and cut off his dominions in the Netherlands from his dominions in Spain. So the way for exploration in North America lay open to England. But Henry and Wolsey, absorbed in winning 'ungracious dogholes' in France, had none of the curiosity about Atlantic adventure which More and Rastell felt. Later, in 1521, Henry showed a transient interest in the New Found Land. It has been suggested that this was due to More, then rising in the king's favour, and discussing with him Geometry and Astronomy (and probably Cosmography). But the French war of 1522 stopped this, as it stopped other useful schemes. Expeditions did indeed set out in 1527 and 1536. The explorers found Portuguese, Breton and Norman vessels before them in the New World, but did nothing useful themselves. North American exploration was left to Jacques Cartier and the French.

Although we need not follow More's German critics in making him the father of British Imperialism, the discovery of Rastell's venture does prove that this criticism has a certain element of truth. Colonization and transatlantic adventure meant much to the writer of *Utopia*.

Yet there is nothing so sinister about it as these German critics have argued. The Utopians only settle where there is 'much waste and unoccupied ground', and they admit to full citizenship any of the natives who care to join them. It would have been well if all Sixteenth-Century colonization had been equally humane. And More's words cannot be twisted into a plea for a monopoly of colonial rights for England; if he is staking out a claim, it is for the common body of Christendom. For *Utopia* is a work of our common Western European civilization, dedicated to subjects of Charles V, Giles and Busleiden, the Latin text published in six great European cities before it was ever published in England, and translated into German,

Italian, and French before, in 1551, the English translation appeared.

We can only understand *Utopia* if we remember the Europe for which it was written; at home John Rastell preaching exploration to the More household; abroad the travels of Vespucci in every man's hands; Vespucci, who had found folk holding property in common, and not esteeming gold, pearls, or jewels. (It is important to remember that the Inca empire of Peru, which in more than one detail had a likeness to Utopia, was not known till some fourteen years later; Cortes had not yet conquered Mexico.)

The problem of poverty and unemployment (destined in England to be aggravated by the Dissolution of the Monasteries) was already a European one. Ten years after *Utopia*, More's friend Vives wrote a tract on it. At the root of More's interest in colonization lies his pity for the unemployed labourers:

> 'Poor silly wretched souls; away they trudge out of their known and accustomed houses; all their household stuff, being suddenly thrust out, they be constrained to sell it for a thing of naught. And when they have, wandering about, soon spent that, what can they do but steal, and then be hanged, or else go about abegging. Whom no man will set awork, though they never so willingly offer themselves thereto.'

But the fact that *Utopia* belongs to its age does not mean that it is the less epoch-making. Some things which may now seem commonplaces to us were less so then. It may seem quite natural to us that in Utopia there should be no class distinctions. It was less obvious to a scholar of the Renaissance. Plato's Commonwealths had been based on class distinction. In the *Laws* the citizens fall into four classes. In the *Republic*, also, there are classes, although so much attention is given to the warrior class, and their common life, that we almost forget the others. Plato is emphatic that every man should have one job only, and he does not waste words on his artisans, except to urge that they must be experts in their own business, and must stick to it. The Middle Ages inherited the same idea of the State: ploughmen and artisans to labour, clerks to pray and study, knights to fight. But the Utopian citizen does all three things;

he labours with his hands, studies in his spare hours, and, though he hates warfare, is, at need, a soldier.

It is noteworthy that, despite his admiration for Greek life and thought, More did not build Utopia after the Hellenic pattern. His free citizens are not a privileged class dependent on slave labour, nor are his bondmen a distinct class. Bondage in Utopia is penal servitude – a humane substitute for the death penalty. The repentant bondman is restored to freedom, the incorrigible bondman is slain.[1] But the citizens themselves are all workers.

Finally the outstanding feature of *Utopia* is implied in the great sentence with which Raphael ends his story:

> When I consider all these commonwealths which nowadays anywhere do flourish, so God help me, I can perceive nothing but a conspiracy of rich men, procuring their own commodities under the name and title of the commonwealth.[2]

The Middle Ages had often been charitable to the poor, and More's age had inherited vast charitable endowments. More altogether approved of these endowments, and, later, we shall find him defending them against the fanaticism of reformers who wished to hand them over to a conspiracy of rich men procuring their own commodities under the title of the commonwealth. But More's claim for *justice* goes far beyond medieval admonitions to charity. Its publication throughout Europe by the printing press marks an epoch.

§ 10. LAST VISITS OF ERASMUS TO ENGLAND

Whilst More was at work on *Utopia*, Erasmus made another visit to England, staying with More in his house at Bucklersbury. Here, in close concert also with his friend Ammonio, Erasmus set to work to overcome the misfortunes of his early days. He needed a papal dispensation to allow him, despite his illegitimate birth, to accept Church preferment; also dispensation from the monastic obedience which he had too rashly vowed in his youth. Erasmus was now a man of importance; the dedication of his *New Testament* had been accepted by Leo X, to whom he now made this petition, from London and with the

---

[1] *Utopia*, p. 230.   [2] The same, p. 309.

help of Ammonio.[1] Then he returned to the Continent, stopping on the way with Fisher at Rochester, whither More rode down to take a second farewell.[2] Back in Antwerp, Erasmus, with Giles, saw to the editing and publishing of *Utopia*.

Just before it was published, More wrote to Erasmus that he had been made King of Utopia. Crowned with a diadem of wheat, carrying a handful of corn as a sceptre, and clothed in his Franciscan friar's frock, he has just been giving audience to foreign ambassadors arrayed in their wretched vulgar gold chains and jewels. But Tunstall and Erasmus are not to fear that More's elevation will turn his head. He will never forget the old friends he had known when he was in a private station. If Erasmus will visit him in Utopia, all those who are subject to his clemency shall show Erasmus that deference which is due to one whom the King delights to honour. But, alas, More writes, the dawn of day had expelled him from his sovereignty, and sent him back to prison, that is, his legal work. But he comforts himself by reflecting that real kingdoms are not much more permanent.[3]

Months passed, and Erasmus was beginning to fear that his dispensations were not going through. At last Ammonio, to whom as Papal Collector in England they were sent, told him that the documents had arrived, and summoned him to England. 'I hate that sea of yours,' said Erasmus; but across he came, post haste; and on 9 April 1517, at Westminster, Ammonio was able to absolve him from ecclesiastical censures incurred by abandoning his monastic dress, and to grant him a general dispensation. Erasmus stuck to the precious document till death.[4]

He had now lived down all his troubles. His greatest works were published; he was at the summit of his fame. But he left England never to return. Henry had made no move, and hope had been deferred too long. Some months before, Colet had written to him sadly, 'I should like you to settle down with us, if we are worthy of so great a man; but you have had all too much experience of what kind of people we are'.[5]

[1] Aug. 1516, ALLEN, II, Nos. 446, 447.   [2] 22 Aug. 1516, ALLEN II, No. 455.
[3] c. 4 Dec. 1516, ALLEN, II, No. 499.
[4] It is now in the University Library at Basel.
[5] 20 June 1516, ALLEN, II, No. 423.

And yet the wants of Erasmus were very simple. A house of his own where he could insist on a greater standard of cleanliness than was usual in English homes, and could have a room sheltered from draughts and a fireplace that would burn well; a skin of Greek wine or a cask of Burgundy, to save him from the odious necessity of drinking English beer; plenty of warm clothing; a scholar-servant who could make him a salad with butter and sour wine; a quiet horse; books and manuscripts; and, above all, a scholarly printer who would work under his direction, importing if necessary a craftsman or two from Germany. These things would have sufficed to make the Royal Library and the Royal Press of London, with its scholar Erasmus, the centre of the world of learning, and would have given Henry VIII a place with Augustus and Charlemagne among the great patrons of letters. It was a reasonable expectation from the humanist prince who despised the ignorance of Charles V. But where Henry could not spare some thousands of pounds to encourage learning, he could squander hundreds of thousands on continental adventure, helping the Pope against France. At the moment that Erasmus was despairing of any support, England was at peace with France. So Henry, to put a spoke in the wheel of Francis I, sent a vast subsidy to hire Swiss mercenaries, who were to co-operate with Maximilian and turn the French out of Milan. They took Henry's money, and Maximilian marched them to within nine miles of Milan. He then marched them back, without striking a blow. Wolsey got a Cardinal's hat for his pro-Papal policy,[1] but no one else was any the better – except, of course, some 15,000 muscular Swiss peasants,[2] whose pockets were lined with good English money. It was just at this time that More was writing in *Utopia* of the Zapoletes, dwelling in woods and high mountains, who would sell their service as soldiers to anyone for a halfpenny more wages by the day.

But there were other reasons why Erasmus would not settle in England, perhaps even more fundamental than Henry's neglect. He wrote from Louvain for More's advice as to where

---

[1] See the extract from the diary of Paris de Grassis (MS. B.M. Addit. 8046 etc.) quoted by CREIGHTON, *History of the Papacy*, 1897, v, p. 315.

[2] *L.P.*, II, No. 2178.

he should settle. 'As to England, I fear its tumults *and I have a horror of servitude.'* [1] Henry called men of learning to his court, till it became, as Erasmus said, almost a university; but he called them, not to a life of learned leisure, but of diplomatic and administrative service. Erasmus was determined to retain his freedom.

And Erasmus, much as he loved some English scholars, disliked and feared the English proletariat. They tapped his wine casks in transit, and left him only the dregs. They did not understand their inferiority to the cultured Netherlanders and Italians who condescended to live among them. Erasmus wrote to the sympathetic Ammonio: 'We have to do, my Andrew, with a kind of men who are utterly uneducated and utterly malicious.'[2] Sometimes his language is untranslatable, and not always limited to the uneducated classes.

But these classes repaid the dislike with interest. Only by a few days did Erasmus miss seeing with his own eyes the tumults which he feared. It was on 1 May 1517, after having stopped a few days at Rochester to give Fisher some lessons in Greek, that he landed on the Continent from his final visit to England. It was a perilous landing, as he wrote to More, made in the middle of the night by the ship's boat on rocks not far from Boulogne; then followed a chilly, wind-buffeted journey by the sea shore.[3]

§ 11. 'EVIL MAY DAY'

Whilst poor Erasmus was jumping from a tossing cock-boat to a slippery rock, More was having an even more adventurous time in the dark hours before the dawn of what was long remembered in London as Evil May Day. The feeling against the strangers had been growing. In Easter week a popular preacher had denounced them, and in the last days of April they were jostled in the streets of London and pushed into the gutter. The authorities were alarmed, and More, together with Richard Brook, the Recorder, his predecessor as Under-Sheriff, was sent to the Cardinal for instructions. They came back to the Guildhall at 8.30 p.m. on 30 April, with the command

---

[1] c. 10 July 1517, ALLEN, III, No. 597.   [2] 11 Nov. 1511, ALLEN, I, No. 240.
[3] ALLEN, II, Nos. 584, 592.

that every man should keep himself and his prentices and servants indoors between 9.0 that night and 7.0 next morning. The command was not likely to be popular with the prentices, for the early revels of May Morning meant a lot to them, and half an hour was short notice.

At 9.0 in the evening an alderman found some young men playing, and told them to stop. One said, 'Why?' 'Thou shalt know', said the alderman, and began to march him off to gaol. The cry of 'Clubs' and 'Prentices' was raised, and the alderman 'fled, and was in great danger'. Ugly mobs came together. By 11.0 there were six or seven hundred in Cheapside, and from St. Paul's Churchyard came three hundred more. 'So out of all places they gathered', broke open prisons and released the prisoners, and ran in a mob till they met Thomas More. The London Chronicler,[1] to whom we owe the vivid account of the rising, tells us that More's eloquence 'had almost brought them to a stay'. But there was some stone throwing, and a sergeant-at-arms, standing at More's side, was hit, lost his temper, and shouted in a fury, 'Down with them'. So the 'misruled persons' dashed off again, and there was much plundering. But no alien was killed, and by 3.0 in the morning the mobs dispersed. The alarm however had been given. Sir Richard Cholmeley, Lieutenant of the Tower, 'no great friend to the City', began to fire his ordnance into London. He did little harm, 'howbeit, his good will appeared', says the sarcastic chronicler. By 5.0 various noblemen, with such strength as they had, and the gentlemen of the Inns of Court, joined the Mayor and heads of the City in enforcing order. But by then the riot had ceased, and it was only a question of arresting the dispersed rioters at daybreak, and sending them to the Tower, to Newgate, and to the Counters.

On 4 May vengeance was taken: the City streets were kept by the old Duke of Norfolk and his son the Earl of Surrey (Surrey, the Lord Admiral, is of course the same as the Duke of Norfolk who was later to be so often associated with More; he came into the title in 1524, on his father's death). They brought thirteen hundred of their men, in harness, into the City. 'Then proclamations were made that no women should

---

[1] HALL's *Chronicle*, ed. WHIBLEY, I, pp. 157-64.

come together to babble and talk, but all men should keep their wives in their houses. All the streets that were notable stood full of harnessed men, which spake many opprobrious words to the citizens, which grieved them sore.' The citizens, the London chronicler takes care to remind his readers, were two hundred to one; 'but, like true subjects, they suffered patiently'. The court met, and 'the prisoners were brought in through the streets tied in ropes, some men, some lads, some children of thirteen year. There was great mourning of fathers and friends for their children and kinsfolk'. Thirteen were executed at one time; their violation of the King's amity with foreign nations was held to be treason; and they were hanged, not at Tyburn, but on gallows erected in divers places where the offences were done. This, and the 'extreme cruelty' showed 'to the poor younglings, in their execution', distressed the City. More, together with the Recorder and various aldermen of London, in black, visited the King at Greenwich to ask when the Mayor and aldermen might present their apologies and 'beseech his Grace to be good and gracious lord unto them, and to accept them now being most sorrowful and heavy'.[1] The King was not easily appeased, and referred them to the Cardinal; and More, with others, was sent to the Cardinal 'to feel My Lord Cardinal's mind concerning the number of persons that shall come to the King's Grace for the said suit to be made'. And so a great scene was staged in Westminster Hall; the Mayor and aldermen appeared in their best livery, and the prisoners were produced. 'Then came in the poor younglings and old false knaves bound in ropes all along, one after another in their shirts, and every one a halter about his neck, to the number of four hundred men and eleven women. All the prisoners together cried, "Mercy, gracious lord, mercy".' According to the old ballad, Queen Catherine, 'disrobed from rich attires, with hairs hanged down', interceded pitifully, till the King gave them a pardon. The Cardinal then gave them an exhortation. 'And when the general pardon was pronounced, all the prisoners shouted at once, and all together cast up their halters into the hall roof, so that the King might perceive they were none of the discreetest sort.' Various offenders who had so

---

[1] Repertory of the Court of Aldermen, III, fol. 143.

far escaped arrest, hoping that the King was inclined to mercy, had come to Westminster 'well apparelled'. They suddenly 'stripped them into their shirts', put halters round their necks, and got their pardon with the rest. And so, after three weeks, the gallows within the City were at last taken down.

More had been on the Commission for investigating the cause of the rising. Many years later he tells us that it was all due to the 'ungracious invention' of two young lads, prentices in Cheapside, who had gone about first among the journeymen, then among the prentices of the mean crafts of the City, telling them that if they were once 'up' there were many others who would be at hand in the night and take their part; two or three hundred serving men of divers lords' houses, and some of the King's too. More quotes this as an example of the harm that can be done by the irresponsible revolutionary.[1]

The two lads escaped, as instigators of trouble so often do; but a month or two later a certain Coo, 'one of the prentices that made the insurrection in London', was serving on John Rastell's ship, the *Barbara*, and fomenting the trouble which prevented her from sailing to the New Found Lands. Coo must have possessed gifts as an agitator which, in more appreciative days, would have carried him to high distinction.

No lives had been lost, except those of the poor executed rioters; the mob seems to have dispersed voluntarily, and without much force being used. How far this was due to More's eloquence, how far to desire to get to bed after four or five hours' excitement, we cannot say. But the London tradition was, that More by his unaided eloquence had first quelled the riot and then obtained pardon for the rioters. This is the story with which the old play of *Sir Thomas More* begins. The griev-ances of the Londoners against the aliens are vividly and sympathetically depicted by the dramatists. More quiets the rioters in a scene of three pages, which is extant in what is certainly the handwriting of its author. And that author is, I think beyond dispute, William Shakespeare.

All lovers of Sir Thomas More ought to read the old play, or at any rate the three pages claimed to be in Shakespeare's handwriting. There is only room to quote a few sentences

[1] *Apology, Works*, 1557, p. 920.

here. The rioters rush on the stage. It was agreed by contemporary visitors to England that Englishmen fed well. The
rioters complain that the aliens are devouring the good English
food, and introducing their own inferior diet:

> 'Our country is a great eating country, *argo*[1] they eat more
> in our country than they do in their own.'
> 'By a halfpenny loaf a day, troy weight.'
> 'They bring in strange roots, which is merely to the un-
> doing of poor prentices, for what's a sorry parsnip to a good
> heart?'

More enters and gradually, in a series of eloquent speeches,
brings the rioters to reason. They ask for the removing of the
strangers:

> MORE   Grant them removed, and grant that this your noise
> Hath chid down all the majesty of England.
> Imagine that you see the wretched strangers
> Their babies at their backs, and their poor luggage,
> Plodding to the ports and coasts for transportation,
> And that you sit as kings in your desires
> Authority quite silenced by your brawl
> And you in ruff of your opinions clothed,
> What had you got? I'll tell you. You had taught
> How insolence and strong hand should prevail,
> How order should be quelled; and by this pattern
> Not one of you should live an aged man;
> For other ruffians, as their fancies wrought
> With self same hand, self reasons and self right
> Would shark on you; and men like ravenous fishes
> Would feed on one another.

The speeches placed in the mouth of More, as he argues with
the rioters, are a most eloquent and impassioned statement of
that respect for authority which was the foundation of the
political thinking alike of Shakespeare and of More.

§ 12. 'THE BUSY TRIFLES OF PRINCES'

The London play makes More's entry into the King's
service the result of his feats in London on Evil May Day.
Roper, a lawyer, gives a different account. King Henry claimed

---

[1] *argo*, vulgar for *ergo*. It is found in contemporary drama in Shakespeare,
II Henry VI, IV, ii, 31; in *Hamlet*, V, i, 13 (as *argal*), and here, but nowhere else.

as a forfeiture a ship of the Pope's, at Southampton. The Papal ambassador retained More as counsel and interpreter, and the case was heard before Wolsey and other judges in the Star Chamber:

> Where Sir Thomas More not only declared to the ambassador the whole effect of all their opinions, but also, in defence of the Pope's side, argued so learnedly himself, that both was the foresaid forfeiture to the Pope restored, and himself among all the hearers, for his upright and commendable demeanour therein, so greatly renowned, that for no entreaty would the King from thenceforth be induced any longer to forbear his service.[1]

Both Roper and the old play agree (wrongly) in representing More as having been made a knight immediately upon entering the King's service. For that he had to wait till 1521.

But Erasmus had, by leaving England, escaped a greater danger than riots. That summer the sweating sickness was raging; four hundred students are said to have died in Oxford within a week. More writes to Erasmus:

> We are in such grief and danger as never before. Many are dying all round us, and almost everybody at Oxford, Cambridge and London has been laid up within the last few days. Many of our best and most honoured friends have perished: among these – I grieve for the grief it will give you – Andrew Ammonio, in whom good letters and all good men have suffered a great loss. He thought himself protected against contagion by his temperance in food. It was due to this, he thought, that his whole household escaped, whilst almost everybody he met had their whole families laid up. He boasted to me and to many others of this, a few hours before he died. For in this Sweating Sickness death always comes, if it does come, on the first day. I, with my wife and children, am as yet untouched: the rest of my household has recovered. I tell you, there is less danger on a battle front than in London. And now, I hear, it is beginning to rage at Calais just as we are being driven there on diplomatic business – as if it were not enough to have lived among infection, but one must follow it when it goes.[2]

More's business at Calais was to negotiate with French

---

[1] ROPER, pp. 9-10.   [2] 19 Aug. 1517, ALLEN, III, No. 623.

merchants. He was associated with Sir Richard Wingfield and Dr. William Knight.[1]

It was whilst More was at Calais that Erasmus and Giles sent him the diptych with their two portraits, painted by the great Flemish master Quentin Metsys. Instead of placing their names on the portraits, Metsys had cunningly recorded their identity by showing the task upon which Erasmus was engaged, and by showing Giles holding a letter addressed to him in More's handwriting. The painter, says More, had proved himself a skilful forger, and he asks for the letter back, that he may put it by the side of the picture and thus double the marvel. More sent verses of thanks to Erasmus and Giles; the fear of war haunts him; what a vast price posterity will place on these fragile panels, if the age which is to come have any care for the arts, if hateful Mars do not grind Minerva to powder.[2] Mars has been kind, and the portraits, though they have suffered divorce, survive; the Erasmus is in Rome, the Giles at Longford Castle, in the keeping of the Earl of Radnor.

In the letter to Giles, More enclosed one to Erasmus: his vanity is pleased, More says, because he knows that by letters, by books and by pictures, posterity will remember him as the friend of Erasmus.[3] For himself, he is kept in Calais; with difficulty can he get leave for a two days' trip to St. Omer. A few weeks later, he is even more weary. He tells Erasmus:

> You are a wise man in keeping yourself from being mixed up in the busy trifles of princes; and it shows your love for me that you wish me rid of them; you would hardly believe how unwilling I am. Nothing could be more hateful to me than this mission. Here I am, banished to this little seaport, with its barren soil and wretched climate. If I hate legal business at home, where it pays me, you can imagine how it bores me here, where I am losing money over it. The Big Man [Wolsey] is kind enough to promise that the King will repay everything. When I have the money, I will let you know.[4]

It was the burst of impatience from a man who felt the ties of

[1] The commission is dated 26 Aug. 1517 (Cotton Caligula D. vi, 522-7; *L.P.*, ii No. 3634).
[2] 7 Oct. 1517, ALLEN, iii, No. 684.   [3] 7 Oct. 1517, ALLEN, iii, No. 68
[4] 25 Oct. 1517, ALLEN, iii, No. 688. See also Nos. 726, 742.

office closing round him. But they had been closing for some time.

In *Utopia* More had represented Peter Giles as urging Hythlodaye to enter the council of some king. Thereby he would be able to help his friends and kinsfolk. Raphael makes short work of that argument. Before he went on his travels he had divided his patrimony among friends and kin, and he thinks they should be satisfied. But Hythlodaye was a bachelor; More had married a wife; and Mistress Alice had to be reckoned with. She 'fell in hand with him, and all to rated him', and asked him:

> 'What will you do, that you list not to put forth yourself as other folk do? Will you sit still by the fire, and make goslings in the ashes with a stick as children do?'
>
> 'What would you do, I pray you?'
>
> 'By God, go forward with the first; for as my mother was wont to say, God have mercy on her soul, it is ever better to rule than to be ruled. And therefore, by God, I would not, I warrant you, be so foolish to be ruled where I might rule.'
>
> 'By my troth, wife,' quoth her husband, 'in this I dare say you say truth, for I never found you willing to be ruled yet.'[1]

But there were stronger reasons than any which Dame Alice could supply. The hopes of the humanists were rising again. In March 1517 Pope Leo X issued a Bull imposing a five years' truce on the monarchs of Europe, and, in England, at any rate, such a Bull carried great weight.

When, at the beginning of the Eighteenth Century, after the War of the Spanish Succession, European princes began to speak of a league of peace, Cardinal Fleury said to the Abbé of St. Pierre, 'Begin by sending a troop of missionaries to prepare the hearts and minds of the contracting sovereigns'.[2] The humanists were such a band of missionaries. Erasmus, attached to no nation or party, preached peace with complete detachment. He was, it is true, a councillor of Charles V, but his duties were as nominal as his salary was precarious. And he

---

[1] HARPSFIELD, p. 95, following More, *Works*, 1557, p. 1224.
[2] POLLARD, *League of Nations in History*, 1918, p. 6.

kept himself from English entanglements; an English friend complains that Erasmus is not as 'good English' as he would have liked.[1] With More it was different. He had won his reputation as a practical diplomatist; and when the King pressed for his service, he could not, without denying all his principles, refuse.

For, when, in any dialogue, More speaks in his own person, he means what he says. Although he gives the other side a fair innings, he leaves us in no doubt as to his own mind. When Hythlodaye has given to Peter Giles conclusive reasons why he should not put himself into bondage to kings, for the sake of either his kinsfolk or himself, More takes up the argument from the standpoint of public duty.

Hythlodaye – one of the most subtly drawn of all More's characters – dissents. He is wise, cynical, somewhat supercilious. An honest councillor, he says, has no place among the jealousies and flatteries of courts, and he gives examples. More sticks to his point. Plato had said that commonwealths might attain felicity if philosophers were kings or kings philosophers; so let philosophers instruct kings. They have done so already in books, replies Hythlodaye (thinking perhaps of Erasmus). But to show how hopeless such advice is, he depicts himself urging the French king to give his attention to governing France, instead of meddling with Italy. He might quote the example of the Achoriens, who won for their king a second kingdom, which he claimed by title of an ancient marriage. But they found it so troublesome a business to keep this kingdom in subjection, that at last they told their king that he must choose which of the two kingdoms he would have, 'alleging that he was not able to keep both, and that they were more than might well be governed by half a king: forasmuch as no man would be content to take him for his muleteer, that keepeth another man's mules besides his'. The story, though nominally directed against French interference in Italian politics, has a much more obvious applicability to the historic claim of the English king to the throne of France.

Then Raphael turns upon More:

[1] *L.P.*, II, No. 616; NICHOLS, II, p. 285.

'This mine advice, Master More, how think you it would be heard and taken?'

'So God help me, not very thankfully,' quoth I.[1]

Well, let us proceed then, says Raphael. And he goes on, in a marvellously prophetic passage, to enumerate some of the ways in which Henry during the next thirty years was to impoverish his subjects in seeking to enrich himself:

'Here again, if I should rise up, and boldly affirm that all these counsels be to the King dishonour and reproach . . . How deaf hearers, think you, should I have?'

'Deaf hearers doubtless,' quoth I.[2]

Nevertheless, More persists in his attempt to persuade Raphael:

'Yet for this cause you must not leave and forsake the commonwealth; you must not forsake the ship in a tempest, because you cannot rule and keep down the winds . . . But you must . . . study . . . to handle the matter wittily, and that which you cannot turn to good, so to order it that it be not very bad.'

Raphael is unconvinced. By this means, he says, whilst I go about to remedy the madness of others, I should be even as mad as they. For a man must praise all the noisome decrees of the King's advisers. If he is merely half-hearted in his praise, he will be counted almost a traitor.

So More had no illusions as to the danger he was running. But, if Raphael Hythlodaye, though he could not turn the matter to good, would not attempt 'so to order it that it be not very bad', then Thomas More must try. Meantime Erasmus kept his freedom, preaching moderation and peace, and refusing to have anything to do with the warring claims of any state or any sect.

For wisdom is justified of all her children.

---

[1] *Utopia*, p. 87.   [2] The same, p. 76.

THE KING'S SERVANT

(1518–1529)

§ 1. THE KING, WOLSEY AND MORE

FOR twelve years More served the King, before his career was
crowned by his succeeding Wolsey in the Chancellorship. To
all appearances, his life during these years was one of steadily
increasing distinction and power. In reality, these years saw
the hopes which More cherished for his country and for
Christendom one after another overthrown. And, as each blow
falls, we can see More's own destruction brought one stage
nearer. The Chancellorship, which to the world may have
looked like the culmination of a successful career, was in reality
the last of many successive strokes of doom.

Fortune's wheel was a medieval commonplace – all the
time that the men tied to it are rising to the summit, they are
drawing nearer to the moment when the revolution of the
wheel must plunge them down. More, in his youth, had written
verses for the beginning of the *Book of Fortune*:

> But, an thou wilt needs meddle with Her treasure,
> Trust not therein, and spend it liberally.
> Bear thee not proud, nor take not out of measure,
> Build not thine house on height up to the sky.
> None falleth far, but he that climbeth high.
> Remember, Nature sent thee hither bare;
> The gifts of Fortune – count them borrowed ware.

Commonplaces, but all very real to More. He was in grim
earnest when he wrote in the same *Book of Fortune*:

> The head that late lay easily and full soft,
> Instead of pillows, lieth after on the block.

Did he think of these lines, when he defrauded sleep by sub-
stituting a block of wood for his own pillow? Anyway, he

followed his own advice: spent liberally, hoarded nothing, saw the gradual defeat of all his hopes, and cherished no illusions. In mind, at least, he never climbed high, and so had never far to fall.

The two men who govern More's political career are Wolsey and Henry. The Cardinal, placed higher on Fortune's wheel, is naturally thrown down first, and leaves More to face his overwhelming master alone, and in the end to suffer a similar fate.

Neither Wolsey nor More could accomplish their very different aims. Each had to watch the destruction of his plans; each, about the age of fifty-eight, was himself destroyed by the master he had served. And there is a strange likeness, and a strange contrast, in their dying words. 'If I had served God', said Wolsey, 'as diligently as I have done the King, he would not have given me over in my grey hairs.'[1] 'I die,' More said on the scaffold, 'the King's servant, but God's first', and men noticed how imprisonment had aged him,[2] as he carefully arranged his long and disordered beard so that the headsman's axe should not touch it. Yet to More, as to Socrates[3] before him, being put to death did not mean being 'given over'.

During his imprisonment More had leisure to recollect, in tranquillity, some of the exciting scenes through which he had passed. Respect for the King's Grace forbids any mention of Henry, but as More lies in the Tower, facing death, he looks back on the career of the great Cardinal, who had died of fear and anxiety when summoned to that same grim lodging. To the known and public scandals of Wolsey's life, More does not refer. He does not remind us that this would-be reformer of the excesses of the Church was himself one great excess; that not content with amassing pluralities on a grandiose scale, Wolsey had contrived that his illegitimate son, whilst still a lad, should be Dean of Wells, Archdeacon of both York and Richmond, in addition to holding two rectories, six prebends, a provostship and a chancellorship.[4]

More's chief complaint is that Wolsey was vainglorious – or 'glorious', as he sometimes calls it (More uses both words,

[1] CAVENDISH, *Life of Wolsey*, p. 244.   [2] STAPLETON, XX, p. 352.
[3] *Apology*, 31-3.   [4] POLLARD, *Wolsey*, p. 309.

and in his day they could both mean the same thing). 'But glorious was he very far above all measure, and that was great pity, for it did harm, and made him abuse many great gifts that God had given him. Never was he satiate of hearing his own praise.'[1] It is true that in this passage More does not mention Wolsey by name. But the 'great man of the church' of whom these words are said, means Wolsey. Of that, there is no more doubt than that the great lady whose racy vernacular so often delights us is Mistress Alice More. Harpsfield, in close touch with More's circle, takes the identification for a certainty, and so does Wolsey's latest and most scholarly biographer.[2] This characterization of Wolsey serves to introduce More's vivid story of a banquet, where each guest was expected to pay for his dinner by a speech of flattery. If, nowadays, after-dinner speeches are a source of misery to well-filled and comatose guests, what must these during-dinner discourses have been? And no one was spared:

> So happed it one day, that he had in a great audience made an oration in a certain manner, wherein he liked himself so well, that at his dinner he sat (him thought) on thorns, till he might hear how they that sat with him at his board would commend it.
>
> And when he had sat musing a while, devising (as I thought after) upon some pretty proper way to bring it in withal, at the last, for lack of a better (lest he should have letted the matter too long) he brought it even bluntly forth, and asked us all that sat at his board's end (for at his own mess in the midst there sat but himself alone) how well we liked his oration that he had made that day.
>
> But in faith, when that problem was once proponed, till it was full answered, no man (I ween) ate one morsel of meat more. Every man was fallen in so deep a study, for the finding of some exquisite praise. For he that should have brought out but a vulgar and a common commendation would have thought himself shamed for ever. Then said we our sentences by row as we sat, from the lowest unto the highest in good order, as it had been a great matter of the common weal, in a right solemn council.

More thought that he had 'quitted himself meetly well', and

[1] *Works*, 1557, pp. 1221-2.   [2] POLLARD, *Wolsey*, p. 373.

hoped to shine in comparison with the next speaker, an unlearned priest; but, nevertheless, this priest

> had been so well accustomed in court with the craft of
> flattery, that he went beyond me too, too far. And then
> might I see by him, what excellence a right mean wit may
> come to in one craft, that in all his whole life studieth and
> busieth his wit about no more but that one.
>
> But I made, after, a solemn vow unto myself, that if ever
> he and I were matched together at that board again, when
> we should fall to our flattery, I would flatter in Latin, that
> he should not contend with me no more. For though I could
> be content to be out-run of an horse, yet would I no more
> abide it to be out-run of an ass.

But the climax came with the guest who, being highest at
Wolsey's board, had the unenviable privilege of speaking last.
He was a great beneficed man, a doctor, learned in the laws of
the Church.

> A world it was to see how he marked every man's word that
> spake before him. And it seemed that every word, the more
> proper it was, the worse he liked it, for the combraunce that
> he had to study out a better to pass it. The man even sweat
> with the labour, so that he was fain, in the while, now and
> then to wipe his face. Howbeit, in conclusion, when it came
> to his course, we that had spoken before him had so taken
> up all among us before, that we had not left him one wise
> word to speak after.

The 'great beneficed man' was in the same plight as Apelles
the painter, in his picture of the sacrifice of Iphigenia. Apelles
had exerted all his powers in painting the distress of the different Grecian noblemen that beheld the sacrifice, and had
left himself no means of expressing the overwhelming grief of
the father, Agamemnon:

> And therefore, to the intent that no man should see what
> manner countenance it was that her father had, the painter
> was fain to paint him, holding his face in his handkerchief.
>
> The like pageant in a manner played us there this good
> ancient honourable flatterer. For when he saw that he
> could find no words of praise, that would pass all that had
> been spoken before already, the wily fox would speak never
> a word. But as he that were ravished unto heavenward with

the wonder of the wisdom and eloquence that my Lord's
grace had uttered in that oration, he fetched a long sigh with
an 'Oh!' from the bottom of his breast, and held up both
his hands, and lifted up his head, and cast up his eyen into
the welkin, and wept.[1]

More's earnest biographers have felt a little uneasy at their
hero's shameless admission that he was outdone in flattery
rather from want of ability than want of will. So Nicholas
Harpsfield writes:

> In this vainglorious pageant of my Lord Cardinal, though,
> as it appeareth, Sir Thomas More was in a manner forced,
> contrary to his sober and well known modest nature, to play
> a part to accommodate himself somewhat to the players in
> this foolish, fond stage play, yet I doubt nothing, if his answer
> were certainly known, he played no other part than might be-
> seem his grave, modest person, and kept himself within
> reasonable bounds, and yielded none other than competent
> praise.[2]

No doubt. But More got his amusement out of it.

He has another and an even more personal tale to tell
about Wolsey:

> The selfsame prelate that I told you my tale of (I dare be
> bold to swear it, I know it so surely) had, on a time, made of
> his own drawing a certain treaty that should serve for a
> league between that country and a great prince. In which
> treaty himself thought that he had devised his articles so
> wisely and endicted them so well, that all the world would
> allow [i.e. approve] them. Whereupon, longing sore to be
> praised, he called unto him a friend of his, a man well learned,
> and of good worship, and very well expert in those matters,
> as he that had been divers times ambassador for that country,
> and had made many such treaties himself –

More is denouncing the sin of vanity, and I think we can see
a smile on his face; for there are several reasons for thinking that
it is himself he is describing in these flattering terms. The
prelate begs his friend to tell him how he likes the treaty, 'But
I pray you heartily tell me the very truth':

> And that he spake so heartily, that the other had weened
> he would fain have heard the truth. And in trust thereof, he

[1] *Works*, 1557, pp. 1221-2   [2] HARPSFIELD, *Life of More*, p. 38.

toId him a fault therein; at the hearing whereof he sware in great anger, 'By the mass, thou art a very fool'. The other afterward told me, that he would never tell him truth again.[1]

The story comes in More's *Dialogue of Comfort*, where it is narrated to Anthony, who represents More himself. Anthony's comment is, that without question he cannot greatly blame the friend who swore never again to tell the truth to the vainglorious prelate. So we have More (in one disguise) agreeing that More (in another disguise) was right in swearing never to speak the truth to Wolsey again.

There are other versions of the story of how Wolsey called More a fool – one version makes More retort by thanking God that the King has only one fool on his council. This sounds authentic.[2]

More had learnt the necessity of flattery. He reports to Wolsey that he has read to the King various letters of state together with Wolsey's draft replies, or, as he calls them,

> your most politic devices and answers unto all the same; among which, the letter which your Grace devised, in the name of his Highness, to the Queen his sister,[3] his Grace so well liked, that I never saw him like thing better, and, as help me God, in my poor fancy, not causeless; for it is, for the quantity, one of the best made letters, for words, matter, sentence, and couching, that ever I read in my life.[4]

'No one,' says Father Bridgett, commenting upon these words, 'will suspect More of flattering with an interested motive, or even of insincerity, He liked to praise when he could.'[5] True – and indeed to praise Wolsey as an able diplomatist was bare justice, not flattery.

But a much more serious matter than this childish love of flattery, was the fact that the Cardinal's policy, as the years passed on, appeared to More to be going desperately wrong. When Wolsey and Henry persuaded More to enter the royal service, there was no apparent cause of difference between the three. But More had twice to see the country plunged into useless wars. And a further charge was whispered: that Wolsey was the man who had first suggested to Henry doubts as to the

---

[1] *Works*, 1557, p. 1223.   [2] STAPLETON, XIII, p. 246.   [3] Margaret, Queen of Scots.
[4] *State Papers*, I, p. 128 (Letter LXXI).   [5] BRIDGETT, *Life of More*, p. 194.

legality of his marriage with Catherine, doubts which brought him, as they did More, to downfall and death. Whatever be the truth of this charge, it is certain that Wolsey sought to obtain credit in the eyes of the French by the claim that it was he who 'first set forth the terms of the divorce', in order thereby to separate England from Spain, and ally England with France. He made this claim more than once.[1] The fact that he publicly denied the charge, during the divorce proceedings, can count for little: he *had* to deny that he was the instigator of the case of which he had become the judge. But his dying warning is significant – that whatever matter the King's counsellors might put in his head, they could never put it out again.[2] We can trace More's feelings towards Wolsey passing from friendship to bitter hostility, and then, after Wolsey's death, to a good natured pity, and a resigned feeling of the vanity of all human concerns.

As to Wolsey's war-policy, we get a flash of insight from words More uttered in the Tower. More's friends were saying that though he was a wise man, he was too obstinate in his own conceit; men should not be so much wiser than their fellows. More's successor in the Chancellorship thought it appropriate to quote the fable of Aesop's wise men. These wise men knew that a rain was about to fall which would make all whom it wetted fools. So they retired into caves, and after the shower had fallen they came out, expecting to lord it over the unwise. But the unwise, though wet, were a majority, and gave the wise men a good beating, to take their conceit out of them. The tale was repeated to More by his daughter Margaret, and it called up recollections of debates in the Council some thirteen or fourteen years before. More said he had often heard the fable:

It was a tale so often told among the King's Council by my Lord Cardinal, when his Grace was Chancellor, that I cannot lightly forget it. For of truth in times past, when variance began to fall between the Emperor and the French King, in such wise that they were likely, and did indeed fall together at war, and that there were in the Council here sometime sundry opinions, in which some were of the mind that they

---

[1] See LE GRAND, *Histoire du Divorce*, III, 186 (21 Oct. 1528); 318, 319 (22 May 1529).
[2] CAVENDISH, III, 245.

thought it wisdom that we should sit still and let them alone;
but evermore against that way, my Lord used this fable of
those wise men, that because they would not be washed with
the rain that should make all the people fools, went themselves
in caves and hid them under the ground. . . . And so said his
Grace, that if we would be so wise that we would sit in peace
while the fools fought, they would not fail after to make
peace and agree, and fall at length all upon us.

I will not dispute upon his Grace's counsel, and I trust
we never made war, but as reason would. But yet this fable,
for his part, did in his days help the King and the realm to
spend many a fair penny.

But that year is passed, and his Grace is gone. Our Lord
assoil his soul.[1]

More was right in refusing to dispute upon Wolsey's
counsel; for he was facing death, and had other things to think
of than reviving these old disputes. But More's biographer
cannot imitate his reticence, if More's outlook is to be understood. More had represented his Utopians as inhabitants of an
almost impregnable island, so well trained in arms that they
could afford to hate war, and despise it. Utopia, as Erasmus
pointed out, was based on England. If they but would,
Englishmen might have the advantages of Utopia. The
English were, it is true, a small nation: Francis of France had
perhaps four subjects to every one of Henry's, and the Emperor
Charles even more. But the English long-bow was still a terrible
weapon in the hands of men trained to use it from childhood;
and Englishmen, from the King downward, were so trained.
Everyone learned 'how to lay his body in his bow, and not to
draw with strength of arms as other nations do, but with strength
of the body'. Scholars like Ascham, lawyers like William
Rastell, preachers like Latimer – they were all expert bowmen.
Archery was a fashion and a passion; the modern craze for golf
affords only a faint parallel. An English bowman could shoot
ten arrows in a minute, with a range of two hundred yards. We
must not think of the bow as antiquated yet. And the English
'brown bill' could be more than a match for the continental
pike.[2] At Flodden it enabled an English army, hungry, weary
with a long day's march, and in spite of disadvantages of ter-

[1] *Works*, 1557, p. 1436.   [2] See W. MACKAY MACKENZIE, *The Secret of Flodden*, 1931.

rain, to annihilate an invader, fresh, equally brave and equally numerous, but armed with the long pike 'in the manner of the Almains'. Englishmen, if united, had no more to fear than had the Utopians, even if any army could have been landed on their shores. Yet they were too few in number to make any serious impression on the Continent. They could win a few strongholds, 'castles in France', to use More's phrase, 'ungracious dogholes' in Cromwell's more picturesque language. But these gains were too expensive to hold; in the end they had to be surrendered in exchange for a sum which represented a tiny fraction of what they cost to win. European war was futile; there was neither danger to be averted nor advantage to be gained.

Yet English historians have felt a glow of national pride in contemplating the vigour with which that wonderful pair, Henry and Wolsey, threw their weight about in the wars and diplomacy of Europe. Creighton is fascinated by Wolsey's prestige in a way which (if one may say so without disrespect) reminds one of the other 'great beneficed man' at Wolsey's banquet, holding up both his hands in admiration, and casting up his eyes into the welkin.

But for More, as time goes on, Peace becomes the passion of his life: Peace between Princes, and Peace in the Church, without which Europe could expect nothing but generations of warfare. More feels about Peace as Erasmus does, but with the added experience of a practical statesman, and with all the passion of his passionate soul.

More did not need to have the *Cambridge Modern History* on the shelves before him to know that the volume on *The Reformation* would be followed by the volume on *The Wars of Religion*, and that by the volume on *The Thirty Years' War*. He had said so: 'After that it were once come to that point, and the world once ruffled and fallen in a wildness, how long would it be, and what heaps of heavy mischiefs would there fall, ere the way were founden to set the world in order and peace again.'[1] And it is this dread which makes More use the passionate and angry language, for which he has been so sternly censured by Bishop Creighton.

[1] *Works*, 1557, p. 274.

More could see then, as, looking back, we can see now, that peace was the great need of Europe. In the East, Selim the Grim was building up a vast Turkish Empire which was shortly to become a threat to Western civilization, such as had not been since Charles Martel hammered back the Saracen attack from the middle of France, eight centuries before. More's generation saw the fall of Rhodes, and of Belgrade, the sea and the land bastion of Eastern Europe; it saw the chivalry of Hungary perish on the field of Mohacz. More could not know how the attack would in time be checked; how it would be rolled back from the fortifications of Malta, and shattered by Don John of Austria in the battle of Lepanto. We cannot enter into the minds of the men of old 'unless we can think away everything that has happened since, and call up a mist over the face of time'.[1] It sounds a commonplace, yet how difficult it is to do. We must dismiss the idea, which the reign of Elizabeth has left ingrained in the English consciousness, of Spain as the foe of Sixteenth-Century England. Spain and the Netherlands were one Empire, and all English prosperity was based upon friendly trade relations with the Netherlands. War with Spain was in More's day almost unthinkable. The Turk was the imminent danger, and that imminent danger was never long absent from More's mind. And, on the other hand, the amazing expansion of European shipping, westward and eastward, had touched More's imagination. It led him to depict Raphael Hythlodaye, the first globe-trotter in literature. To avert the Turkish menace, to take full advantage of the opening possibilities of trade and exploration by sea, Europe needed peace from internal strife. But it was in vain that Erasmus uttered the *Complaint of Peace*, or More in *Utopia* denounced war. The struggle for power between Francis of France and Charles of Spain tore Europe asunder, made combined defence against the Turks impossible, and so, even when the Turkish wave receded, left Europe cursed with an 'Eastern question'. The quarrel 'paralysed German government, brought the landsknechts sweeping into Italy'.[2] We are suffering from its consequences to-day.

---

[1] P. S. ALLEN, *The Age of Erasmus*, p. 224. For similar wise warnings on 'the knowledge of after events', cf. POLLARD, *Cranmer*, p. 307, and FROUDE, *History*, 1870, 1, p. 167.

[2] FISHER, *History of England, 1485-1547*, p. 205.

Francis and Charles were too evenly matched for either to destroy the other, and every English interest demanded that, if they must fight, England should remain at peace. 'Machia-velli's doctrine' that neutrality is dangerous to a weak state did not apply to an island strong in shipping and arms like England. Yet the hoarded wealth of England was squandered in useless continental wars, and the country brought from wealth to beggary. The bloodshed – so far as England was concerned – was not very serious. Considering Henry's limited resources, his campaigns *could* only be intermittent. But he and Wolsey utterly exhausted those resources; 'the spending of many a fair penny', as More calls it, brought misery, destitution, and starvation upon the English poor. England backed first one side, then the other; earned the hatred of both, and gained absolutely nothing.

§ 2. MORE LEAVES THE CITY FOR THE COURT

However, at the moment when More entered the King's service, there was no ground for disagreement, since Wolsey, temporarily converted to the cause of peace, was taking a great share in the pacification of 1518, upon which the humanists were basing their hopes.

'None Englishman gladder than I of this honourable and profitable amity ... Undoubtedly, my Lord, God continuing it, it shall be the best deed that ever was done for the realm of England.' So wrote Bishop Foxe of Winchester. Foxe was a statesman of the old school of Morton, in which More had been brought up; he believed in peace and retrenchment, and he writes to Wolsey concerning the peace that 'After the King's Highness, the laud and praise thereof shall be to you a perpetual memory.'[1] It was a generous tribute; for Foxe, who in the later years of Henry VII was the greatest statesman of England, had been gently pushed out of politics, back into his diocese, by Wolsey, at a time when Wolsey and his master had little use for Foxe's pacific policy.

Wolsey's encouragement of letters was a second bond between him and More; and one which was to remain unbroken to the end.

Now, with peace re-established, the hopes of the humanists

---

[1] 30 Oct. 1518, FOXE's *Letters*, ed. ALLEN, p. 112.

again rose high. The time had come for the triumph of learning, the defeat of obscurantism, the reform of the Church by reason and scholarship. And if, at the price of a little astute praise, the great Cardinal could be persuaded to concentrate his enormous powers upon these things – the Golden Age might come after all. And so Erasmus of Rotterdam writes a letter full of ornate flattery to Thomas, Archbishop of York, Cardinal, Legate, Chancellor of England. Erasmus begins by apologizing for not making his obeisance in person; he is not yet well enough to face the channel crossing. But he cannot refrain from congratulating '*Our* Britain' upon possessing Wolsey. Pope Leo X had but hoped to impose a five years' truce, but Wolsey has brought about the long desired peace. Wolsey is administering justice, reforming the Church, and inviting the most erudite professors by the offer of magnificent salaries. He is collecting books, and fostering the three tongues, Latin, Greek, and Hebrew. All Britain has been placed under an obligation by Wolsey's gift to the famous University of Oxford. (The reference is to the six public readerships; some were destined to be held by four of More's young friends.) Erasmus becomes eloquent over the age which, if only Wolsey's example is followed by other princes, will shortly come:

I see, I see, an Age truly Golden arising, if that mind of yours should prevail with some number of our rulers. He, under whose auspices they are made, will reward your most holy efforts. And eloquence, alike in Latin and in Greek, will celebrate with eternal monuments your heart, born to help the human race.

Erasmus writes in even more enthusiastic terms to Henry, and to his courtiers. The world is coming to its senses, awakening as it were out of a deep sleep. Henry's court is itself a university; Wolsey and Foxe at Oxford, Fisher at Cambridge, are establishing new colleges; under Henry VIII the Golden Age of law, order, universal peace and learning is coming. The only drawback is that Erasmus is too old to enjoy this new world; but it is well for the young. And Erasmus, who has written school-books for them, will, he optimistically asserts, live in their grateful memories.[1]

[1] 15 May 1519: three letters to Henry VIII, Mountjoy, and Guildford; 18 May 1519, to Wolsey. ALLEN, III, Nos. 964, 965, 966, 967.

Erasmus was again thinking of settling in England. The subject occurs a dozen times or more in his correspondence at this period. Yet Henry failed to make a sufficiently tempting offer, for a vein of parsimony and avarice alternated strangely with the King's extravagance. However, Erasmus is enthusiastic about the way in which 'good letters are triumphing in England; the King himself, the Queen, the two Cardinals [Wolsey and Campeggio], almost all the bishops, are protecting and fostering them with all their heart; obscurantist bigots are being put in their right place.'[1]

The hope that Henry was to initiate a new and better age had made Erasmus accept with equanimity More's desertion of literature for politics. The first definite news we have of More's change of status is in Erasmus' letters: 'More has now become a courtier pure and simple, always with the King, on whose Council he is,' and again, 'I should regret what has happened to More, who has been drawn into court life, were it not that under such a King, and with so many learned colleagues, it seems rather a university than a court; still, we shall get no more news from Utopia to make us laugh, and I know that More would rather laugh than be carried in official state.' To More himself Erasmus writes, 'The one thing that consoles me about your going to court is that it is under the best of kings; still you are lost to us and to learning'.[2] More himself writes a pleasant letter to Fisher: 'Everybody knows that I didn't want to come to court, and the King often twits me about it; I sit as uneasily as a clumsy rider in the saddle. The King has a way of making every man feel that he is enjoying his special favour, just as the London wives pray before the image of Our Lady by the Tower till each of them believes it is smiling upon *her*. I am not so lucky as to be a special favourite, or so optimistic as to imagine myself one. But the virtue and learning of the King increase day by day, so that I feel court life less and less of a burden.'[3]

We must be glad that the tragic end of it all did not deter Roper from putting on record a pleasant picture of the relation

[1] 20 May 1519, ALLEN, III, No. 968. Compare Nos. 834, 855, 970, and many others.
[2] ALLEN, III, Nos. 816, 832, 829 (17, 24, 23 April, 1518).
[3] STAPLETON, VII, p. 230.

of monarch and servant in these early days of More's court life. The King, upon Holy Days, when he had done his own devotions, would send for More to his private apartment, and cause him 'there sometime in matters of Astronomy, Geometry, Divinity, and such other faculties, and sometimes of his worldly affairs, to sit and confer with him. And other whiles would he, in the night, have him up into his Leads, there for to consider with him the diversities, courses, motions, and operations of the stars and planets'. The King was interested in navigation, and probably this stimulated his astronomical studies. More's disposition was so pleasant that 'it pleased the King and Queen, after the Council had supped, at the time of their supper, for their pleasure, commonly to call for him to be merry with them'.[1] In order sometimes to get home to his wife and children, More had 'somewhat to dissemble his nature', so that he was not so often sent for.

It is not quite clear from what exact date we ought to reckon More as being in the King's service. The first payment of his annuity was made on 21 June 1518. The annuity (£100 – say £1500 of our money) was however made retrospective[2] as from 29 September 1517, the time when More went to Calais about 'the busy trifles of princes'. By this reckoning, More's career as servant to Henry begins almost exactly at the same time as Luther's career as Protestant Reformer. For it was on 1 November 1517 that Luther nailed his Ninety-five Theses to the door of the Castle Church at Wittenberg. But that, even if he had heard of it, would not have much disturbed More's peace of mind: to propound subjects for academical discussion was a strictly regular proceeding. Luther's act was but a cloud, the size of a man's fist. The tempest was yet to come. Meantime, the four editions of *Utopia*[3] were making More famous throughout Europe, and these early years in the King's service, 1518-1520, mark the height of More's happiness and success. Admired at home and abroad, a man whom the King delights to honour, all his friends are rallying round him.

So all the omens were fair, peace abroad, learning and

[1] ROPER, p. 11.
[2] See ROUTH, *Sir Thomas More*, pp. 92-3, for some useful discoveries on the dates of this annuity, made by Miss C. Jamison.
[3] Louvain, Nov. 1516; Paris, 1517; Basel, March and Nov. 1518.

justice encouraged at home, under the best of kings and his mighty minister, when on 23 July 1518, a month after he had received the King's payment, More finally cut himself adrift from the City. 'Voluntarily and of his own free will', he resigned his office of Under-Sheriff.

The exchange of kindnesses and good offices between More and the City continues. On great occasions More makes public speeches on behalf of the City,[1] and the citizens evidently feel that they have in More a friend at court. A testimonial from More is a valuable asset if a man wants a post under the Mayor and Corporation, especially if More can be persuaded to appear in person to press the claims of his client. These courtesies go on, as More rises in rank, to Under-Treasurer, to Chancellor of the Duchy of Lancaster, and finally to Lord Chancellor. Thus we find in the 'Repertory of the Court of Aldermen' that in 1529 the Chancellor of the Duchy of Lancaster came in person to recommend for the post of sword-bearer his servant, Walter Smith, who had been with him eight or nine years. A few months later we find in the 'Repertory' that the Lord Chancellor of England is to have a tun of good red wine, and his father is to have a hogshead; and next year, at Christmas, More again is to have a tun of good wine.[2]

But, apart from these civilities, More's connection with the City has ceased, and we have to follow the steps of his promotion at court.

The first account of More as one of the King's Council is to be found at St. Mark's, Venice, in the Archives of the Republic. More's relations with the Venetian ambassador, Sebastian Giustinian, make an interesting little story.

More and Giustinian had long been friends. Years before, when More was a City official, they had had to make elaborate Latin orations to each other, clawing each other's backs with compliments, as More puts it in a letter to Erasmus. 'But,' he continues, 'the man charms me: he is an honourable man, versed in the ways of the world, devoted to sacred letters, and, last but not least, devoted to *you*.'[3]

---

[1] To Campeggio (HALL's *Chronicle*, ed. WHIBLEY, I, 167) or to the Emperor (see below, p. 198).
[2] See Repertory, III, fol. 221; VIII, fols. 39, 77, 141.
[3] 3 Sept. 1516, ALLEN, II, No. 461.

Giustinian was now drawing towards the end of his term of office in London,[1] and he was anxious, before his return, to settle up some difficulties about the wine trade. He played on Wolsey's vanity, extolled his justice beyond measure, and assured him that he wanted no favour, but only the justice which could not be denied by so upright a judge. A new Venetian ambassador, he said, was already on the way to replace him, and it would not be worthy of the justice of England to let him return with his errand unaccomplished. Upon this, Giustinian reports, Wolsey 'told me positively that he meant the matter to be settled, and said he would appoint me two commissioners, namely Richard Pace and Thomas More, the most sage and virtuous, and the most linked with me in friendship of any in this kingdom'. Were he to keep this promise, writes Giustinian to the Doge, 'I should deem the matter as good as settled; but I suspect that this resolve will be impeded, both because Pace is known to be most devoted to your Highness and More devoted to justice; and both one and the other are very friendly indeed to myself personally'.[2]

More, however, could be duly cautious, despite his friendships. A few months later Giustinian reports to the Doge how he has paid his respects at Eltham to congratulate the King on his peace with France. Henry told him that his congratulations were premature, as there were still details unsettled, and left the Venetian ambassador very anxious to know exactly how things stood. So, he says,

> After dinner I contrived a conference with the Magnifico Dom. Thomas More, newly made Councillor, who is very much my friend. I adroitly turned the conversation on these negociations concerning peace; but he did not open, and pretended not to know in what the difficulties consisted, declaring that the Cardinal of York [Wolsey] 'most solely', to use his own expression, transacted this matter with the French ambassadors, and, when he has concluded, he then calls the councillors, so that the King himself scarcely knows in what state matters are.

Giustinian tried to work on More's feelings by 'gently

---

[1] Jan. 1515 – Oct. 1519.
[2] 28 Feb. 1518.   *Venetian Calendar*, II, p. 434; *Selection of Despatches by Giustinian*, trans. RAWDON BROWN, 1854. II, p. 162.

complaining' that he had been kept in the dark; only to be blandly assured that everybody else, including even the reverend Spanish ambassador, was equally in the dark. 'So,' says the baffled diplomat, 'perceiving that I could elicit nothing further, I departed.'[1]

It is interesting that this first report on More as Henry's servant should record that gift of discreet silence, even to his best friends, which in the troublesome days to come was to be More's chief defence, and was to make it so difficult for Henry to bring him to the block. But in 1519 nothing had arisen to interfere with the happy relations of Henry, Wolsey, and More. The first of the numerous official letters extant in More's own hand is addressed by Henry's command to Wolsey. It concludes with congratulations from the King to the Cardinal on his excellent health. The King, More reports, claims the credit of this to himself, on account of the advice he has given Wolsey, 'by which ye leave the often taking of medicines that ye were wont to use; and while ye so do, he saith, ye shall not fail of health, which our Lord long preserve.'[2]

Another feature of Wolsey's rule which must have appealed to More was his desire to secure prompt and impartial justice. To Giustinian, Wolsey's vanity and Wolsey's love of justice are his essential characteristics. When he first arrived in England, Giustinian tells his government, Wolsey used to say to him, 'His Majesty will do so and so.' By degrees he forgot himself and began to say, 'We shall do so and so.' But by the time of which we are writing Wolsey had reached the pitch of saying, 'I shall do so and so.' But, Giustinian goes on to say, he has the reputation of being extremely just. He favours the people exceedingly and especially the poor, hears their suits and seeks to dispatch them instantly, and expects lawyers to plead their causes without fee.[3] Cavendish gives a very similar account of Wolsey; on the one hand, his pomp and display are emphasized. But on the other, Cavendish, looking back over more than a

---

[1] 18 Sept. 1518. *Venetian Calendar*, ii, p. 457; *Selections of Despatches*, as before, ii, pp. 215-6. For another example of More's reticence, see *Venetian Calendar*, iii, p. 163.

[2] 5 July 1519. These autograph letters of More, preserved in the British Museum, have been published by J. Delcourt, Paris, 1914.

[3] 10 Sept. 1519. *Venetian Calendar*, ii, p. 560.

quarter of a century of the troubled rule that had followed
Wolsey's fall, asserts, 'Thus much I dare be bold to say, without
displeasure to any person, or of affection, that in my judgment
I never saw this realm in better order, quietness, and obedience,
than it was in the time of his authority and rule, nor justice
better ministered with indifferency'.[1] Much the same story is
told us by the Chronicler Edward Hall, of Wolsey's behaviour
in these halcyon days of his early rule: how he 'punished lords,
knights, and men of all sorts for riots and maintenance . . . that
the poor men lived quietly'. But Hall, a prosperous bourgeois,
had not complete sympathy with Wolsey's favouring of the
poor. When 'the poor people perceived that he punished the
rich, then they complained without number, and brought many
an honest man to trouble and vexation. And when the Cardinal
at the last had perceived their untrue surmises and fained complaints for the most part, he then waxed weary of hearing their
causes, and ordained . . . diverse under courts to hear complaints, by bill, of poor people'.[2] One of the courts for hearing
complaints of poor people came later to be known as the Court
of Requests. It grew out of a standing Committee of the King's
Council which originally followed the King in his progresses,
hough it ultimately became a Court with permanent judges
and a fixed habitat at Whitehall. But at the time when More
was appointed to the Council it still followed the King, now
at Woodstock, now at Greenwich. It was in special attendance
at this Court that More was first employed. Roper is rather
apologetic about it: Henry made More Master of Requests, he
says, 'having then no better room void'. But More probably
found his employment in this Court – the Court of Poor Men's
Causes, as it was called – quite congenial. Unfortunately there
seems to be at the moment little information as to his activities
in this capacity.[3]

His duties as a member of the King's Council also involved
More in diplomatic business: helping to arrange the meeting
between Henry and Charles; attending the meeting between
Henry and Francis in June 1520, 'The Field of Cloth of Gold',

[1] *Life of Wolsey*, p. 3.
[2] *Chronicle*, ed. WHIBLEY, I, p. 152 (Eighth year of Henry, 1516-17).
[3] For the Court see LEADAM, *Select Cases in the Court of Requests*, 1898. *Selden Society*.

but employing his time on the more congenial task of settling commercial disputes between the English merchants and the merchants of the Hanse – negotiations which had their humorous side. The English ambassadors complain that they have had difficulty in discovering the number and names of the towns which made up the body with which they were negotiating.[1] On the Hanse side also we have a full account of the negotiations. More's polite speech and calm bearing are noted. Such politeness is usual with the English, the Hanse negotiators say, but it does not prevent them from at times showing themselves very stiff opponents.[2]

And this visit gave More an opportunity for that meeting with Erasmus, of which he had for months been expressing the hope in his letters. Erasmus came, evidently in the train of the Emperor, and had interviews with Henry and with Wolsey. Erasmus and More met face to face, at Calais and Bruges, and again, next year, at Bruges.[3] They never met later. But till death they continued 'to have but one soul between them'.

At this point in More's career we may perhaps pause, to survey his friends and his home life, as depicted by Erasmus and others.

§ 3. MORE AND HIS HOUSEHOLD

It was a couple of months after he had written his letters to his English friends about the Golden Age now approaching, that Erasmus wrote his famous account of More. Such a courtier of such a king! Good Christians can be found outside monasteries! It is men like More whom the English King allows, nay invites, nay compels, to come to his court; scholars (and Erasmus runs over the list of great names); not dissolute youths and gay women who will corrupt his morals, or sycophantic officials who will teach him to play the tyrant and find new ways of taxing his people.[4]

If anything could make the irony of fate more pointed it is that the letter is addressed to Ulrich von Hutten – the friend of Erasmus who wishes to learn about his friend More. Von

[1] *L.P.*, II, i, Nos. 868, 869 (Field of Cloth of Gold), 979.
[2] *Hanserecesse*, bearbeitet von Dietrich Schäfer, VII, 1905, p. 593.
[3] ALLEN, IV, Nos. 1087, 1096, 1106, 1145, 1184, 1233.
[4] 23 July 1519, ALLEN, IV, No. 999.

Hutten was to become the embodiment of that lawless violence which Erasmus and More most detested, and was destined to attack Erasmus and to be attacked by him with a bitterness which even von Hutten's miserable death could not appease.

Erasmus begins with a description of More's person: he is of medium height, with a bright and clear complexion, auburn hair, thin beard, blue-grey eyes; with a face like his character, friendly, cheerful, ready for fun but without buffoonery or bitterness. Erasmus also mentions More's habit of raising his right shoulder above his left, especially in walking, his rather coarse hands, and his general carelessness about personal appearance. This carelessness extends to food: More eats beef, salt fish and coarse bread rather than delicacies; he likes milk-foods, fruit, and eggs; he drinks small beer or water, merely touching wine with his lips, as a matter of courtesy.

More's speech is clear and his voice penetrating, but not soft or musical. He cannot sing. (Roper tells us that More sang in the choir of Chelsea Church. A witty Frenchman has remarked that the statements are not incompatible.) More dresses simply, never wearing his gold chain, if he can help it, neglecting formalities, loving equality and freedom. He avoided the Court as long as he could – even that of the considerate Henry VIII. Henry dragged him to Court – no one was ever so eager to go to Court as More to avoid it. He hates games of ball, games of chance, and cards.

He loves to study the forms and characters of animals. There is hardly any kind of bird which he does not keep, and all kinds of rare animals: ape, fox, beaver, weasel. Anything from abroad, or otherwise remarkable, he buys at once. His house is full of noteworthy things, and he loves to see others pleased with them. But it is particularly More's gift for friendship which Erasmus emphasizes: the trouble he will take over his friends' affairs, though careless of his own; how his gentle and merry talk cheers the low-spirited and distressed; how he loves especially to jest with women (including his own wife); the charm with which he rules his household, so that quarrels are unknown, and none of his servants have ever fallen into disgrace; the way he uses his influence with the King to serve his friends; the way he relieves one friend with money, another with a timely recommendation in high places. 'You might call him the general patron of all who are hard up.' No one is more ready to serve, or less expects to be served. He is always reconciling those who have quarrelled. When he was in legal practice, he was disinterested enough to urge litigants to avoid expense by making up their quarrels; if they would not, he showed them how to keep down costs. As an official he has arbitrated settlements in most difficult cases. And never has he accepted any gift.

And Erasmus sums it all up in the words of John Colet – that More is the one genius of Britain.

Many and many a passage could be selected from other letters, in which Erasmus speaks of More's kindliness; one, to Polydore Vergil, cannot be passed over. Polydore thought that More was offended with him for some reason, and Erasmus replies: 'What you write about More is all nonsense; why, he does not remember even grave injuries.'[1]

The magnificent encomium of Erasmus set a fashion in public testimonials. Robert Whittinton, in the following year, having occasion to write a book on Latin prose composition, selected certain current topics for translation. Here is what he tells us of More:

> More is a man of an angel's wit and singular learning. I know not his fellow. For where is the man of that gentleness, lowliness, and affability? And, as time requireth, a man of marvellous mirth and pastimes, and sometime of as sad gravity. A man for all seasons.[2]

The great Spanish scholar, Vives, having occasion to quote from the dialogue of Lucian on the *Calling up of the Dead*, quotes from More's translation, rather than make a version of his own, and so has a pretext to expatiate on More's virtues: the keenness of his intelligence, the breadth of his learning, his eloquence, his foresight, his moderation, his integrity, and his *suavitas*, the sweetness of his temper.[3]

Such general adulation must have been a little embarrassing; even More's oddities received the flattery of imitation; we

---

[1] 5 Sept. 1525, ALLEN, VI, 1606.
[2] *Vulgaria*, 1520; ed. WHITE, E.E.T.S., p. 64.
[3] AUGUSTINE, *De civitate Dei*, per I. L. VIVEM, Basel, 1522, p. 41.

hear of a man 'who, being most unlike unto him in wit and learning, nevertheless in wearing his gown awry upon the one shoulder, as Sir Thomas More was wont to do, would needs be counted like unto him'.[1]

We are so accustomed to think of the household of Sir Thomas More at Chelsea that we are apt to follow Froude in his mistake of localizing there the description of More and his household which Erasmus wrote. But More was still dwelling at that time in the very middle of London, at the Barge in Bucklersbury, surrounded by those shops of herb-sellers which made Falstaff speak of young gallants as 'lisping hawthorn-buds, that smell like Bucklersbury in simple-time'.

After More's household had removed to Chelsea, Erasmus, in a famous letter, described it as Plato's Academy on a Christian footing. Chelsea allowed elbow-room, and More's household became a large one. From the letters and the stories which surviving members carried with them into exile, and which were printed more than fifty years after the household had been broken up, it is possible to get a good idea of this small patriarchal, monastic Utopia which came into existence first in the City, and then on Thames side, and to describe what Nicholas Harpsfield calls More's 'private, secret, and domestical life and trade'.

Dice, cards, and flirtation were forbidden to the numerous retinue of men and women; gardening, study, music, and matrimony were encouraged. There was household prayer every night that the master was at home, compulsory church-going on Sundays and feast days, and at the great feasts everyone had to rise to attend the midnight office. Usually More rose at 2 a.m., and gave the time till 7 a.m. to study and devotion. He heard Mass every morning, and once, when repeated and urgent messages came from the King, he refused to leave till Mass was ended – a refusal which the King took in good part.[2] For devotion, More constructed at Chelsea 'The New Building', with its gallery, library, and chapel; there, so far as possible, he spent his Fridays in prayer and study, and on Good Friday the whole household was assembled there to hear the whole of our Lord's Passion read, generally by More's secretary, John

---

[1] ASCHAM, *Schoolmaster*, ed. ARBER, p. 147.   [2] STAPLETON, IV, p. 183; VI, p. 219.

Harris. At ordinary mealtimes one of the family (and particularly Margaret Gigs) read scripture, intoned in the monastic
fashion, with the commentaries of Nicholas de Lyra. After the
scripture had been discussed, Master Henry Patenson, More's
domestic fool, was permitted to bring the conversation down to
a lower level – for More, Utopian also in this, took great
pleasure in fools. We must not sentimentalize Master Patenson,
as some have done, or make him a counterpart of the tragic fool
in *Lear*. Holbein's record of his face, as he stands against the
door in the family group, confirms what anecdote tells us as
to the crudity of his humour. When his jest at the size of a
guest's nose was received with such silence that he realized its
tactlessness, he made amends by protesting that the gentleman
had a very small nose – in fact, no nose at all. More took
Patenson with him to the Emperor's court at Bruges, where he
was observed to be 'a man of special wit by himself and unlike
the common sort', and where his rough method of dealing with
mockers was not calculated to promote international amity.[1]

More thinks of his young children amidst all the distractions of statesmanship, when toiling on missions abroad, or
following the King round from palace to palace, as Henry fled
before the ravages of the sweating sickness. More writes to them
in Latin prose, or in Latin verse composed as he rides drenched
by the rain, on a horse stumbling or sticking fast in the mud.
He reminds them how he has fed them with fruit and cakes,
given them pretty silken clothes, and, if he has ever had to beat
them, has done it with peacock's feathers.[2]

We have seen how More set to work to educate his first wife,
and that with Mistress Alice he succeeded so far as singing was
concerned. More has himself recorded his failure to teach her
science. He tried to explain to her how the earth is the centre
of all things, and how the centre of the earth is consequently
the lowest spot in creation, from which everything ascends in
every direction. (It is the same system, of course, which we
have in Dante, where, after passing the haunch of Satan, which
is fixed in the exact centre of the earth, the explorer feels that
he is no longer moving downwards, but upwards.) Similarly
More makes the husband explain how, if a hole were bored

[1] *Works*, 1557, p. 768.   [2] *Epigrammata*, 1520.

through the earth, and a millstone thrown down it, the millstone would fall to the centre, and there would stop; because
if it went beyond the centre it would be falling upwards, 'from
a lower place to a higher'.

Now while he was telling her this tale, she nothing went about
to consider his words, but as she was wont in all other things,
studied all the while nothing else but what she might say to
the contrary. And when he had, with much work and oft
interrupting, brought at last his tale to an end: 'Well,' quoth
she to him, . . . 'I will argue like, and make you a like
sample. My maid hath yonder a spinning wheel – or else,
because all your reason resteth in the roundness of the world –
come hither, thou girl; take out thy spindle, and bring me
hither the whorl. Lo, sir, ye make imaginations, I cannot
tell you what. But here is a whorl, and it is round as the
world is. And we shall not need imagine an hole bored
through, for it hath an hole bored through indeed. But yet,
because ye go by imaginations, I will imagine with you.
Imagine me now that this whorl were ten mile thick on every
side, and this hole through it still, and so great that a millstone might well go through it. Now, if the whorl stood on
the one end, and a millstone were thrown in above at the
other end, would it go no further than the midst, trow you?
By God, if one threw in a stone no bigger than an egg, I ween
if ye stood in the nether end of the hole five mile beneath the
midst, it would give you a pat upon the pate that it would
make you claw your head, and yet should ye feel none itch
at all.'[1]

So More had to put away his sphere, since Dame Alice
'could see no difference between the world and the whorl,
because both were round'. Yet Erasmus, a witness not preju-
diced in her favour, tells how she helped the 'School' by insisting on everyone performing the allotted task.[2] If no scientist,
Dame Alice had the makings of a headmistress. And when her
daughters had the honour of disputing together on philosophy
before the King,[3] Dame Alice was probably convinced that there
was something in philosophy after all.

We can realize how largely the business management of the

---

[1] *Defence against Tyndale, Works,* 1557, p. 628. Dame Alice is not mentioned by
name; the tale is told as illustrating the kind of logic Tyndale uses.
[2] ALLEN, IV, No. 1233.   [3] *L.P.,* IV, No. 5806.

Great House lay in the hands of Dame Alice, from the letter
which More wrote to her when he learnt, from his 'son Heron',
of the accidental burning of his barns. He cannot come home
till next week, because he is in attendance on the King at
Woodstock. (He had just returned from negotiating the treaty
of Cambrai, and was making his report to the King.) Dame
Alice is to compensate the neighbours to whom the fire has
spread, 'for an I should not leave myself a spoon, there shall no
poor neighbour of mine bear no loss by any chance happened
in my house; I pray you be with my children and your household merry in God'. Dame Alice is to see for provision for corn
for the household, and to decide whether 'we keep the ground
still in our hands'. 'But I would not,' says More, 'that any
man were suddenly sent away, he wot ne'er whither.'[1]

With his children, catching them young, More had better
success than with Dame Alice. Margaret, Elizabeth, Cecily,
John (the names run like a rhyme) were taught Latin, Greek,
Logic, Philosophy, Theology, Mathematics, and Astronomy. At
the end of the Sixteenth Century there were still extant versions
made by More's 'School', both in Latin and English, of the
letter which More had written to the University of Oxford in
vindication of the study of classical literature.[2] It looks as if
More had anticipated Ascham's system of 'double translation',
by urging one daughter to translate, and the other to put the
English back into Latin. All More's correspondence with his
children, till they were quite grown up, seems to have been in
Latin. This may have made their letters a little artificial, and
More advises them to write them in English first, and then to
translate. But he expects a letter every day; no excuses; John
makes none. John, thrown into the shade by his brilliant eldest
sister, is selected for special praise. The sisters are not to say
there is nothing to write about: girls can always talk about
nothing. They are not to say there is no time to catch the post;
they should have the letter ready. To a letter of Margaret,
asking rather timidly for money, More replies that he would
gladly, if he could, repay every syllable with two gold pieces.

More was aware that in giving his daughters the same
education as their brother he was making a new departure,

[1] 3 Sept. 1529, *Works*, 1557, p. 1419.   [2] STAPLETON, X, p. 251.

which would be criticized. He says so in a long letter in which he discusses their education with their tutor, William Gunnell.

Other tutors the children had: Master Drew; Master Nicholas, who taught them (More says slyly) all the astronomy he knew. Master Nicholas was no less than Nicholas Kratzer, a famous astronomer and wit, whose portrait by Holbein is in the Louvre. Born at Munich, Kratzer made England his home; he was a fellow of Corpus, Oxford, before he taught More's children. Many years later, Henry VIII asked him why he spoke English so badly, and he replied, 'Pardon, your Grace, but how *can* a man learn English in thirty years?'[1] Another tutor was Richard Hyrde. When Margaret translated Erasmus' *Treatise on the Pater Noster*, Hyrde contributed an Introduction, in English, which is a justification of the right of women to a scholarly education. With Hyrde, Greek led to medicine, and later, as physician, he accompanied Gardiner on his embassy to the Pope; the party had to ford a river in spate, and Hyrde caught a chill and died.

With such tutors, Margaret's learning grew to be considerable. Latin compositions of hers, now lost, are praised by Stapleton. Classical scholars have praised her as one of the few women to whom we owe a convincing emendation of a corrupt Latin text. Her father gloried in her scholarship, Latin and English. When he wrote on the 'Four Last Things', he gave the same task to Margaret, and applauded her achievement. He showed her Latin writings to fellow scholars – to Reginald Pole, who could hardly believe that a girl could have attained, unaided, to such Latinity,[2] and to Vesey, Bishop of Exeter, who was equally astonished, and who insisted on sending a gold Portuguese coin to Margaret by way of reward. More tried in vain to refuse it, and was a little annoyed, because he had wished to show Vesey the letters of the other girls, which he did not dare to do, lest he should be suspected of trying to extract further largesse from the episcopal pocket.[3]

On 2 July 1521 Margaret was married to William Roper. She is described as of St. Stephen's, Walbrook, so More was

---

[1] The story is told by Carel van Mander; see CHAMBERLAIN, *Holbein*, I, p. 328.
[2] STAPLETON, V, p. 199.   [3] The same, XI, p. 268.

still living in Bucklersbury.[1] When, in 1523, Erasmus dedicated to Margaret his Commentary on the Christmas Hymn of Prudentius, the great scholar sent a kiss to Margaret's first child. Roper belonged to the same aristocracy of the law as did More, but with much longer ancestry behind him. When he married he was a man of twenty-three (possibly rather more), and had been some three years an inmate of More's house; Margaret was not yet sixteen.

One of the most pathetic stories of More's household tells how Margaret fell so ill of the sweating sickness that 'by no invention or devices she could be kept from sleep, so that both physicians and all other there despaired of her recovery, and gave her over'. More, on his knees in prayer in the New Building, thought of a remedy, which, when he told the physicians, they marvelled that they had not themselves remembered:

> Then was it immediately ministered unto her sleeping, which she could by no means have been brought unto waking. And albeit after that she was thereby thoroughly awaked, God's marks, an evident undoubted token of death, plainly appeared upon her, yet she, contrary to all their expectations, was, as it was thought, by her father's fervent prayer miraculously recovered, and at length again to perfect health restored.

More's comment must be remembered. Had Margaret died, he said, he would have withdrawn altogether from the world: would 'never have meddled with worldly matters after'.[2]

Yet the would-be recluse and the author of the communistic *Utopia* was not blind to the advantages of property in seeking marriages for his children. On 29 September 1525 the two younger daughters, Elizabeth aged about nineteen, and Cecily aged about eighteen, were married at Willesden in the private chapel of Giles Alington, the husband of Alice, More's step-daughter. Elizabeth married William Dauncey, son of Sir John Dauncey, Knight of the Body to Henry VIII, and Cecily married Giles Heron, son and heir of Sir John Heron, Treasurer of the

---

[1] From June 1523 to Jan. 1524 More owned Crosby Hall, though we do not know that he ever lived there. In 1524 he was buying land in Chelsea. He refers to having left St. Stephen's parish for Chelsea, in the *Dialogue, Works,* 1557, p. 131.

[2] ROPER, pp. 28-9.

Chamber to Henry VIII. Giles had been a ward of Sir Thomas More.

In 1529 More's son John married Anne Cresacre, only child and heir of Edward Cresacre of Barnborough Hall, Yorkshire. She also was a ward of More's. When Holbein made his sketch, probably early in 1527, she was already betrothed to John, and was then in her fifteenth year. In Holbein's portrait she looks both amused and terrified at the circle of blue-stockings among whom her lot had been cast. We are told that she begged her father-in-law for a 'billement' set with pearls, and that More tried to cure her of vanity by presenting her with one set with white peas, instead. We are further told that the cure succeeded: 'Never after she had any great desire to wear any new toy.'[1] (Erasmus, long before, had told a somewhat similar story, apparently of More and his first wife, Jane Colt.) But Holbein's drawing shows Anne Cresacre wearing a 'billement', and I am sure it is not of peas. From John More and Anne Cresacre ('my loving daughter', as More calls her in his last letter) are descended the present representatives of More's house, Mr. Thomas More Eyston of East Hendred, and his children, Thomas More, Mary, and John. 'Four centuries after More's execution they carry on his name, and a Lord Chancellor's simple drinking-mug and a bishop's wooden walking-staff are their priceless possessions . . . No relic of kingly pomp compares with little Thomas More's inheritance.'[2]

Stapleton enumerates More's twenty-one grandchildren. Through one or other of them, a large number of Englishmen and Englishwomen to-day can trace descent from Thomas More.

Of members of More's school not of his immediate kindred, the most important is Margaret Gigs, the foster-sister of More's daughter Margaret. Margaret Gigs has told how she used as a child to commit small faults in order to have the pleasure of being reproved by More.[3] Perhaps as a foster-child she was afraid of being overlooked; but More is careful in the superscription of his letters to make it clear that 'he numbers her

---

[1] *Life* by Ro. Ba., *Ecclesiastical Biography*, ii, p. 111.
[2] Dr. Elsie V. Hitchcock, in the Preface to Roper's *Life of More*.
[3] Stapleton, ix, p. 248.

among his own'; that she is 'as dear as though she were a daughter'. She was a Greek scholar, with leanings towards Mathematics and Medicine. More tells how, when 'a young girl', she diagnosed a fever of his which had defied his two physicians, and identified it in the works of Galen.[1]

John Clement, as More's boy attendant, had been with him during his Flemish embassy, and so is brought into *Utopia*. He passed to the service of Cardinal Wolsey. Erasmus evidently feared that the Cardinal would work his brilliant young servant to death; he warns Clement against writing late at night: he is to learn to write standing, and upright, when pressed by the Cardinal's business.[2] Clement, however, outlived almost all his friends. He became Wolsey's lecturer in Rhetoric, and Reader in Greek at Oxford, then took to Medicine, and by 1528 was Court Physician. He must have known Margaret Gigs since they were small children, and when Holbein made his drawing she is noted as 'Clement's wife'. Their marriage is probably the first English example of that union between the man and the woman student of medicine, which is one of the most gracious and hopeful products of our modern education.

Clement was studying medicine at Oxford when Reginald Pole was there, and a fragment of a letter is extant[3] in which More thanks them jointly: Clement for the advice upon diet which he had sent to More's household, and Pole for a prescription which he had secured from his mother, the Countess of Salisbury, and had had made up.

Finally, there was John Harris, More's secretary, amanuensis, and faithful attendant, whose business it was to warn him of any mistake he might make. Harris once expostulated with him for going out in shoes badly broken.[4] 'Ask my tutor to buy me a new pair,' was More's reply; the 'tutor' was the servant deputed to look after his clothes and other necessaries, apparently John a Wood, whom More later took with him as servant to the Tower. Harris married Margaret Roper's maid, Dorothy Colly.

It was a charitable household. More followed literally the

[1] *Works*, 1557, p. 1173. Compare HARPSFIELD, p. 90.
[2] 22 April 1518, ALLEN, III, No. 820, to William Gunnell.
[3] STAPLETON, v, p. 198.   [4] STAPLETON, vi, p. 227.

Gospel precept, and invited the poor rather than the rich to his table. Out of doors, Margaret Gigs was the chief agent of his charitable distributions; at Chelsea he established an alms-house which was the special care of Margaret Roper. At a later date William Roper's own charities were on a munificent scale.

But, however pious and charitable, the young people were also strong-willed, self-willed, and courageous, and could enjoy themselves without any excessive regard for decorum. Giles Heron and William Roper could both be as obstinate as their father-in-law, and much more headstrong. Roper's early Lutheranism, about the time he married Margaret, amounted to a public scandal in the household of a great Court official:

> Neither was Master Roper content to whisper it in hugger mugger, but thirsted very sore to publish his new doctrine and divulge it, and thought himself very able so to do, and it were even at Paul's Cross; yea, for the burning zeal he bare to the furtherance and advancement of Luther's new broached religion, and for the pretty liking he had of himself, he longed so sore to be pulpited that, to have satisfied his mad affection and desire, he could have been content to have forgone a good portion of his lands.[1]

Roper, convinced that 'faith only did justify, that the works of man did nothing profit', could hold his own in open argument with doctors of divinity. He consorted with Lutheran merchants, some of them English, some German Hanseatic traders living in London. With them he was convented for heresy before Cardinal Wolsey. His comrades were put to open shame at Paul's Cross, but, as a favour to More, Wolsey discharged Roper 'with a friendly warning'. But Roper still spent his holy days in reading a Lutheran Bible, so as 'to be able among ignorant persons to babble and talk, as he thought, like a great doctor'.

Poor More, in desperation, betook himself to prayer. 'Meg,' he said to his daughter,

> 'I have borne a long time with thy husband; I have reasoned and argued with him in those points of religion, and still given to him my poor fatherly counsel; but I perceive none

[1] HARPSFIELD, p. 84.

of all this able to call him home; and therefore, Meg, I will no longer argue nor dispute with him, but will clean give him over, and get me another while to God and pray for him.'[1]

Roper's subsequent conversion to fervent orthodoxy seemed to the historian Harpsfield to proceed from the hand of the Most High. A Protestant, in whose possession one of Harpsfield's manuscripts has been, adds a marginal note suggesting that it was rather from the hand of the Devil. But whatever the agency, Roper's subsequent generosity to distressed and imprisoned Catholics, and his firmness in his faith, are as indisputable as the courage with which Margaret Roper bore *her* trials. After her father was dead, her husband in the Tower, the messengers sent from the King to search her house found her 'not puling and lamenting, but full busily teaching her children', so that the searchers were astonished, and could not afterward speak too much good of her.[2] And there is no disputing the courage and integrity of a man who could get into trouble with Wolsey for his Lutheranism, and with Henry and Elizabeth for his Romanism.

More had to protest to the German merchants in London against the spreading of Lutheran doctrines; and it was probably because he was an opponent of the new doctrines that certain London merchants were heard liberally to rail against him, much to the distress of the Water Bailiff of London. The Water Bailiff was one of the four esquires or gentlemen attendant on the Lord Mayor. He was, we are told, an old servant of More's, and begged him to call these slanderers before him and punish them for their lewd malice.[3] More refused, with a smile. The Water Bailiff at this time was Sebastian Hillary, and we have no information as to when he was a member of More's household; it was from the Royal Household that he entered the service of the City. But his wife, Margery Hillary, was an old family servant; Margaret Roper and she 'were very great and familiar together, in so much that they called each other sisters'.

The first of the four esquires to the Lord Mayor was the

[1] HARPSFIELD, p. 87.   [2] The same, p. 79.   [3] ROPER, p. 23.
[4] Depositions in Chancery, C. 24/52; Roper *v.* Royden; Pleadings in Chancery, C. 3, 153/1. I owe this reference to Professor C. J. Sisson.

Sword-Bearer, who may still be seen on state occasions in a costume which has changed very little from that worn in Tudor times. More obtained this post for Walter Smith, who had been for nine years his personal servant. This same Walter Smith has left us a peculiarly vivid sidelight on the More household in *The Twelve merry jests of the Widow Edith.* There was much hunting of wealthy widows in the Sixteenth Century, and Edith secured consideration for herself in her wanderings by quite fictitious claims to property. Professor Reed's researches have shown that suitors, whom she is alleged to have deluded, really existed, and we may accept as authentic her Tenth Jest, the visit to the house of Sir Thomas More at Chelsea. Her alleged wealth was such that William and Margaret Roper tried to secure her for Thomas Arthur, their man. Thomas Croxton, Master Alington's man, and Walter Smith, Thomas More's man, also pressed their suit. There was 'revelling, gossiping, and general bumming', as Margaret Gigs called it, in the widow's chamber, till the three suitors, having been duly fleeced and fooled, discovered the fraud, and took their revenge. 'How the merry Edith's food and ale are medicated, and other things that ensued, must be left to the reader, who will learn in this Tenth Jest of the Household of Sir Thomas More things that are not suggested in Roper, but may not be the less true for all that.'[1]

This list of More's household must not conclude without mentioning the monkey, who appears near Lady Alice in Holbein's drawing. The intelligence of this monkey (or more probably of his predecessor) has been immortalized by Erasmus. Rabbit-hutches were kept at the end of the garden, and the monkey, without emotion, watched a weasel trying to make a forcible entry. Only when the weasel was on the point of success did the monkey suddenly intervene, and block the entrance with such skill that a man could not have done it better. From which Erasmus argues that monkeys are by nature friendly to rabbits.[2] But is it not possible that the monkey's object was to annoy the weasel? More would have thought so, for he drew moral lessons from the fact that 'an ape, not well looked unto,

---

[1] REED, *Early Tudor Drama*, p. 153.
[2] *Colloquies, Amicitia; Opera*, Leyden, 1703, Vol. i, col. 877.

will be busy and bold to do shrewd turns, and contrariwise
being spied will suddenly leap back and adventure no farther';
so, said More, the Devil likewise will flee if resisted, lest by
unsuccessful temptation he should minister merit to man.[1]

Little can the happy and busy household have realized the
fate in store for it. The young people became members of
Parliament, or secured appointments at court, and seemed in
the full tide of advancement. But they remained loyal to the
memory of the man whose scruples checked their careers.
Giles Heron was executed in 1540, the victim of the false
witness of a tenant whom he had put out of a farm. But it was
his known sympathy with and loyalty to his father-in-law which
caused his downfall: it was alleged that More· had been heard,
in the parlour of Heron's house at Shackelwell, Hackney, to
'mumble certain words touching the King'.[2] Roper, Dauncey,
John More, and Heywood were imprisoned, but escaped with
their lives. Margaret Clement was probably the most dauntless
of all, and her reckless courage in succouring the Carthusians
will come later into our story. People were liable to be ques-
tioned by Government agents whether they had been 'in
company with Mistress Roper or Mistress Clement', or 'had
communication with either of them touching the death of Sir
Thomas More'[3] – an unintentional tribute to the reputation of
the two ladies for loyalty to More's memory. The Clements and
the Harrises, like the Heywoods and the Rastells, died in exile.

In time of prosperity More had warned them. It was easy,
he said, to be good so long as virtue was rewarded and vice
punished; 'you are carried up to heaven even by the chins':

'But if you live the time that no man will give you good
counsel, nor no man will give you good example, when you
shall see virtue punished and vice rewarded, if you will then
stand fast and firmly stick to God, upon pain of my life,
though you be but half good, God will allow, you for whole
good.

'If his wife or any of his children had been diseased or
troubled, he would say unto them: "We may not look at our
pleasure to go to Heaven in feather beds: it is not the way,
for our Lord himself went thither with great pain and by many

---

[1] ROPER, p. 27.   [2] *L.P.*, VII, No. 290.   [3] *L.P.*, XIII, 2, No. 695, pp. 266-7.

tribulations, which was the path wherein he walked thither; for the servant may not look to be in better case than his master.'[1]

Erasmus, writing to Budé, speaks of the admiration with which he has read the unaided composition of More's daughters. He had once doubted the wisdom of the higher education of women. But More's experiment had convinced him. It is an example, he thinks, which will be imitated far and wide.[2]

That it was not more widely imitated is only one further example of that frustration and arrest which blights the fair promise of the early Sixteenth Century. As we look back, we can see warnings of the evil days coming in a private quarrel of More's, and in a public disaster in England – the controversy with Brixius and the execution of the Duke of Buckingham.

The Brixius controversy shows how explosive, even in this Golden Age, was the atmosphere of Europe. During the first war between England and France, the English ship *Regent* and the French ship *Cordelière* fought. They were two of the finest ships in their respective navies. The French ship caught fire, and, the ships having grappled, the *Cordelière* involved the English vessel in her fate; both captains and most of the two crews perished. It was a tragic incident which, in more chivalrous days, both sides might have joined in lamenting. But the French scholar Germain de Brie [Brixius], in a patriotic poem on the occasion, had bitterly attacked England. More had replied with a number of epigrams, which were not printed at the time. Later, when discussing the publication of his epigrams with Erasmus, More had very rightly suggested that these should be suppressed. But Erasmus had no national susceptibilities, and perhaps hardly realized how bitter they could be. By a really unpardonable oversight, Erasmus published the epigrams. Brixius replied with his *Anti-Morus*, in which he accused More of the greatest crime which a humanist could commit – that of having put false feet into his verses. More would have overlooked that attack, though he resented this reviving of old bitternesses 'after so many years, in a time of such peace and concord'. But Brixius went further, and tried to make bad blood between More and Henry VIII, by emphasiz-

---

[1] ROPER, pp. 26-7.   [2] Sept. 1521, ALLEN, IV, No. 1233.

ing the way in which, in the Latin poems congratulating Henry on his accession, written years before, but only now published, More had reflected on the government of Henry VII, 'impudently attacking the father, when lauding the son'. As Erasmus said, this was no joke; and it is clear that both More and Erasmus were alarmed at Henry's name being dragged into the controversy. More replied in an *Epistle to Brixius*: as to the false feet in his verses, well, if his feet were not sound, he says, neither was his opponent's head; if his metres were barbarous, so were Brixius' manners. Erasmus deplored this civil war among the humanists: 'People call me biting, but I am nothing to this,' he says of More's reply, which he tried in vain to get him to suppress. The incident shows how national passion could shake that solidarity of humanism to which Erasmus keeps on pathetically appealing: 'With all the obscurantists to fight, we lovers of good letters *must* not quarrel among ourselves', is the burden of letter after letter.[1] But these letters also show that More and Erasmus were gravely disturbed at the imputations made by Brixius upon More's loyalty to the throne; they protest that these imputations will be fruitless; yet they are clearly uneasy. No man could afford to be suspected of disloyalty, as the fate of the Duke of Buckingham was soon to show.

§ 4. THE BEGINNING OF SORROWS

The spring and summer of 1521 – More's fourth in the royal service – mark his establishment in a place of responsibility and power at court. They mark also the set-back of everything he had most desired for his country and for mankind, and the movement of forces which were to combine to bring him to his death.

It was a few weeks before More was appointed Under-Treasurer that the Duke of Buckingham was summoned suddenly from his Gloucestershire home. A few weeks after, the Duke was tried, and executed. These judicial murders were to continue for the rest of Henry's reign, and not to end till, more than a quarter of a century later, the Duke of Norfolk (who with all his faults had been a most able and loyal servant)

[1] See ALLEN, II, No. 461 (3 Sept. 1516); III, No. 620 (Aug. 1517); also IV, Nos. 1087, 1093, 1096, 1131, 1133, 1184.

lay sentenced in the Tower, and was saved because Henry died a few hours before he was to have been beheaded. The cause of it all was Henry's growing anxiety about the succession. Buckingham, with royal blood in his veins, a descendant of Edward III, was accused of having cherished hopes of succeeding to the crown, and of having sent his chaplain to consult a Carthusian of Hinton in Somersetshire, who had foretold that he 'should have all'. That had been eight years before, and before the birth of the Princess Mary; yet, together with some other equally flimsy evidence, it was enough to bring the greatest nobleman in England to the block. Wolsey at the time told the French Chancellor that Buckingham had had his head cut off for murmuring against his policy, and trying to defeat it.[1] The duke died amid general lamentations, protesting his innocence: 'An he had not offended no more unto God than he had unto the crown, he should die as true man as ever there was in the world.' There was serious disaffection in London. A few weeks after Buckingham's execution we find More sent to the Court of Aldermen; the City was told that the King was displeased, because divers persons had lamented the death of the Duke, saying he died guiltless. Four days later, More was sent again; it was suggested that all the harness of the City should be brought to certain places in the City, so as to pacify and please the King.[2]

To More, the most terrible thing about Buckingham's fall was that the idle words of a Carthusian, to whom the world should have been nothing, had had so large a share in it, to the 'great slander and infamy of religion'. He used this many years later, as a warning against mixing politics with religion;[3] but at the time Buckingham's death was one further example of the vanity of the world. More wrote (but not for publication) in his Treatise of the *Four Last Things*, of a great Duke, keeping

> honourable court for the marriage of his child, suddenly taken, his court all broken up, his goods seized, his wife put out, his children disherited, himself cast in prison, brought forth and arraigned, the matter out of question . . . con-

---

[1] POLLARD, *Wolsey*, p. 316.
[2] Repertory of the Court of Aldermen, v, fol. 204, 204b, 5 July, 9 July, 1521.
[3] See below, p. 296.

demned, his coat armour reversed, his gilt spurs hewn off his heels, himself hanged, drawn, and quartered . . .[1]

But still more fatal to all More's hopes was the cloud now rising in Germany. We have seen how More was just entering Henry's service when an obscure German university teacher nailed his Ninety-five Theses to the door of the Castle Church in Wittenberg. In three years, Luther had become the greatest power in Europe. Summoned to attend the Diet of Worms, warned that he would be killed if he went, he had said that he would go, if there were as many devils as tiles on the house roofs to prevent him. Now, in April 1521, he had made his great defence before the Diet: 'Here I stand.' By May, Henry had finished his *Assertion of the Seven Sacraments* in answer to Luther's *Babylonish Captivity of the Church*. In the same month, Luther's books were burnt in St. Paul's Churchyard, whilst Fisher preached a sermon denouncing their errors. By October Henry received the title of *Defender of the Faith*.

It was an omen of the troubles that were to quench all the hopes of the Erasmian reformers, that the same letter which begins with Erasmus hailing Wolsey as the restorer of the Golden Age of learning ends with apologies; Erasmus dissociates himself from Luther, and deplores the violence of German polemics. Of this violence Luther was soon to give a notable example in his reply to Henry. A king could not enter into a scolding match with a German heretic, and More took the quarrel off the King's hands, replying to Luther, in Latin as violent as his own, under the pseudonym of William Ross.

In later years Henry (whilst adhering to the title of *Defender of the Faith*) commanded his ministers to accuse More of having villainously and traitorously provoked him to write his book in maintenance of the Pope's authority, and thereby, to his dishonour throughout all Christendom, to put a sword in the Pope's hands to fight against himself. More replied that the King himself knew this to be untrue. He had only been 'a sorter out and placer of the principal matters', after the book was finished:

Wherein when I found the Pope's authority highly advanced, and with strong arguments mightily defended, I said unto his

---

[1] *Works*, 1557, p. 86. The full penalty was not inflicted.

Grace: 'I must put your Highness in remembrance of one thing, and that is this. The Pope, as your Grace knoweth, is a prince as you are, and in league with all other Christian princes. It may hereafter so fall out that your Grace and he may vary upon some points of the league, whereupon may grow breach of amity and war between you both. I think it best therefore that that place be amended, and his authority more slenderly touched.'

'Nay,' quoth his Grace, 'that shall it not. We are so much bounden unto the See of Rome that we cannot do too much honour unto it.'

Then did I further put him in remembrance of the statute of *Praemunire*, whereby a good part of the Pope's pastoral cure here was pared away.

To that answered his Highness: 'Whatsoever impediment be to the contrary, we will set forth that authority to the uttermost. For we received from that See our crown imperial'; which, till his Grace with his own mouth told it me, I never heard of before.[1]

This is the story as Roper gives it – and it is so crucial to an understanding of More that it is fortunate that we have confirmation of it, in all its essential points, from More's own pen. Writing to Cromwell concerning the King's Book and the supremacy of the Papal See, More says:

I was myself sometime not of the mind that the primacy of that See should be begun by the institution of God, until that I read in that matter those things that the King's Highness had written in his most famous book against the heresies of Martin Luther. At the first reading whereof I moved the King's Highness either to leave out that point or else to touch it more slenderly, for doubt of such things as after might hap to fall in question between his Highness and some Pope, as between princes and Popes divers times have done. Whereunto his Highness answered me that he would in no wise anything minish of that matter, of which thing his Highness showed me a secret cause, whereof I never had anything heard before.[2]

More's letter is guarded; it was written to be placed before

---

[1] ROPER, pp. 67-8.
[2] MS. Cotton Cleop. E. vi, fol. 149 etc.; printed from an earlier draft in *Works*, 1557, p. 1427.

Henry himself. But it is in entire agreement with Roper's fuller statement.

We have seen in the last chapter how grievous were the problems presented by the double position of the Pope – at once the head of Christendom, and the head of a small Italian state. On this, the words of a brilliant and saintly scholar of More's own Church may be quoted:

> Remember the Papacy More lived under. He lived under the worst of the Renaissance Popes; Alexander VI ruled and died within More's lifetime. That is to say, the Papacy he knew was not the Papacy that you and I know and reverence – great, purified, outstanding, spiritual. That is the marvel of his faith. That is where so much of his exquisite discernment shews up against his time when the rest of the world went astray. He died for a Papacy that, as far as men could see, was little else than a small Italian princedom ruled by some of the least reputable of the Renaissance princes.[1]

The essential thing is that More warned Henry against committing himself too much to the Italian ruler who is 'a prince as you are'; and that also he gave his life for the spiritual primacy. In this, as in almost everything else, Henry VIII is the exact antithesis of More; Henry devoted the first half of his reign to promoting the interests of the 'small Italian princedom', and the second to destroying the spiritual primacy.

To More the way in which men abuse a great principle never invalidates that principle itself.

More did not arrive at his conviction without long and careful thought. Writing to Cromwell in 1534, he said he had given seven years' study to the subject, and then altered the word to 'ten' in his final copy.[2] He places the King's Book among the authorities which have led him to his decision; but here Thomas More the courtier is speaking, and also Thomas More the lawyer, adroitly manœuvring his Grace into an awkward corner. How More first came to give earnest thought to the subject we know from the Italian merchant and scholar Antonio Bonvisi, More's friend for forty years, 'the apple of his eye'.[3] Bonvisi's precious recollections of More are otherwise lost.

---

[1] The late FATHER BEDE JARRETT in *The Fame of Blessed Thomas More*, p. 113.
[2] MS. Cotton Cleop. E. vi.   [3] *Works*, 1557, p. 1457.

But Cardinal Pole preserved this one.[1] More was discussing with Bonvisi the growth of heresy, and said that his chief anxiety was over 'perverse opinion touching the sacrament of the altar'. Attacks on the Papal supremacy seemed to him of less moment, because he thought that supremacy a mere human ordinance, 'for the more quietness of the ecclesiastical body'. 'This was his sudden and first answer.' But More immediately admitted that he had spoken unadvisedly, and asked Bonvisi to call again within ten or twelve days. Bonvisi did so, and More then 'brake out into a great reproach of his own self. "Alas, Mr. Bonvisi! whither was I falling, when I made you that answer of the primacy of the Church? I assure you, that opinion alone was enough to make me fall from the rest, for that holdeth up all".' And then, says Cardinal Pole, 'he began to shew him what he had read and studied therein, which was so fixed in his heart that for the defence of the same he willingly afterward suffered death; overcoming all Satan's temptation by the light supernatural, and by a supernatural love that the mercy of God had given him for his salvation'.

But for years after writing the King's Book, Henry was to remain firm in his Papal policy, and heedless of More's counsels of moderation. Even after he had reigned for eighteen years it was still true that

> No monarch since Saint Lewis had stood so high in the confidence and the gratitude of the Church. He had varied his alliances between Austria, France, and Spain; but during four warlike pontificates Rome had always found him at its side. He had stood with Julius against Maximilian and Lewis, with Leo against Francis, with Clement against Charles.[2]

Our story has now reached the time when Henry stood with Leo X against Francis. Leo had been applauded by Erasmus as the pacificator of Europe; 'at your instigation', he said, 'did Henry of England lay down the arms which at the instigation of Pope Julius he took up'.[3] But, whilst Henry was preparing the King's Book to present to him, the policy of Leo was changing until 'for reasons which are even now by no means clear, the

[1] STRYPE, *Ecclesiastical Memorials*, 1822, Vol. III, Pt. ii, pp. 491-3.
[2] ACTON, *Historical Essays and Studies*, 1907, p. 27.
[3] 21 May, 1515, ALLEN, II, No. 335.

Pope signalised the last year of his life by abetting Charles V
in his natural ambition to drive the French from Milan, and
convincing the English government that it had "no other choice
but to conclude an alliance with the Emperor".'[1]

The hope of the humanists for a peaceful reformation
vanished. Never again shall we find Erasmus speaking of a
Golden Age.

§ 5 .   THE UNDER-TREASURER

Whilst the war clouds were gathering, but before the storm
had broken, on 2 May 1521, More was appointed to the
responsible post of the Under-Treasurership;[2] the Duke of
Norfolk was Treasurer. The post carried the large salary of
£173 6s. 8d., and the King, Erasmus tells us, might have saved
this money, for there was a competitor who was willing to
serve without pay. Yet More, who had not asked for the post,
was appointed, and, we learn from Erasmus' letter, knighted
also. The office, Erasmus says, is both honourable and pleasant,
as it does not involve too much work.[3] But we hear, in Wolsey's
letters, of More being detained at the Exchequer for four or
five days 'for such great matters, as at the knitting up of this
term be requisite to be ordered';[4] and More's friend Tunstall
dedicated to him his book on arithmetic; it could not be
dedicated to anybody more appropriately, he said, than to
one altogether occupied in calculation in the royal treasury.

But arithmetic was not to occupy all More's time. The King
had commanded his secretary Pace to write to Wolsey, that
'Whereas old men do now decay greatly within this his realm,
his mind is to acquaint other young men with his great affairs,
and therefore he desireth your Grace to make Sir William
Sandys and Sir Thomas More privy to all such matters as your
Grace shall treat at Calais'.[5]

Next year, in May 1522, the Emperor Charles and his lords
visited England on the way to Spain, and were duly impressed by the English navy, and especially by the weight of
the guns mounted on the ships: 'they said they never saw ships

[1] POLLARD, *Wolsey*, p. 122.   [2] ROUTH, *Sir Thomas More*, p. 107.
[3] 11 June, 12 Aug., Sept., 1521, ALLEN, IV, Nos. 1210, 1223, 1233.
    [4] *State Papers*, I, p. 146.   [5] Ibid., I, p. 20.

so armed'.[1] Sixty-six years later Spaniards were to see from
afar the fellows of these heavy guns. But now all was preparation for the joint attack upon France. Clarencieux herald was
sent to Lyons to defy the French King. We hear of More also
at intervals in connection with it all: busy in the City seeing to
the interning of French enemy aliens[2] (some escaped by speaking Dutch and saying that they were Flemings). When the
King and the Emperor visited the City with their retinues,
More made an eloquent oration 'in the praise of the two princes,
and of the peace and love between them, and what comfort it
was to their subjects to see them in such amity, and how that
the Mayor and citizens offered any pleasure of service that in
them lay, next their sovereign lord'. So says the Chronicler,[3]
and the City records give an interesting sidelight.[4] 'It is agreed
that Sir Thomas More, Under-Treasurer of England, for his
labour and pain that he took for the City in making of a
preposition at the coming and receiving of the Emperor's Grace
into this City, shall have towards a gown of velvet £10' – say
£150 of our money; it would seem that the kind of velvet gown
in which emperors were addressed was expensive. From time
to time More was in attendance on the King; carrying to him
Wolsey's letters, and writing the King's instructions back to
Wolsey. It sometimes requires timely badgering to get the
business through. More is instructed that he 'should diligently
solicit the expedition'. But he can only get from his Grace a
laugh and 'Nay, by my soul that will not be, I will read the
·remnant at night'. At night More manages to get some letters
signed, 'putting over all the remnant till the morning'. Meantime Surrey the Lord Admiral (soon to be Duke of Norfolk) is
burning and harrying France, but gaining no military
advantage whatever. The King reads his dispatches to the
Queen in More's presence, and fatuously hopes that King
Francis will have to make way for him on the French throne,
as Richard III had made way for his father on the English
throne. In reporting which to Wolsey, More makes the
comment: 'I pray God, if it be good for his Grace, and for this

[1] HALL's *Chronicle*, ed. WHIBLEY, I, p. 245.
[2] 9 May 1522, Repertory of the Court of Aldermen, IV, fol. 118; V, fol. 285.
[3] HALL's *Chronicle*, ed. WHIBLEY, I, p. 250.
[4] 18 Nov. 1522, Repertory of the Court of Aldermen, IV, fol. 134b.

realm, that then it may prove so, and else, in the stead thereof I pray God send his Grace an honourable and profitable peace.'[1] The war was only just beginning, and it must have required very great courage to utter an opinion like this. We have seen that More had already expressed in *Utopia* what he thought of the historic English claim to the throne of France.

It is now, when More is in the way of fortune, with his Under-Treasurership and his knighthood, that he writes the grimmest of all his books: *The Four Last Things*.

There is so much of Plato in Christian teaching that it is often difficult to say whether certain ideas have reached More from his Greek reading or his orthodox Catholic training. But here they are in combination. Socrates and the Church agree that the true business of life is meditation upon death:

> For some of the old famous philosophers, when they were demanded what faculty philosophy was, answered that it was the meditation or exercise of death. For like as death maketh a severance of the body and the soul, when they by course of nature must needs depart asunder, so (said they) doth the study of philosophy labour to sever the soul from the love and affections of the body while they be together. Now if this be the whole study and labour of philosophy, as the best philosopher said that it is, then may we within short time be well learned in philosophy.[2]

To More, as to Hamlet, the whole world is a prison. And he is a prisoner waiting till the summons comes to execution:

> For if ye took the matter aright, the place a prison, yourself a prisoner condemned to death, from which ye cannot escape, ye would reckon this gear as worshipful as if a gentleman thief, when he should go to Tyburn, would leave for a memorial the arms of his ancestors painted on a post in Newgate. Surely, I suppose that (if we took not true figure for a fantasy, but reckoned it as it is indeed, the very express fashion and manner of all our estate) men would bear themselves not much higher in their hearts for any rule or authority that they bear in this world, which they may well perceive to be indeed no better but one prisoner bearing a rule among the remnant, as the tapster doth in the Marshalsea; or at the

---

[1] *State Papers*, I, p. 110, etc.   [2] *Works*, 1557, p. 77

uttermost, one so put in trust with the gaoler that he is half
an under-gaoler over his fellows, till the sheriff and the cart
come for him.[1]

§ 6. MORE AS SPEAKER

More's dislike of war must have been strengthened by the
fact that, as Under-Treasurer, he had such responsibilities for
the finance of the realm. No Chancellor of the Exchequer is
likely to favour war. But supplies had to be found, and so a
Parliament was called. It was the only one which sat during
Wolsey's fourteen-years of power, and it did not sit for very long.

On 15 April 1523, at the Blackfriars in London, Parliament
was opened by the King in state, with Wolsey and Warham
seated at his feet. More's friend Tunstall made an eloquent
oration, explaining that the King had called the Parliament 'for
making and ordering of new statutes which may be to the high
advancement of the Commonwealth; wherefore he willed the
Commons to repair to the Common House, and there to elect
them a Speaker, or their Common Mouth'. But, says the
Chronicler[2] cynically, despite this talk about statutes for the
advancement of the Commonwealth, no good act was made,
unless the grant of a great subsidy were one.

The duty of the Speaker was not merely to preside at the
debates of the Commons, but to be 'their Common Mouth'. To
be the Mouth of the Commons to the Monarch was indeed,
originally, his main function, and sometimes a difficult one.
(Henry's mighty daughter once asked Mr. Speaker Popham,
'What hath passed in the Commons House?', and he could only
answer, 'If it please your Majesty, seven weeks'.[3]) The
Commons, knowing that he would be an acceptable choice,
chose Sir Thomas More as Speaker, and presented him to the
King in the Parliament Chamber on the Saturday, 18 April.
'According to the old usage,' More 'disabled himself, both in
wit, learning, and discretion, to speak before the King.' The
oration in which he did so is, says Roper, 'not now extant'. But
from various sources we hear how More told the story (which
he got from Cicero) of the vainglorious lecturer Phormio.

---

[1] *Works*, p. 84.   [2] HALL's *Chronicle*, ed. WHIBLEY, I, p. 279.
[3] FRANCIS BACON's *Apophthegms*.

Phormio invited Hannibal to his lecture room, and then discoursed to him on the art of war, much to the disgust of the Carthaginian general, who protested: 'I never heard a more proud, arrogant fool, that durst take upon him to instruct the flower of chivalry in the feats of war.' So, said More, he also might fear rebuke, if he should speak before a King of such learning, wisdom, and experience, concerning the welding and ordering of a Commonwealth.

When the claims of tradition had been satisfied by More's petition to the King that the Commons might choose another Speaker, and Wolsey's reply on behalf of the King that the Commons could not have chosen a better man, More had then to make a second speech. This *is* extant. Roper must have found it among More's papers, and he gives it in full. It falls into two parts. The first is a personal request for the Speaker himself. If, in declaring anything to the King on behalf of the Commons, he should chance 'to pervert or impair their prudent instructions', he asks leave 'to repair again to the Commons House, and there to confer with them, and to take their substantial advice what thing and in what wise I shall on their behalf utter and speak before your noble Grace'. This was a request which had commonly been made by the Speaker in medieval times, and it served to transfer responsibility from him to the Commons, as well as to give the Commons opportunity of second thoughts, if their first message did not please the King. By medieval tradition this first request of the Speaker was followed by a second – that if the Commons (or if the Speaker on their behalf) should say anything not pleasing to the King, or infringe his prerogative, their offence should be pardoned, since it would not be intentional. This was a kind of apology in advance: somewhat parallel to the custom prevalent among certain savage tribes, that the subordinate, in addressing the paramount chief at a palaver, should begin by protesting that he is only talking in his sleep.

More's request on behalf of the Commons is, then, traditional; but it is nevertheless epoch-making. It is not so much a request that a member may be pardoned, if he inadvertently says anything displeasing to the King; it is rather an argument that debate cannot be properly conducted unless members are

free to speak, even though inadvertently they may say something displeasing. 'It is clear that More did not consider his
petition a petition of right: free speech is not yet a formal
privilege, we gather. Parliament is the King's court; he may be
displeased with what members say; and as discipline is his to
maintain, he may punish the too bold or too rash for their
speeches. But, More urges, to instil fear will prejudice the
King's business.'[1]

So More begins by a preamble: Forasmuch as there are a
great number of Commons assembled, and albeit there has been
due diligence used in sending up to Parliament the most
discreet, whereby it is not to be doubted but that there is a very
substantial assembly of right wise and politic persons; yet, since
among so many wise men every man is not equally wise; and
amongst many, equally wise, every man is not equally well
spoken, and as many 'boisterous and rude in language, see deep
indeed, and give right substantial counsel', and since in matters
of great importance the mind is often so occupied in the matter
that a man studieth what to say rather than how to say it, and
so it may happen to the wisest and best spoken man 'while his
mind is fervent in the matter' to speak in a way which he will
afterwards regret, though his good will is just as great while he is
speaking as afterwards while he is regretting, therefore –

But what follows is too important to be given in any words
except More's, verbatim. It is the first recorded plea for
freedom of speech in Parliament, as against an anticipatory
request for pardon. The plea may have been made before, but
here we have the very words recorded:

Therefore, most gracious Sovereign, considering that in your
High Court of Parliament is nothing intreated but matter of
weight and importance concerning your realm and your own
royal estate, it could not fail to let and put to silence from the
giving of their advice and counsel many of your discreet
Commons, to the great hindrance of the common affairs,
except that every of your Commons were utterly discharged
of all doubt and fear how any thing that it should happen

---

[1] J. E. NEALE, 'Free Speech in Parliament' in *Tudor Studies presented to A. F.
Pollard*, edited by R. W. SETON WATSON, p. 267. I am much indebted to Professor
Neale's article for what is written above as to the traditional freedom of speech
in Parliament, and the place of More's speech in that tradition.

them to speak should happen of your Highness to be taken . . .
It may therefore like your most abundant Grace, our most
benign and godly King, to give to all your Commons here
assembled your most gracious licence and pardon, freely,
without doubt of your dreadful displeasure, every man to
discharge his conscience, and boldly in everything incident
among us to declare his advice; and whatsoever happen any
man to say, that it may like your noble Majesty, of your
inestimable goodness, to take all in good part, interpreting
every man's words, how uncunningly soever they be couched,
to proceed yet of good zeal towards the profit of your realm
and honour of your royal person, the prosperous estate and
preservation whereof, most excellent sovereign, is the thing
which we all, your most humble loving subjects, according to
the most bounden duty of our natural allegiance, most
highly desire and pray for.[1]

Both More's petitions were duly granted, and the parliament began. On 29 April Wolsey came down to the Common
House, declared the reasons of the war with France, and
demanded 'no less than £800,000, to be raised of the fifth part
of every man's goods and lands, that is to say four shillings of
every pound'. Next day, 'Thomas More, being speaker,
declared all the Cardinal's oration again to the Commons, and
enforced his demand strongly, saying that of duty men ought
not to deny to pay four shillings of the pound. But for all that it
was denied'.[2] There were heated economic arguments. It was
urged that there was not in the realm the money that was
demanded; gentlemen had lands, merchants silk, wool, tin, or
cloth, husbandmen corn and cattle. If all money were brought
into the King's hands, men would have to live by bartering
cloth for victuals, and bread for cheese. A deputation from the
Commons waited on the Cardinal, to beg him to move the
King's Highness 'to be content with a more easier sum': 'to
the which he currishly answered that he would rather have his
tongue plucked out of his head with a pair of pinsons than to
move the King to take any less sum'. The news of these debates
began to spread outside Parliament, and the Cardinal complained 'that nothing was so soon done or spoken therein, but
that it was immediately blown abroad in every alehouse'. He

[1] ROPER, pp. 15-6.   [2] HALL's *Chronicle*, ed. WHIBLEY, I, pp. 284 etc.

also determined to come down again to the House, to urge the Commons to comply.

> Before whose coming, after long debating there, whether it were better but with a few of his lords (as the most opinion of the House was) or with his whole train royally to receive him there amongst them: 'Masters,' quoth Sir Thomas More, 'forasmuch as my Lord Cardinal lately, ye wot well, laid to our charge the lightness of our tongues for things uttered out of this House, it shall not in my mind be amiss with all his pomp to receive him, with his maces, his pillars, his pollaxes, his crosses, his hat, and Great Seal too; to the entent, if he find the like fault with us hereafter, we may be the bolder from ourselves to lay the blame on those that his Grace bringeth hither with him'; whereunto the House wholly agreeing, he was received accordingly.[1]

The Commons listened in silence to Wolsey; and Wolsey then went so far as to try and debate the matter with individual members. Wolsey's action was an attack on the privilege of the House. They were entitled to debate among themselves, and to reply through their Speaker. Wolsey demanded an immediate answer:

> 'Masters, you have many wise and learned men among you, and sith I am from the King's own person sent hither unto you for the preservation of yourselves and all the realm, I think it meet you give me some reasonable answer.' Whereat every man holding his peace, then began he to speak to one Master Marney (after Lord Marney): 'How say you,' quoth he, 'Master Marney?' Who making him no answer neither, he severally asked the same question of divers others, accounted the wisest of the company.
>
> To whom, when none of them all would give so much as one word, being before agreed, as the custom was, by their Speaker to make answer: 'Masters,' quoth the Cardinal, 'unless it be the manner of your House, as of likelihood it is, by the mouth of your Speaker, whom you have chosen for trusty and wise, as indeed he is, in such cases to utter your minds, here is without doubt a marvellous obstinate silence.'
>
> And thereupon he required answer of Master Speaker; who first reverently upon his knees excusing the silence of the house, abashed at the presence of so noble a personage,

[1] ROPER, p. 17.

able to amaze the wisest and best learned in a realm, and after by many probable arguments proving that for them to make answer was it neither expedient nor agreeable with the ancient liberty of the House, in conclusion for himself showed that though they had all with their voices trusted him, yet except every one of them could put into his one head all their several wits, he alone in so weighty a matter was unmeet to make his Grace answer.

Whereupon the Cardinal, displeased with Sir Thomas More, that had not in this Parliament in all things satisfied his desire, suddenly arose and departed.[1]

Wolsey had merely irritated the Commons: his argument that there was plenty of wealth in the country – sumptuous buildings, plate, rich apparel and fat feasts – seemed to his hearers 'as though he had disdained that any man should fare well, or be well clothed, but himself'.

The debates dragged on; amongst the papers of Thomas Cromwell is the draft of a speech against the war and the tax; whether Cromwell ever delivered the speech we cannot, of course, tell. But it is all excellent common sense. In discussing the policy of the invasion of France, Cromwell alludes to and adopts the apology of More's oration: 'In the reasoning of which matter I shall but utter my ignorance before Hannibal, as our right wise Speaker rehearsed now of late.' This is, so far as we know, the first contact between the two statesmen who were later to be brought into such marked opposition. Cromwell emphasizes the impossibility of attempting to 'recover again by the sword the realm of France, belonging to our most redoubted Sovereign by good and just title'. It would not be safe to advance in France leaving any strongholds behind, and in the last war the winning of Thérouanne 'cost his Highness more than twenty such ungracious dogholes could be worth unto him'. 'Supposed that Almighty God sent our Sovereign his desired purpose, how should we be able to possess the large country of France', when England has so few inhabitants? England has now no confederates or allies in France, as in the days of our earlier triumphs. Cromwell, like Machiavelli, is impressed with the French national spirit: 'there was never nation more

---

[1] ROPER, pp. 18-9.

marvellously linked together than they be amongst themselves'.

There were further disputes between the knights and gentry on the one hand, and the burgesses on the other, as to how the tax was to be paid. But 'at the last the Speaker called them all together, and after long persuading, and privy labouring of friends',[1] an agreement was reached. The upshot of it was explained by Cromwell, in a humorous letter to a friend:

> Ye shall understand that by long time I amongst other have endured a Parliament which continued by the space of seventeen whole weeks, where we communed of war, peace, strife, contention, debate, murmur, grudge, riches, poverty, penury, truth, falsehood, justice, equity, deceit, oppression, magnanimity, activity, force, attemperance, treason, murder, felony, counsel . . . and also how a commonwealth might be edified and also continued within our realm. Howbeit in conclusion we have done as our predecessors have been wont to do, that is to say, as well as we might, and left where we began.[2]

It is clear that More, whilst co-operating quite loyally with Wolsey in persuading the Commons to grant the unpopular subsidy, disliked his bullying methods. If Roper is to be believed, Wolsey still felt resentment against More:

> and after the Parliament ended, in his gallery at Whitehall in Westminster, uttered unto him his griefs, saying, 'Would to God you had been at Rome, Master More, when I made you Speaker'.

Now pilgrimages were one of More's enthusiasms. We are told that he used to go on pilgrimages to the shrines round about London, and always on foot, 'a thing', says Stapleton, 'which in England even the poorest are loath to do'.[3] Yet with all his enthusiasm he had never found time to see Rome. So he made the natural reply to Wolsey:

> 'Your Grace not offended, so would I too, my Lord,' quoth he. And to wind such quarrels out of the Cardinal's head, he began to talk of that gallery, and said, 'I like this gallery of yours, my Lord, much better than your gallery at Hampton

---

[1] HALL's *Chronicle*, ed. WHIBLEY, I, p. 288.
[2] MERRIMAN, *Life and Letters of Thomas Cromwell*, I, p. 313.
[3] STAPLETON, VI, p. 221.

Court.' Wherewith so wisely brake he off the Cardinal's displeasant talk that the Cardinal at that present (as it seemed) wist not what more to say to him.[1]

If Wolsey realized how much More disliked his arrogance, and if there was really the friction between them which Roper records, Wolsey certainly got over his annoyance in a way which does him credit. The letter which he wrote, 24 August 1523, immediately after the dissolution of Parliament, for More to present to Henry, is full of kindly feeling. It is extant in the Record Office in Wolsey's own handwriting:

> Sir. After my most humble recommendations. It may like your Grace to understand, I have shewed unto this bearer, Sir Thomas More, divers matters to be by him, on my behalf, declared unto your Highness, beseeching the same, that at convenient time it may be your pleasure to hear him make report thereof accordingly. And, Sir, whereas it hath been accustomed that the Speakers of the Parliaments, in consideration of their diligence and pains taken, have had, though the Parliament hath been right soon finished, above the £100 ordinary, a reward of £100, for the better maintenance of their household and other charges sustained in the same, I suppose, Sir, that the faithful diligence of the said Sir Thomas More, in all your causes treated in this your late Parliament, as well for your subsidy, right honourably passed, as otherwise considered, no man could better deserve the same than he hath done, wherefore, your pleasure known therein, I shall cause the same to be advanced unto him accordingly. Ascertaining your Grace that I am the rather moved to put your Highness in remembrance thereof, because he is not the most ready to speak and solicit his own cause.[2]

Two days later More writes to Wolsey:

> Furthermore it may like your good Grace to understand that at the contemplation of your Grace's letters the King's Highness is graciously content that beside the £100 for my fee for the office of the Speaker of his Parliament, to be taken at the receipt of his Exchequer, I shall have one other hundred pounds out of his coffers by the hands of the treasurer of his chamber, wherefore in most humble wise I

---

[1] ROPER, p. 19.   [2] Record Office, *L.P.*, III, No. 171.

beseech your good Grace that as your gracious favour hath obtained it for me, so it may like the same to write to Mr. Wiatt that he may deliver it to such as I shall send for it. Whereby I and all mine, as the manifold goodness of your Grace hath already bound us, shall be daily more and more bounden to pray for your Grace; whom our Lord long preserve in honour and health; at Esthamstede the 26th day of August,

    Your humble orator and most bounden beadman,
                                    Thomas More.[1]

There are many letters of More to Wolsey of about this date. They are official letters, in which More conveys the King's wishes; but more than once he takes the opportunity to express his gratitude to the Cardinal: 'Finally, that it liketh your good Grace so benignly to accept and take in worth my poor service, and so far above my merits to commend the same . . . I were, my good Lord, very blind if I perceived not, very unkind if ever I forgat, of what gracious favour it procedeth; which I can never otherwise re-answer than with my poor prayer, which during my life shall never fail to pray to God for the preservation of your good Grace in honour and health.'[2]

§ 7 . THE WINNING OF CASTLES IN FRANCE

It can hardly be that at this date there was any particular ill feeling between the Under-Treasurer and the Cardinal. But Wolsey's whole war-policy must have been hateful to a man who was only wishing for 'an honourable and profitable peace'. Less than a week before the letter above quoted, it had been More's duty to convey to Wolsey the King's wishes as to the conduct of the war in France. Suffolk wanted to conduct the war with humanity, but More was instructed to tell Wolsey that only the hope of plunder would keep the army together:

Finally, where the Duke adviseth that the King's army shall in the marching proclaim liberty, sparing the country from burning and spoil, the King's Highness thinketh, that sith

---

[1] MS. Cotton Titus B.1, fol. 331 [325]; cf. DELCOURT, *Essai sur la langue de Sir Thomas More*, pp. 328-9. Both letters are quoted in *State Papers*, and in the notes to HARPSFIELD's *Life*.

[2] 26 Sept. 1523, DELCOURT as above, p. 348. Compare the letter of 13 Sept. DELCOURT, p. 337.

his army shall march in hard weather, with many sore and grievous incommodities, if they should also forbear the profit of the spoil (the bare hope whereof, though they gat little, was great encouraging to them) they shall have evil will to march far forward, and their captains shall have much ado to keep them from crying, Home!, Home![1]

A few weeks later Wolsey wrote to Henry that never would there be 'like opportunity given hereafter for the attaining of France'.[2]

But Henry did not 'attain' France. All the burning and plundering led to nothing; the English army withdrew without any decisive action. Large areas of France had been devastated, but the wealth of England also had been exhausted. The war seemed like ending in stale-mate. In 1524 England did nothing. The allies, Henry and Charles, distrusted one another, and Henry was meditating a separate peace. Then suddenly, a decision came, in Italy. Francis, besieging Pavia, was caught between the garrison of the town and a relieving force. Though unpaid, starving, and in rags, the forces serving Charles were roused to enthusiasm by their leaders, and before dawn on 24 February 1525, the twenty-fifth birthday of the Emperor, they began to batter down the high wall round the French headquarters. In the rout that followed 'a whole generation of French paladins was swept away'. All the French artillery, and the captured King Francis himself, made such a birthday gift to the Emperor as few armies have ever been able to send to their king.

In a fortnight the news reached England, and ambassadors had to be sent to Spain to arrange for the complete ruin of France. And here Roper's narrative lands us in a difficulty. Roper tells us that Wolsey had been so dissatisfied with More's conduct as Speaker that he,

for revengement of his displeasure, counselled the King to send him ambassador into Spain ... Which when the King had broken to Sir Thomas More, and that he had declared unto his Grace how unfit a journey it was for him, the nature of the country and disposition of his complexion so disagreeing together, that he should never be likely to do his

[1] 20 Sept. 1523, DELCOURT, as above, p. 343.   [2] *State Papers*, I, p. 143.

Grace acceptable service there, knowing right well that if his Grace sent him thither, he should send him to his grave; but showing himself nevertheless ready, according to his duty, all were it with the loss of his life, to fulfil his Grace's pleasure in that behalf; the King, allowing well his answer, said unto him, 'It is not our meaning, master More, to do you hurt, but to do you good would we be glad; we will therefore for this purpose devise upon some other, and employ your service otherwise.'[1]

It is highly probable that Wolsey wished to send More as ambassador to Spain, when his business as Speaker was concluded. Sir Thomas Boleyn had just been recalled, and it was no doubt desirable to send a competent man to assist Richard Sampson at the Spanish court. More had been Sampson's colleague before, and might seem to be an obvious choice. But, also, it was a well known trick of Wolsey's to send on foreign embassies rivals whose power he feared.[2] And we know from Erasmus that Wolsey was none too friendly to More, because he feared him more than he loved him.[3]

But now that Henry was contemplating a joint attack upon France, it was urgently necessary to re-establish close communications with Charles. If More did not wish to go, the other obvious person was Tunstall, and so he was sent, together with Sir Richard Wingfield, Chancellor of the Duchy of Lancaster. So great was their haste that, after landing in Spain, they rode all day, 'which here no man useth this hot time of year', and arrived at Toledo thoroughly knocked up. How they fared then is reported in a letter from Tunstall from Toledo, 10 Aug. 1525:

Please it your Grace to understand that it hath pleased Almighty God to call Mr Wingfield out of this present life. The manner and form of whose death shall appear unto you by the King's letter which shall come to your knowledge. Wherefore I shall not need to repeat it. He hath written a letter unto your Grace commending unto the same his wife and his children, which greatly ran in his mind in his sickness . . . His sickness had well nigh overthrown me also, for lack of rest and sleep, when he drew nigh to his end . . . My

---

[1] ROPER, pp. 19-20.   [2] TYNDALE, *Works*, 1572, p. 368.
[3] *Epistolarum Opus*, Basel, 1538, p. 1071.

companion Mr Sampson, the morrow after his death, fell into a fever and is not yet well recovered. I was, not long before Mr Wingfield's sickness, brought so low by a flux that my legs began to fail me. And my stomach and strength was gone. If the fever had come, as oft it followeth that disease, surely I had not escaped; but lovyd [i.e. praised] be God, now I am better, and Mr Sampson past the worst.[1]

I think we may find, in the ill luck which happened to overtake the legation, the explanation of the revengeful purpose which Roper attributed to the Cardinal. We can imagine that, after the news reached Chelsea, More may have said, 'Now I see, son Roper, why my Lord Cardinal wished to send *me*'. More's jest could never be easily distinguished from his earnest. And Roper was a serious young man.

The embassy to Charles had no success; Charles was not going to invade France in order to restore to Henry VIII the provinces conquered by Edward III and Henry V. And even if he had been so foolish, Henry was not in a position to carry out his part of the campaign. Wolsey's attempt to raise supplies for an invasion of France failed utterly. The Cardinal proposed an enormous capital levy of one-sixth on the goods of the laity and one-third on those of the clergy, with a tax on incomes of the same amount. This was the so-called 'amicable grant', 'perhaps the most violent financial exaction in English history',[2] to be raised, without any parliamentary sanction, on secret instructions from Wolsey to his Commissioners.

An upheaval resulted, the seriousness of which even so loyal a king-worshipper as Edward Hall does not minimize:

All people cursed the Cardinal, and his coadherents, as subversor of the laws and liberty of England. For they said, if men should give their goods by a Commission, then were it worse than the taxes of France, and so England should be bond and not free ... Thus was the muttering through all the realm, with curses and weepings that pity it was to behold.[3]

There were not only curses and weepings; there was open rebellion everywhere. In justice to More, it is necessary to

---

[1] MS. Cotton Vespasian C. iii, fols. 82-4.   [2] POLLARD, *Wolsey*, p. 142.
[3] HALL's *Chronicle*, ed. WHIBLEY, II, pp. 36-7.

note how far his friendly words to Wolsey belong to the period before the Cardinal's worst outrages.

There is abundant evidence of what the feeling of England was. The Archbishop of Canterbury was Chief Commissioner for raising the money in Kent – and this is part of his report to Wolsey:

> It hath been showed me in secret manner of my friends that the people sore grudgeth and murmureth, and speaketh cursedly among themselves, as far as they dare.

People were saying they would never have rest from payments 'so long as *some* liveth' (that is, as long as Wolsey remained alive)

> and that they had liever die than to be thus continually handled; reckoning themselves, their children, their wives, as desperates, and not greatly caring what they do, or what become of them.

People were impugning the whole policy of the war with France, and (what fifteen years ago would have seemed impossible) comparisons were being drawn between Henry and his father, in the father's favour. The Archbishop continues:

> I have heard say, moreover, that where the people be commanded to make fires and tokens of joy, for the taking of the French King, divers of them have spoken that they have more cause to weep than to rejoice thereat. And divers (as it hath been showed me secretly) have wished openly that the French King were at his liberty again, so as there were a good peace, and the King's Grace should not attempt to win France. The winning whereof should be more chargeful to England than profitable: and the keeping thereof much more chargeful than the winning. Also it hath been told me secretly that divers have recounted what infinite sums of money the King's Grace hath spent already invading France . . . and little or nothing hath prevailed: insomuch that the King's Grace at this hour hath not one foot of land more in France than his most noble father had, which lacked no riches or wisdom to win the kingdom of France if he had thought it expedient.[1]

It was probably about this time[2] that the King was an

---

[1] ELLIS, *Letters*, Series III, Vol. I, p. 374.   [2] See HARPSFIELD, Note to p. 24.

unexpected guest at dinner at Chelsea, and after dinner walked for an hour in the garden with his arm round More's neck, much to Roper's delight:

> As soon as his Grace was gone, I, rejoicing thereat, told Sir Thomas More how happy he was, whom the King had so familiarly entertained, as I never had seen him to do to any other except Cardinal Wolsey, whom I saw his Grace once walk with, arm in arm. 'I thank our Lord, son,' quoth he, 'I find his Grace my very good lord indeed, and I believe he doth as singularly favour me as any subject within this realm. Howbeit, son Roper, I may tell thee I have no cause to be proud thereof, for if my head could win him a castle in France (for then was there war between us) it should not fail to go.'[1]

More, one cannot but think, must have been deeply moved to have allowed himself to speak so plainly even to his trusted Roper. Had Henry been trying to persuade his Under-Treasurer as to the possibility of financing the war which was to win him, not merely a castle in France, but the whole realm?

Some historians are confident that Henry cannot have been so foolish as to hope to partition and rule France, 'a martial realm marvellously linked together', the population of which has been estimated at four or five times that of Henry's England. Yet the words of all his leading statesmen, Wolsey, Warham, Cromwell, More,[2] point to their regarding the ambition as serious, at any rate at times. All save Wolsey deprecate it.

More in *Utopia* was not voicing an isolated protest against such wars of conquest, but a feeling which was obviously widespread, at home and abroad. The feeling was shared by More's fellow-humanist Vives, who wrote to Henry[3] from Oxford hoping that Charles and he would make a moderate use of their victory, and not devastate the most flourishing realm of Christendom, or pluck out one of the eyes of Europe. It was not the fault of his people, said Vives, if Francis had made war, against the will of all his council.

But England was in no position to win any castles in France. There remained nothing but to make peace, and to complain

---

[1] ROPER, pp. 20-1.   [2] See above pp. 199, 205, 209, 212.
[3] Vives' letter, No. 3 in *Epistolae Erasmi, Melancthonis, Mori et Vivis*, London, 1642.

that Charles was aspiring to universal monarchy. More was concerned in the negotiation of a truce in August 1525, and with the subsequent treaties.[1] The French were, as usual, expected to pay heavy sums to Henry and Wolsey, and smaller pensions to leading councillors, as the price of English friendship. A small pension of 150 crowns was granted to More.

'Wolsey's unpopularity dates from the pressure of taxation owing to the French War, and the failure to reap any apparent return even from the total defeat and capture of Francis at Pavia.' But unpopularity was to develop rapidly 'when Wolsey's peace with France appeared a mere prelude to war with Charles V'.[2] That time, however, was not yet.

The death of Sir Richard Wingfield, on the embassy from which More had succeeded in excusing himself, left vacant the two important posts of Chancellor of the Duchy of Lancaster, and High Steward of the University of Cambridge, in both of which More succeeded the victim of diplomatic hustling.

The Duchy of Lancaster had its separate administration, carried on from Westminster, and controlling possessions which might be outside the boundaries of the county. More resigned his Under-Treasurership soon after this appointment,[3] but he remained in constant personal attendance on the King. The ordinances made at Eltham about this time provide for the establishment of a Council of twenty members, 'Sir Thomas More, Chancellor of the Duchy', being one. But since many of the Council were often absent from the Court for 'reasonable impediments', ten of the Council, including More, are named for 'continual attendance'. But because some of these may also be absent for 'some reasonable cause', a residuum of four is named (Sir Thomas More again being one) who shall, 'or two of them at the least, always be present, except the King's Grace give licence to any of them to the contrary'. They are to be in the King's dining chamber, or other appointed Council chamber, 'in the forenoon by ten of the clock at the furthest, and at afternoon by two of the clock', in case the King wish to

---

[1] *L.P.*, IV, Nos. 1570, 1600, 2382, 3619; RYMER, XIV, pp. 48, 185.

[2] POLLARD, *Wolsey*, p. 220.

[3] Chancellor of the Duchy, July 1525; resigned Under-Treasurership, Jan. 1526.

confer with them, and also 'for hearing and direction of poor men's complaints and matters of justice'.[1]

For a little more than four years More had the experience of being Chancellor of the Duchy of Lancaster, before he was called to be Lord Chancellor. But very little which interests us to-day is recorded of the business which came before him in the Duchy Court.[2]

§ 8.   MORE'S SCHOLAR-FRIENDS

More had been appointed High Steward of the University of Oxford a year before Wingfield's death led to his also being appointed High Steward of the University of Cambridge. His High Stewardships involved him in important duties, trying persons accused of crimes in those two very unruly universities. But there were other more pleasant occasions, and Roper refers to the great resort of learned men to More. More had been trained in the disputation of the Schools, and availed himself of these opportunities for discussion; but Roper assures us that he did not press his logical tournaments *à l'outrance.* When he found that his donnish visitors 'could not, without some inconvenience, hold out much further disputation against him', then, rather than 'discourage students in their studies', he would 'by some witty device courteously break off into some other matter, and give over'. When the King visited Oxford or Cambridge in his progresses, More had to answer extempore to the eloquent and loyal orations of the universities, and he missed no chance of attending and joining in the official 'readings and disputations'.[3] His services to Oxford varied from those of Sanitary Inspector in time of plague,[4] to the defence of Erasmus and Greek against preachers who attacked both.

More's relations with Bishop Fisher had always been cordial. Fisher had been Vice-Chancellor of Cambridge since 1501, when he was thirty-two (an early age for Vice-Chancellors), and Chancellor since 1504. Fisher wrote to congratulate More when he was called to Court, and again when he was knighted;

[1] Bodleian, MS. Laud 597, fol. 31b.; see also POLLARD in *English Historica Review*, XXXVII, p. 359.
[2] See H. FISHWICK, *Pleadings and Depositions in the Duchy Court of Lancaster,* 1896.
[3] ROPER, pp. 21-2.   [4] *L.P.,* II, No. 4125.

Cambridge had few friends at Court, Fisher said, and of these they reckoned More the chief. But, albeit Fisher was to be so closely associated with More in his death, More's closest associate in life was Cuthbert Tunstall, a fellow-humanist whose praises More delights to sing. One of the many pleasant episodes of their friendship is More's letter to Tunstall thanking him for the gift of a fly preserved in amber. Tunstall lacked More's imaginative genius and his iron resolution; as a scholar and diplomatist he may well have been More's superior, and Henry paid him the compliment of fearing his opposition. But Tunstall's opposition could be undermined (as More warned him).[1] Unwillingly he obeyed Henry, and lived to have a chequered career under Henry's children. But he refused to bow to Elizabeth, as he had bowed to her father, and died in the kindly charge of Archbishop Parker at Lambeth. Tunstall was a gentle soul who had no more desire to make martyrs than to be one. As Bishop of London, he would not burn the persons of heretics, but preferred to buy and burn Tyndale's translation of the New Testament; not, of course, from any objection to an English translation as such, but because Tyndale's version was unauthorized, and was considered tendentious and heretical. It was bad policy, for the purchase-money ultimately reached Tyndale, and helped him to carry on his propaganda. More was cross-questioning a heretic in London as to who was financing Tyndale and the other heretics abroad, and got the reply: ' "Marry, it is the Bishop of London that hath holpen us, for he hath bestowed among us a great deal of money in New Testaments to burn them, and that hath been and yet is our only succour and comfort." "Now, by my troth," said More, "I think even the same; and I said so much to the Bishop, when he went about to buy them." '[2]

The record of their friendship remains in the books they wrote before they were both absorbed by the King's business, and Tunstall also by the cares, first of the bishopric of London, and then of that of Durham. Tunstall's farewell to the sciences was the book on arithmetic, which he published just before his consecration as bishop, and which he dedicated to the Under-Treasurer, Thomas More. A critic, not accustomed to over-

[1] See below, p. 293.   [2] HALL's *Chronicle*, ed. WHIBLEY, II, p. 162.

praise, has said, 'For plain common sense, well expressed, and learning most visible in the habits it had formed, Tunstall's book has been rarely surpassed, and never in the subject of which it treats'.[1]

Of the humanists abroad who were More's friends, three call for special mention: Budé, Vives and Cranevelt.

More's younger friend, Thomas Lupset, printed the second edition of *Utopia* in Paris without his permission. (It was a characteristic act of indiscretion; Lupset was an impetuous young man, and More had to plead Lupset's cause with Erasmus, when his young admirer was not sufficiently careful over the secret of *Julius Excluded*.) Budé, who did not at that time know More personally, contributed an introductory letter in praise of *Utopia* and of More. Later they met face to face when in attendance on their kings at the Field of Cloth of Gold, and continued to correspond afterwards. More presented Budé with English dogs; he passed them on to his friends.[2]

A much closer friendship was that with John Louis Vives, a Spaniard, some fourteen years More's junior. After More had published *Utopia*, the three names familiar among scholars throughout Europe were those of Erasmus the Netherlander, Budé the Frenchman, More the Englishman. But, as More became absorbed in the King's business, 'lost to us and learning' as Erasmus put it, Vives took the place which More might have occupied, as third in the great triumvirate of scholarship. Never does More betray the slightest touch of jealousy or disappointment, at seeing himself outstripped by one so much his junior.

Vives is closely parallel to More in many ways – in his care for education, and especially for the education of women; in his determination that something ought to be done to grapple systematically with the problem of poverty, in his devotion to Queen Catherine.

Vives, like Erasmus, serves to remind us that the career of More cannot be understood save in connection with the circle of humanists of which he was the best-beloved member. It was not their fault if their hopes for a rule of reason, learning, moderation and mercy were frustrated.

[1] A. DE MORGAN, *Arithmetical Books*, 1847, p. 13.   [2] *L.P.*, III, No. 413.

> Even so the gods, whose seeing mind
> Is not as ours, ordained.

It is to John Harris, More's secretary, that we owe the preservation of the text of many of the letters between More and his fellow humanists; the text only, because the actual copies, frail already when the widow of John Harris handed them over to Stapleton, have mostly disappeared. This is not the case, however, with More's correspondence with Cranevelt. Cranevelt had been introduced to More by Erasmus in Bruges in 1520, when More met Erasmus there in the train of Charles V.[1] More, the connoisseur, had delighted Cranevelt by the gift of a gold coin of Tiberius, and a silver one of Augustus, and a gold ring with an English posy for his wife. Cranevelt kept carefully the letters he received from his learned friends, and his son in due time supplied to Stapleton copies of two letters from More. A little more than twenty years ago, two bundles of letters to Cranevelt were discovered in an attic. Rats and mice had gnawed them; water had dripped on them and filtered right through both bundles. But three letters in More's handwriting, and two signed by him, but written by Harris, still remained. Professor Henry de Vocht, of Louvain, was preparing an edition, when in August 1914 the War broke out. He made the letters into a parcel, 'which', he says, 'in those uneasy days I hardly let go out of my sight'. He kept the parcel with him amid the fire-lit streets during the dreadful night of Aug. 25/26, and also when he was led away a prisoner two days later. 'I was only separated from it for a few hours at Tervueren, where I was held up by a company of soldiers stationed on the roadside; being at last released from suspense and anxiety, I was sent onward to the regiment, that had continued its way to Brussels. After some trouble and some palavering, I found my parcel in the bucket of the ammunition waggon where I had left it.' After fourteen years of strenuous labour at deciphering the almost undecipherable, de Vocht published his magnificent edition of Cranevelt's letters.[2] More would have rejoiced to think that once again Minerva had won through, in Mars' despite.

[1] ALLEN, IV, No. 1145.   [2] *Literae ad Franciscum Craneveldium*, Louvain, 1928.

§ 9 .   H A N S   H O L B E I N   V I S I T S   C H E L S E A

Hans Holbein, when probably barely eighteen, had begun to design the woodcuts which adorn books issued from Froben's press at Basel, including More's *Utopia.* He settled in Basel, and joined the Painters' Guild there. But, after seven years, patronage was failing, and Erasmus, who was also settled in Basel, gave him letters of introduction to friends in the north. To Peter Giles Erasmus writes: 'The bearer is the man who painted me; I will not trouble you with a testimonial, but he is a great man at his craft. The arts are freezing here, and he is on his way to England to scrape some angels together. If he wants to visit Quentin Metsys, and you are too busy to introduce him, send your servant to show him the house.'[1] It is pleasant to think of Holbein thus associated with the Flemish master who had painted the diptych of Giles and Erasmus for More nine years before.

Holbein reached England before Christmas. 'Your painter, dearest Erasmus', More writes, 'is a wonderful man; but I fear he won't find England as fruitful as he had hoped. Yet I will do my best to see that he does not find it absolutely barren.'[2] According to his early biographer, Holbein was More's guest at Chelsea. He painted the portrait of More which was long in the Huth collection. It is no credit to England that this portrait, 'immeasurably more beautiful than any reproduction of it', was allowed to go out of the country without a single word of protest. It was purchased by Mr. H. C. Frick of New York, and now looks down on all comers from the walls of that Palace of Art, the gift of which to the public of New York marks an epoch in the study of painting.

Holbein also painted Dame Alice and Margaret Roper – portraits which have been lost, but of which copies, almost contemporary, remain. Some think that the Dame Alice *is* Holbein's panel, though so painted over that the master's own handiwork is not now visible.

More also set Holbein to work on a Family Group. The study for this is reproduced here. The original, in Indian ink, is in the Basel Gallery. It is, perhaps, the family picture by Holbein which we know that More sent to Erasmus, and the

[1] 26 Aug. 1526, ALLEN, VI, No. 1740.   [2] 18 Dec. 1526, ALLEN, VI, No. 1770.

receipt of which Erasmus ecstatically acknowledges.[1] 'Oh that yet once more in life I might see those friends most dear to me!' 'Friends', he writes to Margaret Roper, 'to whom I owe a large portion of such fortune and fame as I have, and to none am more glad to owe it. I recognized all, but none more than you. I saw shining through its beautiful dwelling your yet more beautiful soul.' On the drawing the names and ages are written in Latin, in what I believe to be More's own hand-writing. From left to right, they run: 'Elizabeth Dauncey, Thomas More's daughter, in her 21st year – Margaret Gigs, Clement's wife, fellow student and kinswoman of More's daughters, in her 22nd year – John More, the father, in his 76th year – Anne Grisacre, betrothed to John More, in her 15th year – Thomas More in his 50th year – John More, son of Thomas, in his 19th year – Henry Patenson, Thomas More's fool, in his 40th year – Cecily Heron, Thomas More's daughter, in her 20th year – Margaret Roper, Thomas More's daughter, in her 22nd year – Alice, Thomas More's wife, in her 57th year.' Thomas More entered his fiftieth year[2] on 6 Feb. 1527, and Anne Grisacre or Cresacre had passed out of her fifteenth year by 22 April 1527, so we can date the notes Feb.–April, 1527.

Studies of the heads of Elizabeth Dauncey, Margaret Gigs, Sir John More, Anne Cresacre, Thomas More, John More and Cecily Heron were made by Holbein, and are now in the Royal Library, Windsor.

The little town of Basel watched its citizenship carefully, and Holbein had been given only two years' leave of absence. He had been kept busy in England among More's friends; he painted the magnificent portraits of Archbishop Warham, Nicholas Kratzer, Sir Henry and Lady Guildford, and many others, including probably Sir Thomas and Lady Elyot, besides decorating a banqueting house at Greenwich for Henry VIII. It is possible that the More Family Group had been left unfinished when, in August 1528, Holbein was back in Basel, buying a house with some of the money he had earned in

---

[1] 3 Sept., 6 Sept. 1529; ALLEN, VIII, Nos. 2211, 2212. The interval of more than a year since Holbein's return to Basel is unexplained.

[2] See above, p. 49.   Those who believe that More was born 7 Feb. 1477 will have to date these notes before 7 Feb. 1527.

England. Certain it is that the large canvas of the group (which was long in the possession of the Ropers at Well Hall, and then passed by marriage to Nostell Priory, near Wakefield) is signed, not by Holbein, but by 'Richardus Locky', and dated 1530. Did Locky copy a Holbein canvas now lost, or did he paint over a canvas which Holbein had only begun?[1]

On the Basel study, Holbein notes that Dame Alice is to sit, instead of kneeling. In the Nostell Priory painting she is seated. There are other changes, indicated in Holbein's sketches, and carried out in the Nostell Priory painting. Further, the figure of John Harris, More's secretary, is introduced near the door. But – a cause of much subsequent confusion – despite the Nostell Priory painting being dated 1530, the names and ages are given as they were written into the Basel sketch early in 1527.

John More's descendants possessed two copies of the Group. One, which was kept at their house at Barnborough in Yorkshire, is now in the hands of their representatives, the Eystons of East Hendred in Berkshire. At some date it was cut down to fit a panel, and Lady Alice and the monkey were sacrificed. In 1593 another copy was made, for the family home at Gobions in Hertfordshire.[2] In this copy the figures were rearranged, and those who did not possess More kindred or affinity were summarily ejected. Margaret Gigs, Harris, Patenson, Lady Alice and the monkey all had to go. Room was thus found for Thomas More, John More's son, the Elizabethan recusant who spent his time in and out of prison, for his wife, his eldest son John More and his youngest son Christopher Cresacre More. The painting is therefore a composite group of five generations, seven in Early Tudor, and four in Later Tudor costume. The newcomers are dated 1593, and their ages given accordingly. The original figures are dated 1530, but it was realized that the traditional ages did not quite fit that date. Two years were therefore added to the ages of most of the members of the family, which still left them a year younger than they really were in 1530. But More was described as 50 years of age in 1530; he really was in his 50th year in 1527.

[1] See A. B. CHAMBERLAIN, *Hans Holbein the Younger*, 1913; M. W. Brockwell, *Catalogue of the Pictures at Nostell Priory*, 1915.
[2] This painting, long at Burford Priory, is now (April, 1935) deposited in the National Portrait Gallery.

When Cresacre More came to write the life of his great-grandfather, he had, hanging in his house, this picture of himself, a charming youth of 21, among four generations of his ancestors. He accepted the age there attributed to Thomas More; he could indeed do little else, for Henry VIII had confiscated all the family papers. That is why he wrongly made More born in 1480.

But it is not only the ages of the family group which have been confused. Many portraits of other people have been wrongly described as Thomas More – Holbein's portrait of Sir Henry Wyat in the Louvre, for example, has always been traditionally, though absurdly, named Sir Thomas More. And to trace the progressive deterioration of the engraving of More's face would afford a complicated, though depressing, study. A very fine drawing of an unknown English lady, in the British Museum (Salting Collection) is constantly and confidently reproduced as 'Margaret Roper'. The face is much too old to be that of Margaret Roper at the time of Holbein's first visit; and we have no evidence that Holbein had any relation with the family of his old patron during his later sojourn in England. The expression is one of extraordinary nobility and sadness; but Margaret Roper was not the only sad and noble woman in the days of Henry VIII.

During this first visit to England Holbein probably painted a portrait of Bishop Fisher. But nothing has come down to us save three studies. One of these is now in the British Museum. Another, in the Royal Library at Windsor, is well known, and, though showing precisely the same pose, it gives the Bishop an even more frail and ascetic face. Fisher had yet seven or eight years of sickness, and many months of imprisonment, before he gave his life for resisting the King's will in 'his great matter'. We may well believe that on Tower Hill he appeared (as an eye-witness described him) 'a very image of death, and, as one might say, Death in a man's shape, and using a man's voice'.

§ 10. THE KING'S GREAT MATTER

Meantime, the Cardinal was playing his desperate game, which was to involve first him, and then More, in destruction.

The unwillingness of Charles V to share with Henry the fruits of his triumph had led to a complete change of front. The Cardinal's enemies believed that Wolsey had also a private motive for revenge upon Charles, who had not given the promised support to his claims to the Papacy. Anyway, the new policy now was that England and France, in alliance, should curb the over-great power of Charles. But Henry was married to Charles' aunt; so a divorce from the Spanish consort and a marriage to a French consort seemed to be indicated. And already in September 1526 there is an obscure reference, which has puzzled all the historians, to 'that blessed divorce'.[1] In March 1527 the Bishop of Tarbes arrived in London to negotiate perpetual peace with France and war upon Charles. Before Wolsey set out for France, to carry these negotiations further, the first steps were taken towards securing the 'Divorce'.

Into the complex question of Henry's marriage with Catherine it is fortunately not necessary for us to enter in any detail. But it is important to remember that at the time when the marriage of Henry to the wife of his deceased brother was first suggested, it was felt to be a very dubious matter. Although the Pope granted the necessary dispensation, there was still some feeling of uneasiness. Son after son was born to Catherine, but either they were still-born, or died immediately after birth. Early in Henry's reign political trouble arose between Henry and his father-in-law, accompanied by a growing friendship with France, and in 1514 Catherine's position had grown difficult.[2] But when Francis I came to the throne of France, jealousy led to an estrangement between England and France, and consequent friendship between England and Spain. Then in 1516 Princess Mary was born, and Henry's hopes revived. 'We are both young,' he said, 'if it was a daughter this time, by the grace of God the sons will follow.'[3] But the sons did not follow, and now by the year 1525 all hope had disappeared. It was natural that, as hostility to Spain and friendship with France grew once again, so the idea of a divorce should have grown also.

[1] *L.P.*, IV, No. 2482. Brewer (and Pollard) think this a reference to Catherine; Friedmann (p. 50) and others think not.
[2] *Venetian Calendar*, II, No. 479 (1 Sept. 1514).
[3] *Venetian Calendar*, II, No. 691 (24 Feb. 1516).

Henry's passionate desire for a male heir was natural and justified. The only precedent for a woman ruler in England, that of Matilda in the reign of Stephen, was not encouraging. If we wish to realize how men felt at the time, we must shut out rigidly from our minds all we know of the success of later English queens.

How far the divorce sprang of itself to Henry's mind, how far Wolsey instigated it, we shall never know. It was also stated that the French ambassador, the Bishop of Tarbes, had suggested doubts. But the extraordinary mortality among his children was in itself enough to suggest doubts to Henry. There must be some reason why one so pious and so orthodox, one who might reasonably be regarded as marked out for Divine favour, should suffer such calamities.

Henry had had an illegitimate son, by Elizabeth Blount, the sister of that Lord Mountjoy by whose invitation Erasmus had come to England, and it seems that his first idea, when it became clear that Catherine would never bear him a son to succeed him, was to legitimize the young Henry Fitzroy. More played his part in the elaborate ceremonial by which Fitzroy was first created Earl of Nottingham, then Duke of Richmond and Somerset.[1] More read the patent, as the King girded the young Duke with a sword. The boy was only some six years old, but shortly he was made Lord High Admiral of England, and then given two titles which Henry VIII himself had held when he was very young, those of Lord Warden of the Marches and Lord Lieutenant of Ireland.

But the growing hostility to Spain, and the fact that Henry had fallen in love with Anne Boleyn, combined to lead him to the more violent course of a repudiation of Catherine, and a re-marriage. There were contemporaries who saw in Anne Boleyn the source of all the woe, and made her solely responsible for the deaths of Fisher and of More. 'What laws have been enacted,' says Cavendish, 'what noble and ancient monasteries overthrown and defaced ... how many famous and notable clerks have suffered death, what charitable foundations were perverted from the relief of the poor unto profane uses ... if

---

[1] *L.P.*, IV, No. 1431. Later the King consulted More about the boy's education, IV, No. 5806.

eyes be not blind men may see, if ears be not stopped they may hear, and if pity be not exiled they may lament the sequel of this pernicious and inordinate carnal love. The plague whereof is not ceased (although this love lasted but a while).'[1]

Anne Boleyn's sister, Mary Boleyn, had already been Henry's mistress, and the King's 'inordinate carnal love' would, normally, have led to nothing very revolutionary. It was the abnormal circumstances which produced abnormal results. The quarrel with Spain might well encourage an ambitious woman in the belief that she could deprive Catherine, not merely of Henry's affections, but of her throne. And no mistress could satisfy Henry's desire for a legitimate heir. But, above and beyond everything else, was the conviction growing in the King's mind that by his union with Catherine he had committed a sin which no papal dispensation could excuse. It is true that he had contracted an affinity with Anne Boleyn, by his illicit relations with her sister, very similar to that which he was asserting that Catherine had contracted with him by marriage with his brother. At the very time that he was denying the power of the Pope to remove the one disability, he was seeking a papal dispensation to remove the other. But Henry's conscience was an intricate matter, and we must not deny its terrible power because we cannot follow its logic; he was 'unscrupulous, violent, and crafty, but justifying to himself, by his belief in himself, both unscrupulousness, violence, and craft'.[2] A man may, as Shakespeare says, make 'such a sinner of his memory to credit his own lie'.

So that we must not attribute any conscious insincerity to Henry when he instructed his ambassadors, if the Emperor should suggest that the divorce merely arose out of a political quarrel, to reply

that whereas the King for some years past had noticed in reading the Bible the severe penalty inflicted by God on those who married the relicts of their brothers, he began to be troubled in his conscience and to regard the sudden deaths of his male children as a Divine judgement. The more he studied the matter, the more clearly it appeared to him that

[1] *Life of Wolsey*, ed. ELLIS, pp. 105-6.
[2] STUBBS, *Lectures on Mediaeval and Modern History*, p. 290.

he had broken a Divine law. He then called to counsel men learned in pontifical law.[1]

Amongst the men 'learned in pontifical law' whom Henry began to consult in the early summer of 1527 were some of his bishops; apparently, also Sir Thomas More.

Proceedings began by a secret suit, in which Wolsey, as Papal Legate, and Warham, as Archbishop of Canterbury, cited the King to appear before them to answer to the charge of having lived in incest with his brother's widow for eighteen years. The suit had of course been really instigated by the King. He appeared in person, and then appointed a proctor to continue his defence, whilst the archbishops, on their side, began to consult bishops of known learning as to the lawfulness of the King's marriage. Fisher's answer has been preserved: the authorities differ, he says, but he himself sees no reason to think the marriage prohibited by Divine law; it is for the Pope to decide in ambiguous cases; the Pope has thought fit to dispense, and Fisher has no doubt that such dispensation is within his power.[2]

It was probably about this time that Henry first consulted More, and so began that struggle of wills which was not to cease till, eight years later, the heads of Fisher and More fell on Tower Hill.

A great historian[3] has asserted that More had defended divorce in *Utopia*, and that this had encouraged the King to suppose that More would not resist pressure on a subject on which he had already shown a favourable bias. It is the same strange assumption that meets us at every turn: the assumption that More 'defends' everything which he represents his Utopians as doing. There is something grotesque in the assumption that Henry, in his matrimonial troubles, would have consulted *Utopia* for consolation. Had he done so, he would have found small comfort therein. He would have found the Gordian knot of his marital entanglements severed in a most final way. For in *Utopia* the man who commits adultery twice is invariably punished with death. And it is indisputable that Henry had committed adultery at least twice.

[1] 1529, *L.P.*, IV, No. 5156.
[2] Record Office: *L.P.*, IV, No. 3148; Compare *State Papers*, I, p. 189.
[3] ACTON, *Historical Essays and Studies*, 1907, pp. 30, 31. See also below, p. 354.

Once again, it must be said that the Utopians are heathen philosophers, and, as such, guided solely by the light of reason. Their matrimonial ideas are therefore not binding upon Christian folk, but they are very interesting to us, as showing how More thought that enlightened and righteous heathen ought to behave. The Utopians are the only people in that part of the world who are content every man with one wife apiece: 'And matrimony is there never broken, but by death, except adultery break the bond, or else the intolerable wayward manners of either party.' But Henry never accused Catherine of either adultery or intolerable wayward manners; and since, in Utopia, a husband divorced from his wife by reason of his own intolerable wayward manners was never allowed to marry again, this Utopian regulation would have availed him little. It is true that, in Utopia, divorces are sometimes allowed for incompatibility, but only with the full consent of *both* parties, provided the Council, *and their wives* assent: 'Yea, and then also they be loth to consent to it, because they know this to be the nearest way to break love between man and wife – to be in easy hope of a new marriage.' But the Utopians will on no account allow a husband to put away an innocent wife against her will:

> But for the husband to put away his wife for no fault, but for that some mishap is fallen to her body – this by no means they will suffer. For they judge it a great point of cruelty that anybody in their most need of help and comfort should be cast off and forsaken, and that old age, which both bringeth sickness with it, and is a sickness itself, should unkindly and unfaithfully be dealt withal.[1]

Were it not that More had published *Utopia* ten years before the divorce question arose, the passage might almost be read as a reference to, and a condemnation of, Henry's action. That a historian like Acton should interpret More's words as proving 'that he had already shown a favourable bias' towards Henry's divorce would be puzzling, had not so many other great historians treated More in much the same way.

As a matter of precise terminology, the question of divorce, as we understand it, never arose. The problem was not whether

---

[1] *Utopia*, ed. LUPTON, pp. 227-9.

Henry should be divorced, but whether or no he was a bachelor, living in incest, falsely called marriage, with his brother's wife. Henry was seeking opinions as to whether he was, in fact, wedded to Catherine. Was the prohibition of *Leviticus* xviii. 16, so binding that no papal dispensation could abrogate it? What was the relation of the text in *Leviticus* to *Deuteronomy* xxv. 5? On the face of it, *Deuteronomy* seems flatly to contradict *Leviticus*. These were the questions of Canon Law which had to be decided. It was the books of the Bible and the Fathers, not *Utopia*, which Henry and More turned over together, when Henry consulted his faithful counsellor.

For this first conference we have nothing to depend upon but Roper's recollections of what More must have told him after the divorce proceedings became public. The King showed More 'certain places of scripture that somewhat seemed to serve his appetite'. More excused himself, as 'unmeet to meddle in such matters'. When further pressed, More asked for time, and was told to consult with Tunstall, Bishop of Durham, and Clerk, Bishop of Bath. In due course More had made his report to Henry:

> 'To be plain with your Grace, neither my Lord of Durham nor my Lord of Bath, though I know them both to be wise, virtuous, learned, and honourable prelates, nor my self, with the rest of your Council, being all your Grace's own servants, for your manifold benefits daily bestowed on us so most bounden to you, be, in my judgement, meet counsellors for your Grace herein. But if your Grace mind to understand the truth, such counsellors may you have devised, as neither for respect of their own worldly commodity, nor for fear of your princely authority, will be inclined to deceive you.'

> To whom he named then St. Jerome, St. Augustine, and divers other old holy doctors, both Greeks and Latins; and moreover showed him what authorities he had gathered out of them; which, although the King (as disagreeable with his desire) did not very well like of, yet were they by Sir Thomas More, who in all his communication with the King in that matter had always most discreetly behaved himself, so wisely tempered, that he both presently took them in good part, and ofttimes had thereof conference with him again.[1]

Meantime, a disaster had taken place in Italy which was to have repercussions on the question of Henry's divorce. The Emperor's victorious troops, unpaid, mutinous with hunger, had stormed and sacked Rome, amid horrors greater than those inflicted by Alaric and his Goths eleven centuries before. The Pope had fallen into the power of the Imperialists just at the time when it was most important for Henry that he should be independent of Charles.

So, when Wolsey set out for France, in July 1527, it was with a three-fold purpose: to ratify the treaty of the preceding April; to arrange for war against Charles; and (as he vainly hoped) to get himself appointed Vicar-General for the Pope, so long as the Pope should be in the hands of Charles. If he could have achieved this, then, acting on behalf of the captive Pope, he could have settled 'the King's great matter'.

More accompanied Wolsey on this embassy, the magnificence of which is recorded by Wolsey's gentleman usher. 'Then marched he forward out of his own house at Westminster, passing through all London, over London Bridge, having before him of gentlemen a great number, three in a rank, in black velvet livery coats, and the most part of them with great chains of gold about their necks'. The second night they stopped at Rochester, and lodged in Fisher's palace. Wolsey sounded Fisher on the divorce question, and his report to the King on Fisher's replies is extant at length.[1]

It is an odd coincidence that More should have been staying with Fisher at the time that Fisher was thus being interrogated on the subject which was to be the most anxious preoccupation of both during the next eight years. But it is unlikely that at this time they had any conference together on the subject. Fisher had been sworn to secrecy by Wolsey before the Cardinal began his confidential talk. And More and Fisher would have material enough for anxious talk in the news of the sack of Rome and the captivity of the Pope, besieged in his Castle of St. Angelo.

Canterbury was reached on the fourth day, and a solemn service of intercession for the Pope was held, whereat, says Cavendish, 'I saw the Lord Cardinal weep very tenderly,

[1] *State Papers*, I, p. 198.

which was, as we supposed, for heaviness that the Pope was at that present in such calamity and great danger of the Lance Knights'.[1]

The embassy occupied the whole summer; it culminated in a solemn service in the Cathedral of Amiens on 17 Aug. The elaborate letters of Wolsey to Henry, and the reminiscences written down thirty years later by Cavendish, enable us to reconstruct the whole episode in great detail. No trouble was spared to celebrate the peace by entertainments showered upon Wolsey, More and the other diplomatists. Even Wolsey's gentleman usher shared the reflected glory; he was feted wherever he went, on one occasion by a noble lady with a train of twelve gentlewomen. 'Forasmuch,' said his hostess, 'as ye be an Englishman, whose custom is in your country to kiss all ladies and gentlewomen without offence, and although it be not so here in this realm, yet will I be so bold to kiss you, and so shall all my maidens.' 'By means whereof I kissed my lady, and all her women.'

In the late summer, More duly returned from his embassy, and reported himself at Hampton Court to the King. Pressure was at once put on him to agree to the policy of the divorce. Here we are on firm ground, for we have More's own account, written down some six years later:[2]

> Suddenly his Highness, walking in the gallery, brake with me of his great matter, and showed me that it was now perceived that his marriage was not only against the positive laws of the Church, and the written law of God, but also in such wise against the law of Nature, that it could in no wise by the Church be dispensable.

Hitherto, says More, it had been a question of whether the papal dispensation was sufficient. That the marriage was 'in such wise against the law of Nature' was a new point. The King took graciously More's 'sudden unadvised answer', and told him to confer with Edward Foxe, subsequently his almoner.

§ 11. THOMAS MORE'S THREE WISHES

But More was soon to be sent on another embassy. Wolsey's peace with France had only been a first step towards a joint

[1] *Life of Wolsey*, ed. ELLIS, p. 61.   [2] *Works*, 1557, p. 1425.

war of England and France upon Spain, a war undertaken contrary to the wishes of everyone. The war with France had become unpopular, although France was the hereditary enemy. Still there were plenty of fighting barons, bill-men and archers, willing to plunder up and down France so long as bread, beef, and beer were provided. The difficulty came when the bread, beef, and beer had to be paid for. But war on Spain meant war on the Netherlands – the great market for English goods. Such a war could not be carried on without undermining the whole commercial prosperity of England. Even the French ambassador felt the impossibility of it: 'Wolsey is playing a terrible game', he writes, 'for I think that he is the only man in England who wishes for a war with Flanders.'[1]

To More, the Emperor was always the defender of civilization against the Turk; one to whom he owed 'any pleasure of service that in him lay, next his sovereign lord'.[2] The war against the Emperor was to him not merely – as it was to every Englishman – an economic absurdity; it was a war upon the secular head of Christendom. To see 'folly, doctor-like, controlling skill', made Shakespeare cry for 'restful death'. And there is something of the same indignation against the folly with which human affairs are governed in More's words to Roper:

> So on a time, walking with me along the Thames side at Chelsea, in talking of other things he said unto me: 'Now would to our Lord, son Roper, upon condition that three things were well established in Christendom, I were put in a sack, and here presently cast into the Thames.'
> 'What great things be those, Sir,' quoth I, 'that should move you so to wish?'
> 'Wouldest thou know what they be, son Roper?' quoth he.
> 'Yea, marry, with good will, sir, if it please you,' quoth I.
> 'In faith, son, they be these,' said he. 'The first is, that where the most part of Christian princes be at mortal war, they were all at an universal peace. The second, that where the Church of Christ is at this present sore afflicted with

[1] LEGRAND, *Histoire du divorce*, III, p. 81: *Il joue de terribles misteres, car je pense qu'il est seul en Angleterre qui veult la guerre en Flandres*: du Bellay, à Mr. le grant Maistre.
[2] HALL's *Chronicle*, ed. WHIBLEY, I, p. 250.

many errors and heresies, it were settled in a perfect uniformity of religion. The third, that where the King's matter of his marriage is now come in question, it were to the glory of God and quietness of all parties brought to a good conclusion.' Whereby, as I could gather, he judged that otherwise it would be a disturbance to a great part of Christendom.[1]

Yet, compared with Shakespeare's, More's cry for restful death is a cry with a difference: things must be put right before he is put into the sack.

§ 12.   THE PEACE OF CAMBRAI AND AFTER

Two of More's three wishes were to be utterly frustrated; the third was to be in some measure fulfilled. The blow fell which wrecked Wolsey's foreign policy. Once again he had backed the wrong horse. For four years he had attempted to support French power in Italy as a counterpoise to that of Charles, and at times success had seemed near. But now it began to appear that the result of the defeat of Pavia could not be reversed, and 'the ladies', Louise the mother of Francis and Margaret the aunt of Charles, were meeting at Cambrai to negotiate an arrangement between Francis and the Emperor. As he was wont to do, Wolsey 'staked his head' to Henry that these rumours of a separate peace between the antagonists were 'an invention of the enemy'.[2] They were in fact the complete condemnation of his policy. He had argued that if England was so wise as to keep out of the war of fools, the fools would combine to attack her. Wolsey and Henry had so acted as to secure the hearty hatred of both sides, and if both sides did not combine to attack England, it was no thanks to Wolsey's policy. So far from England being arbiter of the fate of Europe, it was necessary to send ambassadors to Cambrai at once, lest Francis and Charles should come to an agreement leaving England out of account. But Wolsey was busy over the divorce. A commission had been granted by the Pope to him and Campeggio, and as papal legates they were trying the case of Catherine and Henry in London. For this reason, and perhaps for others, Wolsey was kept out of these foreign negotiations. More and Tunstall were once again associated together as

<hr />

[1] ROPER, pp. 24-5.   [2] 28 Jan. 1529, L.P., IV, No. 5231.

diplomatists, and were sent to Cambrai to make the best they could of a bad business.[1]

But nine days before the commission was issued to them a further blow had fallen in Italy. The decisive battle of Landriano confirmed the decision which had been arrived at four years before at Pavia. Once again the army of Francis was destroyed. It was a less spectacular defeat, but final. This time Francis accepted the decision.

Francis was asked to wait for the arrival of Tunstall and More[2] 'as, considering their age and quality, they could not be expected to travel post'. Tunstall, remembering his experience in Spain, probably did not want any further posting at midday under a summer sun. It was a thankless task. But, says Roper, in the negotiations

> Sir Thomas More so worthily handled himself, procuring in our league far more benefits unto this realm than at that time by the King or his Council was thought possible to be compassed, that for his good service in that voyage the King, when he after made him Lord Chancellor, caused the Duke of Norfolk openly to declare unto the people (as you shall hear hereafter more at large) how much all England was bound unto him."[3]

In the epitaph which he wrote for his tomb at Chelsea, and in which, after his career was closed, he summarized the whole meaning of it, the peace of Cambrai is the only public event of which More makes mention; and, as in *Utopia*, he takes the opportunity of his association with Cuthbert Tunstall to sing the praises of his friend. More says that he had been sent on divers embassies,

> and last of all at Cambrai, joined fellow and companion with Cuthbert Tunstall, chief of that embassy (then Bishop of London, and within a while after Bishop of Durham, who so excelleth in learning, wit and virtue, that the whole world scant hath at this day any more learned, wiser, or better) where he both joyfully saw and was present ambassador, when the leagues between the chief princes of Christendom were renewed again, and peace, so long looked for, restored

[1] Commission issued 30 June 1529, *L.P.*, IV, No. 5744.
[2] 30 June 1529, *L.P.*, IV, No. 5741.   [3] ROPER, pp. 36-7.

to Christendom. Which peace our Lord stable and make perpetual.[1]

The peace so long looked for was not to be perpetual, but at least the treaty of Cambrai secured for England thirteen years freedom from foreign war – by far the longest spell of peace in the troubled reign of Henry.

The complete victory of Charles in Italy had its repercussions upon papal policy, and upon the trial of the King's great matter, proceeding in London at the Blackfriars. Whilst More and Tunstall were overseas at Cambrai, the final meeting of the court was held. Campeggio arose; and all expected him to give judgment. Instead, he adjourned the case till the end of the long vacation. It was an adjournment for ever; because in fact, though it was not yet publicly known, the cause had been recalled to Rome, where the King and Queen of England were cited to appear, in person or by proxy.

When Campeggio had spoken: 'With that stept forth the Duke of Suffolk from the King, and by his commandment spake these words, with a stout and hault countenance. "It was never," quoth he, "merry in England, whilst we had cardinals among us": which words were set forth with such a vehement countenance that all men marvelled what he intended; to whom no man made answer.'[2]

The words of Suffolk, the King's boon companion and brother-in-law, meant that the King had thrown the Cardinal to the wolves. They had long been on his track, drawing ever nearer and nearer. Wolsey's fate was sealed, although it was still some months before he was deprived of office.

The King acted rapidly. A fortnight after the scene at the Blackfriars, writs were issued for a parliament. There had been no Parliament since, six years before, More, as Speaker, had had to co-operate with the overbearing Wolsey in somehow squeezing supplies from an unwilling nation.

Another three weeks, and More was back from Cambrai, to report matters to the King.

The King was beginning to feel more hopeful as to the divorce. He had, he told More, been 'in utter despair', but now 'he had conceived some good hope to compass it'. He

---

[1] *Works*, 1557, p. 1421.   [2] CAVENDISH, *Life of Wolsey*, ed. ELLIS, p. 122.

repeated that his marriage was against the law of Nature, and not dispensable by the Church. Such is Roper's account, and subsequent biographers have naturally followed him, in narrating Henry's different attempts to win More over. Yet it is hardly likely that More confided these secret talks to Roper at the time; and even if he did, Roper's chronology is naturally unreliable concerning events which took place long before he wrote. Roper is likely to have made more serious errors here than the venial one of calling Tunstall Bishop of Durham before he had been translated to that see.

The most reliable account is in More's letter to Cromwell, written a few years after these events; and from it I have already quoted. In that letter More says nothing of any discourse with the King on this subject, immediately after his return from Cambrai. He *does* tell us (as does also Roper) of a subsequent interview, soon after he became Chancellor. That will be narrated in the next chapter. At that interview More was told to confer with the Archbishops of Canterbury and York (Cranmer and Lee), with Dr. Foxe, 'now his Grace's almoner', and Dr. Nicholas, the Italian friar. In these conferences More was not able to take the view of 'the King's great matter' which the King himself would have wished; but we gather from More's words that the conference was as friendly 'as reason could in a matter disputable require'.

It may be that Roper is merely giving us a confused reminiscence of this later conference, when he tells us that after his return from Cambrai, More was bidden to confer with Stokesley, whom he calls Bishop of London. (Stokesley did not become Bishop of London till a little later.)

More, as Roper's story goes, could find no reason to change his opinion: Stokesley made a true, yet friendly report of the matter to the King, saying that he found More 'desirous to find some good matter wherewith he might truly serve his Grace to his contentation'.

The service with which More was to content Henry was that of succeeding Wolsey as Chancellor.

THE LORD CHANCELLOR

(1529–1532)

§ 1. MORE ACCEPTS THE GREAT SEAL

WHY did More accept the office of Chancellor, when it was clear that Parliament was being called together in order to carry measures of which he disapproved?

More knew quite well what was coming. Intelligent observers had seen it, as soon as Wolsey's fall drew near. The French ambassador wrote (in cipher) that, after Wolsey was dead or ruined, the great lords meant to attack and plunder the Church. And, he added, 'it is hardly needful for me to write in cipher, for they proclaim it openly. I expect they will do fine miracles'.[1] A little later he writes that 'the clergy are going in this Parliament to have terrible alarms'. He does not think that any priest will ever have the Great Seal again. More was no priest, but he was that even more devoted defender of clerical rights – the ecclesiastically-minded layman. If Henry could bend More to his will, his triumph would be complete. Why then did More accept a post in which he must either break or bend? His acceptance has often been described as his fatal mistake.

But, in fact, More had no choice. Once he had entered the King's service, he was no longer a free man. Before this date he had made it clear to the King that he could not bend in the matter of the divorce. If the King, knowing this, promised to give him freedom of conscience, and to employ him in other matters, More had no option but to serve the King.

'It is one of the few admirable traits of Henry's character,' it has been said,[2] 'that, provided his ministers observed the outward form of his somewhat arbitrary laws, he did not seek

---

[1] *L.P.*, IV, No. 6011.　　[2] POLLARD, *Cranmer*, 1926, p. 132.

to put further burdens on their conscience.' And More has been quoted as a proof of this: 'all the time that he was Chancellor, the King did not employ him on business connected with the divorce of Catherine of Aragon, because he knew that More disapproved of it'.

When Henry's admirable traits are so frankly admitted to be few, it seems uncharitable to make them fewer. But the fact is, that this promise of liberty of conscience to his servants was one of the most powerful weapons in Henry's armoury. It enabled him to insist on their serving him, so long as he needed their services, although they might disapprove of much that he was doing.

Soon after More became Chancellor, the King again asked him to consider 'his great matter'. More fell upon his knees. He would gladly give one of his limbs, he said, to be able to serve the King in that matter, with a safe conscience. Henry promised to use the advice of those 'whose consciences could well enough agree therewith', to use More 'otherwise', and 'never with that matter molest his conscience after'.[1]

It is likely enough that Roper's memory is at fault as to the exact times when the King consulted More, and the words used on each occasion. But we have More's letter to Cromwell to prove that the King, when asking him 'to consider his great matter', repeated the promise of freedom of conscience which he had given him on first entering his service: 'that he should first look unto God, and after God unto him'.[2]

But when Henry's promise to molest More no further, followed by promises of worldly honour and profit, failed to change More's mind, then Henry proceeded to molest him again.[3] The test of a man's generosity lies, not in the promises he makes, but in the promises he keeps.

But one admirable trait Henry indisputably had – patience. He combined it with another, less admirable – dissimulation. They made a powerful combination. Henry would promise freedom of conscience to those whom he could not easily bend to his will, and then later play upon their gratitude to extract a compliance which he could never have extracted by force. The rigidity of More's conscience is shown not so much by

[1] Roper, p. 50.   [2] *Works*, 1557, p. 1426 (1427).   [3] Roper, p. 66.

the fact that it was proof against Henry's threats, as that it was proof against his blandishments. 'Look first unto God, and after God, unto me; nevertheless weigh my great matter once again.' That was Henry's trump card, and it seldom failed to win. But if it failed, Henry had another trump up his sleeve, and the obstinate man was in due time told 'that never was there servant to his Sovereign so villainous, nor subject to his Prince so traitorous as he'.

A piece of evidence, which has hitherto been neglected, goes to prove More's unwillingness to accept the Chancellorship. This is the statement of his nephew William Rastell, in a fragment of his lost *Life* of his uncle. The King, says Rastell, was determined not to give the Chancellorship to a cleric, 'and offered it to Sir Thomas More, who refusing it, the King was angry with him, and caused him to accept it, and laboured to have him persuaded on his side in the matter of his divorce; and because he could not be persuaded, he hated him for it'.[1]

And there was another reason why More could not refuse to be one of the small band of Catherine's friends who were preparing what resistance they could. Even now, at the eleventh hour, he might help to stave off some of the disasters he foresaw. There was always the duty he had represented himself as urging upon Raphael Hythlodaye: 'That which you cannot turn to good, so to order it that it be not very bad.'

When the Dukes of Norfolk and Suffolk appeared at York House to demand the surrender of the Great Seal from Wolsey, the fallen Cardinal refused to deliver it in response to a mere verbal message. There were 'many stout words between them',[2] but in the end the Dukes departed without the Great Seal. Next day they returned with the King's letters, and in due course the Seal was handed at Windsor to Henry, who himself affixed it to certain documents.[3] Suffolk was suggested as a successor to Wolsey, but the jealousy of Norfolk, the High Treasurer, stood in the way.[4] Tunstall was ruled out as an ecclesiastic. To More, no one had any objection. It was rumoured that Wolsey himself had spoken of More as his

---

[1] RASTELL, Fragment A, in Appendix to HARPSFIELD's *Life of More*, p. 222.
[2] CAVENDISH, *Life of Wolsey*, p. 133.   [3] 20 Oct. 1529, *L.P.*, IV, No. 6025.
[4] *Spanish Calendar*, IV, 1, p. 326.

only possible successor. 'The Cardinal,' Erasmus wrote later, 'who, whatever his misfortunes, was assuredly no fool, when he saw that he had no chance of returning to power himself, stated that in the whole island there was no one who was equal to the duty of Chancellor except More alone. And he was not led to that view by any personal friendship; for, all his life long, he was hardly More's friend, and feared rather than loved him.'[1]

And Wolsey's judgment was shared by everyone. The new Imperial ambassador, Eustace Chapuys, had just arrived in England. Readers of Shakespeare will remember him as the Capucius of *Henry VIII*, a gracious figure introduced into the play to speak a few kindly words to the dying Catherine, and to receive her last requests. Chapuys was destined to stay in England through all these troublous times, and his elaborate dispatches, from now on, are a most important source of information. They are honest, though naturally biassed. He writes to Charles,[2] 'The Chancellor's Seal has remained in the hands of the Duke of Norfolk till this morning, when it was transferred to Sir Thomas More. Everyone is delighted at his promotion, because he is an upright and learned man, and a good servant of the Queen.'

There are many references to More's appointment in the letters of Erasmus to his English friends. With considerable foresight, Erasmus keeps on repeating that More himself is not to be congratulated; nor is Learning, which will lose More's services. But for King Henry's sake, for England's sake, and also for the sake of Erasmus himself, there is cause to rejoice. A holier or better judge, Erasmus says, could not be.[3]

The official account tells us that the Seal was delivered by the King at East Greenwich on 25 October 1529 to Sir Thomas More, in the presence of the Attorney General, and that next day More took the oath as Chancellor in the great hall at Westminster, in the presence of the Dukes of Norfolk and Suffolk and other peers, spiritual and lay.[4] Roper has recorded that the Duke of Norfolk, on the King's behalf, declared 'how much all

[1] To Faber, *Epist. Opus*, Basel, 1538, p. 1071.
[2] 25 Oct. 1529, *L.P.*, iv, No. 6026 (p. 2684).
[3] ALLEN, viii, Nos. 2263, 2287, 2295.   [4] *L.P.*, iv, No. 6025.

England was beholden to Sir Thomas More', and 'how worthy he was to have the highest room in the realm'. More in reply 'disabled himself as unmeet for that room, wherein, considering how wise and honourable a prelate had lately before taken so great a fall, he had, he said, thereof no cause to rejoice'.[1]

Stapleton has preserved two speeches of very doubtful authenticity. In the first the Duke of Norfolk dilates, rather tactlessly, on More's lack of noble birth, but explains that his virtues compensate for this. In his reply, More dwells upon the great qualities of Wolsey, which nevertheless have not saved him from his fall; and draws the obvious moral that fate is hanging over his own head.[2] Both speeches are probably nothing but the rhetorical exercises of the biographer, and we must reject them, much as we should wish to believe that More had taken this occasion to emphasize 'the incomparable prudence, skill, and experience in affairs' of his luckless predecessor.

§ 2. MORE'S ATTACK ON WOLSEY

What we know More to have actually said about Wolsey, when Parliament opened a few days later, was indeed something very different from the generous words Stapleton makes him use on receiving the Seal.

Parliament met at the Blackfriars.[3] The Rolls of Parliament tell us that, in a long and eloquent speech, More explained that Parliament had been called together to reform abuses. We are fortunate in having an account of More's opening speech by a member of Parliament, 'the first historian who, as an M.P., deals with its proceedings',[4] the Chronicler Edward Hall. The King had come by water to his palace of Bridewell, where he and his nobles had put on their robes of Parliament, and so came to the Blackfriars. There, after solemn mass, the Commons were summoned into the Parliament chamber, and Sir Thomas More, standing at the right hand of the King seated in his throne, made an eloquent oration. The first part of the speech, as reported by Hall, agrees with the summary in the *Rolls*, and

---

[1] ROPER, pp. 39, 40.   [2] STAPLETON III, pp. 173-7.   [3] 3 Nov. 1529.
[4] PROF. A. F. POLLARD, *The First M.P. Journalist*, contributed to *The Times*, 1 Oct. 1932.

deals with the reformation of abuses (not specifically defined). More then went on (in words which remind us of what, years before, he had written in *Utopia*) to develop the comparison of the King to a shepherd:

> For if a prince be compared to his riches, he is but a rich man; if a prince be compared to his honour, he is but an honourable man. But compare him to the multitude of his people and the number of his flock, then he is a ruler, a governor of might and puissance. So that his people maketh him a prince, as of the multitude of sheep cometh the name of a shepherd.

And this leads up to a bitter attack upon the fallen Wolsey:

> As you see that amongst a great flock of sheep some be rotten and faulty, which the good shepherd sendeth from the good sheep, so the great wether which is of late fallen, as you all know, so craftily, so scabbedly, yea and so untruly juggled with the King, that all men must needs guess and think that he thought in himself that the King had no wit to perceive his crafty doing, or else that he presumed that the King would not see nor know his fraudulent juggling and attempts. But he was deceived, for his Grace's sight was so quick and penetrable that he saw him – yea and saw through him, both within and without – so that all thing to him was open. And according to his desert he hath had a gentle correction. Which small punishment the King will not to be an example to other offenders, but clearly declareth that whosoever hereafter shall make like attempt to commit like offence shall not escape with like punishment.

More then passed on to direct the Commons to elect a Speaker as their 'common mouth'.[1]

Admirers of More have doubted the accuracy of this speech, because of its bitter attack upon a fallen man.[2] Admirers of Wolsey, on the other hand, have reproached More because he could not resist 'the temptation to catch a passing cheer by unworthy taunts at a defeated adversary'.[3] Nevertheless, that the speech is accurately reported there is, I think, no reason to doubt. Chapuys gives a summary of More's speech which,

[1] Hall's *Chronicle*, ed. Whibley, ii, pp. 164-5.
[2] Bridgett, 3rd ed., pp. 231-2, and Appendix D
[3] Creighton, *Wolsey*, p. 190. Compare Brewer, *Henry VIII*, ii, p. 391.

though less detailed, agrees with Hall's. 'The Chancellor,' he
says, 'went on enumerating the misdeeds of the Cardinal.'[1]

It is all very unchivalrous, and quite contrary to our feelings
to-day, when political life has become something of a game,
and one of the rules of the game is that the reputation of a
deceased or defeated adversary must not be attacked too
bitterly. But More's age was unchivalrous. Years before, More
had offered, and Henry VIII had accepted, congratulations
upon the royal accession which reflected upon the memory of
Henry VII. More's good taste was not infallible. But neither
then nor now was More acting from mere vindictiveness, still
less sycophancy. In each case there is the implication that the
new rule is going to break away from the mistakes and crimes
of the old. In each case he is preaching to Henry VIII, rather
than reviling the fallen.

Wolsey's pro-French and anti-Spanish policy laid him open
to the suspicion of having instigated the divorce, for the divorce
was the natural corollary of that policy. More's circle believed
this, and moreover they believed that Wolsey was moved by
personal motives.[2] More has left us nothing in writing on the
subject; but we may well suppose that he had come to regard
Wolsey as the evil genius of Henry and of England – the man
who had impoverished his country by useless wars with France,
and then embroiled her in war with Charles V, that is with
England's traditional friends, the house of Burgundy. Those
things Wolsey indisputably had done, and they were enough to
have earned from More the bitterest hatred he was capable of
feeling. But if Wolsey, in addition to this, had put doubts
about his union with Catherine into Henry's mind, then, More
would feel, he had endangered the unity of Christendom, and
the salvation of Henry's soul. The danger to his own career
and head More would probably have thought little of, in
comparison with those two mighty issues.

The wonder is that here, and elsewhere, More deals as
leniently with Wolsey as he does.

Besides, although More probably felt about Wolsey even

---

[1] *Spanish Calendar*, I, pp. 323-4.
[2] ROPER, pp. 29-31; HARPSFIELD, *Life of More*, pp. 39-44, *Pretended Divorce*,
pp. 175 etc.; STAPLETON, XVIII, p. 343. See also above, pp. 162-3, 223.

more bitterly than he spoke, we must remember that he was speaking as Henry's servant. Wolsey had admitted himself guilty of unlawfully vexing the King's subjects, and of having incurred the penalties of *praemunire*. Only four days earlier he had submitted to the King's mercy. The Chancellor spoke as the King's mouthpiece. And he had to explain to Parliament why this man, who for so many years had been ruling the realm with the King's approval, had now been disgraced by the King. Had the King then been deceived? No, he had seen through Wolsey, More assured the Commons.

§ 3. 'A PARLIAMENT—GOD KNOWETH WHAT MANNER OF ONE'

The passage in which the Chancellor spoke of the reform of errors and abuses may have given him more uneasiness than his references to Wolsey. Parliament, he said, had been called to reform 'divers new enormities sprung amongst the people', and as he uttered these words he must have felt most unhappily conscious that his idea of the 'enormities' which the Parliament ought to reform might not in all respects coincide with that of his King. 'Reform' was indeed to be the business of this Parliament, which has come to be known in history as the 'Reformation Parliament', or sometimes as Henry's Long Parliament. And it has left a permanent mark on English history such as no other Parliament has ever done, not even the Long Parliament of Charles I.

In the last chapter, our story turned on the relation of More to Henry and to Wolsey. Wolsey is now out of the story; the tale turns upon the relation of More to Henry, Thomas Cromwell, and Parliament. At his trial, nearly six years later, More was blamed for 'stiffly sticking' to his own private judgment against an act of this same parliament, at the pompous opening of which he was now assisting. He replied that 'against this one parliament of yours (*God knoweth what manner of one*), I have all the councils of Christendom, made these thousand years'.[1] Now in the mouth of Thomas More the phrase 'God knoweth what manner of one' must mean a good deal. During the whole controversy on the questions of the Matrimony and the

[1] HARPSFIELD, *Life of More*, p. 196. See below, p. 341.

Supremacy, More refrained from dropping any ungenerous word against those who thought differently from himself. And he was an ex-Speaker, with a knowledge of parliaments which went back thirty years, to the days when he had been 'a beardless boy'. The words are weighty.

More's words may well reflect rather on the pliability of Parliament than upon its composition. Very rightly have Henry and his Parliament been compared to Ulysses and 'the bow which he alone could bend'.[1] The secret of Henry's skill had been expressed by More when he first entered the royal service; the King could make every man feel that he was enjoying his special favour, just as the London wives each thought that the image of Our Lady by the Tower was smiling specially upon her.[2] But, if blandishments failed, then all Henry's great men knew that, in the words so often on the lips of Tudor statesmen, 'The wrath of the King is Death'. And Henry, with his extraordinary personal powers as a ruler of men, was born into an age when the king was recognized as 'a god on earth'. 'It was an enormous strength to Henry to begin with, that he himself had no doubt that to withstand him was to withstand God: much more, that most of his subjects uneasily felt that he was right.'[3] How the rank and file of Parliament could be dealt with, we learn from the member for Much Wenlock, Edward Hall the Chronicler. Hall is in many ways More's opposite number. Both of them combined a University training with a training in one of the Inns of Court; both were great historians; both were Under-Sheriffs of London. Hall was a king-worshipper, and his complete admiration of Henry allowed him in his *Chronicle* to express only a very tempered admiration for More. Hall tells us how the King had borrowed money in the fifteenth year of his reign, and how in the twenty-first (the first year of More's chancellorship) a Bill was introduced to release the King from his debts:

This bill was sore argued in the Common House; but the most part of the Commons were the King's servants, and the other were so laboured to by other, that the bill was assented to. When this release of the loan was known to the commons

---

[1] POLLARD, *Henry VIII*, p. 258.   [2] See above, p. 169.
[3] PICKTHORN, *Early Tudor Government*, p. 369.

of the Realm, Lord, so they grudged, and spake ill of the whole Parliament . . . but there was no remedy.[1]

We need not suppose Hall to mean that an actual majority of Commons were the King's servants. He need only mean that the King's men were sufficient to convince the rest. This 'labouring' of the other members, by those upon whom the King could rely, is the essential thing. We shall find that the law under which More was executed was only carried after much 'sticking', and even then in a somewhat modified form. But carried it was, and in a form which enabled the King to do what he wanted.

When the whole of the North of England, a little more than a year after More's death, burst into rebellion against the legislation of this Reformation Parliament and its brief successor, there was violent language about the 'King's servants', and the unrepresentative character of Parliament. And these reflections on either the independence or the character of members of Henry's later Parliaments were echoed by enthusiasts both on the Catholic and Protestant side; writers like More's nephew Rastell or the biographer of Fisher might be quoted from the one party, Reformers like Brinklow from the other.[2] 'Be he never so very a fool, drunkard, extortioner, adulterer, never so covetous and crafty a person, yet if he be rich, bear any office, if he be a jolly cracker and bragger in the country, he must be a burgess of Parliament.' The writer is a strong Protestant. 'Roisting courtiers, parasites and flatterers, lightly furnished with either learning or honesty.' The writer is a strong Catholic. Perhaps the godly on both sides were somewhat wanting in charity. Let us turn to the more measured words of the modern historian. 'In Henry's reign the English spirit of independence burned low in its socket, and love of freedom grew cold.' 'A few noble examples, Catholic and Protestant, redeemed, by their blood, the age from complete condemnation, but, in the mass of his subjects, the finer feelings seem to have been lost in the pursuit of wealth.'[3]

---

[1] Ed. WHIBLEY, II, p. 169.

[2] See *Rastell Fragments* in Appendix to HARPSFIELD, p. 222; *Analecta Bollandiana*, x, 1, 1891, pp. 335-6; BRINKLOW's *Complaynt of Roderyck Mors*, p. 13. Brinklow was writing about 1542, but is referring also to earlier Parliaments.

[3] A. F. POLLARD, *Henry VIII*, 438, 431.

Parliament was recruited from that class of Henry's subjects among whom the pursuit of wealth was a possibility. But there were others who could only hope to earn a bare living, 'not the wise and well-bespoke, but the mere uncounted folk', who were never elected to Henry's Parliaments, and were seldom even electors. Amongst them the confiscatory legislation of Henry's Reformation Parliament and its successors can hardly have been as popular as it was among the 'rich bearers of office' who profited by it. John Palmer, twice sheriff of Surrey and Sussex, obtained a grant in Sussex of monastic land, and, it was said, proceeded to convert to his proper use the holdings of the peasants. When they protested, he was alleged to have replied: 'Do ye not know that the King's Grace hath put down all the houses of monks, friars and nuns? Therefore now is the time come that we gentlemen will pull down the houses of such poor knaves as ye be.'[1] Of course, against the rapacity of profiteers (which had become a serious problem long before the Reformation Parliament and its confiscations) the poor had an appeal to the Star Chamber or the Court of Poor Men's Causes. And so long as Wolsey and More were in power, that meant much. More's conduct as a judge – which extended in his various capacities over a period of twenty-two years – gained him the reputation of being 'the best friend that the poor e'er had'. But after More's fall it became more and more the case that the men before whom redress had to be sought were the very men who were profiting by the Great Spoliation legalized by the Reformation Parliament and its successors.

The gentlemen, the 'jolly crackers and braggers' who expected to make their profit out of the dissolution of the monasteries, might be opposed to More, but there is little doubt that amongst the mass of the people there was the deepest sympathy both for him and for the cause for which he died. And the·tradition persisted, with the odd result that, even after England had become Protestant, More remained a popular hero.

But More, when he used the words 'Parliament – God knoweth what manner of one', was a condemned man, with only five days to live. He meant exactly what he said. He had

---

[1] TAWNEY and POWER, *Tudor Economic Documents*, 1924, I, pp. 20-1.

used similar words of his own condemnation some moments before: 'Seeing ye are determined to condemn me, God knoweth how.'

Anyway, there were members of this Parliament who were very dear to More. His own family was well represented in it. The husbands of his three daughters, and of his step-daughter, all had seats. William Roper sat for Bramber in Sussex, Giles Heron and William Dauncey for Thetford in Norfolk, Sir Giles Alington for the County of Cambridge.

§ 4. THE ATTACK ON THE CLERGY

And so the Parliament got to work. Thomas Audeley was chosen Speaker. He was a somewhat colourless and very typical servant of Henry; he had stepped into More's shoes as Chancellor of the Duchy of Lancaster, and was destined to succeed him as Chancellor. He went through the usual form of 'disabling himself for lack of wit, learning and discretion', as More had done before, when elected Speaker in the last Parliament. More was now in the place of Wolsey, and it fell to him to reply, on behalf of the King, that Audeley's 'own oration, there made, testified the contrary'. Then the Commons, assembled in the Lower House, 'began to commune of their griefs' against the clergy. How far these were spontaneous complaints, how far, as Rastell tells us, they were suggested 'by the King's own drift', we shall never know. What is certain is that the bishops 'frowned and grunted', and Bishop Fisher of Rochester complained that now with the Commons it is nothing but 'Down with the Church'; and all this, said Fisher, 'me seemeth is for lack of faith only'. The Commons 'took the matter grievously', and sent their Speaker to complain to the King that they 'which were elected for the wisest men of all the shires, cities and boroughs within the realm of England, should be declared to lack faith, which was equivalent to say that they were as ill as Turks or Saracens'. Fisher was called before the King and had to explain his words away, 'which blind excuse pleased the Commons nothing at all'.

The quarrel had begun, though for the moment matters rested there.

On 29 Nov. 1530, Wolsey died at Leicester, on his way to the

Tower under arrest. But the evil that he had done lived after him, to Henry's profit. His usurpations of authority, by which he had incurred a *praemunire*, had been tolerated by clergy and laity, whereby they might be held to have connived at his illegalities. It seems hardly fair, since, but for Henry's protection, clergy and laity would long ago have made short work of Wolsey. The suggestion that they should be made to pay for having endured Wolsey's tyranny was too much even for the faithful Commons. Violent words were uttered: 'The King had burdened and oppressed the kingdom with more imposts and exactions than any three or four of his predecessors, and should consider that his strength lay in the affections of his people.'[1] Henry realized this, and he granted the Commons the pardon they desired. For the moment the clergy were his concern. *They* could only atone for their errors by voting handsome supplies for the crown – £100,000 from the Convocation of Canterbury, and some £19,000 from the Convocation of York. But the King would not accept this, nor pardon the clergy, unless they recognized him as 'sole protector and supreme head of the Church and clergy of England'.

§5. SUPREME HEAD OF THE CHURCH

What did such a title mean? Probably none of the clergy to whom the claim was made anticipated that in eight years the King would be claiming to define by proclamation what was, and what was not, heresy. But the title was sufficiently alarming. Anne Boleyn's brother was sent by the King to suggest an amendment, 'Supreme Head after God'; but the admission that Henry was subordinate to God seemed to the clergy insufficient. It was suggested on behalf of the King that he, being a temporal prince, would not intermeddle with spiritual matters; and Fisher, seizing upon this, suggested the addition of the saving clause, 'So far as the law of God allows'. And so, in this form, on 11 February 1531, the Convocation of Canterbury acknowledged, on the motion of Archbishop Warham, that the King was

> 'their singular protector, only and supreme Lord, and so far as the law of Christ allows, even Supreme Head'.

[1] *L.P.*, v, No. 171.

It was the title which, a little more than four years later, was to cost Fisher and More their lives.

§6. THE KING'S GREAT MATTER ONCE MORE

Relations with Rome were growing strained, but were not yet broken. It turned on what the Pope might yet do in the matter of the divorce.

Meanwhile on the suggestion of a middle-aged Cambridge don, Thomas Cranmer, the universities of Europe had been canvassed as to the legality of the King's marriage with Catherine. Some amusing episodes had occurred in the university contest of Charles V, supported by Deuteronomy, *versus* Henry VIII, supported by Leviticus. 'On the one side, a library catalogue was forged, in order to throw the Englishman off the scent of a Greek father; on the other, needy rabbis were fished out of their ghettos to opine against Deuteronomy at a minimum charge of twenty-four crowns. It is not necessary to suppose that all the learned men were dishonest, though the atmosphere was not favourable to strict scientific integrity.'[1] The preceding summer, Henry's leading noblemen had signed a joint letter to the Pope urging him to give sentence, and declaring that many famous universities held the King's marriage unlawful. Wolsey, a few months before his death, signed the document. More's name is conspicuously absent. And now, a few weeks after More had been mortified by the action of the clergy in granting the title of Supreme Head, he had to announce to Parliament the result of all this university research into the law of marriage. More began in the Lords, by saying that the King was pursuing the divorce from scruples of conscience, and not because he was in love with any other lady. Obviously the King's motives were locked in the royal breast, and his Chancellor could only speak as the King's mouthpiece, reporting what the King told him. And, indeed, it is likely enough that the scruples of conscience *were* the King's original motive, and preceded his passion for Anne. More has been blamed for this speech; but if anyone was to blame it was the King, who had promised More that he would employ in the matter of the divorce only those whose consciences were per-

[1] FISHER, *History of England, 1485–1547*, pp. 302-3.

suaded. And the employment of More led to an awkward episode. Someone asked him for his own opinion. He replied that he had many times already declared it to the King, and said no more. The answer made More's disapproval clear, for, had he approved of the divorce, he could hardly have done other than say so, after such a question. The Chancellor then descended to the Commons, with some of the leading peers, and repeated what had been said before the Lords, adding that the Commons were to report these matters in their districts when they returned home. Next day, Parliament was prorogued, and More, on behalf of the King, had to make a speech to the members expressing Henry's satisfaction with them.[1]

However loyal and discreet More might be, his opposition to the divorce could not be kept secret. The ambassador of Charles V reported that More had spoken so much in the Queen's favour that he had had a narrow escape of being dismissed; at another time he reported that More was so distressed by Henry's claim to be Supreme Head of the English Church that he was anxious above all things to resign the Chancellorship, whilst Fisher was ill from grief. This news naturally moved Charles, for all the troubles of More and Fisher were closely linked with their championship of the Emperor's aunt. So Charles wrote directly to More, sending the letter through his ambassador.[2] But More very properly refused to receive it. He begged Chapuys 'for the honour of God' not even to pay him a visit. He protested that, although his loyalty to Henry ought to have placed him above suspicion, any communication with Charles would be unwise; 'it might deprive him of the liberty which he had always used, in speaking boldly to King Henry in those matters which concerned Charles and Queen Catherine of Aragon'. And More went on to tell Chapuys that these things concerned him no less than his life, not only for the sake of Charles and the Queen, but for the sake of Henry and the kingdom of England. But he could receive no private

---

[1] CHAPUYS' report, 2 April 1531, *L.P.*, v, No. 171.
[2] Chapuys to Charles, reporting More's distress, 21 Feb. 1531, *L.P.*, v, No. 112. Letters were taking about a week to pass from London to Charles' court, which was then in or near Brussels. Charles wrote a personal letter to More about 12 March which Chapuys acknowledged on 22 March (*Spanish Calendar*, IV, ii, p. 98). On 2 April, Chapuys reported More's refusal to receive Charles' letter (*L.P.*, v, No. 171).

communication. If the letter were shown to him, he must show it to Henry. And More evidently anticipated that the tenor of the letter would not be such as to make it suitable reading for Henry.

When the prorogued Parliament met again, the great attack was made on the Church, in the form of a Supplication or Complaint of the Commons against the bishops. Corrected drafts in the handwriting of Thomas Cromwell sufficiently show the origin of this attack. Such an attack was only the opening move of a sustained campaign. It shows how little the Commons realized the character of the revolution which they were beginning, that, at the very time of laying this Supplication before the King, they asked him to consider the great inconvenience they had incurred by their long attendance in Parliament, and begged for a dissolution. The King very reasonably pointed out that they must wait and hear the answer to their grievances – in fact they had to serve for another four years. Whilst the Commons were waiting for the reply of the bishops, the Act was passed withholding the payment of annates to Rome. When the answer of the bishops came, the King handed it to his Commons with the words, 'We think their answer will smally please you, for it seemeth to us very slender'. The Commons were to look into the matter, carefully, and the King assured them that he would be impartial! The clergy made a second answer, but still the King was not satisfied. Then the King made the discovery of a lifetime. He sent for the Speaker and twelve other members of the Commons and announced it: 'Well beloved subjects, we thought that the clergy of our realm had been our subjects wholly; but now we have well perceived that they be but half our subjects – yea, and scarce our subjects. For all the prelates at their consecration make an oath to the Pope clean contrary to the oath they make to us, so that they seem his subjects and not ours.'

The King's demands were again placed before Convocation; and on 15 May 1532, a date memorable in English history, the clergy made their complete surrender to Henry. By emphasizing that they did this in view of his 'excellent wisdom and fervent zeal', they tried to make it a personal grant, hoping that in some future reign they might recover their position.

Next day More resigned his office. It was the end of his political career. As a statesman, he had not been able to defend the clergy or the Faith. It remained for him to give the whole of his time, so long as he was a free man, to defending them by his writings.

§7. BOOKS OF CONTROVERSY

Why should the Reformation have moved More to such a passion of wrath and fear? He had composed a beautiful prayer, supposed to be uttered by the men of different religions assembled for common worship in Utopia, and in it he had hinted that there may, perhaps, be something in the variety of religious worship which is pleasing to the inscrutable will of God.[1] Like Milton, More believed that 'it is not impossible that Truth may have more shapes than one'. During his imprisonment in the Tower, he loved to recall how, although two Fathers of the Church had of old taken different views, yet now 'they be both twain holy saints in Heaven'. He repeats, a dozen times or more, that he condemns the conscience of no other man.

It is precisely More's tolerance that makes him, on true Utopian principles, intolerant of the Reformers. As the disciple of Colet, and the friend of Erasmus, More was as convinced as any Bible-Christian of the necessity of the intelligent study of the New Testament. Few could read Erasmus' Greek text, and many could not read Erasmus' Latin paraphrase; therefore More wished that the Bible should be translated into English. He admits that some people would misuse such a translation – but the misuse should not take away the use: 'a commodity ought not to be kept back for the harm that may come of it'.[2] Under strict episcopal licence, More would permit individuals to use Bible translations. But when Reformers would abolish pilgrimages, or the veneration of images and relics, as nothing but superstitious idolatry, then More opposes them. Here also he considers that the abuse should not take away the use. Bible reading is not everything. Forty per cent of the population, and more, he urges, cannot read at all.[3] All religious experience is sacred to More. He honours the scholarship of an

ed. LUPTON, p. 298.   [2] *Works*, 1557, p. 244.   [3] *Works*, 1557, p. 850.

Erasmus, poring over the Greek Testament to get the meaning of every word, till he sees Christ preaching, healing and dying before his eyes. But More equally honours the devotion of some illiterate old woman, bowed in silent adoration at the foot of a crucifix. And when the religious Reformer would denounce the old woman as an idolater, and smash the crucifix before her eyes, then More stands up in wrath. Dante, skilled in all the learning of his age, when he has reached at last the Heaven of Light beyond all space, and is to enjoy the Beatific Vision, compares himself to some pilgrim from Croatia, in silence before the Veronica; just so More, with all his learning, respects the devotion of the humble and ignorant.

More's controversial works on matters of religion fall into two classes. There are the Latin letters to his old friend Edward Lee, or to Martin Dorp, in which More defends Erasmus and his New Testament against the attacks of the old-fashioned and strictly orthodox. Here the controversy was thoroughly friendly, More's opponents were not unworthy of his steel. Occasionally we get some interesting autobiographical details. In his Letter to Dorp, More tells how he listened at table to a dispute between a contradictious monk and a learned Italian merchant – clearly Antonio Bonvisi. Bonvisi was as firmly orthodox as More himself, but played upon the theologian's ignorance of the New Testament by inventing spurious texts, always quoting a chapter, but 'if there were only sixteen chapters in the book, he would quote from the twentieth'. The poor theologian never detected the fraud, but brought forward his rival interpretation of the bogus texts, and even asserted that the famous commentary of Nicholas de Lyra supported his interpretation.

In his controversy with Dorp, More had the greatest and rarest reward that can fall to an honest disputant. He converted his antagonist. To More, with his passionate belief in Reason, this was a special joy. Against the Reformers, More argues that 'Reason is servant to Faith and not enemy'.[1] This devotion to Reason is one of the many striking likenesses between Thomas More and Jonathan Swift. To both of them it appears a tragedy that Reason does not lead men at once to the same conclusions. When Gulliver visited the virtuous horses, he found things

[1] *Works,* 1557, p. 152.

different: 'Neither is reason among them a point problematical as with us, where men can argue with plausibility on both sides of the question; but strikes you with immediate conviction; as it must needs do where it is not mingled, obscured, or dis-coloured by passion and interest.' So More rejoices when Dorp and he at last arrive at the same conclusions.[1]

The letter to an anonymous monk, in defence of Erasmus, is less friendly.[2] Here again there are some interesting personal touches – notably More's story of his encounter with an ignorant friar, when he visited his sister Elizabeth Rastell at Coventry.

Old-fashioned bigots, like the friar at Coventry or the monk at the table of Bonvisi, did not really matter. They might annoy, but could not seriously check the Erasmian reformers. The real danger to More came, not from that side, but from the Lutherans, who would sidetrack the reform he looked for, and turn it into what he most hated.

More's argument that the Bible should be translated into the English tongue is a noble one; he would have the bishops print it at their own expense, and distribute it for devotional reading. But it must be a translation made by scholars of stand-ing; and it is not to be disputed in taverns for 'every lewd lad to keep a pot-parliament upon'.[3] And it is not for irresponsible individuals like Tyndale to make tendentious translations of their own.

In March 1528, a year and a half before More became Chancellor, Tunstall, as More's bishop, gave him licence to read Lutheran books in order to confute them. Working rapidly, More in the same year produced his massive *Dialogue concerning heresies*, against Luther and Tyndale, in four books. It is a true debate. The antagonist, a man of 'a very merry wit' and 'of nature nothing tongue-tied', is cleverly drawn. More allows him to score some shrewd points, and he does this quite deliberately. But in the end he is like Dr. Johnson, who took care that the Whig dogs should not have the best of it. Then came the *Supplication of Souls* (1529), an answer to the

---

[1] Letter to Dorp, quoted in STAPLETON, v, p. 206.
[2] The letter to Lee and to the monk are both in *Epistolae aliquot Eruditorum*, Antwerp, 1520. More's visit to Coventry was probably about 1506.
[3] *Works*, 1557, p. 246; 'lewd' of course simply means 'ignorant'.

Supplication for the Beggars, in which Simon Fish had urged the confiscation of all church property. Whilst Chancellor, More found time to meet Tyndale's *Answer* with the first part of a *Confutation* (1532). During his retirement he continued the *Confutation of Tyndale's Answer,* replied to John Frith's treatise on the Sacrament, wrote his *Apology* in defence of the clergy, the *Debellation of Salem and Bizance,* and the *Answer to the book which a nameless heretic hath named the supper of the Lord* (the last three in 1533).

A great collection was made by the clergy to reward More for his labours in defence of the Church. Roper says it amounted to four or five thousand pounds – say £70,000 of our money. His friends, Tunstall, by now Bishop of Durham, Clerk of Bath, and Veysey of Exeter joined to urge him that, if he would not take it for himself, at least his wife and children might have it. For More had by his resignation become a poor man. But he realized that the whole moral force of his defence would be gone, if he were in the pay of the clergy. So he refused:

'Not so, my Lords,' quoth he, 'I had liefer see it all cast into the Thames, than I, or any of mine, should have thereof the worth of one penny. For though your offer, my lords, be indeed very friendly and honourable, yet set I so much by my pleasure, and so little by my profit, that I would not, in good faith, for so much, and much more too, have lost the rest of so many nights' sleep as was spent upon the same. And yet wish would I, for all that, upon condition that all heresies were suppressed, that all my books were burned and my labour utterly lost.[1]

Roper's narrative is confirmed by More's own words: that he 'would rather have cast their money into the Thames';[2] that he wished people 'neither to read these heretics' books nor mine, but occupy their minds better' with 'such English books as most may nourish and increase devotion'.[3] He mentions some of these books – Hilton's *Scale of Perfection,* a translation of the *Life of Christ* attributed to St. Bonaventura, and the *Imitation of Christ,* which, to us, goes under the name of Thomas à Kempis.

[1] ROPER, p. 48.   [2] *Works,* 1557, p. 867.   [3] The same, pp. 356-7.

§8. UTOPIAN RELIGION AND HENRICIAN 'REFORM'

It is because More's English works have been inaccessible, that the idea has arisen that there is an incompatibility between More's earlier views, and his writings in defence of the Church, the clergy, clerical celibacy, monasticism, miracles, prayers to the saints and pilgrimages. The more we read *Utopia* together with More's treatises against the heretics, the more they reveal the same mind. The idea that they are opposed springs from a mechanical outlook. To take an obvious example: Protestant ministers may marry, Roman priests are celibate; but the priests in Utopia are married; *argal*, say More's critics, when he wrote *Utopia* he was a Protestant before Protestantism. But More had thought the matter out, which his critics have not. More, when he defended clerical celibacy in the *Dialogue*, had to meet the Pauline text that 'the bishop should be the husband of one wife'.[1] Quite so, said More; that was among the first converts, at a time when the Apostles could make no priests except 'such as either were, or had been, married'. Celibacy, More argued, was a regulation enforced *later* by the Church. Now in Utopia the fundamental laws of nature and human reason prevail. If the celibacy of the clergy is to be regarded as a law of nature and reason, then the Pauline text can only be taken as abrogating the law of nature. It would then amount to a command that the clergy must marry – the very view which Tyndale urged, and which More denied.

'Reason is servant to Faith.' *Utopia* gives us the foundation of Reason, before the Faith is erected upon it. We have seen that in Utopia the clergy are inviolate. But, although themselves inviolate, the Utopian priests have power to excommunicate, and this power is dreaded, for if the person excommunicated do not quickly repent, the secular arm intervenes and punishes him. Utopia has two religious orders, devoted to good works; members of these orders are normally not priests; and here again, this is in conformity with what More advocates later, when defending the Church.[2] One of these orders is celibate, one (like the Franciscan Third Order) permits marriage. The

---

[1] 1 Tim. iii. 2; see *Works*, 1557, pp. 228-9.   [2] *Dialogue*, *Works*, 1557, p. 227.

Utopians have magnificent and solemn churches, which, by the counsel of the priests, have been deliberately built so that the light within may be dim and doubtful, 'because they thought that over much light doth disperse men's cogitations'. Though they have no image of God in their churches, it is not from antipathy to images as such, but because they do not agree as to His likeness; but we have seen that they have an elaborate ritual of vestments, candles, frankincense and music. So far was More, when he wrote *Utopia*, from being even able to comprehend the position of the Reformers, that he allows these things their place in the public worship of the Utopians, *because they are things that can offend no one.*

Utopia is the work of a man who felt that love of ritual and beauty were natural and reasonable instincts.

A great German scholar has distinguished between the two sharply contrasted ideals brought into open conflict as the Middle Ages ended: the Church-ideal, with its visible institutions, and the Sect-ideal, with the emphasis laid upon the individual soul.[1] Now, apart from everything else that we know of More, and of his austere and lifelong orthodoxy, *Utopia* alone should suffice to show us on which side he was likely to find himself in this quarrel. The Protestant reformer placed his hopes in every man being allowed to study for himself the Word of God; but King Utopus brings about reform by compelling men to submit to 'the laws and institutes of the Island of Utopia'. It is not always realized how very medieval those laws are.

Again, from the economic side, the man who depicted so sympathetically the communism of Utopia was bound to distrust the changes of the early Sixteenth Century. It was observed by our great Utopian of the Nineteenth Century, William Morris, that More is rather the last of the old than the first of the new. The spirit of association, as it existed in medieval times, was still strong in him, and led him to denounce the 'ugly brutality of the earliest period of commercialism', the revolution which was altering the peasant life of England.[2] Morris was thinking

---

[1] E. Tröltsch, *Gesammelte Schriften*, I, p. 371 (*Die Soziallehren der christlichen Kirchen und Gruppen*). See E. F. Jacob, *Nicolas of Cusa* in *Some Great Thinkers of the Renaissance*, ed. Hearnshaw, 1925, p. 33; Bryce, *Holy Roman Empire*, 1912, p. 373.

[2] See Introduction to Kelmscott Press edition of Robinson's translation of *Utopia*.

especially of More's denunciation of the grasping landlords,
and the enclosure of the open fields. But a Utopian was equally
bound to dislike the proposal to make over to a grasping king
and to grasping landlords the abbeys, friaries and hospitals.

We may admit that, by the Sixteenth Century, most of the
medieval experiments in corporate life badly needed overhaul-
ing and mending. But More had laid it down in *Utopia* that a
physician must be foolish, if he can only cure a patient of one
disease by giving him another; and that likewise the king, who
can amend the life of his subjects only by confiscation, shows
that he knows not how to rule freemen. *Utopia* proclaims that,
whilst he realized the faults of individual friars or monks, More
believed their community houses to be on the right lines. In
such institutions, as Burke put it later, there was 'a great *power*
for the mechanism of politic benevolence, what our workmen
call a *purchase*. There were revenues with a public direction;
there were men without the possibility of converting the estate
into a private fortune. In vain shall a man look for the possibility of making such things when he wants them. The winds
blow as they list. These institutions are the products of enthusiasm; they are the instruments of wisdom'. How was the
man who wrote *Utopia* 'changing', because he dreaded the
prospect of these revenues with a public direction being converted to private fortunes, and to the upkeep of the very things
he thought most useless, armaments, great households, and idle
serving men?

Medieval collectivism had been wrapped up with medieval
religion. The storm that was brewing threatened both. The
Guilds prayed for the souls of the dead, and this brought them
under the ban of the Reformers. The very existence of the
hospitals was threatened by some Reformers, because of their
connection with the Church. 'The more hospitals the worse',
said Simon Fish. Surely such words might move a Utopian to
wrath. They moved More to fear also. Of all the heretical
pamphlets, he had most to dread that of Simon Fish; before
More became Chancellor, it had apparently reached the
hands of the king, and the king was considering if he should
act on it.[1]

---

[1] Foxe, ed. Townsend, IV, 658; cf. *L.P.*, IV, No. 5416.

Whether the London hospitals were well or ill managed is not the point. Statements made by flatterers, after the king's wish for an excuse for confiscation had become publicly known, are not evidence. The point is, that More and his circle believed that 'the products of enthusiasm' should be made 'the instruments of wisdom'. More outlined this in *Utopia*; his friend and fellow-courtier, Vives, showed more in detail how it might be done. 'Reactionaries' like More and Vives could not see the logic of the argument that, because funds left for the aid of the sick were alleged to be badly administered, therefore they should be taken from the sick and given to the wealthy. The advice of Fish and of Cromwell proved in the end more to Henry's mind. More had not been dead many months when one of the four great London houses for the sick was given to Henry by Parliament. It became the dwelling-house of Sir John Williams, Master of the Jewels, and the 'lodgings for the poor' became stables: a grim commentary on what More had said in *Utopia* twenty years before – that the sick and aged poor were cared for no better than beasts of burden, and that the rich were daily seeking, under form of law, to take from them even what they had. Soon the three other hospitals were also laid waste. The inmates sometimes received a pittance for some weeks or months; sometimes they were in mercy allowed to remain in any odd corners of the buildings where they could find shelter, and were 'supported by the casual alms of the charitable'.[1] But the staff were turned away; each 'late hospital' lay 'vacant and altogether destitute'. So things continued for years, till Henry, 'divine mercy inspiring us', restored for charitable purposes the site of *one* of the four hospitals, Rahere's great foundation of St. Bartholomew's. But Henry retained the endowments, and as there was equipment for only three or four patients,[2] a mere site was not much use. Therefore Henry resumed possession. But the protests of the City were too strong to be quite ignored, and on his deathbed Henry re-granted the hospital buildings and most (not all) of the endowments. Thus he became the 'Founder'. The vulgarity by which Henry claimed to be the donor of charities

---

[1] Norman Moore, *History of St. Bartholomew's Hospital*, ii, p. 126.
[2] Ibid., p. 153.

he did not destroy has even shocked his admirers; but many years before, in *Utopia*, More had depicted flatterers instilling into a king that he is the gracious donor of whatsoever he does not confiscate. Years of flattery had convinced Henry in all sincerity that this was so; but why is More said to have 'changed' because in 1529 he opposed what in 1516 he had asserted it to be the plain duty of a councillor to oppose?

Ten years elapsed between the date when Henry began the sack of the London hospitals, and the date when he re-endowed St. Bartholomew's.

The city, later, recovered St. Thomas's from Edward VI; the two other hospitals were for ever destroyed. Yet one of these, St. Mary's outside Bishopsgate, had a much larger revenue than either St. Bartholomew's or St. Thomas's; at the Dissolution 'there were found 180 beds, well furnished, for the receipt of the poor; for it was an Hospital of great relief'. [1]

Now every modern reader is struck by the picture of the four great hospitals which stand outside the chief town of Utopia, Amaurot. But in this, as as in other details (to some of which the marginal notes of *Utopia* call attention), More is merely giving a glorified picture of 'the flower of cities all', that most beautiful (if most insanitary) London which he loved. The proposal to destroy the spacious churches, halls, and hospitals which were the honour of his town, moved him to indignant protest against the railing rhetoric of Simon Fish:

But now to the poor beggars: what remedy findeth their proctor [Simon Fish] for them? To make hospitals? Nay, ware of that! Thereof he will none in no wise. For thereof, he saith, the more the worse, because they be profitable to priests. What remedy then? Give them any money? Nay, Nay, not a groat. What other thing then? Nothing in the world will serve but this: that if the king's grace will build a sure hospital, that never shall fail to relieve all the sick beggars for ever, let him give nothing to them, but look what the clergy hath, and take all that from them. Is not here a goodly mischief for a remedy? Is not this a royal feast, to leave these beggars meatless, and then send more to dinner to them? [2]

---

[1] STOW, *Survey* (1603), p. 168.   [2] *Works*, 1557, pp. 301, 302.

This is no caricature. Fish contemplates no re-endowment; he does really suggest the confiscation of all the property of the Church, and apparently the abolition of the clergy themselves, as the one remedy for social evils. But, in Utopia, a citizen who had privately suggested such things to the prince as Fish suggested to Henry would have been put to death. Why, then, wonder at More's indignation?

When it was too late, More's indignation was echoed by English writers of every party: and the most vocal of all were the extreme Reformers themselves. Latimer has too many associates in his 'protest against the Protestant tyranny'[1] for their evidence to remain for ever ignored. The difference between More and the Reformers is this: More protested beforehand against the policy of 'leaving beggars meatless, and then sending more to dinner to them'; the Reformers bewailed the results of that policy. One of them rejoices 'for the Faith's sake' that the Abbeys have been taken from the 'Imps of Antichrist', but he admits that *'it had been more profitable for the Commonwealth that they had remained still in their hands'*.[2] The monasteries, another Reformer groans, at least 'kept hospitality, let out their farms at a reasonable price, nourished schools, brought up youth in good letters'; but the laity who have got the monastic lands 'do none of all these things'.[3] 'The state of England was never so miserable, as it is at this present.' The same complaint, that schools had been ruined, and charitable provision for the poor made away, was bluntly stated by a preacher before Edward VI and his Council.[4] More had gone so far as to say that the oppression with which Christian people were threatened by the spread of these new ideas was worse than the tyranny of the Turks.[5] It was left for an extreme Reformer to tell how a merchant, returning home after many years abroad, was surprised to see the old almshouse gorgeously rebuilt, till he was undeceived by a beggar, who explained that the inmates had been turned out to die in corners, and that men of great riches now owned the house:

---

[1] W. P. KER in CRAIK's *English Prose*, I, 226.
[2] BRINKLOW, *Roderick Mors*, ed. COWPER, E.E.T.S. (1874), pp. 9, 32, etc.
[3] BECON, *Jewel of Joy* (1553), H. ii, verso.
[4] LEVER, *Sermons*, ed. ARBER, 81.   [5] *Works*, 1557, p. 275.

Lord God, quoth this merchant,
    In Turkey have I been,
    Yet among those heathen
    None such cruelty have I seen.[1]

Mr. R. H. Tawney puts it that 'the classes whose backing was needed to make the Reformation a political success had sold their support on terms which made it inevitable that it should be a social disaster.'[2] More saw the bargain being made, though he did not live to see its fruits. He watched the court of Henry VIII with that uncanny insight which enabled him to make forecasts such as Roper has recorded. He must have realized exactly what was threatened, when Fish's *Supplication of Beggars* was passed from one greedy courtier to another, from Rochford to Anne Boleyn, and from Anne to Henry himself. At the very time that More was publishing his reply to Simon Fish, foreign observers were struck with the open way in which the great lords were planning to take the property of the Church.[3] Where the modern economic historian speaks of 'social disaster', More, in his more picturesque Tudor English, calls it 'a devilish desire of noyance both to poor and rich; priest, religious and layman; prince, lord and people; as well quick as dead'.[4]

To describe the 'progressive' author of *Utopia* as having 'changed into a reactionary', because he did not wish to tread 'the path of progress' exactly as Henry and Thomas Cromwell were planning to tread it, seems unreasonable, whether we think of the religious houses and their beautiful ritual, or of social problems and the growth of capitalism. From the political point of view there was not more ground for sympathy. The essence of Henry's revolution was to sweep aside one of the two sets of rulers, ecclesiastical and civil, who, in theory, had governed Christendom. One medieval ideal, which Marco Lombardo explained to Dante in the Third Circle of Purgatory, had been that the temporal and spiritual powers should guide and check each other.[5] And we have seen that this dual control seemed so much a matter of course to More when he

---

[1] Crowley, *Selected Works*, ed. Cowper, E.E.T.S. (1872), pp. 11, 12.
[2] *Religion and the Rise of Capitalism* (1926), p. 142.
[3] *L.P.*, IV, No. 6011; Le Grand, *Histoire du Divorce*, III, 374 (1688).
[4] *Works*, 1557, p. 290.   [5] *Purgatorio*, xvi, 106-8.

wrote *Utopia* that, although the Utopians are heathen, they reflect the medieval theory, with the two parallel authorities, civil magistrates and priests. But Henry's revolution left the king supreme. So it was natural that a Reformer like Tyndale should write, 'The king is, in this world, without law, and may at his lust do right or wrong, and shall give account but to God only'. It was equally natural that Henry should say of Tyndale's book, 'This book is for me, and all kings, to read'.[1] And it was equally natural that the deviser of *Utopia* should disapprove of Tyndale and his book, seeing that in Utopia the prince is hedged in by laws which it means deposition for him to break, and may be excommunicated by priests whom he cannot touch.

Now all these things which have been mentioned are not among the beliefs which a Utopian may accept or reject at will. The solemn dark churches, with their elaborate ritual of music, vestments, candles, and frankincense, are part of that state religion which remains, when everything has been removed which can offend any particular sect. So, too, the dual authority, ecclesiastical and civil, the limited power of the prince, and the inviolability of the priest, are not tenets of any sect, but part of the fundamental constitution of Utopia.

More's critics have not realized how many of the things in defence of which he, at the end of his life, stepped forward, had already seemed to him so vital when he wrote *Utopia*, that he made them part of that greatest common measure of all religions which is the official creed of Utopia.

What is remarkable, then, about the religion of *Utopia* is not the extent to which it differs from the practice of the medieval Church, but the extent to which it coincides with it. There *are* differences, and they follow, inevitably, from the postulate that Utopia is a 'philosophical city' grounded upon reason alone: the Utopians, ignorant of revelation, naturally have views on worship, asceticism, suicide, and divorce which differ from those of the orthodox in the Middle Ages. And 'the verses in the Utopian tongue', added apparently by Peter Giles, with a Latin translation, emphasize this point. King Utopus 'has offered to men a pattern of a philosophical city. In his turn

---

[1] STRYPE, *Ecclesiastical Memorials* (1822), I, i, 172.

he is willing to receive better'. More is sketching a system of
what Francis Bacon, in the *Advancement of Learning*, calls
Natural Theology ('that rudiment of knowledge concerning
God obtained by a contemplation of his creatures') as against
Divine Learning, which is 'grounded on the word and oracle
of God'. Bacon has little interest in Natural Theology; it
suffices to disprove Atheism, but beyond that he will not go.
In *Utopia* More goes a great deal further: ritual, symbolism,
and sacerdotalism have their place in the Natural Religion of
Utopia.

What would have happened to a Protestant reformer seeking
to evangelize Utopia? Such a reformer would have objected to
the solemn churches. These pope-holy works, he would have
said, by their darkness prevent us from reading the Word of
God.[1] He would have called 'the curiosity of their dainty
singing' nothing but 'a mockery with God'.[2] The tapers offered
in these dark churches, for purposes of ritual, would have drawn
from the reformer the scoff which irritated More – 'Does God
need candlelight?'[3] A reformer would have seen only an out-of-
date abuse in the inviolability of the Utopian priests; and still
more in their vestments, in the varied colours of which they
asserted that various divine mysteries, of which the priests held
the key, were symbolized. Could a thoroughgoing reformer
have abstained from assailing such 'conjuring garments'?[4] He
would have ascribed to the Devil[5] the miracles which the
Utopians asserted to happen often, and which they 'highly
esteemed'. But, had he 'contended thus vehemently and fer-
vently', our Protestant reformer would have been deported
from Utopia, or else condemned to penal servitude, with the
threat of death if he were still recalcitrant.

Utopia tolerates those who worship Sun or Moon; but if a
man declares any recognized religion to be profane, impious,
and sacrilegious, Utopia does not tolerate *him*; he is punished
cruelly. This is very much the same view as that which More
put forward later, when writing against the Reformers: that it

---

[1] Compare *Works of Tyndale, Frith, and Barnes*, 1572, p. 279.
[2] BILNEY, quoted by FOXE, ed. TOWNSEND, IV, p. 621.
[3] *Dialogue, Works*, 1557, p. 118.
[4] CROWLEY, quoted in STRYPE, *Life of Parker*, 1821, I, p. 301.
[5] cf. MORE, *Dialogue, Works*, 1557, p. 286.

'were peradventure none evil way' to allow Turkish missionaries in Christendom, if the Turk would receive Christian
missionaries in Turkey, 'violence taken away by assent on both
sides'; but that this is no reason for tolerating heretics, who *are*
violent.[1]

Anyway, Utopia would have tolerated no reformer in
religion, if 'reformer' implies persistent censure of the unre-
formed. We must never allow ourselves to forget the kind of
arguments More had to meet. One of his antagonists, after
bringing every filthy accusation he can think of against all the
clergy, demands that they be tied to carts, to be whipped naked
about every market town, and then married. Whereby, says
More, 'what opinion he hath of wedding ye may soon perceive:
for ye see well that if he thought it good he would not wish it
them'.[2] Tyndale and many of the other martyrs had used
words hardly less violent. Such language, quite apart from any
question of the doctrines they are maintaining, places Tyndale
and Fish outside the toleration of Utopia. More is simply
echoing *Utopia* when he blames the heretics for being raisers-up
of dissensions; or again, when, in defence of the severe words he
feels bound to use, he says:

> If they [the heretics] will not . . . be heretics alone themself
> and hold their tongues and be still, but will needs be babbling
> and corrupt whom they can, let them yet at the leastwise
> be reasonable heretics, and honest, and write reason and
> leave railing, and then let the brethren find the fault with
> me, if I use them not after that in words as fair and as mild
> as the matter may suffer and bear.[3]

But, More adds, this way will the heretics never take. 'In
railing standeth all their revel.'

Again, the same feeling for European solidarity which runs
through *Utopia* runs also through More's treatises against the
Reformers. The Lutheran teaching, that it would be better to
have Germany Turkish than Catholic, and that the Turk was
a divinely appointed scourge whom it was sinful to resist, has
been denounced by an English historian as treachery to
Germany – it was dangerous, he says, to the peace and unity,

---

[1] *Works*, 1557, pp. 275-6. [2] The same, p. 307. [3] The same, p. 866

nay to the very existence of the German nation.[1] It is characteristic of the modern historian that he attacks such teaching as a
threat to German nationality. It is characteristic of More that
he attacks it[2] as dangerous to the peace, unity, and existence
of Christendom.

Like Fisher, More could never forget that Islam had won
from Christendom Asia, Africa, nearly half Europe, and was
still advancing. From the age of Bede to the Fifteenth Century,
Europe had held its own. Now, once more, it seemed to be
retiring. The heretics who would rend Christendom asunder
at the moment when the Turk was at the gates of Vienna are,
in More's view, traitors to the common cause. Almost equally
so are the Christian kings, who are censured in *Utopia* because
they think of nothing but war among themselves.

From *Utopia* to the scaffold, More stands for the common
cause, as against the private commodity of the single man, or
even the single kingdom. He will not accept the new statesmanship which regards the nations as totally independent,
'gladiators in the European arena', and which makes one
nation look on with complacency, and almost with satisfaction,
at the prospect of another being destroyed by the Turkish
hordes.

Yet it is not enough merely to think of More as one who
struggled to keep down the barriers rising to divide Christendom, and as the advocate of the poor against a growing commercialism, and as a humane lover of animals and men. It is
easy, by selection, to make a picture of More, as of St. Francis
of Assisi, which is but a half-truth. What seemed to More the
most terrible thing in the clamour for the plunder of Church
endowments was that it involved, not only social injustice, but
the cessation of prayer for the dead: 'that any Christian man
could, for very pity, have founden in his heart to seek and study
the means, whereby a Christian man should think it labour lost,
to pray for all Christian souls'.[3] The average man to-day feels
that a dissolution of the monasteries should have preserved all
the monastic libraries; should have made arrangements for the
carrying on of the philanthropic and educational work, much

---

[1] ARMSTRONG, *Charles V*, I, p. 260.   [2] *Dialogue, Works*, 1557, p. 278.
[3] *Works*, 1557, p. 290.

of which was so brutally interrupted; should have left standing for public use, as places of preaching and assembly, all those great London churches, the want of which was bitterly felt when the nobles had turned them into storehouses for herrings and wine. We all regret the destruction of historical monuments: 'spoiled, broken and ruinated, to the offence of all noble and gentle hearts', as the proclamation of the second year of Queen Elizabeth put it. But if all these things had been safeguarded, More would still have disapproved of a wholesale dissolution. He believed in the religious houses as places of prayer, and of prayer for the souls of the dead. None have ever felt more earnestly that the noble living and the noble dead are branches of one society. This characteristic of More struck Erasmus: 'He talks with his friends in such a way about the world to come that you can see that he is speaking from his heart, not without good hope.'[1] This is the meaning of More's words on the way to the scaffold, when he assured the Winchester man who had been sustained by his prayer, that there need be no fear lest such prayer was now about to cease.

This belief in the communion of saints is a fundamental article of the Utopian creed. Not only must the Utopian believe in immortality. The Utopians further

> suppose the dead to be present among them when they talk of them, though to the dull and feeble eyesight of mortal men they be invisible. For it were an unconvenient thing, that the blessed should not be at liberty to go whither they would. And it were a point of great unkindness in them, to have utterly cast away the desire of visiting and seeing their friends ... Therefore the Utopians go more courageously to their business, as having a trust and affiance in such overseers.

§9. 'THAT WORTHY AND UNCORRUPT MAGISTRATE'

But it was not as a statesman or a writer or a defender of the Church that More was best remembered. It is as 'that worthy and uncorrupt magistrate' that Sir John Harington sums him up, sixty-one years after his death. And Erasmus

[1] ALLEN, IV, 999, p. 21.

had said the same thing when he heard of More's appointment as Chancellor: 'a holy and righteous judge'.

Too righteous, some of his family thought. Roper tells us that, he being at leisure, as seldom he was whilst he was Lord Chancellor, one of his sons-in-law (it must have been William Dauncey) pointed out that even the very doorkeepers of the Cardinal had got great gain. But he could not honestly receive anything from his friends and kinsfolk for giving them access to More, because he knew that More was so accessible that no introduction was necessary: 'Which condition, although he thought in Sir Thomas More very commendable, yet to him, said he, being his son, he found it nothing profitable.' More congratulated Dauncey on being so scrupulous, but said that there *were* means by which he could help a friend of Dauncey's, by word or letter: 'or if he have a cause depending before me, at your request I may hear him before another. Or, if his cause be not all the best, yet may I move the parties to fall to some reasonable end by arbitrement'.[1]

It shows how much judicial etiquette has changed, that More's Nineteenth Century lawyer biographers are scandalized at the mild favouritism, by bestowing which More thought he might mollify his son-in-law: 'such practices would now be matter of severe censure or impeachment',[2] says one. More would have recoiled from such breaches of equality if he had been called upon to perform them, says another.[3]

But More's conclusion was quite uncompromising:

Howbeit, this one thing, son, I assure thee on my faith, that if the parties will at my hands call for justice, then, all were it my father stood on the one side, and the Devil on the other, his cause being good, the Devil should have right.

And More was as good as his word:

That he would for no respect digress from justice well appeared by a plain example of another of his sons-in-law called Master Heron. For when he, having a matter before him in the Chancery, and presuming too much of his favour, would by him in no wise be persuaded to agree to any

[1] ROPER, p. 42.   [2] LORD CAMPBELL, *Lives*, 1856, p. 33.
[3] SIR JAMES MACKINTOSH, *Life*, 1844, p. 139.

indifferent order, then made he in conclusion a flat decree against him.[1]

The details of this case are preserved in the Record Office, and those who feel tempted to further research may go to Chancery Lane and consult Early Chancery Proceedings, Bundle 643, No. 32: Giles Heron *versus* Nicholas Millisante.

It was well for More that he kept his hands clean. For otherwise, as Roper remarks, when he comes to tell of More's retirement from office, 'it would, without doubt, in this troublous time of the King's indignation towards him, have been deeply laid to his charge and of the King's Highness most favourably accepted'.

As in the case of one Parnell it most manifestly appeared; against whom, because Sir Thomas More, while he was Lord Chancellor, at the suit of one Vaughan, his adversary, had made a decree, this Parnell to his Highness most grievously complained that Sir Thomas More, for making the same decree, had of the same Vaughan (unable for the gout to travel abroad himself) by the hands of his wife taken a fair great gilt cup for a bribe. Who thereupon, by the King's appointment, being called before the whole Council, where that matter was heinously laid to his charge, forthwith confessed that forasmuch as that cup was, long after the foresaid decree, brought him for a New Year's gift, he upon her importunate pressing upon him therefore, of courtesy refused not to receive it.

Then the Lord of Wiltshire[2] (for hatred of his religion preferrer of this suit) with much rejoicing said unto the Lords, 'Lo, did I not tell you, my Lords, that you should find this matter true?' Whereupon Sir Thomas More desired their Lordships that as they had courteously heard him tell the one part of his tale, so they would vouchsafe of their honours indifferently to hear the other. After which obtained, he further declared unto them that, albeit he had indeed, with much work, received that cup, yet immediately thereupon he caused his butler to fill it with wine, and of that cup drank to her; and that when he had so done, and she pledged

---

[1] ROPER, pp. 42-3.

[2] Thomas Boleyn, Earl of Wiltshire, Queen Anne's father. Roper, in using the words 'for hatred of his religion' is thinking of the Boleyns' feud with More in the matter of the Supremacy. Roper does not say that Wiltshire was a Lutheran.

him, then as freely as her husband had given it to him, even so freely gave he the same unto her again, to give unto her husband for his New Year's gift; which, at his instant request, though much against her will, at length yet she was fain to receive, as herself, and certain other there, presently before them deposed. Thus was the great mountain turned scant to a little molehill.[1]

The details of the Parnell-Vaughan case are extant.[2] We may note that, four and a half years later, a John Parnell, gentleman, was a member of the jury that found More guilty.

Other anecdotes of Roper illustrate the difference of standard between More's time and our own. It is clear that to have rejected a proffered bribe too brusquely might have hurt the feelings of a worthy litigant.

At another time, upon a New Year's Day, there came to him one Mistress Crocker, a rich widow, for whom, with no small pain, he had made a decree in the Chancery against the Lord of Arundel, to present him with a pair of gloves, and forty pounds in angels in them, for a New Year's gift. Of whom he thankfully receiving the gloves, but refusing the money, said unto her: 'Mistress, since it were against good manners to forsake a gentlewoman's New Year's gift, I am content to take your gloves, but as for your money I utterly refuse.' So, much against her mind, enforced he her to take her gold again.

And one Master Gresham likewise, having at the same time a cause depending in the Chancery before him, sent him for a New Year's gift a fair gilt cup, the fashion whereof he very well liking, caused one of his own (though not in his fantasy of so good a fashion, yet better in value) to be brought him out of his chamber, which he willed the messenger, in recompence, to deliver to his master; and under other condition would he in no wise receive it.[3]

Here again the modern lawyer is apt to be a little shocked. Some six years ago Lord Justice Russell wrote: 'Sir Thomas More's integrity emerged unscathed from these charges; but I confess his conduct over the Gresham cup strikes me as in-

[1] ROPER, pp. 61-3.
[2] C 1/685/39. The case was heard 20 Jan. 1531 (Richard and Geoffrey Vaughan *v.* John Parnell).
[3] ROPER, pp. 63-4.

judicious, and I should have liked to have seen Mistress Crocker committed for contempt of court.'[1]

More used to sit in his open hall every afternoon, to receive suitors and hear complaints,[2] and it was here that he delivered one of his judgments which, though not amongst the best authenticated, at least bears the closest resemblance to that which made the reputation of Solomon:

> Sir Thomas his last wife loved little dogs to play withal. It happened that she was presented with one, which had been stolen from a poor beggar woman. The poor beggar challenged her dog, having spied it in the arms of one of the serving men, that gave attendance upon my lady. The dog was denied her; so there was great hold and keep about it. At length Sir Thomas had notice of it; so caused both his wife and the beggar to come before him in his hall; and said, 'Wife, stand you here, at the upper end of the hall, because you are a gentlewoman; and goodwife, stand there beneath, for you shall have no wrong.' He placed himself in the midst, and held the dog in his hands, saying to them, 'Are you content, that I shall decide this controversy that is between you concerning this dog?' 'Yes,' quoth they. 'Then,' said he, 'each of you call the dog by his name, and to whom the dog cometh, she shall have it.' The dog came to the poor woman; so he caused the dog to be given her, and gave her besides a French crown, and desired her that she would bestow the dog upon his lady. The poor woman was well apaid with his fair speeches, and his alms, and so delivered the dog to my lady.[3]

Wolsey's passion for the administration of impartial justice had been one of the good features of his rule, upon which the few friends he left behind him felt free to dilate. The abuses of the common law (and they were many) were controlled by Wolsey as Chancellor: 'He did a good deal in detail by means of injunctions staying the execution of what the judges called law in the interests of what Wolsey called equity.'[4] In the words of Wolsey's biographer, the Chancellor by Wolsey's day had become

---

[1] *The Fame of Sir Thomas More*, p. 74.   [2] Roper, p. 43.
[3] The story comes from the life by 'Ro. Ba.', written at the end of Elizabeth's reign. *Ecclesiastical Biography*, II, pp. 102-3.
[4] Pollard, *Wolsey*, p. 95.

the King's principal agent for the purpose of mitigating the rigour and the rigidity of the common law, filling the growing gaps which the archaism of that ancient structure exhibited to the needs of a newer age and a subtler civilization, and welding into a system and into a constitution heterogeneous practices and ideas derived from the law of God and the law of nature, common law and statute, canon law and civil law, the law merchant and the law martial, the custom of the country and the practice of the seas. The chaos, with which this conflict of laws menaced good government during the later middle ages, needed as strong a hand and as firm a treatment as the conflict of arms which came to a head in the wars of the roses. The 'new' monarchy was a response to that need and an impersonation of the modern state; its agent in respect of the conflict of laws was the chancellor; and the chancellor *par excellence* was Wolsey.[1]

When More succeeded Wolsey as Chancellor, he inherited two problems: firstly there was the friction which had arisen between the common lawyers and the Chancellor by reason of Wolsey's injunctions staying the execution of law; secondly, there was the congestion of business. Roper, a lawyer, assures us that More was careful to issue as few injunctions as he could; but the judges were in a state of irritation, and Roper had to warn his father-in-law that some of them 'misliked' his action. More dealt with the problem in a peculiarly modern manner – an invitation to dinner, followed by an informal discussion. But before issuing the invitation, he carefully prepared the ground over which the discussion would range. Among the principal officers of the Court of Chancery were the Six Clerks, whose duty it was to file all bills, answers, replications, and other records, in causes on the Equity side of the Court of Chancery. More caused the chief of the Six Clerks

to make a docket containing the whole number and causes of all such injunctions as either in his time had already passed, or at that present depended in any of the King's Courts at Westminster before him. Which done, he invited all the judges to dine with him in the council chamber at Westminster: where, after dinner, when he had broken with them what complaints he had heard of his injunctions, and more-

over showed them both the number and causes of every one
of them, in order, so plainly that, upon full debating of those
matters, they were all enforced to confess that they, in like
case, could have done no other wise themselves, then offered
he this unto them: that if the justices of every court (unto
whom the reformation of the rigour of the law, by reason of
their office, most especially appertained) would, upon
reasonable considerations, by their own discretions (as they
were, as he thought, in conscience bound) mitigate and
reform the rigour of the law themselves, there should from
thenceforth by him no more injunctions be granted. Whereunto when they refused to condescend, then said he unto
them: 'Forasmuch as yourselves, my Lords, drive me to that
necessity for awarding out injunctions to relieve the people's
injury, you cannot hereafter any more justly blame me.'
After that he said secretly unto me, 'I perceive, son, why they
like not so to do, for they see that they may by the verdict
of the jury cast off all quarrels from themselves upon them,
which they account their chief defence; and therefore am I
compelled to abide the adventure of all such reports.'[1]

The second difficulty – the congestion of business – was the
natural result of Wolsey's distractions; for Pooh Bah himself
hardly held a more heterogeneous or a more important collection of offices than More's predecessor had done. The office
upon which Wolsey had most prided himself had not been that
of Chancellor, but of Papal Legate. As Papal Legate, Archbishop of York, Bishop of Winchester, Abbot of St. Albans, and
from time to time Ambassador abroad, Wolsey must have found
the time very limited which, as Chancellor, he could devote to
legal affairs. It was asserted that, when More took office,
cases were pending which had been introduced twenty years
before.[2]

Here More had an immense advantage over his predecessor.
The King used him as little as possible on business on which
his conscience was not persuaded, and the King's business
became more and more of that character. We can imagine the
relief it must have been to More, as everything he loved was
threatened, to be able to concentrate his mind upon his
intricate legal duties. He had, what Wolsey had not, a legal

[1] ROPER, pp. 44-5.   [2] STAPLETON, III, p. 179.

training; and he now applied to the legal business of Chancery that peculiarly rapid mind which in earlier days had enabled him to grasp the meaning of a Greek sentence with a quickness which astonished his humanist colleagues.

His day of triumph came when, having taken his seat and settled a case, he called for the next, and was told that there was no man or matter to be heard. 'This,' we are told, 'he caused to be enrolled in the public acts of that Court.' Two generations later it remained a marvel. 'It is strange to them that know there have been causes there depending some dozen years.'[1]

It was this, together with his humour, which gave More his traditional reputation:

> When More some time had Chancellor been,
>   No more suits did remain.
> The like will never more be seen
>   Till More be there again.

Clearly, it could not be done without arousing some enmities; and we know that on his way to the scaffold More was reviled by a disappointed suitor. But the verdict of his fellow countrymen on this subject was definite.[2] Roper could have given, he tells us, many more instances of his father-in-law's 'innocency and clearness from all corruption'. But he left it to his readers 'with their own judgments wisely to weigh and consider' the few examples he gave.

§ 1 0.   THE CHANCELLOR AND THE HERETICS

A further series of charges turns upon More's alleged cruelty to heretics; and it would have been well if More's critics had (in Roper's phrase) 'wisely weighed and considered' these charges.

More, while denying indignantly the cruelties attributed to him, 'wills all the world to wit on the other side' that he believes that it is necessary to prohibit 'the sowing of seditious heresies', and to punish, in extreme cases with death, those who defy such prohibition.[3] It was the view, held by all parties alike,

---

[1] 'Ro. Ba.', *Life of Sir Thomas More: Ecclesiastical Biography*, II, p. 80.
[2] e.g. John Owen's Epigrams, ed. Leyden, 1628, p. 172; London, 1633, p. 137. Many other instances might be quoted.
[3] See especially *Works*, 1557, pp. 274-88, 926.

that open defiance of authority in spiritual matters, of such a kind as to lead to tumult and civil war, might be punished with death. I have tried to show above that there is nothing in this inconsistent with the Laws of Utopia.

After Wolsey was succeeded by More as Chancellor, there was a sudden revival of religious persecution. It has been the custom to blame More for this. The charge against More overlooks the obvious fact that in their capacity of Chancellor, neither Wolsey nor More could have burnt a heretic. The trial of heretics was entirely a matter for the bishops and the Ecclesiastical Courts. In the very rare cases in which the death sentence was inflicted on an obstinate heretic, the civil power actually carried out the sentence, but the sheriff or other officer had nothing to do with condemnation or acquittal. As a layman, More could not have tried and sentenced heretics. It was the bishops' duty to try heretics, and More was very firmly of opinion that it ought to remain so.[1] For brief periods, however, heretics were in More's temporary custody.

The charge of persecution turns on a passage in More's *Apology*, where (as it is asserted) More admits that he had twice flogged for heresy. Accordingly, his denial of further 'enormities' is dismissed as mere forgetfulness; 'he under-estimated his activity'. Now More's *Apology* was never printed between 1557 and 1930, and More has been condemned unheard. What More admits is this. He accepted into his household a child from a heretical home. He once ordered this child to be flogged – not for holding heretical dogmas, but for teaching them to another child in the house. The households of great men filled in Tudor days some of the functions of a public school. Now, even if More had been the philosophic agnostic which some people think the author of *Utopia* ought to have been, yet, in fairness to the orthodox parents who had trusted their children to him, he could not have allowed these children to be taught an illegal doctrine, the holding of which might have made them liable to the death penalty when they grew up.

The second case is more serious; in a passage, twice reprinted in the nineteenth century, More tells, with what reads like callous brutality, how he caused a heretic, admittedly half-

[1] *L.P.*, v, No. 1013 (13 May 1532).

witted, to be flogged. But the appearance of brutality is due to
the fact that the passage has been twice bowdlerized in the
interests of propriety. More flogged the man, not for holding
heretical views, but for making indecent attacks upon women,
in church, at the time of the Elevation. I will venture to restore
the expurgated passage:

> And if he spied any woman kneeling at a form, if her head
> hung anything low in her meditations, then would he steal
> behind her, and, if he were not letted, would labour to lift
> up all her clothes and cast them quite over her head.[1]

More, 'being advertized of these pageants', at the request
of 'very devout religious folk' intervened, and had a sound
thrashing administered, making sure that the man had enough
wits to know why he was being flogged. Nowadays, the culprit
might have been sent to prison, or perhaps for life to an asylum.
More's rough and ready method was effective, and more merciful. 'God be thanked,' he writes later, 'I hear none harm of
him now.'

Yet three eminent writers have quoted this case as proving
that heretics were 'persecuted', 'beaten into orthodoxy' and
punished 'for religious opinion', by More.

Which proves that, when we expurgate, we should always
insert asterisks.

Though he was not flogged for heresy, the culprit was
indisputably a heretic, and was indisputably flogged against a
tree outside More's garden. But there were also trees inside
the garden (one is asserted to be still standing in Chelsea to-day).
Why should not those trees have been used for flogging heretics?
More tells us how the story grew:

> . . . so farforth that one Segar, a bookseller of Cambridge,
> which was in mine house about four or five days, and never
> had either bodily harm done him, or foul word spoken him
> while he was in mine house, hath reported since, as I hear
> say, to divers, that he was bounden to a tree in my garden,
> and thereto too piteously beaten, and yet beside that bounden
> about the head with a cord and wrungen, that he fell down
> dead in a swoon.

And this tale of his beating did Tyndale tell to an old

[1] *Apology*, cap. 36; *Works*, 1557, p. 901.

acquaintance of his own, and to a good lover of mine, with one piece farther yet, that while the man was in beating, I spied a little purse of his hanging at his doublet, wherein the poor man had (as he said) five mark, and that caught I quickly to me, and pulled it from his doublet, and put it in my bosom, and that Segar never saw it after. And therein I trow he said true, for no more did I neither, nor before neither. Nor, I trow, no more did Segar himself neither, in good faith.[1]

And of all that ever came in my hand for heresy, as help me God, saving, as I said, the sure keeping of them, (and yet not so sure neither, but that George Constantine could steal away) else had never any of them any stripe or stroke given them, so much as a fillip on the forehead.[2]

Now we cannot get round this denial by suggesting that More is mistaken: that 'it is clear that he under-estimated his activity'. The charge is that, as Chancellor, More illegally tortured luckless heretics who were in his keeping for a few days before being given into the custody of the bishop. More, writing a few months after his resignation, says that he gave them 'not so much as a fillip on the forehead'. Either he is speaking the truth, or he is telling a peculiarly deliberate and peculiarly cowardly lie. Dean Swift calls More the person 'of the greatest virtue this kingdom ever produced',[3] and Dean Swift did not give testimonials recklessly: when our *Dictionary of National Biography* asserts that this most virtuous Englishman who ever lived was a liar, Englishmen are entitled to ask for the evidence. What is the evidence?

There are two petitions, extant in the Record Office, which accuse More of illegal imprisonment. Froude treats these charges as true.[4] Froude cannot have known that, in the *Apology*, More deals with this very question, mentioning by name one of the petitioners, Philips, and telling how the king ordered a scrutiny, and how the accusation had to be dismissed as frivolous.

More challenged his traducers to produce the evidence at a time when he was in retirement and poverty. If he really *had* instructed his officers to inflict illegal torture and imprisonment,

[1] *Apology*, cap. 36; *Works*, 1557, p. 902.   [2] The same, p. 901.
[3] *Works* (ed. Temple Scott), iii, 301.   [4] *History*, ii (1856), pp. 76-83.

he was in no position to have closed their mouths. It would, as Roper says, 'in this troublous time of the king's indignation towards him have been deeply laid to his charge, and of the king's highness most favourably accepted'.

Yet all the efforts of More's foes procured no such evidence of illegal floggings and torturings. After More's execution a wave of protest against his death passed over Europe; and there is evidence that the Government tried to counter this by inventing, and circulating in Germany, stories of More's cruelty to heretics.[1] And the story of Segar the bookseller was not forgotten, though it got attached to other names. A generation later, when the tales of the Protestant martyrs were collected, More was charged with having abused his power as Chancellor against four heretics, Tewkesbury, Frith, Petit and Bainham. We know the dates when these atrocities must have occurred, if they did occur, *and in three cases they do not fall within More's chancellorship.* The fourth case is possible, chronologically; but it rests on the same basis of irresponsible gossip as the others, and falls with them.

But I must leave the fuller consideration of these charges to another place, where there may be room to quote and examine them in detail.

It may be said that, granting these tales of illegal 'enormities' to be untrue, More might have instigated persecution, without going outside the existing law. But the play of *Sir Thomas More* gives the London tradition concerning him. London was unlikely to have forgiven or forgotten a persecutor: the Bishop of London, Fitz James, described his diocese as maliciously set in favour of heresy.[2] Yet the old play gives no hint of anything in More's life needing apology, except that he, 'a very learned worthy gentleman, seals error with his blood'. And Erasmus states that, whilst More was Chancellor, no one suffered death for heresy in England.[3] This is not true; Erasmus was not in a position to know exactly what was going on, especially in the provincial dioceses of England; but he knew More too well to make it likely that he could have said this, if More really had

[1] See FRIEDMANN, *Anne Boleyn*, 1884, II, p. 87.
[2] *The enquirie and verdite of the quest paneld of the death of Richard Hune.*
[3] *Epist. lib. xxxi* (Lond. 1642), col. 1505.

been a persecutor. Since More lived in the London diocese, a persecution encouraged by him would have been particularly felt in London. And Froude tells us that 'no sooner had the seals changed hands [from Wolsey to More] than the Smithfield fires recommenced ... encouraged by the Chancellor.'[1] But, thanks largely to the pious care of Foxe, we have details of the burnings for heresy in London. Froude's statement is not true: it is, in fact, only a reminiscence of a rather different statement of Burnet, that, whereas Wolsey was no great persecutor of heretics, More, as soon as he came into favour, pressed the king much to put the laws against heretics in execution.[2] What *is* true is that, as More rose in favour, he became a leader against the heretics. In 1519 the king was 'making it his study how to extirpate Luther's heresy'; and More was soon helping him to revise his book against Luther; later, More stepped in, and took the whole controversy off the king's shoulders (1523). Then we find More associated with Wolsey in trying to stop the importation of Lutheran books[3] (1526). Then More's close friend Tunstall, Bishop of London, handed over to him the task of refuting all heretical books (1528). Then More was made Chancellor (1529), and certainly remained 'in favour' till February, 1531, when the trouble came, over the king being made 'Supreme Head of the Church'.

All this time, More's exertions against the heretics must have given him special opportunities of encouraging 'the Smithfield fires'. *But in all these twelve troubled years there was (so far as our very ample information goes) not one death sentence pronounced on a heretic in the diocese of London.*

The Smithfield fires recommenced only after the date when an unwilling clergy had conferred on the king the title of Supreme Head (February, 1531). And from that date More, though still in office, was no longer in power. Chapuys writes that More is so distressed that he is anxious above all things to resign his office.[4] More's friend, Tunstall, had become Bishop of Durham, and had been succeeded as Bishop of London by Stokesley. Stokesley was not personally unfriendly to More,

---

[1] *History* (1856), II, 83.   [2] Ed. POCOCK, I, 262.
[3] Leaflet addressed *Den wirdigen ... heren Burgemeysteren und Rait Mannen der Sta Coelln.* (Brit. Mus. C. 18. e. 1 (94)).
[4] *L.P.*, v, No. 112 (21 Feb. 1531).

but he was the principal promoter of the measures which were making office intolerable to him.[1] Yet More could not resign without seeming to censure the King; and it was another fifteen months before failing health justified him in retiring.

During the last six months of More's chancellorship three[2] heretics *were* burnt at Smithfield. We know from More's words that in some cases, at least, he had been present at the trial, as had many other officials, clerical and lay.[3] But Stokesley was responsible. More refers to these three cases in the *Apology*: he writes as a layman defending *the clergy* from the charge of administering the law harshly, and he argues that the sufferers had a fair trial according to the laws of the realm.[4] More's words, written about a year after these trials, seem quite incompatible with the assumption that he (or any layman) was held responsible. Foxe, writing thirty years later (1563), makes More largely responsible. But the official documents, which Foxe quotes at length, do not bear this out. Foxe, however, also quotes a dying speech of one of the martyrs (Bainham) blaming More for his death. This speech, if authentic, would be evidence. But Foxe omitted it from later editions, presumably because he no longer believed it authentic. Modern editors have reinserted it.

For two years More was in retirement, writing against heretics of various kinds, Tyndale, Frith, and Barnes. During this time Stokesley handed over to the secular arm, for capital punishment, two heretics, one of whom was Frith. The chronological error has already been noticed by which Foxe makes More, as Chancellor, arrest and ill-use Frith. Frith's examination before Stokesley makes it clear that Frith did not even land in England till after More had surrendered the seals.

Then Stokesley, in May 1535, sentenced either thirteen or fourteen anabaptists. His colleague in this severity was More's antagonist, the Lutheran Barnes. More had nothing to do with it; he had been in prison over a year, and a few weeks later he followed the heroic and nameless anabaptists to death.

---

[1] *L.P.*, v, No. 62 (23 Jan. 1531).

[2] If the *Grey Friars' Chronicle* (*Monum. Franc.*, ii, 194) is to be interpreted that two * o*thers were burnt *with* Bainham, this would make five. But neither Foxe nor More knows of more than three in all, within this period.

[3] *Works*, 1557, p. 348.   [4] *Works*, 1557, p. 889.

To recapitulate: during the dozen years when More was increasingly in power and favour, there were no death sentences for heresy pronounced in his diocese; during the few months when he was still in office, but certainly neither in power nor favour, there were three; during the three years of his retirement, disgrace, and imprisonment there were fifteen or sixteen. During these last three years Lord Audeley held the seals: and he was supposed to be friendly to the Reformers. The figures do not suggest that the London persecution had anything to do with More; they suggest that it depended upon Stokesley replacing Tunstall as bishop. The bishops who, willingly or unwillingly, were separating the Church of England from the Church of Rome, persecuted heretics in order to persuade themselves and others that they were orthodox. So did the King. And Froude, in a passage curiously at variance with the general trend of his argument, admits that this was so.[1]

Those who have given currency to the myth of More's 'enormities' have shown that they possess neither the perspicacity of Mr. Justice Stareleigh (who ruled that hearsay evidence is no evidence) nor the legal acumen of Mr. Weller senior (who understood the value of an alleybi).

But, although More as a layman had no immediate responsibility for putting any heretic to death, he held that the ultimate responsibility rested not with the Church, but with the State. He argued that the Church tried and condemned the heretic, but inflicted no punishment beyond excommunication. It was not the Church, but secular princes, More insisted, who, for the preservation of the peace among their people, had passed laws inflicting the death penalty on such an excommunicated heretic. More made his antagonist in the *Dialogue* reply, 'Marry, but as methinketh, the bishop doth as much as though he killeth him, when he leaveth him to the secular hand'.[2] And this is one of the cases where the modern reader will feel that More has put into the mouth of his antagonist arguments which he fails to answer. But the thing for us to note is that, in More's view, the heretic was not punished by the Church (save in so far as he was excommunicated) but by the laws which the State, for reasons of state, had passed, because

[1] *History*, 1870, II, p. 256.   [2] *Works*, 1557, p. 277.

it had been found that seditious heresy led to tumult and civil war. 'I would little rigour and much mercy showed, where simpleness appeared, and not high heart or malice',[1] More says. It was *seditious* heresy which More hated; to those in doubt or spiritual trouble he was the gentlest of advisers. How tolerant he could be is shown by his treatment of Simon Grinaeus, a Lutheran scholar, who had come to England to consult manuscripts of Plato, and commentaries, in the College libraries of Oxford. More was then Chancellor, and at the height of his controversy with the Lutherans; he entertained Grinaeus hospitably and gave him all the help he could, only insisting on a promise that his guest would not spread his heresies in England. To make sure that he did not, More accompanied Grinaeus when possible; when he could not go himself, he sent his secretary, John Harris, with the German scholar. The tale is told from opposite sides in a rather amusing way. Grinaeus tells it in dedicating the edition of Plato, published at Basel in 1534, to More's son John, in acknowledgement of his father's kindness; Harris told Stapleton. Both More and Harris were determined to help Grinaeus all they could, but to see that he issued no pernicious propaganda; had he done so, More would have turned him out of the kingdom very quickly. Yet, amid all the cares of office, More spent many hours in a vain effort to win Grinaeus back to orthodoxy, first by discussion at Chelsea, later by correspondence.

More's hatred of heresy has its root, not in religious bigotry, but in the fear of sedition, tumult and civil war characteristic of Sixteenth-Century statesmen.

§ II. MORE'S RETIREMENT

More had been too proud to supplement his rather meagre official salary by perquisites and gifts. He told Roper that he had never asked the King for himself the value of one penny. He had always realized that his position was too risky to make it worth while to accumulate much: he did not need to be told what Hamlet told Rosencrantz – that the officers soaking up the King's rewards are only sponges: 'when he needs what you

---

[1] *Works,* 1557, p. 279.

have gleaned, it is but squeezing you, and, sponge, you shall be dry again'.

The first duty of the ex-Chancellor was to provide for his dependants. He 'placed all his gentlemen and yeomen with bishops and noble men, and his eight watermen with the Lord Audeley, that in the same office succeeded him, to whom also he gave his great barge'.[1] 'After his debts paid,' says Roper, 'he had not, I know, his chain excepted, in gold and silver left him the worth of one hundred pounds.' His annuity of £100 from the King continued to be paid in full, though at irregular intervals, up to the time of his arrest;[2] apart from what he had 'of the gift of the King's most noble grace', More estimated that he had not 'yearly full fifty pounds'.[3] Not exactly poverty, when we make the necessary multiplication by fifteen; but with the Great House to be maintained it was hardly sufficient to find 'meat, drink, fuel and apparel' for 'such as necessarily belonged unto him'. It was fourteen years since More had abandoned his post in the City, and it was too late to return to legal practice. His health was breaking down, and his industry in controversy was making it worse. Some year and a half later, More writes to Cromwell of 'this disease of mine, whereof the chief occasion is grown, as it is thought, by the stooping and leaning on my breast, that I have used in writing'.[4]

But his bad health gave More the great advantage of being able to leave the King's service without open scandal. The Duke of Norfolk remained his sympathetic friend, until later More carried his resistance to lengths which the Duke considered silly. More had parted from the King in all friendship, the King assuring him that in any suit which might concern his honour or profit he would be good and gracious lord to him.[5] Nevertheless, rumours that the King had 'thrust More out of the Chancellorship' spread, not only in England, but abroad. More wrote to Erasmus that his resignation was due to sickness, that as the doctors told him that he must either resign office or run the risk of dying, which would also have involved resigna-

[1] ROPER, p. 52.   [2] ROUTH, Sir Thomas More, p. 93.
[3] Works, 1557, p. 867. ROPER (p. 53) gives More's yearly revenue as 'little above an hundred pounds'.
[4] British Museum, MS. Arundel 152, fol. 299.
[5] ROPER, p. 52; Works, 1557, p. 1423.

tion of office, he preferred to abandon one thing rather than both. The King, More further told Erasmus, had proclaimed, first by the mouth of the Duke of Norfolk, and secondly by that of Lord Audeley, that he had only unwillingly permitted More's resignation at More's own request. The second declaration had been made in the King's presence, in Parliament. More indicated that he sent this information to Erasmus for publication.[1]

More discussed with 'us all that were his children', to use Roper's phrase, how they were to continue to live in the Great House, descending to Lincoln's Inn fare, and then by annual degrees, if necessary, to New Inn fare and Oxford fare. At worst they could become beggars 'and so still keep company and be merry together'.[2] He slyly chaffed poor Dame Alice upon the loss of her accustomed ceremony on the first day that they were in church together after the dismissal of his retinue. The congregation in Chelsea parish church was no doubt separated (as in Utopia), men sitting on the right, women on the left.

> Whereas upon the holy days, during his high Chancellorship, one of his gentlemen, when service at the church was done, ordinarily used to come to my lady his wife's pew, and say unto her 'Madam, my lord is gone', the next holy day after the surrender of his office and departure of his gentlemen he came unto my lady his wife's pew himself, and making a low curtsey said unto her 'Madam, my lord is gone'.[3]

It was natural that More, now that all his pomp was a thing of the past, should have gone to his wife's pew to escort her home. The jest lies in the words, and the specially deferential manner. The story is spoilt by a later biographer,[4] who tells us that this was More's method of first acquainting his wife with his resignation, in order to break the news to her gently. Not satisfied with this, family tradition went further.[5] More, finding Dame Alice taken aback by the news, was alleged to have found fault with her dressing, and, chiding his daughters that they could find none, to have said, 'Do you not perceive that your mother's

---

[1] *Epist. Opus*, 1538, p. 1073 (14 June 1532), p. 1076.   [2] ROPER, pp. 53-4.
[3] ROPER, p. 55.   [4] STAPLETON, XIII, between pp. 285 and 286.
[5] CRESACRE MORE, 1726, p. 187.

nose standeth somewhat awry?' It is a silly amplification of More's innocent jest. That all More's gentlemen could have departed, and that so good a housewife as Dame Alice should have failed to notice the fact, or, noticing it, to ask the reason, is not believable.

More's age liked horse-play, and we can trace anecdotes of him deteriorating as they pass. His intimate friends knew better. More's character, Erasmus says, was like his face, cheerful and ready to smile, for More was inclined rather to merriment than gravity, 'though very far removed from silly buffoonery'.[1] And his friend Pace tells us the same: More's fun was tempered by urbanity.[2] In most cases it is best silently to ignore stories which cannot be traced back to contemporary sources, and I have usually done so.[3] But the 'nose-awry' story was unfortunately interpolated into an Eighteenth-Century edition of Roper's *Life*, although there is no trace of it in any one of the thirteen manuscripts or in the first two editions. Accordingly it is found in the current texts of Roper, and in many biographies, including the standard *Life* by Father Bridgett. Bridgett disliked the story, and said so; but, as he believed that it had Roper's authority, he was too honest to suppress it.

This buffoonery gives a quite wrong impression of More's relations to Dame Alice. She was not in his confidence as Margaret was, or even as Roper was, but when troubles began to thicken, during this time of retirement, More tried to comfort her as well as them:

> In the time somewhat before his trouble, he would talk with his wife and children of the joys of heaven and the pains of hell, of the lives of holy martyrs, of their grievous martyrdoms, of their marvellous patience, and of their passions and deaths that they suffered rather than they would offend God; and what a happy and blessed thing it was for the love of God to suffer loss of goods, imprisonment, loss of lands and life also. He would further say unto them that, upon his faith, if he might perceive his wife and children would encourage him to die in a good cause, it should so comfort him that, for very joy thereof, it would make him merrily run to death.

[1] 23 July 1519, ALLEN, IV, No. 999, p. 14.   [2] *De Fructu*, p. 82.
[3] See above, p. 45.

He shewed unto them afore what trouble might after fall unto him; wherewith and the like virtuous talk he had so long before his trouble encouraged them, that when he after fell into the trouble indeed, his trouble to them was a great deal the less.[1]

Upon retirement More, like some modern ex-premiers, set to work on a piece of autobiography and vindication. But instead of the modern two to five volumes, this is compressed into a single page; thrown into the form of an epitaph, inscribed on the tomb which he had built in Chelsea Church for Dame Alice and himself. Thither he conveyed the bones of 'dear Jane, his little wife'. He added to the epitaph some verses which he had composed many years before, and published among his Epigrams, to the effect that he cannot tell which is dearer to him, the wife who bore him his children, or the wife who brought them up. 'Oh how well could we three have lived together in matrimony, if fortune and religion would have suffered it.' But the tomb will bring them all three together,[2] and he prays that Heaven may do the same: 'So death shall give us that thing that life could not.'

That More wished his prose epitaph also to have wide currency among his humanist friends is shown by his having sent a copy to Erasmus – which meant publication. He enumerates his public offices under Henry, 'which alone of all Kings worthily deserved both with sword and pen to be called Defender of the Faith, a glory afore not heard of'. (This is a shrewd thrust to deliver in the summer of 1532.) He celebrates Cuthbert Tunstall,[3] and then turns to his own career:

When he had thus gone through this course of offices or honours, that neither the gracious prince could disallow his doings, nor he was odious to the nobility nor unpleasant to the people, but yet to thieves, murderers and heretics grievous –

More had his critics, and he knew it; he wrote these words (as he said to Erasmus) *ambitiosè*,[4] which I think we might be allowed to translate 'out of swank'. King, nobles, and commons

---

[1] ROPER, pp. 55-6.
[2] Actually, More's body was buried in St. Peter's in the Tower, his head in the Roper vault, St. Dunstan's, Canterbury: two appropriately dedicated places.
[3] See above, p. 233. I quote from the English version of the 'Epitaphy' given by Rastell, *Works*, 1557, p. 1421.   [4] *Epist. Opus*, 1538, p. 1076.

have approved of him; hostile critics can choose whether they will write themselves thieves, murderers, or heretics. Then, in more serious vein, he praises his father, 'a civil man, pleasant, harmless, gentle, pitiful, just and uncorrupted', who, having lived to see his son Lord Chancellor of England, 'thinking himself now to have lived long enough, *gladly* departed to God'.

And More himself, now no longer 'young More', but with four children and eleven grandchildren, 'began in his own conceit to wax old'; and this feeling of age creeping upon him was increased 'by a certain sickly disposition of his breast':

> He therefore, irk and weary of worldly business, giving up his promotions, obtained at last by the incomparable benefit of his most gentle prince (if it please God to favour his enterprise) the thing which from a child in a manner alway he wished and desired, that he might have some years of his life free, in which he, little and little withdrawing himself from the business of this life, might continually remember the immortality of the life to come.

This monument is every day to put him in memory of death:

> And that this tomb made for him in his life time be not in vain, nor that he fear death coming upon him, but that he may willingly for the desire of Christ die, and find death not utterly death to him, but the gate of a wealthier life, help him (I beseech you good reader) now with your prayers while he liveth, and when he is dead also.

The epitaph was a gesture, emphasizing the friendly relations between Henry and his old servant, and proclaiming More's determination not to annoy his King by meddling further in worldly concerns. It was also much more.

§ 12. THE EMPEROR'S PRAISE

Sir Thomas Elyot, More's friend, had been ambassador with the Emperor Charles V. He had left the Emperor's court in April 1532, if not in March, and was back in London in May, to find More's resignation everywhere the subject of conversation. He repeated to a group of More's young friends the great Emperor's words in praise of More. Roper remembered the words, and repeated them more than twenty years after:

'And this will we say, that if we had been master of such a servant, of whose doings our self have had these many years no small experience, we would rather have lost the best city of our dominions than have lost such a worthy counsellor.' Which matter was by the same Sir Thomas Elyot to my self, to my wife, to Master Clement and his wife, to Master John Heywood and his wife, and unto divers other his friends accordingly reported.[1]

When Elyot left the Emperor's court, More had not actually resigned, but the Emperor knew that More's loyal support of Catherine was making his position impossible; some time before the Emperor had written to him that private letter which More did not feel it discreet to receive.[2] When giving Elyot an audience, Charles would inevitably have asked after More, and might naturally have said that he himself would value such a counsellor above the best city of his dominions. Even so wary a diplomatist as Elyot might allow himself to repeat this praise, in the summer of 1532, in the company of More's young friends. Clement was at that time court physician, Heywood was in receipt of a court pension which he had earned as singer and player of the virginals, Roper held an important legal post; their wives were respectively adopted daughter, niece and daughter of Thomas More. And More himself was enjoying, in his retirement, the King's benevolent favour.

It was an intimate little society, that of the Ropers, Clements, and Heywoods. They must have met often in Clement's house, 'The Barge', in Bucklersbury, the same house in which More himself had lived with his young children before he moved to Chelsea.

But, writing twenty years afterwards, Roper has telescoped together two meetings of this little band of familiar friends — one just after More's resignation, and another, sadder, meeting not long after his execution. He has transferred Elyot's words from the one to the other, and has given them a preface which twists them into a reference to More's death:

Soon after whose death came intelligence thereof to the Emperor Charles. Whereupon he sent for Sir Thomas Elyot our English ambassador, and said unto him: 'My Lord

---

[1] ROPER, p. 104.   [2] See above, p. 250.

Ambassador, we understand that the King, your master. hath put his faithful servant and grave wise counsellor, Sir Thomas More, to death.' Whereunto Sir Thomas Elyot answered that he understood nothing thereof. 'Well,' said the Emperor, 'it is too true. And this will we say . . .'[1]

No middle-aged man who has checked his own lapses of memory over a period of a quarter of a century need feel surprise at this. An attempt was at one time made to support the story, as Roper tells it, by supposing that Elyot returned to the Emperor for a second term of office as ambassador. But we now know the name of the English ambassador who was with Charles at the time of More's death, and it was not Elyot.

But, indeed, the story only becomes rational and credible when we have corrected it in the way chronology demands.

As told by Roper, the tale has been solemnly repeated in histories of England and biographies of More. Yet, for an expression of the feelings of Charles, upon first hearing of the execution of More, it seems inadequate. Henry, it is true, weighed the lives of his servants against material values; Henry, when examining Cavendish as to the whereabouts of the fifteen hundred pounds which Wolsey had left, began by 'wishing that liefer than £20,000 he had lived'. But would Charles V have descended to this level, by saying that he would rather have lost the best city of his dominions than – what? From Charles' point of view, rather than have put to death the most wise and loyal counsellor he had, for having given him such advice as would save him from the danger of immediate excommunication and ultimate damnation. Indeed, to talk of Henry as having 'lost' More in July 1535, as he might have lost a town, is a little absurd. It reminds one of the American schoolgirl's description of Henry, 'a great widower, having lost several wives'.

Besides, the story, as Roper tells it, is improbable to us who know the secret history of the time in a way which he could not. Elyot certainly sympathized with More, but he had been cowed by the stern measures meted out to those who would not bow to the King's will. About a year after More's death we find him writing to Cromwell, asking him 'to put away the remembrance of the amity which was between me and Sir Thomas More'. It is very unlikely that any time after More's death Elyot would have dared to be in the company of Mistress Roper or Mistress Clement. Years later a man might be called to account for having been with those ladies, still more for having spoken with them touching the death of Sir Thomas More.[1] And in any case it would have been going very far for an ex-ambassador to have reported such a censure by a foreign sovereign upon an act of his own King.

The Emperor's praise marks More's position as a man eminent in European, as well as English, history.

---

[1] See the examination of Sir Geoffrey Pole upon this very point, *L.P.*, xiii, 2, No. 695, pp. 266-7.

'THE KING'S SERVANT, BUT GOD'S FIRST'

(1532–1535)

§ I.   MORE FACES CROMWELL

Soon after More's retirement Cromwell came to him with a message from the King. When they had thoroughly communed together, More said:

'Master Cromwell, you are now entered into the service of a most noble, wise and liberal prince; if you will follow my poor advice, you shall, in your counsel-giving unto his Grace, ever tell him what he ought to do, but never what he is able to do . . . For if a lion knew his own strength, hard were it for any man to rule him.'[1]

Thomas Cromwell was not likely to take More's advice; as a student of Machiavelli's *Prince* he knew that 'the man who leaves what *is* done, for what ought to be done, learns sooner his ruin than his preservation'.[2] So Cromwell swept on, to become 'the hammer of the monks', to make the King supreme over his cowed nobles and helpless clergy, to aim at making him, out of the monastic spoils, 'the richest King in Christendom', and even at putting into his head to 'take upon him to have his will and pleasure regarded for a law'.[3] We may think of the interview between More and Cromwell as one where the Utopian faced the Machiavellian, provided we use those words without prejudice – and few words have accumulated more. It was not necessarily idealism facing villainy. Cromwell may have honestly believed in an autocratic monarchy, and to him the advice that the lion should be kept from learning his strength, in order that he might be ruled, may have sounded

---

[1] Roper, pp. 56-7.   [2] Cap. xv.
[3] Foxe, *Acts and Monuments*, ed. Townsend, 1838, vi, p. 45.

villainous. But, however we choose to allot praise or blame, the contrast is there.

Now, why should it be propounded as 'one of history's perplexing ironies' that 'the man who devised the ideal of *Utopia*' died as an opponent of the revolution carried through by Henry and Cromwell?

One competent observer did not so regard it. We have met in our story Antonio Bonvisi, a scholar, a wealthy merchant from Lucca, living in London, and for about forty years a friend of More. Bonvisi had the foreigner's privilege of standing aloof from English politics, and, says Harpsfield, would often talk of More,

> and also of Sir Thomas Cromwell, with whom he was many years familiarly acquainted, and would report many notable and as yet commonly unknown things, and of their . . . un-like . . . natures, dispositions, sayings and doings, whereof there is now no place to talk. [1]

I sometimes think that Archdeacon Harpsfield deserved his sixteen years in the Fleet, for having left untold these anecdotes of Bonvisi, showing the different tempers of those two mighty opposites, Thomas Cromwell and Thomas More.

The rest of our story is that of the struggle between these two men.

For a year, all was quiet, and More concentrated his efforts upon his controversy with the heretics. Then at last, on 23 May 1533, the 'divorce' business was brought to an end, and at the convent of Dunstable Cranmer gave sentence that the marriage of Catherine and Henry was null; five days later, after a secret enquiry at Lambeth, he declared the marriage between Henry and Anne valid; on 1 June Anne Boleyn was crowned in Westminster Abbey. More's good friends and warm admirers, Tunstall Bishop of Durham, Clerk Bishop of Bath, and Gardiner Bishop of Winchester, asked him to bear them company in the coronation ceremony, and sent him twenty pounds to buy a gown for the occasion. More accepted the money, but stopped at home, and at their next meeting said that as he had granted one of their requests he thought he might be the bolder to deny the other. And he told them one of his tales, of an Emperor who

[1] *Life of More*, p. 138.

wished to put a maiden to death for some offence, but could not, because he had himself decreed that no virgin should suffer death for that offence, 'such a reverence had he to virginity'.

> Suddenly arose there up one of his Council, a good plain man, among them, and said: 'Why make you so much ado, my Lords, about so small a matter? Let her first be deflowered, and then after may she be devoured.' . . . Now my Lords (quoth he), it lieth not in my power but that they may devour me; but God being my good lord, I will provide that they shall never deflower me.[1]

More professed that he did not remember the details of his tale, or what the girl's offence was. But More was a student of history, and of Tacitus. Who, having read the story, can forget it? The crime of the poor child was that she was the daughter of Sejanus, and she kept on asking 'What had she done? She would never do it again. Could she not be whipped for it like any other child?' – and then the unutterable sequel.[2] Was More's irony here so deep that it has escaped notice for four centuries? Was it an unspoken parallel between the despotism of Tiberius and that which Henry was building up? Yet the obvious irony is clear enough, and must have made Tunstall and his fellows wince. The 'good plain man', who can teach the autocrat how he may break his own laws, destroy innocence, and yet keep his conscience safe! Henry had surrounded himself with such 'good plain men'. The Great Seal, which Warham, Wolsey and More had held, was now held by that 'good plain man' Audeley, who boasted that, unlike his predecessor, he had no learning. Scholars like Tunstall and Gardiner had to toe the line. And so, with a jest, as his manner was, More made the decision which was to cost him his life, and parted from the scholars who had been the friends and colleagues of a lifetime. Presence at the coronation, he warned them, would be followed by their being asked to preach and write books in defence of the new order. More had no illusions as to what was in store for him. 'God give grace, son,' he said to Roper, 'that these matters within a while be not confirmed with oaths.' Whereat Roper was much offended. So we are all apt to be, when one

[1] ROPER, pp. 58-9.
[2] More may have read the story in the edition of Tacitus by BEROALDUS, Rome, 1515, fol. 63b,

whose judgment we must respect prophesies an evil we ourselves had not foreseen. We feel, as Roper naïvely says,[1] that the prophecy brings the evil nearer.

But More's resistance was passive. About Christmas 1533 a book of nine articles was published by the King's Council justifying his marriage. More was accused of having made an answer to this book, and having delivered it to his nephew William Rastell to print. He wrote to Cromwell indignantly denying the charge. The letter marks clearly More's view of his duty as a member of the King's Council – to discharge his conscience faithfully when consulted, but to abstain from any public opposition:

> I will by the grace of Almighty God, as long as it shall please Him to lend me life in this world, in all such places as I am of my duty to God and the King's Grace bounden, truly say my mind and discharge my conscience as becometh a poor, honest, true man, wheresoever I shall be by his Grace commanded. Yet surely if it should happen any book to come abroad in the name of his Grace or his honourable Council, if that book to me seemed such as myself would not have given mine own advice to the making, yet I know my bounden duty to bear more honour to my prince, and more reverence to his honourable Council, than that it could become me for many causes to make an answer unto such a book, or to counsel and advise any man else to do it.[2]

More was molested no further on this count. It was found possible to bring against him a much more serious charge – complicity in the treasons of the Holy Maid of Kent.

Elizabeth Barton, a Kentish serving maid, was alleged to have been miraculously cured of the falling sickness, and then to have received divine revelations. She became a nun, at Canterbury, and, long before these troubles arose, Archbishop Warham had thought it worth while to report to the King words which she was said to have spoken in her trances. The King referred the matter to More, who found in these revelations nothing but what 'a right simple woman might speak of her own wit'. But, in view of the nun's reputation for sanctity, 'he durst not, nor would not, be bold in judging the matter'.

[1] ROPER, p. 57.   [2] Works, 1557, p. 1422.

After the question of the King's divorce arose, the nun's revelations began to be political, and they were spread abroad by several ecclesiastics, including two Franciscan Observant friars.

The Carthusians and the Franciscans were the two orders which More in his youth had thought of joining – they were now almost the only two orders among whom any resistance to the King's innovations was found. Friar Peto, of the Observants of Greenwich, told the King when preaching before him that, if he behaved like Ahab, it might come to pass that the dogs, after his death, would lick his blood, as they had licked the blood of Ahab. Indignant courtiers threatened to sew Peto and his brother friars in sacks and throw them into the Thames, only to be told that the way lay as open to Heaven by water as by land. Peto's threat was astute, for there was no means of refuting it during the King's lifetime; he got away with it, and lived to be a cardinal. The Holy Maid, to her misfortune, ventured on more short-dated prophecies; one of which was that if the King married another woman he should not be King seven months – six months – one month later. After the lapse of due time, the prophet was clearly in the power of her enemies, and in the autumn of 1533 she was arrested with her adherents, including Father Risby, Friar Observant, formerly of Canterbury, and Father Rich, Friar Observant of Richmond. They were charged with treason, and ultimately executed at Tyburn on 21 April 1534. A number of more important people, including Bishop Fisher of Rochester and Thomas More, were charged with misprision of treason: with having known of the treason, and failed to denounce it. This was not a capital offence, but it involved forfeiture of all goods, and imprisonment during the King's pleasure.

Fisher had, unwisely, allowed the nun to repeat some of her prophecies to him, and thereby had placed himself in a difficult position. The nun, who did not at this date lack courage, had seen the King, and alleged that she had told these prophecies to him. If Fisher went to the King, and repeated the prophecies, he would lay himself open to the charge of joining with the nun and her adherents in their attempt to intimidate him. If he did not, he laid himself open to the charge of misprision of treason.

More showed greater wisdom. Father Risby, staying a night at his house, began to tell him that the nun had had a revelation on the King's great matter; but More stopped him, saying that 'any revelation of the King's matters he would not hear of'. Father Rich, paying a visit to More, asked him if Father Risby had told him any of the nun's revelations concerning the King's Grace. 'Nay forsooth', said More, 'nor if he would have done, I would not have given him a hearing.' More himself had an interview with the nun. Though they 'talked no word of the King's Grace', More thought it well to write a letter to her afterwards, reminding her how the Duke of Buckingham had met destruction largely through talking with 'one that was reported for an holy monk'. Therefore, he warned the Holy Maid,

> keep you from talking with any person, specially with high persons, of any such manner things as pertain to princes' affairs, or the state of the realm, but only to commune and talk with any person, high and low, of any such manner things as may to the soul be profitable.

More's letter is remarkable for its tone of humility towards the Holy Maid; he conveys this warning, but writes as if the nun really had received divine revelations, and were spiritually in a plane above his own. But the fact that he kept a copy of his letter shows that he realized how dangerous things had become.

We have all these details from a long letter which More wrote to Cromwell.[1] Cromwell had told Roper that More had been in communication with the nun, and had been giving her advice and counsel; which was indeed quite true, though not in the sense that Cromwell meant. Cromwell evidently did not believe More's explanation. Father Rich was interrogated. He confirmed More's statement and confessed that he had 'showed other revelations to Sir Thomas More, but none concerning the King, for he would not hear them'. But this passage was struck through, and the name of More was inserted by Cromwell himself in the list of those to whom revelations about the King had been divulged.[2] Nevertheless More's letter, with its warning

---

[1] MS. Arundel 152, fol. 296; MS. Royal 17 D. xiv, fols. 376-83. The letter was not printed by Rastell in MORE's *Works*, 1557.
[2] *L.P.*, vi, No. 1468.

against mixing religion and politics, drawn from the story of the Duke of Buckingham, was confirmed down to minute details by the evidence of one of the prisoners.[1]

When the Bill of Attainder was introduced into the House of Lords on 21 Feb. 1534 More's name was included. He wrote both to Cromwell and to Henry protesting his innocence.

Up to this date Henry had treated More well, and More's letter to Henry is such as a man might write in excusing himself from a charge of treason to a friend and benefactor. If he loses Henry's good opinion, he says, nothing else will give him any pleasure. His only comfort would be 'that after my short life and your long . . . I should once meet your Grace again in Heaven, and there be merry with you; where, among mine other pleasures this should yet be one, that your Grace should surely see there that . . . I am your true beadsman now, and ever have been'.

To be suspected of having instigated an ignorant woman to promulgate bogus prophecies against his sovereign, was a thing which revolted More, alike as a loyal Catholic, as a loyal subject, as a scholar, and as an honest man. From the time when he had heard the nun make her confession at Paul's Cross on 23 Nov. 1533, More had complete contempt for her. She is 'the lewd nun', 'the wicked woman of Canterbury'. More wished to defend his own character publicly before the Lords. The King, 'not liking that', appointed a Committee, Cranmer, Audeley, Norfolk and Cromwell, to call More before them; and Roper begged him to ask for their help to get himself discharged from the Bill. But the Committee gave him no chance of answering the charges – instead, they began by assuring him that 'he could ask no worldly honour nor profit at his Highness' hands that were likely to be denied him', if he would but consent to what the Parliament, the Bishops and the Universities had already approved. More replied:

I verily hoped that I should never have heard of this matter more, considering that I have, from time to time, always from the beginning so plainly and truly declared my mind unto his Grace, which his Highness to me ever seemed, like

[1] The same, No. 1467; MS. Cotton Cleopatra E. vi, fol. 159. The writer is apparently Rich or Risby.

a most gracious prince, very well to accept, never minding, as he said, to molest me more therewith. [1]

When they could not shake him by offers of kindness, the Commissioners began 'more terribly to touch him',

telling him that the King's Highness had given them in commandment, if they could by no gentleness win him, in his name with his great ingratitude to charge him, that never was there servant to his sovereign so villainous, nor subject to his prince so traitorous as he.

But the treason alleged was not that of having instigated the Holy Maid, but of having instigated the King's Grace to write the *Assertion of the Seven Sacraments*. More had no difficulty in meeting this accusation:[2] 'My Lords, these terrors be arguments for children, and not for me.'

So More and the Commissioners parted, as Roper says, 'displeasantly'. The interview had been a complete repudiation of that liberty of conscience which Henry had promised More when he entered his service, and again when he undertook to study and report on the marriage question. Yet More's previous 'grateful acknowledgement' of Henry's promise is solemnly quoted by historians as evidence of Henry's kindness to his servants. It would be as reasonable to quote the grateful acknowledgement of the oysters as evidence of the kindness of the Walrus and the Carpenter.

More realized that he would be, as he put it, 'devoured'; but he returned from the interview, Roper tells us, in high spirits:

Then took Sir Thomas More his boat towards his house at Chelsea, wherein by the way he was very merry, and for that was I nothing sorry, hoping that he had got himself discharged out of the parliament bill. When he was landed and come home, then walked we twain alone into his garden together; where I, desirous to know how he had sped, said, 'I trust, Sir, that all is well because you be so merry.'

'It is so indeed, son Roper, I thank God,' quoth he.

'Are you then put out of the parliament bill?' said I.

'By my troth, son Roper,' quoth he, 'I never remembered it.'

'Never remembered it, Sir,' said I. 'A case that toucheth yourself so near, and us all for your sake. I am sorry to hear it; for I verily trusted, when I saw you so merry, that all had been well.'

Then said he, 'Wilt thou know, son Roper, why I was so merry?'

'That would I gladly, Sir,' quoth I.

'In good faith, I rejoiced, son,' quoth he, 'that I had given the devil a foul fall, and that with those Lords I had gone so far, as without great shame I could never go back again.'

At which words waxed I very sad, for though himself liked it well, yet liked it me but a little.[1]

On 5 March, immediately after this interview, More wrote both to Henry[2] and to Cromwell,[3] asserting his loyalty and defining his views.

The King was so offended that he was determined that More's name should remain in the list of those guilty of misprision. But if a man, whose conduct had been as correct as More's, was to be judged guilty of misprision, and not even heard in his defence, then the liberty and goods of even the most submissive statesman would not be safe. Probably few had been as discreet as More, in refusing even to hear the nun's prophecies. The Lords, in giving a third reading to the Bill of Attainder, sent a polite request to the King to ask whether it squared with the royal wishes that the accused should be heard by the Lords in the Star Chamber.[4] This, the King's advisers were convinced, would ruin all: 'For in this case of the nun, he was accounted, they said, so innocent and clear, that for his dealing therein men reckoned him far worthier of praise than reproof.'[5] Henry said that he would be personally present himself to overawe his Lords; but Lord Audeley and the rest, following the medieval custom, fell on their knees in protest before him: 'considering that if he should, in his own presence, receive an overthrow, it would not only encourage his subjects ever after to contemn him, but also throughout all Christendom

---

[1] ROPER, pp. 68-70.

[2] Works, 1557, p. 1423; MS. Cleopatra E. vi, fol. 176; Record Office, State Papers, Henry VIII, §82, p. 254 (both these are autograph); Royal 17.D.xiv, fol. 383.

[3] Works, 1557, p. 1424; MS. Cleopatra E. vi, fol. 149; Harleian 283, fol. 120b.

[4] 6 March 1534, Lords' Journal, i, p. 72.   [5] ROPER, pp. 70-1.

redound to his dishonour for ever'. So More's name was withdrawn, before the Bill was read by the Lords the fourth time.[1] Cromwell, meeting Roper in the Parliament House, told him the good news, which Roper sent at once to his wife at Chelsea. More's comment was that the trouble was deferred, not removed; and Roper asserts that Henry's advisers, when they persuaded the King to remove More's name, had said 'that they mistrusted not in time to find some meeter matter to serve his turn better'. But Roper was not present when Henry met his advisers; and it is more charitable to suppose that Norfolk and the rest honestly meant well by More, and felt that they had done all they could to save him. Roper has recorded Norfolk's warning after this incident (a warning never absent from the minds of Tudor statesmen), that 'the indignation of the Prince is death':

'By the mass, Master More, it is perilous striving with princes. And therefore, I would wish you somewhat to incline to the King's pleasure; for by God's body, Master More, *Indignatio principis mors est.*'

'Is that all, my Lord?' quoth he. 'Then in good faith is there no more difference between your Grace and me, but that I shall die today and you tomorrow.'[2]

In the same month of March 1534, the 'confirmation with oaths' which More had feared was enforced. An Act was passed[3] fixing the succession on the offspring of Henry and Anne Boleyn; and all subjects arrived at full age could be compelled 'to make a corporal oath' to observe and maintain 'the whole effects and contents' of the Act. The penalties of refusal were to be those of misprision of treason – imprisonment and confiscation of goods.

More recognized the right of the King and Parliament to fix the succession; if they disinherited the legitimate princess Mary in favour of Henry's children by Anne Boleyn he might regret, but, as a loyal subject, he must comply. He would doubtless have complied, though with regret, if Henry and Parliament had fixed the succession upon his illegitimate son Henry Fitzroy, as at one time Henry seems to have meant to do.

---

[1] 12 March 1534.   [2] ROPER, pp. 71-2.
[3] 25 Henry VIII, cap. 22; *Statutes*, III, p. 474; *Journals of the Lords*, I, p. 82.

But Audeley and Cromwell, to please the King, amplified the oath 'of their own heads, to make it appear unto the King's ears more pleasant and plausible'.[1]

§ 2. 'BEFORE THE LORDS AT LAMBETH'

On the Sunday after Easter,[2] 12 April 1534, More had come to London with Roper to hear the sermon at St. Paul's. He then went to John Clement, now living in More's old house, in Bucklersbury. Here, amid reminders of his early married life, and in the presence of three of his dearest friends, Roper, Clement, and Clement's wife Margaret, the blow fell on More. The officer whose duty it was to cite him to appear before the Commissioners at Lambeth had learnt of his being in London, and served the notice upon him. More returned at once to Chelsea.

That evening, he took his farewell of his family. Next morning, as had been his custom before undertaking any weighty matter – his embassies, or the office of Speaker, or of Lord Chancellor – he went to Chelsea Church, was confessed, heard mass, and received the communion. But this time he would not suffer his wife and children to bring him to his boat outside his garden gate, to kiss him and bid him farewell,

> but pulled the wicket after him, and shut them all from him; and with a heavy heart, as by his countenance it appeared, with me and our four servants there took he his boat towards Lambeth. Wherein sitting still sadly a while, at the last he suddenly rounded me in the ear, and said, 'Son Roper, I thank our Lord the field is won.' What he meant thereby I then wist not, yet, loth to seem ignorant, I answered, 'Sir, I am thereof very glad.'[3]

At Lambeth Roper parted from More, and we have no evidence that they ever saw each other again. Some five anxious days went by. Then the family at Chelsea received, from the Tower, the long letter which told them how More had fared. The Commissioners had shown him the oath, under the Great Seal, and the Act of Succession in a printed roll. He was willing to swear to the succession, but could not take the oath as

[1] ROPER, p. 78.
[2] STAPLETON, XV, p. 305. By a slip, *in palmis* has been miswritten for *in albis*.
[3] ROPER, p. 73.

offered him. He was shown the names of the Lords and
Commons who had subscribed already, and, as he still refused,
was commanded to go down into the garden.

> And thereupon I tarried in the old burned chamber that
> looketh into the garden, and would not go down because of
> the heat. In that time saw I Master Doctor Latimer come
> into the garden, and there walked he with divers other
> doctors and chaplains of my Lord of Canterbury. And very
> merry I saw him, for he laughed, and took one or twain
> about the neck so handsomely, that if they had been women,
> I would have weened he had been waxen wanton. After
> that came Master Doctor Wilson forth from the Lords, and
> was with two gentlemen brought by me, and gentlemanly
> sent straight unto the Tower.[1]

Dr. Nicholas Wilson had held the very important post of
chaplain and confessor to the King. Like More, he had been
bidden to study the divorce question, and he and More had
studied it together, and together had arrived at the same
conclusion. More had been impressed by Wilson's learning,
judgment, loyalty to the King, and above all by his secrecy.
Except Fisher, there can have been no man in whose fate More
was more interested; and to Fisher More's mind at once returns:

> What time my Lord of Rochester was called in before them,
> that can I not tell. But at night I heard that he had been
> before them, but where he remained that night, and so forth
> till he was sent hither, I never heard.

More watched, with quiet amusement, the demeanour of
the London clergy. The Vicar of Croydon (the same who long
ago had wished to be sent as missionary to Utopia) either for
gladness or for dryness, or to show his intimacy with the Archbishop, went to the buttery bar of the palace and called for
drink. When they had played their pageant, More was called
in again, and again refused to swear; but without giving his
reasons, or blaming any who had sworn. Cranmer seized upon
this, and attempted to save More. If he did not condemn the
consciences of those who swore the oath, that, said Cranmer,
showed that he must hold the swearing or not swearing to be
a thing uncertain and doubtful; but for a certainty, without

[1] *Works*, 1557, p. 1429.

doubt, he was bound to obey his King. More confesses himself staggered by this argument, 'which seemed suddenly so subtle', and modern historians have quoted this admission as a proof of Cranmer's ability in debate.[1] But I am not sure that More is not here being a little ironical. The argument seemed, he says, so subtle, especially 'as coming out of so noble a prelate's mouth'. For the argument is that in all matters wherein we are not prepared to condemn the consciences of others, we are bound, for ourselves, to accept the orders of the state. Such an argument would mark the end of religious freedom, of academic freedom, of all freedom. More was staggered that it should be put forward by the Primate of England, the successor of Warham and Becket, of Anselm and Dunstan, of Lawrence and Augustine. Not all these men had been always heroic, but every one of them had braced himself to stand up for the truth, as he saw it, against any earthly potentate. And More had no difficulty in reducing Cranmer's argument to an absurdity. For, said More, if we accept that view, we have a ready way to avoid all perplexities:

> For in whatsoever matter the doctors stand in great doubt, the King's commandment, given upon whither side he list, solveth all the doubt.

And indeed, four years after More's death, this *reductio ad absurdum* was actually accepted by the English Parliament, which left it to the King to define by proclamation what men should believe, on pain of death.

To the argument that he was opposing the Council of the realm, More replied by appealing to the general Council of Christendom. That went to the root of the matter, and at once brought the mighty opposites face to face. Cromwell, says More,

> sware a great oath, that he had liever that his own only son (which is of truth a goodly young gentleman, and shall I trust come to much worship) had lost his head, than that I should thus have refused the oath. For surely the King's Highness would now conceive a great suspicion against me, and think that the matter of the nun of Canterbury was all contrived by my drift. To which I said that the contrary was true and well known.

[1] POLLARD, *Cranmer*, pp. 238, 364.

More repeated that he was willing to swear to the succession, if the oath were framed in such a manner as might stand with his conscience. And he concludes his letter:

> Howbeit, as help me God, as touching the whole oath, I never withdrew any man from it, nor never advised any to refuse it, nor never put, nor will put any scruple in any man's head, but leave every man to his own conscience. And methinketh in good faith that so were it good reason that every man should leave me to mine.

The four days between More's refusal of the oath at Lambeth and his committal to the Tower were spent in the custody of the Abbot of Westminster. Meantime there was discussion as to his fate. More had refused to say definitely why he would not swear the oath; but the preamble to the Act of Succession contained a statement (which he certainly did not believe) that Henry's marriage with Catherine was invalid; and the oath, as it had been tendered to him, involved the repudiation of the Papal Supremacy. Roper tells us that the King and his Council were at first willing to meet More by waiving the question of the Papal Supremacy, provided More would swear not to let it be known whether he *had* sworn to the Supremacy or not; 'yet did Queen Anne, by her importunate clamour, so sore exasperate the King against him, that contrary to his former resolution he caused the said oath of the Supremacy to be ministered'.[1] Here again, people have perhaps taken Roper's assertion too seriously, as if he had been present at the secret councils of Henry and Mistress Anne. But certain it is that Cranmer suggested some such compromise; he proposed that Fisher and More should be excused from denouncing either the marriage with Catherine or the Papal Supremacy, provided they would accept the succession of Anne Boleyn's children, and swear 'to maintain the same against all powers and potentates'.[2] Cranmer further suggested that the form of oath taken by Fisher and More should be 'suppressed', i.e., kept secret; which of course would have involved an oath of secrecy from them such as Roper mentions. We need not suppose that Cranmer realized how More would have been trapped; we may credit the Archbishop with intentions more

[1] p. 74.   [2] 17 April 1534, *L.P.*, VII, No. 499.

merciful than treacherous. More would certainly have agreed to swear to recognize Elizabeth as heir to the throne. He says so. If he had done this, and if further he had sworn to keep complete silence as to what oath he had sworn, there were plenty of royal officials who would have given out that he had sworn the same oath as everyone else. More could not have contradicted this; his oath would have been 'suppressed'. And so he might have gone down to history as one of the men who, despite a brave resistance at the outset, had not had the courage to stand out to the last.

Anyway, his enemies saved him from this horrible dilemma – and it is a remarkable proof of the truth that he was fond of preaching, that a man's 'most enemies' are often his best friends. Whether or no it was Mistress Anne who hardened Henry's heart against More, certain it is that in the end the King decided conclusively against any such compromise. His decision was announced in a letter of Cromwell to Cranmer commanding him not to urge his suggestion further, as it would 'be a reprobation of the King's second marriage' – which indeed is true enough. From his own point of view, the King was right. It would not satisfy Henry that More and Fisher should recognize the right of Parliament to fix the succession on Anne's offspring, although illegitimate. What Henry wanted was an oath declaring belief that the offspring was legitimate

§ 3. IN THE TOWER

More was accordingly committed to the Tower.

Whom, as he was going thitherward, wearing, as he commonly did, a chain of gold about his neck, Sir Richard Cromwell, that had the charge of his conveyance thither, advised him to send home his chain to his wife, or to some of his children. 'Nay, Sir,' quoth he, 'that I will not; for if I were taken in the field by my enemies, I would they should somewhat fare the better by me.'

At whose landing Master Lieutenant at the Tower gate was ready to receive him, where the porter demanded of him his upper garment. 'Master Porter,' quoth he, 'here it is'; and took off his cap, and delivered it him, saying, 'I am very sorry it is no better for you.' 'No, Sir,' quoth the porter, 'I must have your gown.'[1]

[1] ROPER, pp. 74-5.

It seems a poor, forced jest; and there is wisdom and sympathy in the suggestion that, for the moment, even More's high spirits had failed him.[1]

More had his personal servant John a Wood to wait on him, and was able to send the long letter describing his examination at Lambeth. After that, writing material seems to have been taken away from him, and we get the first of his letters pencilled in charcoal. He writes to Margaret, 'of worldly things I no more desire than I have'. 'Written with a coal by your tender loving father, who in his poor prayers forgetteth none of you all, nor your babes, nor your nurses, nor your good husbands, nor your good husbands' shrewd wives, nor your father's shrewd wife neither, nor our other friends. And thus fare ye heartily well for lack of paper.'[2] 'Our Lord keep me continually true, faithful and plain', he adds.

After some time Margaret wrote her father a letter 'wherein she seemed somewhat to labour to persuade him to take the oath'. William Rastell is anxious to defend his cousin's firmness; 'She nothing so thought', he tells us, but wrote this letter 'to win thereby credence with Master Thomas Cromwell, that she might the rather get liberty to have free resort unto her father.' The letter has not been preserved. It drew from More the most acute cry of pain which came from him in all his sufferings:

> If I had not been, my dearly beloved daughter, at a firm and fast point, I trust in God's great mercy this good great while before, your lamentable letter had not a little abashed me, surely far above all other things, of which I hear divers times not a few terrible toward me. But surely they all touched me never so near, nor were so grievous unto me, as to see you, my well beloved child, in such vehement piteous manner labour to persuade unto me the thing wherein I have, of pure necessity for respect unto mine own soul, so often given you so precise answer before.[3]

Margaret replied with a letter of passionate love from 'your daughter and beadswoman, which desireth above all worldly things to be in John a Wood's stead, to do you some service'.

[1] CHRISTOPHER HOLLIS, Sir Thomas More, 1934, p. 249.
[2] Works, 1557, p. 1430.   [3] The same, p. 1431.

Her letter achieved its object, and after More had been over
a month in prison, she (though usually no one else) 'obtained
licence of the King that she might resort unto her father in the
Tower'. After the prayers with which these interviews always
began, More said:

'I believe, Meg, that they that have put me here ween they
have done me a high displeasure. But I assure thee on my
faith, my own good daughter, if it had not been for my wife
and you that be my children, whom I account the chief
part of my charge, I would not have failed long ere this to
have closed myself in as straight a room, and straighter
too . . . Me thinketh God maketh me a wanton, and setteth
me on his lap and dandleth me.'[1]

The Lieutenant of the Tower, Sir Edmund Walsingham,
an old friend, apologized because he could not, without the
King's indignation, make him better cheer. 'Assure yourself,
Master Lieutenant,' More replied, 'I do not mislike my cheer;
but whensoever I so do, then thrust me out of your doors.'
Yet More allowed himself to speak to his daughter with some
indignation of the illegality of his imprisonment:

'I may tell thee, Meg, they that have committed me hither,
for refusing of this oath not agreeable with the statute, are
not by their own law able to justify my imprisonment. And
surely, daughter, it is great pity that any Christián prince
should by a flexible Council ready to follow his affections,
and by a weak clergy lacking grace constantly to stand to
their learning, with flattery be so shamefully abused.'[2]

That More's indignation was justified is proved by the fact
that an Act of Parliament had to be passed to legalize retro-
spectively the oath for refusing which he was imprisoned.[3]

So the summer days passed, till in August Dame Alice's
daughter, Lady Alington, tried to intercede for her step-
father with Lord Audeley, More's successor in the Chancellorship. She writes to her 'Sister Roper' to tell of her ill-
success. The Lord Chancellor had

come to take a course at a buck in our park, the which was
to my husband a great comfort, that it would please him so

---

[1] ROPER, p. 76.   [2] The same, p. 78.
[3] 26 Henry VIII, cap. 2. See below, p. 319.

to do. Then when he had taken his pleasure and killed his deer, he went to Sir Thomas Barnston's to bed: where I was the next day with him at his desire, the which I could not say nay to, for me thought he did bid me heartily: and most especially, because I would speak to him for my father. And when I saw my time, I did desire him as humbly as I could, that he would (as I have heard say that he hath been) be still good lord unto my father.

Audeley, a typical servant of the New Monarchy, was not too sympathetic. We must remember that he had been on his knees before Henry to get More put out of the Bill of Attainder, and he not unnaturally thought it was time that More did something to help himself. He said he would do as much for More as for his own father (which is likely enough to have been true), but he marvelled that More was so obstinate in his own conceit. For himself, he had no learning, but in a few of Aesop's fables, two of which he proceeded to relate to Lady Alington. One of them is Wolsey's old fable of the wise men who sought to rule the fools, and for their pains were flogged by the foolish majority. 'Now, my good sister,' poor Lady Alington concludes,

> hath not my Lord told me two pretty fables? In good faith they pleased me nothing, nor I wist not what to say, for I was abashed of this answer. And I see no better suit than to Almighty God. For he is the comforter of all sorrows, and will not fail to send his comfort to his servants when they have most need.[1]

§ 4. MARGARET PLEADS WITH MORE

At her next visit to the Tower Margaret took this letter to show her father. It led to a long dialogue, thrown into the form of a letter from Margaret to Lady Alington. The Margaret speeches in the dialogue are pure Margaret, the More speeches pure More. When Rastell published the letter, long years after the death of both, their nearest and dearest could not say which had written it. This seems to show that the copy which Rastell used was not in More's handwriting, which he knew well. More was for the moment out of pain, free from the

[1] *Works*, 1557, p. 1434.

intermittent suffering of chest attacks, gravel and cramp. So, after the seven psalms and the litany said, and talk of the friends left at home, Margaret mentioned Lady Alington's news that More had little further to expect from his friends at court.

> With this my father smiled upon me and said, 'What, Mistress Eve (as I called you when you came first), hath my daughter Alington played the serpent with you, and with a letter set you awork to come tempt your father again, and for the favour that you bear him labour to make him swear against his conscience, and so send him to the devil?' And after that he looked sadly again, and earnestly said unto me, 'Daughter Margaret, we two have talked of this thing ofter than twice or thrice. And the same tale in effect that you tell me now therein, and the same fear too, have you twice told me before, and I have twice answered you too, that in this matter if it were possible for me to do the thing that might content the King's Grace, and God therewith not offended, there hath no man taken this oath already more gladly than I would do.'

Still hoping to move him, Margaret handed her father Lady Alington's letter, which he read twice, with grateful acknowledgement of his step-daughter's love, and of the good offices of Audeley and Cromwell in the matter of the Maid of Kent. He then discussed Audeley's fables at more length than they deserved, for he was obviously nettled at the suggestion that his obstinacy was due to a desire to rule. He was equally nettled by the suggestion that his obstinacy was due to Fisher's example:

> 'For albeit that of very truth I have him in that reverent estimation, that I reckon in this realm no one man, in wisdom, learning, and long approved virtue together, meet to be matched and compared with him, yet that in this matter I was not led by him, very well and plain appeareth, both in that I refused the oath before it was offered him, and in that also that his Lordship was content to have sworn of that oath (as I perceived since by you when you moved me to the same) either somewhat more, or in some other manner than ever I minded to do. Verily, daughter, I never intend (God being my good lord) to pin my soul at another man's back, not even the best man that I know this day living: for I know not whither he may hap to carry it.

There is no man living, of whom while he liveth, I may make myself sure.'

Some might take the oath with a mental reservation, convinced

'that if they say one thing and think the while the contrary, God more regardeth their heart than their tongue, and that therefore their oath goeth upon that they think, and not upon that they say: as a woman reasoned once, I trow, daughter, you were by.'

Was this Dame Alice? Anyway More cannot go with those who so argue. And he tells a tale of a suit between a Londoner and a Northern man, which had to be settled by a quest of twelve men, 'a jury, I remember they called it, or else a perjury'. (Surely this is More, writing in Margaret's name, and exaggerating her ignorance of the law.) The perjury was packed with Northern men, all but a poor Southerner called Company. The Northerners were agreed upon their verdict, when Company dissented. 'Company,' quoth they, 'play the good companion, come thereon forth with us, and pass even for good company.' 'But', retorted Company, 'when we shall hence, and come before God, and that he shall send you to Heaven for doing according to your conscience, and me to the Devil for doing against mine, if I shall then say to all you again, "Go now for good company with me," would ye go?'

'I meddle not with the conscience of any man that hath sworn,' More repeats, 'nor I take it not upon me to be their judge.' And then again we come to the eternal question of the supremacy of the state. Margaret repeats the doctrine of More's court friends:

'And sith it is also by a law made by the Parliament commanded, they think that you be upon the peril of your soul bounden to change and reform your conscience, and confirm your own, as I said, unto other men's.' 'Marry, Marget,' (quoth my father again), 'for the part that you play, you play it not much amiss. But, Margaret, first, as for the law of the land, though every man being born and inhabiting therein is bounden to the keeping in every case upon some temporal pain, and in many cases upon pain of God's displeasure too, yet is there no man bounden to swear that every law is well made, nor bounden upon the pain of God's displeasure to perform any such point of the law as were indeed unlawful.'

But *why* he refuses the oath More doggedly refuses to say, even to Margaret: 'that thing (as I have often told you) I will never show you, neither you nor nobody else, except the King's Highness should like to command me'. Many who had before agreed with More have now sworn, but again he refuses to judge their conscience, 'which lieth in their own heart far out of my sight'. It cannot be that they have complied from fear,

'For if such things should have turned them, the same things had been likely to make me do the same: for in good faith I know few so faint hearted as myself.'

Against Margaret's argument that those who have sworn are so many, and those who have refused so few, More replies,

'I nothing doubt at all, but that though not in this realm, yet in Christendom about, of those well learned men and virtuous that are yet alive, they be not the fewer part that are of my mind.'

And then seeing Margaret sitting very sad,

He smiled upon me, and said, 'How now, daughter Marget? What how, Mother Eve? Where is your mind now? Sit not musing with some serpent in your breast, upon some new persuasion, to offer father Adam the apple yet once again.'

Margaret confessed that she had but one argument left, and that was 'the reason Master Harry Patenson made'. Harry Patenson, once More's household jester, had been preferred to the service of the Lord Mayor. Master Harry, Margaret said,

'met one day one of our men, and when he had asked where you were, and heard that you were in the Tower still, he waxed even angry with you, and said, "Why, what aileth him that he will not swear? Wherefore should he stick to swear? I have sworn the oath myself." And so I can in good faith go now no further neither, after so many wise men whom ye take for no sample, but if I should say like Master Harry; "Why should you refuse to swear, father? For I have sworn myself." At this he laughed, and said, "That word was like Eve too, for she offered Adam no worse fruit than she had eaten herself." '

Margaret was doing herself an injustice, and More knew it.
She had sworn the oath with the exception 'as far as it would
stand with the law of God'. This of course rendered the oath
meaningless, and with this saving clause Fisher and More
would, I suppose, have been willing to take it. But in their
case no compromise was to be allowed, as More had all along
known:

'I counted, Marget, full surely many a restless night, while
my wife slept, and weened I had slept too, what peril were
possible for to fall to me, so far forth that I am sure there
can come none above. And in devising, daughter, thereupon, I had a full heavy heart. But yet, I thank our Lord
for all that, I never thought to change, though the very
uttermost should hap me that my fear ran upon.'

Margaret could only reply that More might repent when it was
too late:

'Too late, Margaret? I beseech our Lord, that if ever I make
such a change, it may be too late indeed. For well I wot the
change cannot be good for my soul, that change I say that
should grow but by fear. And therefore I pray God that in
this world I never have good of such change.'

But More trusts that God will give him strength to take any
suffering he may have to bear patiently, 'and peradventure
somewhat gladly too'.

'Mistrust him, Meg, will I not, though I feel me faint. Yea,
and though I should feel my fear even at point to overthrow
me too, yet shall I remember how Saint Peter with a blast
of a wind began to sink for his faint faith, and shall do as he
did, call upon Christ and pray him to help. And then I
trust he shall set his holy hand unto me, and in the stormy
seas hold me up from drowning. Yea, and if he suffer me to
play Saint Peter further, and to fall full to the ground, and
swear and forswear too (which our Lord for his tender
passion keep me from, and let me lose if it so fall, and never
win thereby): yet after shall I trust that his goodness will cast
upon me his tender piteous eye, as he did upon Saint Peter,
and make me stand up again, and confess the truth of my
conscience afresh, and abide the shame and the harm here
of mine own fault. And finally, Marget, this wot I very well,

that without my fault he will not let me be lost . . . And therefore, mine own good daughter, never trouble thy mind, for
any thing that ever shall hap me in this world. Nothing can
come, but that that God will . . . And if anything hap me
that you would be loth, pray to God for me, but trouble not
yourself: as I shall full heartily pray for us all, that we may
meet together once in heaven, where we shall make merry for
ever, and never have trouble after.'

And here, as in some of Plato's dialogues, the discussion
ends suddenly.[1] There is indeed nothing more to be said.

§ 5 . MORE'S WRITINGS IN THE TOWER

More has been often blamed, and often excused, for his
harsh words about heretics. It has not been sufficiently realized,
I think, how, from the time he enters the Tower, those harsh
words cease. He had said that he hated the vice of the heretics,
and not their persons.[2] But now he is 'Thomas More, prisoner',
with no more responsibility for repressing any of the errors of
the world. He might say, with another Thomas, 'I am beyond
all that'.[3] 'Stone walls do not a prison make' – it is a commonplace. More's writings in the Tower are more carefree than
those which he wrote in freedom; a collection of More's merry
tales would draw heavily from the *Dialogue of Comfort*. There is
a marked contrast between the happiness of the *Dialogue* and
the grim tone of the *Four Last Things*, written when More was
rising to power in the King's service.

In the *Dialogue of Comfort*, More has retreated from the out-
works to the inmost citadel. He is no longer defending this
dogma or that; he is defending the right of the individual soul,
against the command of the civil power, to hold any dogma
at all.

In doing this he was, in fact, touching upon the King's
matters more closely than if he had continued to write controversial works against the heretics. More and Henry had
still so much in common in matters of doctrine that More might
have gone on writing books to which the King would not have
objected, though he might not have wished the works of an

---

[1] *Works*, 1557, pp. 1434-43. Compare the end of the *Gorgias*.
[2] *Apology*, cap. 49; *Works*, 1557, p. 925.
[3] LASCELLES ABERCROMBIE, *Sale of St. Thomas*.

attainted prisoner to be published. Instead, More chooses a really dangerous subject. The *Dialogue of Comfort* is a debate between a pious and humorous old Hungarian nobleman, Anthony, and his rather weak young nephew, Vincent, as to how they are to behave in face of the Turkish conquest. Even the most stupid could not fail to see that most of what More wrote concerning the proper bearing of Catholics under the Turkish tyranny had the most intimate reference to his own case; and it involved a parallel between Henry and the Turk. The *Dialogue* had to be kept very secret; it was a denial of the thesis that the head of the State might dictate the religious belief of his subjects.

More returns to the topic of *Death the Tyrannicide*, with which he had played in his Latin epigrams when, as a youth, he lay under the displeasure of Henry VII. There is no king so great but is very sure that he must die:

And therefore, but if he be a fool, he can never be without fear, that either on the morrow, or on the selfsame day, the grisly, cruel hangman, Death, which, from his first coming in, hath ever hoved aloof, and looked toward him, and ever lain in await on him; shall amid all his royalty, and all his main strength, neither kneel before him, not make him any reverence, nor with any good manner desire him to come forth; but rigorously and fiercely gripe him by the very breast, and make all his bones rattle, and so by long and divers sore torments, strike him stark dead, and then cause his body to be cast into the ground in a foul pit, there to rot and be eaten with the wretched worms of the earth, sending yet his soul out farther unto a more fearful judgment, whereof at his temporal death his success is uncertain.[1]

.   .   .   .   .

St. John the Baptist was, you wot well, in prison, while Herod and Herodias sat full merry at the feast, and the daughter of Herodias delighted them with her dancing, till with her dancing she danced off St. John's head. And now sitteth he with great feast in heaven at God's board.[2]

.   .   .   .   .

Now to this great glory can there no man come headless. Our head is Christ: and therefore to him must we be joined,

[1] *Dialogue of Comfort, Works*, 1557, p. 1244.   [2] The same, p. 1248.

and as members of his must we follow him, if we will come thither. He is our guide to guide us thither . . . Knew you not that Christ must suffer passion, and by that way enter into his kingdom? Who can for very shame desire to enter into the kingdom of Christ with ease, when himself entered not into his own without pain?[1]

It is the same stern, ascetic creed which we find in the noblest Middle English religious literature. And it was therefore natural that when More had finished his *Dialogue of Comfort* he wrote the *Treatise on the Passion*, preparing himself for the end which he saw to be inevitable.

The medieval Saints' Legends are full of the stories of martyrs who have courted (or even demanded) persecution, like the Spanish girl Eulalia who, when her judge, moved by her youth and beauty, wished to acquit her, spat in his face to bring him up to the scratch. More must have read of this action of the saintly maiden in Prudentius,[2] but I am sure that he regarded it with the highest measure of disapproval consistent with complete orthodoxy. More lays no claim to such 'high degree of stout courage'. He turns for encouragement to the story of the Passion. To those like himself, filled with fear, he imagines Christ as saying:

'Pluck up thy courage, faint heart; what though thou be fearful, sorry and weary, and standest in great dread of most painful torments, be of good comfort; for I myself have vanquished the whole world, and yet felt I far more fear, sorrow, weariness, and much more inward anguish too, when I considered my most bitter, painful Passion to press so fast upon me. He that is strong-hearted may find a thousand glorious valiant martyrs whose ensample he may right joyously follow. But thou now, O timorous and weak, silly sheep, think it sufficient for thee only to walk after me, which am thy shepherd and governor, and so mistrust thyself and put thy trust in me. Take hold on the hem of my garment, therefore; from thence shalt thou perceive such strength and relief to proceed.'[3]

More began the treatise in English, and continued it in Latin; but just as he came to write of the arrest of Christ in the

---

[1] *Dialogue of Comfort, Works*, p. 1260.   [2] *Peristephanon*, III, 121.
[3] *Treatise on the Passion, Works*, 1557, pp. 1357-8.

Garden, his books and writing material were taken from him. One of Margaret Roper's children, Mary Basset, translated her grandfather's Latin into English, and this version is printed in More's *Works*. As the printer there says, Mary Basset's translation goes so near More's English phrase, that she is no nearer to him in kindred than in his English tongue. The reader can judge for himself, for the extract just quoted is from Mary Basset's rendering of More's Latin.

More had inherited his prose style from the great English devotional writers of the Fourteenth and Fifteenth Centuries. He had immensely broadened the scope of English prose, but now, in the last year of his life, we find him returning to the traditional style and the traditional topics. For nearly four hundred years More's devotional books, like those of his predecessors, have been almost forgotten. Within the last dozen years, they have been reasserting their power once again. The time will come when, as William Rastell said, they will be 'joyously embraced and had in estimation of all true English hearts'.

The Meditations which More wrote in the Tower on a *Book of Hours* have been hardly known from that day to this. Now, suddenly within the last three years, they have been circulated in tens of thousands of copies. They mark his farewell to the world:

> Give me Thy grace, good Lord, to set the world at nought,
> To set my mind fast upon Thee,
> And not to hang upon the blast of men's mouths ...

These prayers are written in ink; a luxury which was not always allowed to More in the Tower. 'Within a while after he was prisoner' he had to use a piece of charcoal as a pencil. Then more liberty was allowed; he could see Margaret and Dame Alice, and was even allowed to walk with them in the Tower garden. But, as the year 1534 wore on, conditions became harder. Margaret writes, 'Father, what moved them to shut you up again, we can nothing hear'. Occasional letters could still be exchanged. Margaret says that if the whole world had been given her, it had been a small pleasure compared with More's letter, which, 'though it were written with a coal, is

worthy in mine opinion to be written in letters of gold'. And
More replies:

> If I would with my writing (mine own good daughter)
> declare how much pleasure and comfort your daughterly
> loving letters were unto me, a peck of coals would not suffice
> to make me the pens. And other pens have I (good Mar-
> garet) none here; and therefore can I write you no long
> process, nor dare adventure, good daughter, to write often.

More has been warned that there may be further legislation to
deal with him. He trusts that God will not allow the King's
noble heart and courage to resort to 'such extreme unlawful and
uncharitable dealing'.[2] 'But,' he concludes, 'take no thought
for me, whatsoever you shall hap to hear, but be merry in God.'

§6. MORE AND DR. WILSON'S SECOND THOUGHTS

Meantime we must turn to Dr. Nicholas Wilson, sometime
chaplain and confessor to King Henry, whom More, when he
was before the lords at Lambeth, had seen 'gentlemanly sent
straight unto the Tower'. And now Wilson wrote to his fellow-
prisoner for advice — advice which More could not give him,
despite Wilson's 'agony and vexation of mind'. For More,
having 'signified his own poor opinion' to the King, had
determined 'to discharge his mind of any further studying or
musing on the matter'. 'As touching the oath,' he replies to
Wilson, 'the causes for which I refused it, no man knoweth
what they be ... Finally, as I said unto you, before the oath
offered unto us, when we met in London at adventure, I would
be no part-taker in the matter ... so say I to you still.' If only
on the score of health, More feels that he is now face to face with
death. 'I have, since I came in the Tower, looked once or twice
to have given up my ghost ere this; and in good faith mine
heart waxed the lighter with hope thereof ... I beseech God
give me and keep me the mind, to long to be out of this world
and to be with him. For I can never but trust, that whoso long
to be with him shall be welcome to him. And on the other
side, my mind giveth me verily, that any that ever shall come to
him, shall full heartily wish to be with him, ere ever he shall

[1] *Works*, 1557, p. 1446.   [2] The same, p. 1448.

come at him.'[1] Long ago, More had said just the same concerning his Utopians, who were horrified at the death of those who died unwillingly, but rejoiced at the funerals of those who departed merrily and full of good hope.[2] And at the time that he was writing to Wilson, More was saying the same thing in his *Dialogue of Comfort*: that a man could hardly be welcome to God who, when called, came unwillingly; but that on the other hand,

> he that so loveth him, that he longeth to go to him, my heart cannot give me but he shall be welcome, all were it so that he should come ere he were well purged. For charity covereth a multitude of sins, and he that trusteth in God cannot be confounded.[3].

More ends his letter to Dr. Wilson with words of the tenderest friendship: 'For our Lord's sake, good Master Wilson, pray for me, for I pray for you daily, and sometimes when I would be sorry but if I thought you were asleep.'

Despite More's wish to avoid discussion, Wilson wrote to him again, and it was clear that he meant to swear the oath. More replied to him this time very briefly, reminding him again that he had never given any man counsel to the contrary, and that, whilst they were both at liberty, he had told Wilson that he would neither know his mind nor no man else's; and that no man else should therein know his. More's letter is final, yet it is very friendly: 'as long as my poor short life shall last, anything that I have, your part shall be therein'.

Poor Wilson did not escape too easily. He was kept in prison for two years more, and had another imprisonment in the Tower during the troubles of 1540-1. But so far as More is concerned, he is now out of the story.

Early in the New Year, More wrote to a certain Master Leder, of whom we know nothing save that Rastell tells us that he was 'a virtuous priest'. Leder had heard a tale that More had sworn the oath, and had written to congratulate him on the end of his troubles. More thanks him for his good will; but 'the tale', he says, 'is a very vanity'. The letter reveals More's fear (which he expresses here more openly than in his letters to Margaret) that he might be put to the torture. 'If ever I should

---

[1] *Works*, 1557, p. 1445.   [2] *Utopia*, p. 277.   [3] *Works*, 1557, p. 1168.

mishap to receive the oath (which I trust our Lord shall never suffer me) ye may reckon sure that it were expressed and extorted by duresse and hard handling.' 'I trust both that they will use no violent, forcible ways, and also that if they would, God would of his grace (and the rather a great deal through good folks' prayers) give me strength to stand.'[1]

More repeats in this letter what he is always saying: that he will not meddle with other men's consciences. Yet the fact that More and Fisher were suffering imprisonment rather than swear, could not but influence the consciences of others, and form a grave embarrassment to Henry and his advisers. At the end of 1534 the Government strengthened itself by putting a number of measures on the Statute Book.

§ 7 . THE ACTS OF SUPREMACY AND TREASONS

The Act of Supremacy declared the King Supreme Head of the Church of England, ignoring the limitation 'so far as the law of Christ allows', subject to which qualification alone Convocation had approved the title. Another Act made the imprisonment of More and Fisher more regular by defining the oath which Parliament was to be reputed to have meant and intended. The Act of Treasons made it High Treason, after 1 Feb. 1535, by words or writing maliciously to deprive the King of his dignity, title, or name of his royal estate. Finally, Acts of Attainder were passed against Fisher and More for having refused the oath. In the Act against More his offences are alleged to date from 1 May preceding. Why that date was chosen is not clear. These Acts of Attainder did not touch the lives of Fisher or More, but, under the Act of Treasons, any words denying the Royal Supremacy would, after 1 Feb. 1535, render the speaker liable to all the horrors of a traitor's death by disembowelling.[2]

That such an Act was passed shows how Parliament was overawed: that it was not passed without difficulty shows that Parliament was not a mere body of nominees automatically registering the King's wishes. We have an echo of the parliamentary debate in the report which Robert Fisher brought to his brother in the Tower about Candlemas (2 Feb.) 1535.

---

[1] *Works*, 1557, p. 1450.   [2] 26 Henry VIII, caps. 1, 2, 13, 22, 23.

The bishop, when told of the Act of Supremacy, held up his hands in horror: 'Is it so?' and was then told concerning the Act of Treasons: 'But there was never such a sticking at the passing of any Act in the Lower House as was at the passing of the same; and they stuck at the last to have one word in the same, and that was the word *maliciously*, which, when it was put, it was not worth ***; for they would expound the same statute themselves at their pleasure.'[1]

Judge Rastell, in his life of his uncle, emphasizes the legal point:

> Note diligently here that the bill was earnestly withstood, and could not be suffered to pass, unless the rigour of it were qualified with this word *maliciously*; and so not every speaking against the Supremacy to be treason, but only maliciously speaking. And so, for more plain declaration thereof, the word *maliciously* was twice put into the Act. And yet afterwards, in putting the Act in execution against Bishop Fisher, Sir Thomas More, the Carthusians, and others, the word *maliciously*, plainly expressed in the Act, was adjudged by the King's Commissioners, before whom they were arraigned, to be void.[2]

§8. THE CARTHUSIANS STAND FIRM

A community of Contemplatives was naturally not concerned, as Fisher and More had been, with the King's matrimonial affairs. But about the time that Fisher and More were committed to the Tower, in the Spring of 1534, Commissioners demanded the oath from the Prior of the London Charterhouse, John Houghton. He refused, and, with the Procurator or Steward of the Community, Humphrey Middlemore, he was sent to the Tower. But after a month they were persuaded to relent, largely through the influence of their bishop, Stokesley. They were released, and some kind of oath (the exact terms we do not know) was sworn by the Community, apparently with the saving clause 'so far as lawful'.

'Our hour is not yet come,' Houghton told his brethren,

---

[1] *L.P.*, viii, No. 856, 2, p. 326. The statement is that of Fisher's servant, Richard Wilson, under examination; confirmed by Fisher's evidence, MS. Cotton Cleop. E. vi, fol. 165 (169).

[2] *Rastell Fragments*, HARPSFIELD, App. I, p. 229.

'but within a year I shall complete my course.' Great as More's
sufferings had been, those which now beset Prior Houghton
were beyond measure greater. 'A deadly grief unto me,' More
had written to Margaret, 'and much more deadly than to hear
of mine own death, is that I perceive my good son your husband,
and you my good daughter, and my good wife, and mine other
good children and innocent friends in great displeasure and
danger of great harm thereby.'[1] But Houghton was responsible
for a Community of some thirty choir-monks and lay-brethren;
and under the Act of Treasons he was faced, after 1 Feb. 1535,
not merely by an ignominious death, but by the horror of leaving his Community unprotected; it might be dissolved, and his
monks cast upon the world.　What shall I say, brethren, or
what shall I do, if at the Judgment I can show no fruit of those
whom God has given me?' 'Let us all die in our simplicity,' his
monks replied; and Prior Houghton would gladly have led
them out to one common martyrdom. 'But,' he said, 'I do not
think that they mean to do so much good to us, or so much
harm to themselves.' He saw that the Court policy would be to
kill him and the seniors, and then to win over the younger
monks, many of whom were well-born, by contact with their
courtly kinsfolk. The Prior ordered three days of solemn
preparation for the coming trial; the first was a day of general
confession. On the second, Prior Houghton knelt in the Chapter
House before each monk in succession, from the senior at his
side to the last lay-brother, asking forgiveness for any offence;
and one by one his monks did likewise before each other. On
the third day, whilst Houghton was celebrating Mass, there
came 'a soft whisper of air, which some perceived with their
bodily senses, while all experienced its sweet influence upon
their hearts'. The words are those of Maurice Chauncy, the
historian of the Community, who must himself have been
present. Houghton was so overcome that for some time he was
unable to continue the Mass.

　　Houghton, as Visitor of the English Province, was head of
the Carthusians of England. The Priors of the Charterhouses of
Axholme in Lincolnshire and Beauvale in Nottinghamshire had
come up to the London house to consult their head. All three

[1] *Works*, 1557, p. 1431.

together visited Cromwell, and Houghton began to state their difficulties: 'How could a layman be Head of the Church of England?' 'You would make the King a priest then?', Cromwell retorted, and all three Priors were soon lodged in the Tower. Richard Reynolds, of the Monastery of Sion, had also denied the Supremacy, and was sent to the Tower. Reynolds had been a student of Christ's College, Cambridge, one of the colleges founded by the Lady Margaret under the auspices of Fisher; he was the most learned monk in England, skilled in Latin, Greek, and Hebrew;[1] a man 'of angelic spirit and of angelic countenance'. On 20 April Robert Laurence of Beauvale, Augustine Webster of Axholme, and Richard Reynolds of Sion were again interrogated, and said that they could not take the King to be Supreme Head. On 26 April Houghton, Laurence, Webster and Reynolds repeated their refusal. Preparations were already being made for the Special Commission which was to try them, consisting of the Chancellor Audeley, Norfolk, Cromwell, and nearly a score of the leading peers and judges. At the trial, Reynolds said that 'he had intended to keep silence, following the example of Christ before Herod' (not a very conciliatory beginning). But 'to clear his conscience' he made a speech which was an anticipation of that which More was to make two months later, appealing to the past history of Christendom, and to the Church outside England. Most Englishmen even, he claimed, at heart agreed with him. When asked who, he replied, 'All good men of the Kingdom', and was commanded to keep silence.

All four, whilst refusing to take the King as Supreme Head, pleaded 'Not Guilty',[2] on the ground that they were not refusing *maliciously*. It was on this one word, which had been inserted into the Statute to save them and men like them, that the lives, not only of these four monks, but of Fisher and More also, were now depending. Judge Rastell rightly included in the *Life* of his uncle a full account of the trial of the Carthusians; for it was the test case which established the precedent fatal to More himself. Rastell's words are:

---

[1] POLE, *Pro unitatis defensione*, 1538, fols. 103, 104.
[2] *L.P.*, VIII, No. 609. It is erroneously stated in *L.P.* that on the 29th the monks pleaded *Guilty*. This is wrong; on the 29th they were found *Guilty*.

The four religious persons were arraigned, and the Carthusians by the mouth of John Houghton, their Prior, confessed that they denied the King's supremacy, but not maliciously. The jury could not agree to condemn these four religious persons, because their consciences persuaded them they did it not maliciously. The judges hereupon resolved them that whosoever denied the Supremacy denied it maliciously; and the expressing of the word 'maliciously' in the Act was a void limitation and restraint of the construction of the words and intention of the offender. The jury, for all this, could not agree to condemn them; whereupon Cromwell, in a rage, went unto the jury, and threatened them, if they condemned them not. And so, being overcome by his threats, they found them Guilty, and had great thanks; but they were afterwards ashamed to show their faces, and some of them took great thought for it.[1]

Maurice Chauncy, the Charterhouse monk, who has recorded the sufferings of his fellows, tells the story more in detail: Cromwell sent a messenger threatening the jury with death; but they remained stubborn, and only gave way when he appeared in person.

Reynolds asked his judges to obtain for him a few days' respite that he might prepare his conscience, and die like a good monk.

§ 9. FURTHER EXAMINATIONS IN THE TOWER

The day after the monks had been sentenced, Cromwell and various councillors visited the Tower to get a definite answer from More. More wrote a full account of the meeting[2] to Margaret, to allay her fears, 'she being, as he thought, with child'.[3] Summoned by the Lieutenant to meet Master Secretary and the rest, he had 'shifted his gown', passed many in the gallery, 'some known and some unknown', and, reaching the chamber, had been invited to sit down with the Councillors, 'which in no wise I would'. Cromwell said that More's friends, resorting to him, had doubtless showed him the new statutes; More said they had. Then, seeing that Parliament had made the King Supreme Head, the King, Cromwell said, wished to know what More's mind was therein:

---

[1] *Rastell Fragments*, HARPSFIELD, App. I., pp. 229-30.
[2] *Works*, 1557, pp. 1451-2.   [3] *L.P.*, VIII, No. 867, iii, 2; *State Papers*, I, 435.

Whereunto I answered, that in good faith I had well trusted that the King's highness would never have commanded any such question to be demanded of me ... And now I have in good faith discharged my mind of all such matters, and neither will dispute kings' titles nor popes': but the King's true faithful subject I am, and will be, and daily I pray for him, and all his, and for you all that are of his honourable council, and for all the realm. And otherwise than this, I never intend to meddle.

But, said Cromwell, the King was merciful, and would wish to see More take such conformable ways that he might be abroad in the world again among other men:

Whereunto I shortly ... answered ... that I would never meddle in the world again, to have the world given me, ... but that my whole study should be upon the passion of Christ, and mine own passage out of this world.

More was commanded to withdraw, and when he was called in again, Mr. Secretary Cromwell went to the root of the matter – it was More's demeanour that was making others 'so stiff as they be'. This was no doubt true, and the resistance of the Carthusians has a most intimate connection with More's fate. More replied, with equal truth, that he had given no man advice or counsel one way or another:

I am (quoth I) the King's true faithful subject and daily beadsman, and pray for his Highness and all the realm. I do nobody no harm, I say none harm, I think none harm, but wish everybody good. And if this be not enough to keep a man alive, in good faith I long not to live. And I am dying already, and have since I came here been divers times in the case that I thought to die within one hour. And I thank our Lord I was never sorry for it, but rather sorry when I saw the pang past. And therefore my poor body is at the King's pleasure. Would God my death might do him good.

This touched even Cromwell, who closed the interview by saying 'full gently' that no advantage should be taken of anything More had spoken. And so More ends his letter by bidding Margaret and all his friends to pray for him, and to take no thought whatsoever shall happen to him.

On receiving More's letter Margaret must have sought

permission to visit him again; for on 4 May, a day or two after, she was in the Tower with him. Probably Cromwell chose the day and hour, and it was no accident that father and daughter together saw Reynolds and the Carthusians setting out on their terrible journey to Tyburn. More, 'as one longing in that journey to have accompanied them', said to Margaret:

> Lo! dost thou not see, Meg, that these blessed fathers be now as cheerfully going to their deaths as bridegrooms to their marriage? Wherefore thereby mayest thou see, mine own good daughter, what a great difference there is between such as have in effect spent all their days in a straight, hard, penitential and painful life religiously, and such as have in this world, like worldly wretches, as thy poor father hath done, consumed all their time in pleasure and ease licentiously. For God, considering their long continued life in most sore and grievous penance, will no longer suffer them to remain here in this vale of misery and iniquity, but speedily hence taketh them to the fruition of His everlasting Deity; whereas thy silly father, Meg, that like a most wicked caitiff hath passed forth the whole course of his miserable life most sinfully, God, thinking him not worthy so soon to come to that eternal felicity, leaveth him here yet still in the world, further to be plunged and turmoiled with misery.[1]

Neither father nor daughter had the least assurance that the full horrors of a traitor's death would not be exacted in More's case also, and these gentle words were chosen to cheer Margaret at the preparations taking place before her eyes. The words seem exaggerated, but in very truth, compared with the austerities of Houghton's life, and his mental agonies, More's lot had almost been easy; and he was to be spared the physical agonies which Houghton was now to undergo.

With the four monks there had been tried, and with them suffered, a secular priest, John Hale, Vicar of Isleworth. His offence was different; he had been delated for repeating scandals about the King's amours, for expressing sympathy with Fisher and More ('thus ungodly doth he handle innocents, and also highly learned and virtuous men, thrusting them into perpetual prison, so that it is too great pity to hear'), for calling the King a heretic, and for wishing him an evil death. The

[1] ROPER, pp. 80-1.

poor Vicar threw himself on the King's mercy, but found none.
The monks were of different stuff. Their fate roused consterna-
tion and admiration as news of it passed to the different
capitals of Europe. They were dragged on hurdles, in their
religious habits, to Tyburn, where the Duke of Norfolk, and a
crowd of noblemen and courtiers were assembled. Houghton
was offered pardon if he would submit to the King's laws. He
refused, protesting his loyalty to the King, but his inability to
accept him as Supreme Head of the Church, lest he should
offend the Majesty of God.

He was hanged, cut down, and disembowelled while still
alive; as his entrails were torn out, he was heard to say gently
'Oh most merciful Jesus, have pity upon me in this hour!' The
other monks had to watch his tortures, and, as each awaited
his turn, also those of their fellows. Whilst waiting, they urged
the crowd to obey the King in all that was not against the
honour of God and the Church.[1] Reynolds, last to die, especially spoke at length to the thousands assembled, without any
sign of distress or fear. Pole records the 'alacrity' of the death
of this famous preacher and scholar, his friend and More's.[2]

We are told that after these executions Cromwell came to
More, with a message from the King, that his Highness 'minded
not with any matter wherein he should have any cause of
scruple, from henceforth to trouble his conscience'. The story
is likely enough; it was a part of the royal technique to alternate
exhibitions of frightfulness with professions of generosity. But
More was not shaken by the gentleness of either Cromwell or
Henry. Over thirty years before, he had written 'for his
pastime' verses on Fortune,[3] and he now added 'for his pastime'
(Rastell repeats the phrase) one stanza more as a pendant,
writing 'with a coal, for ink then had he none'.

> Eye-flattering Fortune, look thou never so fair
> Nor never so pleasantly begin to smile,
> As though thou wouldst my ruin all repair,

---

[1] The authorities or the story of the Carthusians are the official documents
in the 'Secret Bag' at the Record Office; Maurice Chauncy, *Historia aliquto
martyrum*, Mainz, 1550, some details of which Chauncy subsequently corrected
in his briefer *Passio minor*; the *Rastell Fragments*; and various reports sent
abroad at the time. See *L.P.*, VIII, Nos. 609, 661, 666, 675, 683, 726.

[2] For Reynolds, see *The Angel of Syon*, by Adam Hamilton, O.S.B.

[3] See above, pp. 92, 157.

During my life thou shalt not me beguile.
Trust shall I God, to enter in a while
His haven of Heaven, sure and uniform;
Ever after thy calm look I for a storm.[1]

The storm was not slow in coming, and, if we can trust the
dates given in More's indictment, More was examined again
before Cromwell on 7 May, a week after his previous examination, and made the same reply which he had reported to
Margaret: 'I will not meddle with any such matters, for I am
fully determined to serve God, and to think upon his passion
and my passage out of this world.' It is quite clear that on 7
May Fisher was examined. More seems to have sent a message
to Fisher (through George Golde, the Lieutenant's servant) that
he was himself 'in a peck of troubles', and would like to know
what answer Fisher had made. Fisher replied that his answer
had been according to the statute, 'which condemneth no man
but him that speaketh maliciously against the King's title; and
that the statute did compel no man to answer to the question
that was proposed him; and that he besought them that he
should not be constrained to make further or other answer than
the said statute did bind him, but would suffer him to enjoy
the benefit of the same statute'. The point is, of course, that
the Statute of Treasons made it capital to assert that the
King was *not* Supreme Head. But that was a different thing
from refusing to assert that he *was*; that refusal Fisher and
More had already made. They were suffering the penalty of
their refusal, which, although severe, was not capital. But the
unfortunate prisoner in the course of cross-examination by
members of the Council might easily slip, from merely persisting
in his refusal to take the oath, into a denial that the King *was*
Supreme Head, which would have been fatal. Fisher, however,
was quite convinced that he had not done this.

Then, apparently on this same 7 May, Richard Rich, the
Solicitor-General, came privately to Fisher. The King, he
said, for the satisfaction of his own conscience, wished to know
Fisher's opinion. No advantage should be taken, and Fisher's
answer should never be revealed to anyone save the King
only. Under this promise of secrecy, Fisher replied that 'He

[1] ROPER, p. 82; *Works*, 1557, p. 1432.

believed directly in his conscience, and knew by his learning precisely, that the King was not, nor could be, by the Law of God, Supreme Head in earth of the Church of England'.

From that moment Fisher's life was in the power of Rich. We need not suppose that the King prompted this treachery; Rich was quite capable of acting on his own initiative.

Meantime, the resistance of the London Charterhouse had not been broken. After the death of their Prior, the leadership fell into the hands of the surviving officials, Middlemore and Exmewe. With them was associated Sebastian Newdigate, who had been a courtier and favourite of Henry. Ten years before, he had been taking part in the Christmas sports at Greenwich, joining in the jousts in which the King shared and, together with men who were to be the leading statesmen of the latter part of Henry's reign, defending the Castle of Loyalty on behalf of four maidens of the Court. But, distressed at the turn things were taking, he had entered the London Charterhouse. On 25 May all three monks were brought to Cromwell's house at Stepney, 'and refusing constantly to acknowledge the King's supremacy, were imprisoned in the Tower of London; where they remained seventeen days, standing bolt upright, tied with iron collars fast by the necks to the posts of the prison, and great fetters fast rived on their legs with great iron bolts; so straitly tied that they could neither lie nor sit, nor otherwise ease themselves, but stand upright, and in all that space were they never loosed for any natural necessity'.

How far More knew of the torture which was going on so near him we cannot tell. For nine days and nights, Middlemore, Exmewe, and Newdigate had been standing bolt upright, and they were to stand for eight days and nights longer, when on 3 June More was again summoned before the Council, Audeley, Cromwell, Cranmer and others. He was told either to acknowledge and confess it lawful, that his Highness should be Supreme Head of the Church of England, or else plainly utter his malignity. 'Whereto I answered,' says More (in the letter in which he reported the interview to Margaret), 'that I had no malignity, and therefore I could none utter.' 'I thanked God that my case was such here in this matter, through the clearness of mine own conscience, that though I might have pain, I could not have harm. For a man may, in such a case, lose his head and have no harm.' Cromwell said that it was quite fair to compel More to make a plain answer, because More himself, as he thought, 'and at the leastwise bishops, did use to examine heretics, whether they believed the Pope to be Head of the Church, and used to compel them to make a precise answer thereto'. Probably More had not examined heretics in this way himself; he rather slyly remarks that in this matter Cromwell 'gave him a great praise above his deserving'. But he would have been the last to deny that the bishops were within their rights in so doing. Because, as he went on to explain to Cromwell, 'at that time, as well here as elsewhere through the corps of Christendom, the Pope's power was recognized for an undoubted thing; which seemeth not like a thing agreed in this realm, and the contrary taken for truth in other realms'. How rigid were More's views as to discipline, any reader of *Utopia* should know. So long as all ecclesiastical authority, throughout Western Christendom, recognized the Papal Supremacy, any individual who defied that authority was guilty, in More's view, of deadly sin. More would not have considered it right for the bishops to compel a man to say whether he thought the Pope's authority of divine or human institution. We know that More himself for a long time believed that the Papal supremacy was a mere human ordinance, 'for the more quietness of the ecclesiastical body'.[1] But, human or divine, authority must be obeyed. More believed, though he would not say it, that the English Parliament was usurping authority in a matter which belonged to 'the Common Corps of Christendom'. And Mr. Secretary Cromwell knew he believed it. 'In conclusion Master Secretary said that he liked me this day much worse than he did the last time. For then, he said, he pitied me much, and now he thought I meant not well.' And so More concludes with a final message to Margaret, 'take no thought for me, but pray for me'.

The authorities had discovered that Fisher and More had been carrying on a correspondence in the Tower. It had been harmless enough; More had communicated to Fisher his reply

[1] See above, pp. 194-6.

to his questioners: that he was determined not to meddle, but to think upon the Passion of Christ, and his passage out of this world; he had agreed with Fisher that the word *maliciously* should afford protection, but warned him not to trust to that, for the interpretation of the statute would not be according to his mind, or Fisher's either; he had warned Fisher that, when examined, each should avoid using phrases which the other had used, lest the Council should think one had 'taken light' of the other. George Golde, the Lieutenant's servant, carried the letters to and fro, and More, that there might be evidence of their harmlessness, would have him keep them; but George always said there was no better keeper than the fire, and so burned them. The servants were examined, and we hear of the little gifts that passed between More and Fisher; how Fisher sent More half a custard and long since greensauce; how More sent Fisher an image of St. John, and apples and oranges after the snow that fell in winter. On New Year's Day, More sent Fisher a paper with two thousand pounds in gold in writing, and an image of the Magi visiting the infant Christ. During the first year of his imprisonment, we learn that Bonvisi sent More meat and a bottle of wine two or three times every week, and to Fisher a quart of French wine every day, and three or four dishes of jelly. The servants no doubt loyally helped their ascetic masters in the consumption of these dainties. We hear incidentally that George Golde was not always sober.

Further questions were put to the servants about the news which had come through to London, that Pope Paul III had created Fisher a Cardinal, on 20 May. The Pope had hoped, no doubt, that the Cardinal's hat, as evidence of his European reputation, would be a protection to Fisher in his trouble. It only increased Henry's wrath: 'I will so provide', said the King, 'that if he wear it, he shall bear it on his shoulders, nor any head shall he have to put it on.' We are also told on good authority that Anne Boleyn urged him on: she 'made the king a great banquet at Hanworth, twelve miles from London, and allured there the King with her dalliance and pastime to grant unto her this request, to put the bishop and Sir Thomas More to death'. But, in fact, it is probable that the fate of both Fisher and More had already been sealed by the resistance of the

Carthusians. On 1 June a special commission was appointed, to inquire and determine treasons; on 11 June Middlemore, Exmewe and Newdigate were brought before it; and on 19 June they were executed at Tyburn in their religious habits, and with the same barbarities as their Prior had suffered.

A tradition preserved in Newdigate's family, and recorded more than a century after his death, tells how Henry visited his former courtier in prison, in the hope of shaking his determination. A curious Spanish Chronicle, supposed to be contemporary with the events it records, but full of inaccurate gossip, tells how Henry visited More in the Tower in the same way.[1] Both stories are unlikely, but there may be truth in the rumour that Henry paid a visit to the monks who were still in the Charterhouse. If so, the visit was in vain, and it was not till after another two years of struggle that almost half the monks were persuaded to submit. Ten who remained obdurate were sent to Newgate, where, as one of Henry's clerics said, they were 'despatched by the hand of God': that is to say, they were tied to posts, as Middlemore, Exmewe and Newdigate had been, but in this case they were left to their fate. For many days they were fed by More's adopted daughter, Margaret Gigs. Her husband, John Clement, was now court-physician, and she bribed the gaoler to allow her to enter the prison disguised as a milkmaid, 'with a great pail upon her head full of meat [i.e. food], wherewith she fed that blessed company, putting meat into their mouths, they being tied and not able to stir, nor to help themselves; which having done, she afterwards took from them their natural filth'. When the terrified gaoler refused to admit her any more, she made unsuccessful efforts to feed the prisoners from the roof. All but one died, 'what with the stink and want of food'. The survivor, a lay-brother, William Horn, was removed to the Tower. Five years after the death of his companions, he was still refusing to recognize the Supremacy. So he was drawn to Tyburn, and died under the knife of the executioner at the same time as More's son-in-law, Giles Heron. Thirty-five years to a day after the death of More, Margaret Clement, 'not less dear to him than a daughter',

[1] *Crónica del Rey Enrico Otavo de Ingalaterra*, Madrid, 1874 (Spanish Academy of History: *Libros de Antano*).

lay dying in exile at Mechlin. But it was not the figure of More that hovered before her dying eyes on the Utas of St. Peter, 1570. 'Calling her husband, she told him that the time of her departing was now come, for that there were standing about her bed the Reverend Fathers, monks of the Charterhouse, whom she had relieved in prison in England, and did call upon her to come away with them, and that therefore she could stay no longer, because they did expect her.'

And so the monks of the Charterhouse are out of the story.

§ 10. TRIAL AND DEATH OF FISHER

On 12 June Fisher was again subjected to a long examination in the Tower. According to More's Indictment, it was on the same day that the Solicitor General, Rich, had the conversation with him in which (as Rich falsely asserted) More denied the King's Supremacy. Rich had come, Roper tells us, with others, to fetch away More's books from him.

Two days later, 14 June, a final attempt was made to get a definite answer out of both Fisher and More. Fisher, when asked why he would not answer resolutely, replied, 'lest he should fall thereby into the dangers of the Statutes'. More replied, 'that he can make no answer'.

The Government had however got a reply from Fisher, which had been given on 7 May, under a pledge of secrecy alleged, truly or falsely, to come direct from the King. From More they had got nothing, and had to rely on simple perjury.

On 17 June Fisher was tried before the same Commission which had condemned the Carthusians six days earlier, and in the presence of 'a great number of people gathered to see this woeful tragedy'. Fisher did not deny that he had used the fatal words, but appealed to the pledge of secrecy from the King. The messenger, according to Judge Rastell, admitted the pledge: 'But all this', he said, 'does not discharge you any whit.' Rastell was possibly present at the trial of Fisher, as he certainly was at his execution, and Rich was still living when he wrote. He does not mention Rich by name as the messenger: another account, written a few years later, gives Rich's name, and varies slightly as to his answer, though it comes to the same thing. Rich, it is there stated, neither denied Fisher's words for false nor confessed them for true, but said, 'If I had said to you in such sort as you have declared, I would gladly know what discharge this is to you in law'. It was in vain that Fisher asked how 'by all equity, all justice, all worldly honesty, and all civil humanity' he could be charged with denying the Supremacy *maliciously* when he spoke at the request of the King, and under a pledge that his reply should be divulged to none save the King. Judge Rastell says grimly, 'Pity, Mercy, Equity nor Justice had there no place'. Fisher was found guilty, and condemned to the full penalty of Treason. The sentence was commuted to beheading; indeed, had Fisher been dragged on a hurdle to Tyburn, he would probably have died on the way.

On 22 June, early, the Lieutenant of the Tower came to Fisher's chamber, and 'after some circumstance unto him used, with persuasion to remember that for age he could not long live', he told him that the King's pleasure was that he should suffer in that forenoon.

'Well,' quoth the bishop, 'if this be your errand hither, it is no news unto me; I have looked daily for it. I pray you what is it a clock?'

'It is,' quoth the Lieutenant, 'about five.'

'What time,' quoth the bishop, 'must be mine hour to go out hence?'

'About ten of the clock,' said the Lieutenant.

'Well then,' quoth the bishop, 'I pray you let me sleep an hour or twain. For I may say to you, I slept not much this night – not for fear of death, I tell you, but by reason of my great sickness and weakness.'

The Lieutenant returned about nine, and found Fisher up, putting on his clothes. Fisher asked the Lieutenant to reach him his furred tippet. 'Oh! my Lord,' the Lieutenant said, 'what need you be now so careful of your health? Your time is very short, little more than half an hour.' 'I think none otherwise,' said the bishop, 'but I pray you, yet give me leave to put on my furred tippet, to keep me warm for the while until the very time of execution. For I tell you truth, though I have, I thank our Lord, a very good stomach and willing mind to die at this present, yet will I not hinder my health in the mean

time not a minute of an hour.' He mounted the scaffold unaided, and Rastell describes how he saw him: 'a long, lean
slender body, nothing in a manner but skin and bare bones, so
that the most part that there saw him marvelled to see any man,
bearing life, to be so far consumed; for he seemed a lean body
carcass, the flesh clean wasted away, and a very image of
death, and, as one might say, Death in a man's shape, and using
a man's voice'. Fisher, with a strong and clear voice, asked for
the prayers of the bystanders: 'Hitherto', he said, 'I have not
feared death. Yet I know that I am flesh, and that St. Peter,
from fear of death, three times denied his Lord. Wherefore help
me, with your prayers, that at the very instant of my death's
stroke, I faint not in any point of the Catholic faith for any
fear.' On the scaffold pardon had been offered him more than
once in the King's name, if he would comply. After execution,
his body was stripped naked, and left all day, till, about eight
in the evening, commandment to bury it came to the guard who
tarried about the scaffold with halberds and bills. They dug a
shallow grave with their halberds under the north wall of All
Hallows, Barking, tossed the headless corpse in, very con-
temptuously, as the King had commanded, and scraped the
earth over. The head was placed on London Bridge, 'as though
it had been alive, looking upon the people coming into London,'
till folk began to talk of a miracle. So when, a fortnight later,
the executioner placed More's head upon the Bridge, he threw
that of Fisher into the river.[1]

---

[1] The documents for the trial and death of Fisher and More are calendared in *L.P.*
VIII, and Dr. Hitchcock and I have printed the more important of them in the
Appendix and Notes to HARPSFIELD's *Life*. The account given above is from
strictly contemporary sources, largely narrative of an eye-witness. The pathetic
stories of how Fisher, tarrying for the sheriffs, opened his New Testament at
adventure, and what he read there, and how the sun shone on his face as he
mounted the scaffold, come from an informant who at the time was a young scholar
of Cambridge. They are probably true, but are not as well authenticated as the
details I have given.

The primary authority for More's trial and death is the News Letter sent to
Paris. Roper's account of the trial (based on the reports of Sir Antony St. Leger,
Richard Heywood and John Webbe) is of great value. Both accounts are combined by Harpsfield, and I use his Tudor translation of the Paris News Letter
rather than make a modern version. The official documents relating to Fisher
and More are extant in the 'Secret Bag' at the Record Office; they confirm the
accounts of Rastell, the News Letter, Roper and Harpsfield. Stapleton's account
of More's execution is important; it was derived from Margaret Clement, an eye-
witness.

§ 11. TRIAL OF MORE

A little before his trial, More, feeling that ere long he might not have liberty to write, sent a farewell greeting to Antonio Bonvisi, in whose house he had been 'almost this forty years, not a guest, but a continual nursling'. The letter, in Latin, is More's farewell to the world of humanist international friendship. I quote from William Rastell's English translation. It ends with a prayer that God may bring them both from this stormy world

> into his rest, where shall need no letters, where no wall shall dissever us, where no porter shall keep us from talking together, but that we may have the fruition of the eternal joy with God the Father, and with his only begotten son our Redeemer Jesu Christ, with the Holy Spirit of them both, the Holy Ghost procceding from them both. And in the mean season, Almighty God grant both you and me, good Master Bonvisi, and all mortal men everywhere, to set at nought all the riches of this world, with all the glory of it, and the pleasure of this life also, for the love and desire of that joy. Thus of all friends most trusty, and to me most dearly beloved, and as I was wont to call you the apple of mine eye, right heartily fare ye well. And Jesus Christ keep safe and sound and in good health all your family, which be of like affection towards me as their master is.
>
> Thomas More: I should in vain put to it, 'Yours', for thereof can you not be ignorant, since you have bought it with so many benefits. Nor now I am not such a one that it forceth whose I am.[1]

On 1 July More was brought to Westminster Hall for trial. After his indictment had been read, he was told by Audeley the Lord Chancellor and by Norfolk that, though he had heinously offended the King's Majesty, they hoped (such was the King's clemency) that, if he would forthink and repent of his obstinate opinion, he might still taste the King's gracious pardon.

'My Lords,' More replied, 'I humbly thank you for your great good will. Howbeit, I make my petition unto God Almighty that it may please him to maintain me in this my honest mind, to the last hour that I shall live. And concerning

---

[1] *Works*, 1557, p. 1457; 'forceth' = 'matters',

the matters you charge me withal, the articles are so prolix and long that I fear, what for my long imprisonment, what for my disease and present weakness, that neither my wit, nor memory, nor voice will serve to make sufficient answer.'

More was leaning upon a staff; but a chair was placed for him, and he sat to answer the articles of his indictment one by one.

On the first charge, he denied having maliciously resisted the King's second marriage; he had only spoken according to his conscience, in that he would not conceal the truth from his Prince. If he had not done as he did, he would have been an unfaithful and disloyal subject. For this error (if error it were) his goods had been confiscated, and he had been adjudged to perpetual prison, where he had now been shut up for fifteen months. More then came to the main charge: that of having incurred the penalty of the Act made since he was imprisoned, in that he had maliciously and traitorously deprived the King of the title of Supreme Head which Parliament had granted him. He was charged with having done this in the first instance by maliciously refusing, on 7 May, to answer Mr. Secretary Cromwell, Bedell, Tregonwell and others, saying, 'I will not meddle with any such matters, for I am fully determined to serve God, and to think upon his passion and my passage out of this world'.

To this More replied that treason lay in word or deed, not silence: 'For this my silence neither your law nor any law in the world is able justly and rightly to punish me.'

The answer of the prosecution was, 'This very silence is a sure token and demonstration of a nature maligning against the statute; yea, there is no true and faithful subject that, being required of his opinion touching the said statute, is not deeply and utterly bound, without any dissimulation, to confess the statute to be good, just and lawful.'

More replied that the maxim of the Civil Law, *Silence gives consent*, would construe his silence rather as ratification than condemnation. He then made his great plea for the liberty of silence: .

Ye must understand that, in things touching conscience, every true and good subject is more bound to have respect to his said conscience and to his soul than to any other thing in all the world beside; namely when his conscience is in such sort as mine is, that is to say, where the person giveth no occasion of slander, of tumult and sedition against his prince, as it is with me; for I assure you that I have not hitherto to this hour disclosed and opened my conscience and mind to any person living in all the world.[1]

The second article charged More with having corresponded with Fisher and thereby encouraged him against the statute. Fisher had burned the letters, but More said that he remembered the contents:

In one of them there was nothing in the world contained but certain familiar talk and recommendations, such as was seemly and agreeable to our long and old acquaintance. In the other was contained my answer that I made to the said bishop, demanding of me what thing I answered at my first examination in the Tower upon the said statute. Whereunto I answered nothing else but that I had informed and settled my conscience, and that he should inform and settle his. And other answer, upon the charge of my soul, made I none.

The third article sought to prove that More had encouraged Fisher by writing to him that 'The Act of Parliament is like a sword with two edges; for if a man answer one way it will confound his soul, and if he answer the other way it will confound his body'. It was claimed as a proof of their collusion that both Fisher and More, when separately examined on 3 June, had used this same phrase. More replied that any resemblance between his answer and Fisher's was due to 'the conformity of our wits, learning, and study'.

The case against More was not going well. What was wanted was not evidence of how he justified his silence, but evidence that he had broken it.

Rich stepped forward.

He asserted that in the Tower, on 12 June, More had uttered the fatal words to him. Rich had said to More, 'Admit that there were an Act of Parliament that all the realm should take me, Richard Rich, for King; would not you, Master More, take me for King?' 'That would I,' More had replied, 'but take a

---

[1] HARPSFIELD, *Life of More*, p. 186.

higher case; how if there were an Act of Parliament that God should not be God?' 'That cannot be,' Rich had replied. 'But I will put a middle case: you know that our King has been made Supreme Head. Why will you not take him as such, even as you would take me as King?'

Then, Rich asserted, More had replied that, though a King could be made by Parliament, and by Parliament deposed, it was not so with the Head of the Church.

More denied the conversation:

> If I were a man, my Lords, that did not regard an oath, I needed not, as it is well known, in this place, at this time, nor in this case, to stand here as an accused person. And if this oath of yours, Master Rich, be true, then pray I that I never see God in the face; which I would not say, were it otherwise, to win the whole world.[1]

More then gave his own version of what had passed. This, unfortunately, has not been preserved. More added, 'In good faith, Master Rich, I am sorrier for your perjury than for my own peril'. He gave a scathing account of the character of Rich. Was it likely that he would utter to such a man the secrets of his conscience, 'the special point and only mark at my hands so long sought for', which he had refused to reveal to the King or to any of his Council? And yet, even if he *had* denied the King's title, he had not *maliciously* denied it; and where there is no malice there can be no offence, just as in 'forcible entry', where there is no force, there is no offence.

Rich called upon Southwell and Palmer, who had been present in the chamber, to support his evidence. It is quite certain that if Rich had really trapped More into uttering the words, he would instantly have called upon Southwell and Palmer to witness them. Richard Southwell was a young man who had two years before been pardoned for complicity in a murder.[2] It remains very much to his credit, and to that of Palmer, that they would not support the evidence of Rich:

> Master Palmer, upon his deposition, said that he was so busy about the trussing up of Sir Thomas More's books in a sack, that he took no heed to their talk. Sir Richard Southwell likewise, upon his deposition, said that because he was

---

[1] ROPER, p. 87.   [2] *Statutes of the Realm*, 25 Henry VIII, cap. 32.

appointed only to look unto the conveyance of his books, he gave no ear unto them.[1]

The jury, after an absence of a quarter of an hour, found a verdict of 'Guilty', and Lord Audeley at once began to pass sentence, without going through the formality of asking More if he had anything to say. Audeley has been harshly censured for this. But for months More had preserved silence, despite all that Audeley and others could do to make him break it, and it probably never occurred to any of them that More now wished to 'discharge his conscience'. Henry's statesmen had, from time to time, to pass capital sentence on their best friends, and all Audeley wished was to get the wretched business over.

But More had thought it all out, and he knew that his time had come.

Only a month before he had been taunted with cowardice, because he would not 'speak even plain out'. He had replied that he had not been a man of such holy living that he might be bold to offer himself to death, and therefore he put himself not forward, but drew back, 'lest God for my presumption might suffer me to fall'. 'Howbeit', he added, 'if God draw me to it himself, then trust I in his great mercy that he shall not fail to give me grace and strength.' More was probably thinking of the Carthusians, men of holy living who had spoken plain out, and who, as he probably knew, had been standing 'tied with iron collars fast by the necks, and great fetters fast rived on their legs'. He did not dare deliberately to incur such torments as they were suffering, lest, when these torments continued week after week, he might fail to show the constancy they showed.

Seven years before, he had said the same thing, when discussing Christ's command to his disciples that, when persecuted in one city, they should flee into another. It was not the business of Christians, More said, to court martyrdom, and thus foolhardily to put themselves in danger of denying Christ 'by impatience of some intolerable torments'. Rather they should flee to some place where they could serve God in quiet, 'till he should suffer them to fall in such point that there were no way of escape, and then would he have them abide by their tackling

[1] ROPER, p. 91.

like mighty champions, wherein they shall not in such case fail of his help'.[1]

After the verdict of 'Guilty' there was no way to escape. It was the sign for which More had been waiting, the sign that help would not fail him, and that now he should 'abide by his tackling'. Let there be no mistake as to the courage needed. For the sentence about to be pronounced was the horrible one of death by disembowelling at Tyburn; it rested with the King's grace whether that sentence were commuted to a dignified and merciful death by beheading on Tower Hill. To Fisher alone of all the nine sufferers had that mercy been shown; and men thought the reason was that Fisher was already so feeble that he would have died outright before the full sentence could be executed. Even Sebastian Newdigate, one of Henry's personal friends, had not been spared. But, at whatever risk of infuriating Henry, More must speak now, or never.

He interrupted Lord Audeley: 'My Lord, when I was toward the law, the manner in such case was to ask the prisoner, before judgment, why judgment should not be given against him.'

Audeley stayed his judgment, and demanded what More had to say. He answered:

Seeing that I see ye are determined to condemn me (God knoweth how) I will now in discharge of my conscience speak my mind plainly and freely touching my indictment and your Statute withal.

And forasmuch as this indictment is grounded upon an Act of Parliament directly repugnant to the laws of God and his holy Church, the supreme government of which, or of any part whereof, may no temporal prince presume by any law to take upon him, as rightfully belonging to the See of Rome, a spiritual pre-eminence by the mouth of our Saviour himself, personally present upon earth, only to St. Peter and his successors, bishops of the same see, by special prerogative granted; it is therefore in law, amongst Christian men insufficient to charge any Christian man.[2]

Thomas More was an intensely loyal Londoner. But just as

[1] *Dialogue, Works,* 1557, p. 278; the same thing is said in the *Treatise on the Passion, Works,* 1557, pp. 1355 etc.
[2] HARPSFIELD, p. 193.

London, 'being but one poor member in respect of the whole realm', could not make a particular law against England, neither could England against 'Christ's universal Catholic Church'. He appealed to the immunity promised to the Church in Magna Carta, to the King's coronation oath, and to the continuity of English Christianity:

> For, as St. Paul said of the Corinthians, 'I have regenerated you, my children in Christ;' so might St. Gregory, Pope of Rome, of whom, by St. Augustine his messenger, we first received the Christian faith, of us English men truly say: 'You are my children, because I have given to you ever-lasting salvation.'

Audeley replied by appealing, as More's opponents appealed all along, to 'the bishops, universities, and best learned of this realm', and More made the reply he always made – that, on a true view of the case, he was not in a minority:

> For I nothing doubt but that, though not in this realm, yet in Christendom about, of these well learned bishops and vir-tuous men that are yet alive, they be not the fewer part that are of my mind therein. But if I should speak of those that are already dead, of whom many be now holy saints in heaven, I am very sure it is the far greater part of them that, all the while they lived, thought in this case that way that I think now; and therefore am I not bounden, my Lord, to conform my conscience to the Council of one realm against the general Council of Christendom. For of the foresaid holy bishops I have, for every bishop of yours, above one hundred; and for one Council or Parliament of yours (God knoweth what manner of one), I have all the Councils made these thousand years. And for this one kingdom, I have all other Christian realms.

It was the inevitable conflict between the national and the super-national outlook. 'We now plainly perceive that ye are maliciously bent,' said Norfolk. 'Nay,' replied More,

> very and pure necessity, for the discharge of my conscience, enforceth me to speak so much. Wherein I call and appeal to God, whose only sight pierceth into the very depth of man's heart, to be my witness. Howbeit, it is not for this Supremacy so much that ye seek my blood, as for that I would not condescend to the marriage.

Audeley was so far shaken that he turned to FitzJames, the Lord Chief Justice, asking whether the indictment were sufficient. FitzJames replied 'like a wise man': 'My Lords all, by St. Julian, I must needs confess that if the Act of Parliament be not unlawful, then is not the indictment in my conscience insufficient.' 'Lo, my Lords, lo, you hear what my Lord Chief Justice saith,' exclaimed Audeley, and so gave judgment.

Convocation had made Henry Supreme Head 'as far as the law of Christ allows'. Parliament omitted the saving clause, but tried to provide some barrier against tyranny by putting the saving word 'maliciously' into the Act of Treasons. The lawyers interpreted 'maliciously' as a void word, and threw back responsibility on Parliament.

The Commissioners courteously asked if More had any further defence. He replied:

> More have I not to say, my Lords, but that like as the blessed apostle St. Paul, as we read in the Acts of the Apostles, was present, and consented to the death of St. Stephen, and kept their clothes that stoned him to death, and yet be they now both twain holy saints in Heaven, and shall continue there friends for ever, so I verily trust, and shall therefore right heartily pray, that though your Lordships have now here in earth been judges to my condemnation, we may yet hereafter in Heaven merrily all meet together, to our everlasting salvation.[1]

Sir William Kingston, Constable of the Tower, brought More back from Westminster to 'the Old Swan toward the Tower', and

> there with an heavy heart, the tears running down by his cheeks, bade him farewell. Sir Thomas More, seeing him so sorrowful, comforted him with as good words as he could, saying: 'Good Master Kingston, trouble not yourself, but be of good cheer; for I will pray for you, and my good Lady, your wife, that we may meet in heaven together, where we shall be merry for ever and ever.'

Soon after, Sir William Kingston, talking with me of Sir Thomas More, said: 'In good faith, Master Roper, I was ashamed of myself, that, at my departing from your father, I found my heart so feeble, and his so strong, that he was

[1] ROPER, p. 96.

fain to comfort me, which should rather have comforted him.'[1]

As More was led back, with the edge of the axe towards him, his son John threw himself at his feet to ask a blessing. At Tower Wharf Margaret Roper was waiting, with Margaret Clement:

> As soon as she saw him, after his blessing on her knees reverently received, she hasting towards him, and, without consideration or care of herself, pressing in among the midst of the throng and company of the guard that with halberds and bills went round about him, hastily ran to him, and there openly, in the sight of them all, embraced him, took him about the neck, and kissed him.[2]

One of the crowd of bystanders has told us how Margaret, unable to speak, held her father 'tightly embraced'; but how More only said, 'Have patience, Margaret, and trouble not thyself. It is the will of God. Long hast thou known the secrets of my heart.'[3] Margaret withdrew ten or twelve paces from her father, and then, 'not satisfied with the former sight of him, and like one that had forgotten herself, being all ravished with the entire love of her dear father, having respect neither to herself, nor to the press of the people and multitude that were there about him, suddenly turned back again, ran to him as before, took him about the neck, and divers times together most lovingly kissed him'.[4] More showed no discomposure, asking only that she should pray for his soul.

Tales of More's bearing during his last days in prison seem to show that both his austerities and his humour were already becoming somewhat legendary. We are told that he scourged himself, and meditated upon death, wrapping a linen sheet round him like a shroud. When informed that the King had commuted his sentence to beheading, More is said to have prayed, 'God forbid that the King should use any more such mercy unto any of my friends'.[5] We are also told that Cromwell made a last attempt to force him to change his mind, and that More replied that he *had* changed it; for whereas he had meant to be shaven he would now let his beard share the fate of his

---

[1] p. 97.   [2] p. 98.   [3] *Paris News Letter*, HARPSFIELD, App. II, p. 265
[4] ROPER, pp. 98-9.   [5] STAPLETON, XX, p. 352; XVIII, p. 340.

head.[1] (This is the earliest of a number of beard-anecdotes, which perhaps have no other foundation than the well-authenticated fact that More, on the scaffold, laid his beard over the block so that it should not be cut.)

Rastell included in More's *Works* a collection of prayers which he says were made by Sir Thomas More after he was condemned to die. More embodied in them sentences which were certainly written not by him but by Margaret Roper. Months before, father and daughter had exchanged these words. 'Good Marget, when you pray it, pray it for us both, and I shall on my part the like,' More had written. And so, when they could no longer enjoy each other's company, they had both used Margaret's prayer, 'continually to have an eye to mine end, without grudge of death'.[2] Yet, though some of these sentences were Margaret's writing, others *were* probably composed by More after sentence had been pronounced upon him:

> Good Lord, give me the grace, in all my fear and agony, to have recourse to that great fear and wonderful agony that Thou, my sweet Saviour, hadst at the Mount of Olivet before Thy most bitter passion, and in the meditation thereof, to conceive ghostly comfort and consolation profitable for my soul. . . .
>
> Almighty God, have mercy on N. and N., and on all that bear me evil will, and would me harm, and their faults and mine together, by such easy, tender, merciful means, as Thine infinite wisdom best can devise, vouchsafe to amend and redress, and make us saved souls in heaven together where we may ever live and love together with Thee and Thy blessed saints. O glorious Trinity, for the bitter passion of our sweet Saviour Christ. Amen.
>
> Lord, give me patience in tribulation and grace in everything to conform my will to Thine; that I may truly say: 'Fiat voluntas tua, sicut in coelo et in terra.'
>
> The things, good Lord, that I pray for, give me Thy grace to labour for. Amen.

Margaret Roper was still allowed to send messages to her father through her maid Dorothy Colly. On Monday, 5 July,

---

[1] Latin *Chronicle of the Divorce*, ed. BÉMONT, p. 72 (this is a very early but most untrustworthy document).

[2] Compare *Works*, 1557, p. 1417, with p. 1449.

More sent to Margaret the hair-shirt which she had washed so often, and a letter 'written with a coal', 'which was the last thing that ever he wrote'.

Our Lord bless you, good daughter, and your good husband, and your little boy, and all yours, and all my children, and all my godchildren and all our friends. Recommend me when ye may to my good daughter Cicely, whom I beseech our Lord to comfort. And I send her my blessing, and to all her children, and pray her to pray for me. I send her a handkerchief: and God comfort my good son her husband. My good daughter Dauncey hath the picture in parchment that you delivered me from my Lady Coniers, her name is on the backside. Shew her that I heartily pray her that you may send it in my name to her again, for a token from me to pray for me. I like special well Dorothy Colly, I pray you be good unto her. I would wit whether this be she that you wrote me of. If not, yet I pray you be good to the other as you may in her affliction, and to my good daughter Joan Aleyn too. Give her, I pray you, some kind answer, for she sued hither to me this day to pray you be good to her. I cumber you, good Margaret, much, but I would be sorry if it should be any longer than tomorrow. For it is Saint Thomas' even and the Utas of Saint Peter; and therefore tomorrow long I to go to God: it were a day very meet and convenient for me. I never liked your manner toward me better than when you kissed me last: for I love when daughterly love and dear charity hath no leisure to look to worldly courtesy. Farewell, my dear child, and pray for me, and I shall for you and all your friends, that we may merrily meet in Heaven. I thank you for your great cost. I send now to my good daughter Clement her algorism stone, and I send her and my godson, and all hers, God's blessing and mine. I pray you at time convenient recommend me to my good son John More. I liked well his natural fashion. Our Lord bless him and his good wife my loving daughter, to whom I pray him be good as he hath great cause: and that if the land of mine come to his hand he break not my will concerning his sister Dauncey. And our Lord bless Thomas and Austen and all that they shall have.[1]

§ 12. DEATH OF MORE

More's wish was fulfilled. Early in the morning of the next day, 6 July, Thomas Pope, 'his singular friend', came with a message from the King and Council that he should suffer death before nine. As a young official of the Court of Chancery, Pope had been well known to More, and there was much to unite them in friendship, in addition to that love of learning which in later years led Pope to found Trinity College, Oxford, in the chapel of which his alabaster effigy may still be seen. That Pope should have been chosen to carry the message was an act of kindness to More. More replied:

'Master Pope,' quoth he, 'for your good tidings I most heartily thank you. I have been always much bounden to the King's Highness for the benefits and honours that he hath still from time to time most bountifully heaped upon me; and yet more bound am I to his Grace for putting me into this place, where I have had convenient time and space to have remembrance of my end. And, so help me God, most of all, Master Pope, am I bound to his Highness that it pleaseth him so shortly to rid me out of the miseries of this wretched world. And therefore will I not fail earnestly to pray for his Grace, both here and also in another world.'

'The King's pleasure is further,' quoth Master Pope, 'that at your execution you shall not use many words.'

'Master Pope,' quoth he, 'you do well to give me warning of his Grace's pleasure, for otherwise I had purposed at that time somewhat to have spoken, but of no matter wherewith his Grace, or any other, should have had cause to be offended. Nevertheless, whatsoever I intended, I am ready obediently to conform myself to his Grace's commandments. And I beseech you, good Master Pope, to be a mean unto his Highness that my daughter Margaret may be at my burial.'

'The King is content already,' quoth Master Pope, 'that your wife, children, and other your friends shall have liberty to be present thereat.'

'O how much beholden then,' said Sir Thomas More, 'am I to his Grace, that unto my poor burial vouchsafeth to have so gracious consideration.'[1]

Pope burst into tears. More comforted him:

[1] ROPER, pp. 100-1.

'Quiet yourself, good Master Pope, and be not discomforted; for I trust that we shall, once in Heaven, see each other full merrily, where we shall be sure to live and love together, in joyful bliss eternally.'[1]

Roper no doubt had this from his friend Pope, just as he had further details from the Lieutenant. Bonvisi had sent More a silk camlet gown, and he began to change into it, partly to please his old friend, partly that the executioner should not lose his perquisite. Mr. Lieutenant protested – the executioner was but a 'Javill':

'What, Master Lieutenant,' quoth he, 'shall I account him a Javill that shall do me this day so singular a benefit? Nay, I assure you, were it cloth of gold, I would account it well bestowed on him, as St. Cyprian did, who gave his executioner thirty pieces of gold.' And albeit at length, through Master Lieutenant's importunate persuasion, he altered his apparel, yet after the example of that holy martyr St. Cyprian did he, of that little money that was left him, send one angel of gold to his executioner.[2]

No one in England dared to make public any account of More's execution, and it was not till the first year of the reign of Edward VI that the story was published, as told, very unsympathetically, by the chronicler Edward Hall. Hall gives many instances of what he calls the 'mocks'[3] with which More ended his life. They all ring true; it was characteristic of More to see the humorous side of martyrdom. Two of these sayings are also recorded by Roper: More's words to the Lieutenant (Hall says it was to one of the Sheriff's officers) going up the shaky stairs on to the scaffold, 'I pray you, Master Lieutenant, see me safe up, and for my coming down let me shift for myself'; and his encouragement to the executioner, 'Pluck up thy spirits, man, and be not afraid to do thine office; my neck is very short, take heed therefore thou strike not awry, for saving of thine honesty'. It is to be expected that Roper's account should be scanty; naturally he was not present. The only member of More's household who had the endurance to be there was the dogged and heroic Margaret Clement, waiting till afterwards she could be joined by Margaret Roper and

[1] ROPER, pp. 101-2.   [2] p. 102.   [3] See above, p. 19; below, p. 353.

Dorothy Colly, when the three were to bury More's body in the chapel of St. Peter ad Vincula in the Tower.

Margaret Clement saw More come forth from the Tower clad in a coarse garment of frieze, with long disordered beard, haggard from imprisonment, and carrying a red cross in his hand. Later she made, or caused to be made, from her memory, a representation of More going to execution, which she showed to Stapleton. As More passed on his way, a woman offered him a cup of wine. It may well have been Margaret Clement herself. The Thursday before she had, like Margaret Roper and John More, broken through the circle of halberds and bills to embrace her foster-father, and the guards may well have made way for her once again. She was a person of importance, and would be known to Tudor officials. But if it were she, she has chosen not to record her name. Instead there is recorded More's answer, as he put the cup aside, 'My master had easell and gall, not wine, given him to drink'.

Another woman reviled him:

'Do you remember, Master More, that when you were Chancellor you were my hard friend, and did me great injury in giving wrong judgment against me?' 'Woman,' (quoth he) 'I am now going to my death. I remember well the whole matter; if now I were to give sentence again, I assure thee, I would not alter it. Thou hast no injury, so content thee, and trouble me not.'

The Winchester man pushed his way through the crowd: 'Master More, do you know me? I pray you for our Lord's sake help me. I am as ill troubled as ever I was.' 'Go thy ways in peace, and pray for me, and I will not fail to pray for thee.'

So Margaret Clement watched More mount the scaffold, slowly and painfully, and saw him kneel down to repeat the Fifty-first Psalm: 'Have mercy upon me, O God, after thy great goodness; according to the multitude of thy mercies do away mine offences.' She saw him rise up briskly; as the executioner knelt and made the customary request for pardon, More embraced him. (He had already told his friends to do to the executioner what acts of kindness they could.) The executioner wished to bind More's eyes; but, saying, 'I will cover them myself,' he bound them with a linen cloth he had brought with him. The saying of More's, that a man might 'lose his head and have no harm' was evidently known, for, says Edward Hall the chronicler, striving to be ironical, 'his head was stricken from his shoulders, and had no more harm'.

More had made only a very brief speech from the scaffold, and this surprised the bystanders, and the foreigners who knew English customs. We know the reason, though they did not. Mr. Pope's warning to More not to use many words was, it would seem, repeated by the Sheriff on the scaffold. Perhaps it is better so; had the speech been longer we should have been dependent upon the selective memory of More's hearers. As it is, we have two or three sentences, in which More flashed out the justification of his life and death. Not even Father Bridgett has given them quite fully. Yet we ought to dwell upon them carefully. Henry had forbidden verbosity, believing (as the heathen do) that men are heard for their much speaking. It was a challenge, which More's quick wit would not be slow to accept, to see how much he could pack into a few dozen words.

Yet it is not More's nearest who have recorded those words. Only Margaret Clement was there, and she, we may believe, was looking on afar off, like the faithful women at another death. All that Roper knew was that More asked those present 'to pray for him, and to bear witness with him that he should now there suffer death, in and for the faith of the Holy Catholic Church'. The words are supremely important. But there were other words, and they were placed on record by the man who sent the news-letter to Paris, a man of whose minute and verbal accuracy we have abundant proof. In a few days the words were to ring through Europe.

He spoke little before his execution. Only he asked the bystanders to pray for him in this world, and he would pray for them elsewhere. He then begged them earnestly to pray for the King, that it might please God to give him good counsel, protesting that he died the King's good servant but God's first.

It was fifty years after More's execution that Stapleton, collecting his information from Margaret Clement and her fellow refugees, first put down on paper the words of comfort, in which More assured the Winchester man who had been sustained by his prayer, that there need be no fear lest such prayer were now about to cease. It may be that More saw the Winchester man still lingering, like another sorely tempted man, at another time, 'to see the end', and chose these words to give him a second assurance of his continued prayer 'elsewhere'. We cannot tell. But we, who would understand More, must note that the quite independent accounts of the Paris news-letter and of Stapleton show him occupied in the moments before his death with this thought of continued intercession on behalf of the friends he was leaving behind. And twenty years before, he had told how his Utopians trusted in their communion with their dead friends, 'though to the dull and feeble eyesight of mortal men they be invisible'.

More's other phrase brings us to the fundamental question with which he had also dealt in *Utopia*. Is the State supreme, or is there a moral law, above the laws which the State makes? The Utopians placed the rights of the State very high; the State might forbid propaganda and impose silence; nevertheless they recognized that there was a power above the State, the man 'in whom remaineth no further fear than of the laws' might not be a citizen of Utopia.

More's words are in striking contrast to the usual speech from the scaffold in Tudor times. The words of Thomas Cromwell are normal: 'I am by the Law condemned to die; I have offended my Prince, for the which I ask him heartily forgiveness'; the victim admits the supremacy of the State which is demanding his head. More's words are the most weighty and the most haughty ever spoken on the scaffold. Dante could not have bettered them. 'The King's good servant, but God's first.'

MORE'S PLACE IN HISTORY

§ I. MORE'S FAME IN ENGLAND THROUGH
FOUR CENTURIES

THE parallel between Thomas More and Socrates, so often suggested, is true also in this: that both are figures of world-history, and cannot be judged merely from the point of view of the history of their particular countries, great and glorious as the histories of Athens and of England are. In the case of Socrates this is recognized, but we are still too near to see the full greatness of More.

More is a hero of whom the whole of England is proud. Strangely enough, this has not been altogether to the advantage of his reputation. We are all of us prone to make our heroes in our own image, and Liberal Protestant England has had such a genuine admiration for Sir Thomas More that a good deal has been read into *Utopia* which is not really to be found there. A picture of More has thus been formed which had somehow to be harmonized with his martyrdom; and so arose the conception of Sir Thomas More which is still dominant in non-Catholic circles, and is, I think, to be found explicit or implicit in English history, whether written by avowed Protestants or by that numerous and influential class which has abandoned everything of Protestantism except its prejudices. So we have More depicted as a Renaissance scholar of that liberal type imagined by Mr. Seebohm; but we are to believe that later, as More's arteries hardened, so did his views. It is a common phenomenon: everyone who still remembers the discussions of his College Debating Society or University Union can name leaders of revolt at the age of twenty who have settled down into middle-aged defenders of society. It is with many of us as it was with Mr. Pepys, when he met his old schoolfriend, Mr.

Christmas, after the happy restoration of Charles II. 'He did remember that I was a great Roundhead when I was a boy, and I was much afraid that he would have remembered the words that I said the day the King was beheaded (that, were I to preach upon him, my text should be "The memory of the wicked shall rot").' So More is excused as an example of the common lapse.

The view of More which regards his life as 'a bundle of antitheses' remains dominant. It would be an interesting and useful study to trace More's fame at length throughout English history; there is room here only for a few headings.

The first writer to emphasize the antitheses and changes of More was William Tyndale, a heroic soul who was puzzled to find that More could share so much of what he himself felt, without sharing his impatience. Tyndale heard of the collections made in England to reward More for his labours in defending orthodoxy; he did not know that More was to refuse the gift. His explanation of what seemed to him to be More's change was that 'Covetousness blinded the eyes of that gleering fox, with the confidence of his painted poetry, as true and authentic as his story of Utopia'. John Foxe inherited this idea of More. *Utopia* is 'poetry', and More a fantastic writer of fiction whom the godly cannot take quite seriously. The idea that *Utopia* is a 'liberal' and 'progressive' work, and that its author ought therefore to have been on the 'liberal' and 'progressive' (i.e. Protestant) side, would have surprised Tyndale or Foxe. It was not because More was the author of *Utopia*, but because he was the friend of Erasmus, that Tyndale thought he had changed.

The majority of King Henry's political supporters naturally did not feel towards More exactly as did that single-minded Reformer, William Tyndale. But these rising men thoroughly approved of a King who was, so far as England was concerned, King, Pope, and Emperor in one. Many of them were London lawyers or merchants, and the confiscation of the monasteries gave them the opportunity they had long desired of acquiring land, and founding families. They loved the brilliant pageantry of the Court, and the foundation of their fortunes rested on Henry's assumption of power as Supreme Head of the Church,

and on what they called his 'Triumphant Reign'. Their spokes-
man is the chronicler Edward Hall, whose book has been so
often quoted above. Hall voices the feelings of a body of
politiques which, although small, was destined to have enormous
weight in the moulding of future opinion. It is remarkable
how Hall has placed the stamp of his convictions upon
following historians of the reign of Henry, by means of what
Mr. H. A. L. Fisher has justly called his 'gorgeous chronicle'.[1]
Like his fellows, Hall has no patience with More's conscientious
scruples. 'I cannot tell whether I should call him a foolish
wise man, or a wise foolish man', is Hall's verdict.

The view which has been held by the historians of the
Eighteenth and Nineteenth Centuries was formulated by Burnet
in his *History of the Reformation*. Burnet, an admirer of *Utopia*,
held that, when he wrote *Utopia*, More had 'emancipated himself, and had got into a scheme of free thoughts'; later he was
'entirely changed', and became the tool of 'the blind and
enraged fury of the priests'. It was probably under the influence
of Burnet that Horace Walpole wrote of More as of one who
'persecuted others in defence of superstitions that he himself
had exposed'.

Yet, all this time, tradition had depicted More as 'that
worthy and uncorrupt magistrate', 'the best friend that the
poor e'er had'. By the early Nineteenth Century, sectarian
bitterness had to a great extent died down; the 'No Popery'
cry was losing its appeal. The Evangelical and Protestant
outlook was so victorious that it could afford to be generous.
And the Bar has always cherished the memory of More.
Consequently the second quarter of the Nineteenth Century saw
three excellent and tolerant little biographies by three lawyers,
Mackintosh, Lord Campbell, and Foss. All three are infuriated
at the injustice of More's trial: Henry is the villain. 'We may
be amused,' says Campbell, 'by a defence of Richard III, but
we can feel only indignation and disgust at an apology for
Henry VIII.'

Yet the apology was not slow in coming. The Oxford Movement and the Catholic Revival reopened the ancient quarrel,
and Froude, in his defence of Henry, attacked More as the

[1] *History*, 1485-1547, p. 210. For HALL see above, pp. 66, 244.

'genial philosopher' transformed into the 'merciless bigot',[1] who 'destroyed the unhappy Protestants' and 'fed the stake with heretics'. And yet, with all his bitter partisan misrepresentation, there is in Froude sympathy and respect for heroism, wherever it is found. When we come to the end of the story of the martyrdom of the Carthusians and of More, as Froude tells it, I am not sure that we are not left with a feeling of admiration and awe, even deeper than that left by a perusal of Father Bridgett's noble delineation of More and Fisher as faultless Catholic martyrs.

Certainly the picture of More drawn by the Protestant Froude leaves a nobler impression than that drawn by the Catholic Acton. According to Acton, More, the apostle of Toleration, had allowed his sentiments to be moulded by the official theology of the Court. It was 'under that sinister influence' that he defended persecution. He had, says Acton, 'defended divorce' in *Utopia*,[2] and Henry 'supposed that a man whose dogmatic opinions he had been able to modify, would not resist pressure on a subject on which he had already shown a favourable bias. More was steadfast in upholding the marriage, *but never permitted his views to be known*'. 'He put off the hour of trial that was to prove the heroic temper of his soul.' (Yet we have More's own word for it that as a private counsellor and minister of the King he spoke to him boldly, and that these matters were as dear to him as his own life.) This very liberty of private advice to the King depended, as More pointed out to the Emperor's ambassador, upon his abstaining from contact with external critics. Acton demands that More should have been simultaneously Chief Minister and Leader of the Opposition.

But the judgment of Creighton[3] is even harsher than that of Acton. Froude's Sir Thomas persecutes from mistaken zeal; Acton's Sir Thomas abandons his previous liberal opinions under the sinister influence of Henry; but Creighton's Sir Thomas because it was convenient for the moment to do so, whilst his real belief forbade persecution. Creighton quotes, or

---

[1] *History of England from the Fall of Wolsey to the defeat of the Spanish Armada*, 1856, etc. See especially I, pp. 344-5; II, pp. 73-4, 227.
[2] See above, p. 226.   [3] *Persecution and Tolerance*, pp. 107-8.

rather grievously misquotes, the passage from *Utopia* about
religious toleration, and then denounces More as 'the official
engaged in justifying what was convenient for the moment',
'putting his principles aside', 'till the King was ready to apply
to him the same measure of justice as himself had applied to
others'. Creighton concludes: 'It was neither mistaken zeal nor
intellectual error that fostered persecution, it was merely
expediency and the thirst for power.' Some years before,
Creighton had been severely reprimanded by Acton, both
publicly and privately, for the leniency of his historical judgments. The Bishop seems to have selected More as a whipping-
boy, upon whose vile body he might demonstrate that he could
be more magisterially severe than Acton himself.

From year to year the traditional verdict is repeated. Our
historian of the Reformation, Principal Lindsay, can only see
in More one who 'turned his back on the ennobling enthusiasms
of his youth'. The tireless organizer of English biography, Sir
Sidney Lee, tells us that 'miscalculation and inconsistency were
the moving causes of the vicissitudes of Thomas More's career'.
And even those who do not join in the stern censures of Froude
or Acton or Creighton or Lindsay or Sidney Lee admit themselves puzzled. The first translator of *Utopia*, sixteen years after
More's death, lamented that a man of so absolute learning was
yet nevertheless so blinded that he could not, or rather would
not, see the shining light of God's holy truth. Protestant has
passed into Whig, and Whig into Liberal, and the same lament
has been made, generation after generation: 'So wise, and yet
he could not, or rather would not, see things as I do.' The
foolish-wise man! The Progressive-Reactionary! And so, only
last year, what claims to be the twenty-fifth biography of
More sets out by expressing the old contrast in new language: 'His life is – if one may coin a phrase – a bundle of
antitheses.'

The puzzled feeling of contrast, expressed by Dame Elizabeth Wordsworth in these words in 1934, had been expressed by
Dame Alice More, in her vigorous Tudor English, in 1534:
'What the good year, Master More, I marvel that you, that
have been always hitherto taken for so wise a man, will now so
play the fool – ' And there is no denying it – apart from James

Gairdner and the small Catholic minority, most Englishmen have held with Dame Alice, and not with Sir Thomas. And it would be ungrateful to deny how much the world owes to its Dame Alices. Anyway, Dame Alice is English through and through. A mother was recently telling her son, 'You have not the honour of being descended from Sir Thomas More; but from Dame Alice, his second wife, through the Alingtons, you *are* descended'. 'Glad of that,' said the boy. 'She was the only one of the crowd that had any sense.'

Our great modern English historians do not put it exactly in that way, but there is no doubt of their verdict.

One reason for the difficulty in understanding More has been that the evidence was not forthcoming. But now that his English works are being published (mostly for the first time since 1557) and the early lives printed or translated, the time has come to ask – was More the Progressive-Reactionary, the 'bundle of antitheses', which most Englishmen and English-women have held him to be?

§ 2.   PROGRESS AND REACTION

'Progress' has seemed so straightforward during the four centuries, now drawing so near their close, which have passed since More's death. It is admitted that there have been regrettable incidents in this advance; it is admitted that there are many features in the life and policy of Thomas Cromwell 'which deserve execration'; nevertheless, we are told, by his sympathies and his interests alike, Cromwell was 'propelled along the path of progress'.[1]

What were abbeys for, in the Sixteenth Century, save to provide endowments for the servants of Henry Tudor, and stones for their country mansions; till those mansions were transformed in due time into the seats of Eighteenth Century noblemen, with some monastic remnant serving to make their landscape gardens picturesque? So in due time a Duke of Bedford, 'a young man with very old pensions',[2] could rejoice at Woburn Abbey over the victories of Jacobinism, under the shade of the oak from which the last abbot had been hanged; and, later, a Lord Byron

[1] FISHER, *History of England, 1485-1547*, p. 446.
[2] BURKE, *Letter to a Noble Lord* (*Works*, 1801, VII, p. 406).

could inherit Newstead Abbey, become 'the poet of the Revolution', and initiate that illustrious sequence of Liberal men of letters which forms one of the chief glories of our Nineteenth Century. In this case also, friends of progress admit regrettable incidents. John Morley deplores the 'dissolution of domestic feeling' in Byron, which dissolution he nevertheless demonstrates to be 'not entirely without justification', because, if Byron had been less dissolute and more domestic, he would have been less unlike George III.[1] Comforted by this, we pursue the path of progress till, for his *Essay on Byron* and other services to that path, John Morley in due time becomes Viscount Morley of Blackburn, and a member of the House of Peers, which in due time is deprived of its veto by Mr. Asquith, who in due time becomes Earl of Oxford and Asquith, till in due time the Upper House welcomes Socialist recruits, and –

Against this pleasant, cultured, literary background, of country mansions, statesmen peers and scholar statesmen, how are we to place the figure of a Chancellor, also a scholar, but kept awake by the pricking of his hair-shirt, whilst he spent most of his nights in writing long treatises intended to obstruct the path of progress? The Chancellor even argues, among other absurdities, that abbeys ought to remain abbeys; hoping for his own part that he may have some months for quiet meditation before his death, and not caring overmuch whether this meditation be in the cell of a monastery or of a prison. Can we wonder that such a figure appears respectable indeed, but grotesquely out of date? Even at the time, More's merry little daughter-in-law, Anne Cresacre, giggled at the hair-shirt, and Dame Alice went to More's father confessor to tell him to tell More to stop such nonsense. Yet More took his hair-shirt with him to the Tower, and was '*content* to be shut up among mice and rats'. What can More's critics, from poor Dame Alice down to the present day, make of a man who would 'sit still by the fire and make goslings in the ashes as children do', when he might, if he had wished, have gone forward with the first along the path of progress, have had first dip into the lucky bag of monastic plunder, and have left a family of which the younger branch might have become leaders of liberal thought, and the

[1] MORLEY, *Byron*, 1887, reprinted in *Critical Miscellanies*, 1923, p. 164.

elder branch ground-landlords of half SouthKensington and
Mayfair and perhaps even Dukes of Chelsea?

Progress has seemed so obvious and so inevitable, as the
historian at each stage has looked back upon the past from the
vantage ground of the immediate present.

And now our momentary present, which we somewhat
arrogantly treat as a fixed point of outlook, whence we can
discern what has been and what has not been the 'path of progress', is itself shifting under our feet with startling speed. It
was on 15 May 1532, that the clergy made their submission to
Henry. Next day More resigned. In eight years there was not
a House of Religion left in England, and by the first half of the
Nineteenth Century another sage of Chelsea had arisen, to whom
a monk was 'an extinct species of the human family'. 'The
Gospel of Richard Arkwright once promulgated,' says Carlyle,
'no Monk of the old sort is any longer possible in this world.'[1]
Yet to-day, if there are not as many monks in England as when
Henry dissolved the monasteries, there are many more women
leading the community life. And Thomas More's hair-shirt has
its place of honour, and is a principal treasure of the House
where the canonesses of Newton Abbot lead their life of ab-
stinence, prayer and adoration. And on the other side of the
Dart the Monastery Church of Buckfast, of which not one stone
was left above ground, has slowly risen on its old foundations.
Four hundred years after More's resignation, in the summer of
1932, it was again consecrated. A monk said to me: 'Henry
VIII destroyed five hundred and twenty-seven monasteries
and nunneries, and you may see their ruins up and down the
land. They are dead, but this is alive.' And now it is the
stately homes of England, which have stood so beautifully for
four hundred years, which are being threatened by the Thomas
Cromwells of to-day. The path of progress would seem to be
constant at least in this, that it entails the senseless destruction
of beautiful (and often useful) things, leaving our England
happier perhaps (for some people are never happy unless they
are destroying) but, as Ruskin said, not handsomer.

But, for the rest, Progress is beginning to look like the
amphisbænic snake with its two heads pointing in directions

[1] *Past and Present*, Book II, Chap. 1.

diametrically opposite, as celebrated in an anonymous poem attributed to Alfred Housman,

> Until it starts, you never know
> In which direction it will go.

Or, as a Russian philosopher and social reformer puts it:

> We still go on with our endless tedious discussions about progress and reaction, just as though everything in the world had not been turned upside down, and as though our old criteria had not lost every shred of significance. Just try to judge world-history with reference to reaction or revolution, try to place your 'right' or your 'left'. The absurdity of this sort of thing will strike you immediately, and the pathetic procession of your conceptual categories takes on an air of sheer provincialism.[1]

'Provincialism' is a harsh word. But is it not the right word here, and has not More been judged against too narrow a background, both of time and place? Both as a medieval Catholic, looking towards Rome, and as a Renaissance scholar, the friend of Erasmus, More had a patriotism which was European as well as English. His critics have scarcely weighed the drift of More's great defence when he appealed, from the narrow issues of the present, to the great event from which the history of England, as a portion of modern world-civilization, has its origin – the mission sent by Gregory the Great from Rome to Canterbury; one of the noblest victories ever won for the unity of culture.

§3. SOME COMPARISONS WITH OTHER ENGLISH WRITERS

More, then, connects Medieval England with Modern England, and he connects England with Europe. Think of him first in connection with the continuity of the English speech, English prose, English literature. To the student of the English language he is a vital link between Middle and Modern English. To the student of English prose his work is the great link which connects modern prose with the medieval prose of Nicholas Love, Walter Hilton, and Richard Rolle, and so with the older English prose of the earlier Middle Ages. To the student of

[1] N. Berdyaev, *The End of Our Time: The New Middle Ages*, 1933, p. 77.

English thought More is equally vital: he points forward to our own times; but he also points back to William Langland, and More and his writings help us to see a continuity running through English literature and history. The late Sir Walter Raleigh said, 'Nothing is more striking than the way English people do not alter'. However that may be, Langland and More deal with somewhat similar problems in a way which does not much alter.

The modern statesman is struck with the modernity of Langland. 'In Piers Plowman is to be found the Englishman of to-day, with the same strength and weakness, the same humour, immutable.'[1] Yet Langland is a Catholic poet of the Middle Ages. So with More. We think of More, and rightly, as our first great modern; as the first great English vernacular historian; or as the first and greatest of an illustrious line of writers of *Utopias*; or as the greatest member of our first group of modern scholars, a man skilled in calling bad names in good Latin; and Dr. Reed has shown us how we have to look to him and his circle for the beginnings of Modern English drama. But More was also the last great man who lived the whole of his life with the England of the Middle Ages yet undestroyed around him; a land of great libraries which had been accumulating since Anglo-Saxon times; of ancient religious houses where the walls were covered with paintings, and the windows shone with the glorious English glass of the Fourteenth and Fifteenth Centuries; a land of schools and hospitals more plentiful than they were to be again for many a day. More is a product of those late Middle Ages of which Dante is the supreme figure; he is the consistent opponent of the new ideas which found literary expression in *The Prince*, and were embodied in the person of Thomas Cromwell.

I have been trying to show how the description of the Utopian state, with its communism, its sacerdotalism, its love of beauty and of symbolic ritual, remains in touch with the Middle Ages. The charges of inconsistency against More arise from our forgetting all this; from our forgetting that his life falls in this last age of English medieval Catholicism, and from our reading back, into his earlier writings, the experience, and

[1] Mr. Stanley Baldwin, July 19, 1929.

even the propaganda, of later generations. Burnet or Froude[1] feel that *When More wrote the 'Utopia', he was in advance of his time. None could see the rogue's face under the cowl clearer than he.* It is just because More *is* medieval that he can 'see the rogue's face under the cowl' without thereby attacking monasticism as an institution. Froude could not; so he calls More a bigot. We might as well think that Fra Angelico was anti-clerical, because, among the group which he depicted as being carried off to Hell from the Last Judgment, we can see the tonsured head, the cardinal's hat, and the bishop's mitre.

In a very similar way the English Reformers misunderstood William Langland. The modern Catholic historian sees in Langland 'the Catholic Englishman *par excellence*, at once the most English of Catholic poets and the most Catholic of English poets',[2] and no one to-day would dispute this judgment. But to John Bale it was clear that William Langland was one of the first disciples of John Wiclif, and that he wrote *Piers Plowman* to reprove the blasphemies of the Papists against God and his Christ. *Piers Plowman* was printed by a Reformer, as good Protestant propaganda.

A little more than a century after More wrote *Utopia*, Francis Bacon wrote his imitation, the *New Atlantis*. A comparison of *Utopia* with the *New Atlantis* may put More's book into its right perspective. It is an odd coincidence, and a helpful one, that our two greatest Lord Chancellors should each have depicted an imaginary commonwealth.

The simplicity of *Utopia*, with its citizens clothed in their Franciscan garb, belongs to an age when voluntary poverty was still an ideal, and an ideal sometimes practised. We have seen that it was an ideal which More always had before him; we have noticed the spirit of St. Francis in his satisfaction when he finds himself a quite penniless prisoner, dependent for his food upon the charity of that great lady, Mistress Alice: 'Me thinketh God maketh me a wanton, and setteth me on his lap, and dandleth me.' Therefore it is natural that the Prince and the Bishop in Utopia are dressed with the same simplicity as their subjects, distinguished only by a little sheaf, or taper of wax,

---

[1] *History*, 1856, II, p. 344.
[2] CHRISTOPHER DAWSON in *The English Way*, ed. by M. WARD, 1933, p. 160.

carried before them. Bacon, on the other hand, combined a
rather childish love of pomp with that very real zeal for the
welfare of his fellow-men which was the motive power of his
life. When he was married to his 'young wench', a contemporary gossip[1] tells us, 'he was clad from top to toe in purple,
and made himself and his wife such store of raiments of cloth
of silver and gold that it drew deep into her portion'. It is
characteristic of Bacon that when he discusses 'philanthropy' he
feels it necessary to utter a warning against unwise self-denial.
And so in the *New Atlantis*, a Professor from the College wears
gloves set with precious stones, and shoes of peach-coloured
velvet; and (what would have shocked More yet further) our
Professor has fifty attendants, 'young men all, in white satin
loose coats up to the mid-leg, and stockings of white silk, and
shoes of blue velvet, and hats of blue velvet, with fine plumes of
divers colours set round like hatbands'.

The austerity of the attire of the citizens of Utopia is set off
by the ritualistic pomp of the priests' vestments during worship.
But we hear nothing of any such Church ritual in the *New
Atlantis*.

On the other hand, whilst More does not make his Utopians
Christian, and does not give them any sacred book, Bacon
invents an outrageous piece of 'miraculous evangelism', in
order to ensure that the *New Atlantis* shall have the canonical
books of the Old and New Testament, wrapped in sindons of
linen, floated over the ocean in a small ark of cedar wood. It
is not that More neglected his Bible; his devotional works con-
tain long passages of translation from the Gospels which should
have given him high rank among English Bible-translators.
And his interest in Erasmus' *New Testament* is shown, among
other things, by his epigrams. Nevertheless, the library which
Hythlodaye took with him to Utopia consisted of Greek works
of literature and science. Hythlodaye and his companions instructed the Utopians in Greek; and also in the mysteries of the
Christian religion; but we hear nothing of any evangelical
literature, as yet, in Utopia. Whilst More was writing *Utopia*,
the Greek *New Testament* of Erasmus had appeared; here was a
chance for More to have brought 'his darling' into his book,

[1] Carleton to Chamberlain. Cf. CHURCH, *Bacon*, p. 78.

as he has brought his other friends. Yet he does not take the opening. The immediate problem of the Utopian converts, as it appears to More, is not how the text of the Gospels can be got out to them, but how a priest is to be appointed to minister the sacraments.[1] Bacon does not bother his head about the apostolic succession among his New Atlanteans. They have got the Word of God.

Surely this difference alone should have been sufficient to show how far More was, at the time of writing *Utopia*, from the Protestantism which has so light-heartedly claimed *Utopia* for its own.

In secular affairs the contrast of Bacon and More is equally marked: Bacon trusts, for the relief of man's estate, to the growth of science; More looks to a more equal distribution of wealth.

Now in England 'Progress' for many centuries moved, not in accordance with the Catholic, medieval, collectivist hopes of More, but along the path indicated by Bacon, the Protestant man of science. And that path *has* led to the 'relief of man's estate', in material things at any rate. Nevertheless, all that had been hoped had not been accomplished, and so the Nineteenth Century saw a revolt, of which the Oxford Movement and *News from Nowhere* were different manifestations. Now it was just because of this return to medievalism that *Utopia* made a strong appeal to the Nineteenth Century, and still makes its appeal. The solemn churches of Utopia move us, while the evangelical miracle of the *New Atlantis* only excites our scepticism. The voluntary poverty of Utopia meets what we feel to be our need. But the wealth lavished upon the Research Professor by the naïve inhabitants of the New Atlantis is bound to cause searchings of heart in the breast of any moderately modest professor; and I speak from thirty years' experience when I say that it always rouses laughter when read to his class. We look back on the *New Atlantis* as a great landmark we have left behind: *Utopia* is still before us.

And so we call *Utopia* 'progressive'. And then we wonder that More resisted 'the progressive movement of his time', forgetting that the charm of *Utopia* lies exactly in the fact that

---

[1] *Utopia*, ed. LUPTON, p. 269.

it championed the things, all trace of which 'the progressive movement of his time', in its haste for change and wealth, was sweeping away. Is it not because we are ourselves too inconsistent to appreciate his consistency, that we blame Sir Thomas More? Like those persons wearing green spectacles of whom Hooker speaks, we think that which we see is green, when indeed that is green whereby we see.

Thomas More ranks with William Langland before him, and Edmund Burke after him, among the greatest of our Reforming Conservatives. Langland, More and Burke are alike in their hatred of oppression and corruption – a hatred which in each case is too fierce to be always just. Yet each, when he finds this hatred leading to revolution, shows marked want of sympathy with the revolutionaries. 'It is no inconsiderable part of wisdom,' said Burke, 'to know how much of an evil ought to be tolerated.'[1] And Burke said this, it is to be noted, not in his Conservative old age, but in the book in which he began his career as a Whig statesman. Burke's sentence might be taken as a motto for much of More's controversial writing against the Reformers; More's constant plea is that the misuse of a good thing does not justify us in abolishing the thing itself.[2]

Langland, More, and Burke place almost first among the order of things which has come down to them, and which they feel it their duty to preserve, such a measure of unity, small or great, as the Christendom of their age has been able to inherit.

The First Book of *Utopia* points back to the medieval ideal of a common Christendom; it is this ideal which makes More hate war among Christian princes, just as it made Langland speak of Edward's French wars as contrary to conscience. This ideal of a united Christendom made Chaucer, who had himself fought in those French wars, pass over as unworthy of record the achievements of his perfect gentle knight in France, whilst he enumerated at length that knight's rather desultory crusades. It is this longing for Unity, Holy Church, and passion against the schism which is destroying it, that inspire the great closing section of *Piers Plowman*:

---

[1] *Thoughts on the Present Discontents: Works*, 1801, II, p. 322.
[2] *Works*, 1557, p. 198, and *passim*.

Quoth Conscience to all Christians then, my counsel is, we wend
Hastily into Unity, and hold we us there
And pray we that a Peace were . . .

It is for 'the common corps of Christendom' that More is
always pleading; and for it he died. It might seem that by the
death of More and his fellow martyrs, the 'common corps' had
been shattered beyond possibility of recovery. Yet by the
Eighteenth Century the bitterness of the Wars of Religion had
died down. As in the early Sixteenth Century, men might hope
for an age of Peace and Reason. Abroad, after the Peace of
Utrecht, people were talking, as they had talked in the days of
Erasmus two hundred years before, of a League of Peace among
Christian Princes. The Eighteenth Century was in a better
position to understand More than the later Sixteenth or the
Seventeenth, and Addison gloried in More's heroism and in his
virtues. From some aspects Swift seems to be More come to
life again; in *Gulliver* he gives to *Utopia* the honour, rare with
him, of direct and repeated imitation, and he repays his debt
by depicting Thomas More as the one modern man worthy to
rank with the five noblest men of antiquity. Swift has been
described as the soul of Rabelais in a dry place; we might think
of him as the mind of Sir Thomas More without More's patience
or More's faith, wandering through desert places seeking rest,
and finding none. But in nothing is the likeness more strong
than in the passion shown by Swift against the futile wars of
Christian nations which, when narrated, arouse the disgust
alike of the virtuous Houyhnhnms and of the magnanimous
giants of Brobdingnag. Few things are more remarkable than
the salute passed from Jonathan Swift to Thomas More across
the two intervening centuries of futile religious strife; it is a
sign that, with the cessation of the Wars of Religion, the standpoint of a common European civilization is again becoming
intelligible. At the end of the Eighteenth Century, it is possible
for Burke to conceive Western Europe as a unit, before the
upheaval of the French Revolution. We cannot but be reminded of More when reading the great passage near the end
of the *First Letter on a Regicide Peace*, where Burke eulogizes
Europe as 'virtually one great state'.[1] Langland's lament over

[1] BURKE, *Works*, 1801, VIII, pp. 108-9.

the Papal schism, More's difference with Henry VIII, Swift's hatred of the Whig war-party, Burke's quarrel with the Jacobins, are all at bottom one: the complaint of the man who longs for unity and peace in Europe against those whom, justly or unjustly, he regards as, in Burke's words, 'making a schism' in the European system.

There is another sentence of Burke which may be a help towards the understanding of Sir Thomas More. When well over sixty,[1] Burke recalled how 'pretty early in his service' he had told the House that 'he had taken his ideas of liberty very low; in order that they should stick to him, and that he might stick to them, to the end of his life'. More had taken his ideas of liberty very low; so low that, one might think, there should have been little difficulty in sticking to them. Yet he stuck to them only at the cost of his life.

More, if we can trust his biographer, spoke freely in Parliament during the reign of Henry VII; his plea for freedom of speech in the parliament of Henry VIII is classic; but, as a Tudor statesman, he necessarily placed the rights of authority very high indeed; if he died for liberty, it was only for that last stronghold of liberty – the right of the free man not to be compelled to say that which he does not believe.

Of course, first and foremost, More gave his life, not for liberty at all, but for Unity, 'in and for the Faith of the Holy Catholic Church'. So he said on the scaffold; at his trial he was able to speak more at length, and it was *then* that he put forward the plea of liberty of conscience. It seems to be agreed that thereby he was claiming for himself a liberty which he denied to others: most of our great historians who have dealt with his trial say so.

Now, as we have seen, More in the *Utopia* depicted the State as laying down what doctrines might be publicly preached and how they might be preached. To disobey is to be guilty of tumult and sedition, and to incur the severest punishment. More held that the heretics *were* so guilty, and deserved severe punishment. More's consistency was put to the extreme test when he found himself faced with the same problem which the heretics had had to face; when the State decided against

[1] *Appeal from the New to the Old Whigs: Works,* 1801, vi, p. 118.

the view which he held to be true. More allowed himself to be silenced. He maintained this silence both to his fellow-sufferers[1] and to his enemies.[2] His enemies were puzzled. They could not see why a man who submitted so far should not submit farther. More's strictly Utopian attitude comes out at his trial. He is entitled to plead conscience, he asserts, *just because* he has given no occasion of tumult or sedition.[3]

Not long before his own imprisonment, More had enumerated the cases of the only heretics (seven in all) who, so far as he knew, had suffered death in England in recent times – actually within the preceding eighteen years. He had maintained that, under the law, they had had no wrong.[4] Now, thanks chiefly to Foxe, it is easy to control More's judgment in all seven cases. All these martyrs seem to have been devoted and heroic men, and some of them were assuredly saintly men. But they had all used that 'contentious rebuking and inveighing' which More, when he wrote *Utopia*, thought a penal offence. Further, they had all either recanted, and then deliberately broken their oath, or else they had 'given occasion of tumult and sedition'; most of them had done both these things. His adversaries tried to force More to 'give occasion of tumult and sedition'; by saying that he was afraid of death, they tried to taunt him into uttering treason. If More had publicly and violently denounced the Act declaring the King Supreme Head, after it had been made high treason to do so; if he had then been forgiven, upon making his submission to the King, and swearing to oppose him no more; if he had then quite deliberately broken his oath; it might have been said of him, as he says of the heretics, that he had brought his death upon himself.

I am not saying that these Protestant martyrs were the less heroic because of their momentary weakness. It increases our sympathy, and should not diminish our respect. But More had

---

[1] CRESACRE MORE, 1726, p. 241.   [2] *Works*, 1557, p. 1454, C.E.

[3] See above, p. 337. Harpsfield is here following the contemporary account of More's trial and death in the News-Letter sent to Paris. The French original brings out the point even more clearly than Harpsfield's version: *pourveu que telle conscience, comme est la mienne, n'engendre scandale ou sédition à son Seigneur: vous asseurant que ma conscience ne s'est descouverte à personne vivante.* There is no doubt as to the authenticity of this: the same statement occurs a dozen times in More's letters.

[4] *Works*, p. 890. There were at least five other cases, of which More was ignorant.

a strictly legal mind, and could not tolerate such weakness, either in himself or others. In Burke's words, he took his idea of liberty low, and stuck to it. It is just because More kept his claim for freedom of conscience within the narrow limits which he had himself defined twenty years before, in *Utopia*, that we can regard him as a consistent martyr for his ideal of freedom. A low ideal, you may say. Anyway, it was too high for More to hold it and live, in the days of Henry VIII.

§4. AGES OF TRANSITION

More, then, has affinities with many English writers, medieval and modern; but his closest links are with the men of the Middle Ages, and with those moderns who have striven to preserve something of the Legacy of the Middle Ages – first and foremost, the conception of the unity of Civilization.

Fundamental to an understanding of More are two sentences of our great historians:

> Such is the unity of all history, that anyone who endeavours to tell a piece of it must feel that his first sentence tears a seamless web.[1]

> Of all the schisms which rend the woven garment of historical understanding, the worst is that which fixes a deep gulf between medieval and modern history.[2]

Not only have we made a deep gulf where none should be, but further, in so far as we *must* make a gulf, we have put Thomas More on the wrong side of the gulf. The year 1485 has hypnotized us. We have, as Professor Pollard says, imagined the Middle Ages as rolling away when the crown rolled off the head of Richard III on Bosworth field. Yet, in fact, the reign of Henry VII and the early years of the reign of Henry VIII belong more to the Middle Ages than to modern times.

More would perhaps have been differently judged if our text-books, instead of beginning the modern period of English history with 1485, had begun it with the Reformation Parliament of 1529-36. With these years a new world begins; and the whole previous period, from the introduction of printing into England, is rather a prelude to modern times than a part of them.

[1] POLLOCK and MAITLAND, *History of English Law*, i, p. 1.
[2] POLLARD, *Wolsey*, 1929, p. 8.

For it is obvious that the age of Thomas More grows, by a natural series of evolutions, from the Middle Ages, without, as yet, any violent break. It is separated from the following Elizabethan period by a succession of violent and fundamental revolutions. The epoch of More is not the beginning of the modern period of English history as we know it. It is the beginning of a modern period of English history as it might have been, if the Reformation could have been the Reformation of Erasmus, instead of the Reformation of Luther; Reformation by evolution and reason, instead of Reformation by revolution and violence. It is the gigantic figure of Luther, not the comparatively commonplace figure of the victorious Henry VII at Bosworth field, that begins a new age, after which nothing can be the same. To link pre-Lutheran and post-Lutheran together under the convenient name 'Tudor Period' is misleading.

So, if such men as Froude and Jowett, Lindsay and Creighton, Acton and Sidney Lee, scholars and historians of every possible point of view, Roman Catholic, Presbyterian, Anglican, agnostic, have agreed in their inability to see a consistent purpose running through all More's life, I suggest that the main reason for this is that they judged More as belonging to the Post-Reformation age in which they themselves lived. Finding that they agreed with More in many things, they assumed that there ought to have been complete agreement in all things, and they accused More of inconsistency if he acted in a way inconsistent with the way in which they themselves would have wished to have acted in his place. Bishop Creighton,[1] indeed, seems to admit this, in a remarkable letter in which he tries to defend his thesis that More was a 'pseudo-liberal'. The foundation of his criticism of More lies in the conviction that More, belonging to the Tudor period, therefore belongs to the first stage of our modern era, as a figure of which he must be judged.

And now it is we ourselves who are passing into an age which will look back upon the age of Froude and Acton and Creighton as something strangely remote. Future historians will need a word to characterize the period which begins with the generation of Luther, and ends with the generation now

[1] *Life and Letters*, 1904, II, pp. 184 etc. (Letters to Mr. W. S. Lilly).

growing old. This modern era, which under our eyes is ceasing
to be modern and is passing into history, has been marked by
many distinct characteristics. It has seen the development of
nationalism; of optimistic confidence in its growing intellectual,
political, industrial and scientific progress. It has been an age
of unbridled capitalism; an age when government, in England
at any rate, has been in the hands of country gentlemen,
lawyers, and men of business; an age when learning has been
dominated by Hellenic scholarship. It has been an age when,
as Dr. Johnson said, every man got as much Greek as he could.
It has been an age when every statesman got as much land
round his country seat as he could. And to this modern age of
aristocratic learning, based on the classics, Thomas More, the
Greek scholar, the lawyer-statesman, buying land and building
a house among the meadows of Chelsea, also belongs. But he
does not belong entirely to it. How many of More's successors
among the scholars, lawyers, and squires of England could have
confessed, as he did, that but for wife and children they would
long ago have left their Great Houses for monastic cells? How
many would have comprehended that an eminent lawyer, a
scholar of European fame, a prosperous squire, *could* have said
such a thing?

In many ways More stands nearer to St. Francis or St.
Bruno than he does to the later Tudors of Elizabeth's reign.

Thomas More belongs, then, not to the modern period, but
to the last transitional era of the Middle Ages. Of course all
ages are ages of transition – but that does not alter the fact that
there are certain periods when changes huddle closely one upon
another; when the gradient becomes so steep as to be almost a
precipice. More was born within a few months of the issue in
this country of the first printed book; yet he lived to use the
printing press in Latin and English controversy in a way which
cannot be paralleled among the great writers of England till,
more than a century later, we come to Milton. As a boy of
five More heard foretold the last deposition in those dynastic
struggles with which our Middle Ages close; yet he lived to
pray for the princess who was to be Queen Elizabeth. More was
a youth of nearly fifteen when the New World was discovered;
yet he lived to discuss in *Utopia* the ethics of colonization with

such foresight that his words have been regarded by a German historian as a Machiavellian device intended at once to predict and to justify the yet unborn British Empire.[1] More was forty when Luther appeared; yet before More's death all the essential steps had been taken in the revolution which was to separate the Anglican from the Roman Church.

And now, four hundred years later, the modern world, which More watched growing up, is in its turn passing away, with some odd coincidences of date. If the last decade of the Fifteenth Century saw the discovery of America, the last decade of the Nineteenth Century saw the not less revolutionary conquest of the air. We may perhaps date the modern world, for Europe as a whole, from the day when Luther nailed his ninety-five theses to the door of All Saints Church, Wittenberg, 1 November 1517. On 3 November 1917 the Bolshevik revolution began, destined to alter, even more fundamentally than Luther's revolution, the lives of an even greater number of people, and to have repercussions even more world-wide.

But perhaps the most striking resemblance of all is that men, in the opening years of the Sixteenth Century, as in the opening years of the Twentieth, rejoiced over the growth of knowledge, and felt that at last an age of peace and learning was coming, little realizing the troubled times ahead. For ten years, from 1509 to 1519, this optimism prevailed among scholars in England. In the happy years 1517 and 1518 More's friends, Tunstall and Erasmus, were speaking of the Golden Age at hand, and how their posterity would rival the ancients in every branch of learning. But the ninety-five theses were already on the church door at Wittenberg, destined to bring not peace but a sword. Yet in 1518 Henry, Francis and Charles were treating for universal peace.

But though the sky was clear, the weather was what Oxfordshire folk call foxy. Strife of nations, strife of creeds cannot in a moment be allayed. Suddenly the little clouds upon the horizon swelled up, and covered the heaven with the darkness of night, and before the dawn broke into new hope, Erasmus had laid down his pen for ever, and was at rest from his service to the Prince of Peace.

[1] See above, p. 140.

So wrote the greatest of all students of the age of More and
Erasmus, Dr. P. S. Allen, in the book on *The Age of Erasmus*
which he published in 1914. But the weather in 1914 was as
foxy as it was in 1518. And when now, twenty-one years after
he published it, we read Dr. Allen's wise and noble book, we
come across passage after passage which, in the optimistic confidence of its scholarship, points us back to a pre-war age which
seems happier than our own. Again the clouds swell up, and
a good many people seem strangely wanting in confidence that
the dawn will ever break into new hope. Yet few of us have
reason to feel a disappointment as keen as that which More
and Erasmus felt. More watched, without wincing, the destruction of the hopes which he, like Erasmus, had cherished for
mankind. Like Erasmus, though in a different way, he struggled
tirelessly to the very end; unlike Erasmus, he did not complain.

And now we are drawing near to the four hundredth anniversary of the day when More's head fell from the block. A
world, perplexed and afraid at the transition and uncertainty
which it sees everywhere around, might do well to look back
for some word of encouragement to that quiet and unafraid
figure standing on the scaffold on Tower Hill, about nine in the
morning of 6 July 1535.

§5. SOCIALIST AND CATHOLIC ESTIMATES

The changes which are taking place should make it easier
to appreciate More, by ridding us of some of the prejudices
which have hampered his admirers for four hundred years.
Protestantism has grown less consciously intolerant. The biographer of More no longer finds it necessary to suppress all
mention of his hero having wished 'to bury himself' in a
monastery; nor, on the other hand, does he claim special credit
to himself for broadmindedness in not so suppressing it, and
for feeling that retirement into a cloister '*really* is not discredit-
able'.[1] And, in much the same way, some of the apologies for
the 'political chimeras'[2] of *Utopia* are beginning to look un-
necessary. In the course of one lifetime *Utopia* has passed out

[1] LORD CAMPBELL, *Lives of the Lord Chancellors*, Chap. xxx, *Life of Sir Thomas
More.*
[2] MACKINTOSH, *Life of Sir Thomas More*, p. 55.

of the realm of fantastic 'poetry', as Tyndale called it, and has become a text-book of practical politicians.

The veteran of European Socialism has described More as 'a man of genius who understood the problems of his age before the conditions existed for their solution'; a man who 'championed the oppressed classes even when he stood alone':

> And nothing speaks more eloquently for the greatness of the man, nothing shows more clearly how, like a giant, he towered over his contemporaries, than the fact that it needed more than three hundred years before the conditions have come about which show us that the aims which More set before himself are not the fancies of an idle hour, but the result of a deep insight into the actual economic tendencies of his age. Already More's four hundredth birthday is past, *Utopia* will soon be four hundred years old, but still his ideals are not defeated, still they lie before struggling mankind.[1]

So wrote Karl Kautsky forty-five years ago; and he repeated these words only the other day, merely bringing the chronology up to date. It is some six years since Mr. Gilbert Chesterton, writing as an English Catholic, said:

> Blessed Thomas More is more important at this moment than at any moment since his death, even perhaps the great moment of his dying; but he is not quite as important as he will be in about a hundred years time. He may come to be counted the greatest Englishman, or at least the greatest historical character in English history.[2]

Such a judgment is itself a portent. 'We are accustomed', writes Father Henry Browne, 'to Mr. Chesterton's sudden flashes of spiritual intuition, yet we wonder if he ever delivered a more inspired utterance than this.'[3]

It is instructive to put side by side these two judgments on More, that of the German Socialist and that of the English Catholic, and to observe how, from their different standpoints, they agree on this essential verdict – that More has had to wait four hundred years for his real importance to be fully discerned, that his ideals still lie before striving mankind, and will make him more and more important as the years pass on.

---

[1] KARL KAUTSKY, *Thomas More*, 1890, p. 340.
[2] *The Fame of Blessed Thomas More*, p. 63.   [3] The same, p. 92.

Indeed, the love of Sir Thomas More is one which joins together many and diverse spirits, as does the love of the mountains, or of St. Francis of Assisi. Who but St. Francis could have united in devoted love of himself such different men as Benito Mussolini and Mr. Laurence Housman, Ernest Renan and the Capuchin who said of Renan, 'Il a écrit sur Jésus autrement qu'on ne doit, mais il a bien parlé de Saint François. Saint François le sauvera!'

In the same way, men of every creed and nation gather in the evening in a lodging among the mountains, and feel that their common love of the high places makes them at one. And among them are those who next morning will be passing over glaciers and snowfields in the inmost recesses, or breathing the clean thin air of the peaks. And there are others of us who will never rise above the thicker atmosphere of the lower slopes; but we get refreshment and strength by looking up to the heights above us: 'I will lift up mine eyes unto the hills, from whence cometh my help.'

I am not forgetting that More died for the Papacy, 'suffering death in and for the faith of the Holy Catholic Church', that his blessing belongs of right to those of the faith for which he died, and that the rest of us can only have such blessing as poor Esau claimed, who had lost his birthright: 'Hast thou but one blessing: bless me, even me also, oh my father.'

And indeed some very strange and hairy Esaus are clamouring for the blessing of Saint Thomas More. That the love of Thomas More unites those who might seem to be separated by a considerable gulf is shown by the fact that the *Karl Marx-Engels Institute of the Central Executive Committee of the Union of Soviet Republics* should have been seeking for information about that great Communist Sir Thomas More, from the Sisters of the Beaufort Street Convent, who maintain ceaseless adoration, with prayer that the crime of our people in slaying Sir Thomas More may be forgiven. 'It proved impossible for us to find out the name and the address of these ladies,' says the letter from the *Marx-Engels Institute* which ultimately reached my hands. 'We would be infinitely obliged to you for letting us know what you have found out in this direction.'

§6. THE ENGLISH ESTIMATE

But the average Englishman, in this year 1935, is neither a Bolshevik nor a Roman Catholic, whatever he may become in the future; and his judgment still remains what it has always been, wonder that so wise a man as More could have been so wanting in common sense. The charge of impracticability is repeated from generation to generation. 'What an infinitely wise – infinitely foolish – book *Utopia* is; making its own wisdom folly for evermore.' So wrote John Ruskin,[1] echoing, though he did not know it, the very antithesis of 'wise' and 'fool' uttered in More's day by Dame Alice and by Edward Hall. It is not here a question of More having changed from wise to foolish. If the reader is not convinced of the consistency of More's opinions, at this 375th page of the book, little will be gained by dragging on the discussion for the few remaining pages. But the question still stands: was More striving to stop that which a wiser man might have seen could not be stopped? It is to this question that I wish to devote those few remaining pages. In the words of the greatest living historian of More's period:

> Political movements are often as resistless as the tides of the ocean; they carry to fortune, and they bear to ruin, the just and the unjust with heedless impartiality . . . Fisher and More seeking to stem the secularization of the Church, are like those who would save men's lives from the avalanche by preaching to the mountain on the text of the sixth commandment . . . That is the secret of Henry's success.[2]

But is it quite true that 'Henry's measures were crowned with whatever sanction worldly success can give'? And is 'ruin' quite the correct word to use of More's end?

After four hundred years, Henry's masterful personality still stands him in good stead. That is a fact, with which any biographer of More finds himself confronted. He must face it squarely.

We all of us feel a natural unwillingness to revile, in death, a man whom none of us would have dared to revile in life. This honourable feeling accounts, no doubt, for the efforts

[1] *Letter to F. S. Ellis*, 1870, *Works*, XXXVII, p. 12.
[2] POLLARD, *Henry VIII*, 1913, pp. 437-40.

which historians make to find something which they can say in praise of Henry. It is not their fault if such apologists some-times remind us of the medieval tale of the kindly angels at the Judgment, trying to rescue the soul of Piers the Usurer; the fiend loaded his side of the balance with Piers' black and innumerable sins; the good angels could find nothing save that Piers, in a fit of temper, had once hurled a crusty loaf at a beggar's head: thus, indisputably, Piers *had* once given a loaf to a beggar. So they laid that in the balance against Piers' sins:

> They had nought else, they must needs.[1]

The shifts to which historians are put to find something in praise of Henry is, in itself, Henry's condemnation, and often enough More's vindication. Thus, one historian tells us that the multifarious energies of his people found in Henry a leader of wide aptitude and congenial force.[2] The praise is impressive; but unfortunately the historian also gives particulars. Mr. Fisher's enumeration of these energies of his people, which Henry led with aptitude and force, is as follows. The paintings of Holbein. (Holbein was not one of Henry's people, and he owes his acclimatization in England chiefly to Thomas More.) The lyrics of Wyatt and Surrey. (Henry imprisoned and broke the spirit of the first, and decapitated the second.) The fact that *one* London merchant did press upon Henry the advantage of piercing the North-West passage to the Indies. (Henry's reign is remarkable by being 'almost barren of mercantile ex-pansion, maritime discovery, or any other form of oversea enterprise';[3] the theoretical interest of More in transatlantic adventure, and the practical interest of More's brother-in-law, received little encouragement from Henry.[4])

Yet even this absence of transatlantic enterprise, which would have been derided in anyone else, is applauded in Henry, on the ground that Spain would not have approved of his following up the American adventures of his father.[5] And, strangest of all, Mr. P. S. Allen, the greatest of the admirers of More, even says of Henry VIII that 'it is a testimony to the

---

[1] ROBERT MANNING of BRUNNE, *Handlyng Synne*, 5668.
[2] FISHER, *History of England, 1485-1547*, p. 483.
[3] CALLENDER, *The Naval Side of British History*, p. 47.
[4] See above, pp. 139-42.   [5] TREVELYAN, *History of England*, p. 295.

greatness of that amazing man that, at the end, More could look forward to being "merry in heaven" with the master who required his death'.[1] Such a judgment from such a scholar must carry weight. Yet, in fact, this phrase was used by More of Henry not 'at the end' but whilst he was still at liberty, at a time when Henry was *not* requiring his death.[2] After his trial, More spoke of being merry in heaven with the judges who had condemned him, Norfolk, Audeley and the rest (a solemn lot, one would think, to be merry with anywhere); but, so far as our information goes, More rather markedly avoided using any such phrase of Henry. He said that he would continue to pray for Henry, but not that he either expected or hoped that his prayers in the next world would be interrupted by His Grace's conversation. He probably anticipated inhabiting another mansion.

§7 . THE SUCCESS OF HENRY

But, so far as this world is concerned, *were* Henry's measures 'crowned with success'? In estimating a man's success, we must ask – at what did he aim? Henry aimed, naturally and rightly, at securing a male heir who should ensure the permanency of his dynasty. In this he failed. He aimed at establishing uniformity in religion, but on a basis odious alike to devout Protestants and devout Catholics: he 'destroyed the Pope, but not popery',[3] or, as Harpsfield more picturesquely put it, he cut off St. Peter's head and set it, an ugly sight to behold, upon his own shoulders. Such a settlement was not, and could not be, successful. Idolized by his people, Henry had inherited an undisputed succession and a vast treasure; after thirty-two years he said that he had an evil people to rule, and that he would make them so poor that it would be out of their power to rebel.[4] He certainly succeeded in making his people poor. England when he came to the throne had been a treasure-house of art; he left it a chaos of fragments. Yet all his spoliation made him so poor that, to the utter misery of his people and embarrassment of his successors, he had to debase the coinage,

---

[1] Sir Thomas More, *Selections*, p. ix.
[2] 5 March 1534: sixteen months before More's death
[3] Hooper to Bullinger, Robinson, *Letters*, Parker Society, 1, p. 36.
[4] Pollard, *Henry VIII*, p. 402.

the excellence of which had been one of England's great traditions; it 'had remained intact throughout the humiliations of the kingdom under John, and the confusion of the Wars of the Roses'.[1] Henry had inherited an England in friendship with all other kingdoms, and in alliance with the one most potentially formidable; he left England at war, exposed to the open hostility or covert dislike of every foreign state.

One great inheritance Henry had not destroyed. His father, keenly interested in the navy, had left him a great fleet; Henry strengthened it enormously. It has been suggested that the great guns which were being made by the craftsmen of Mechlin 'appealed in a subtle and peculiar way to Henry's destructive instinct';[2] anyway, he ordered his shipwrights to devise how they could be mounted on his vessels. Thus he produced a navy with which he could defy Europe, and he left it as a sure shield to his successors. If we believe that British sea power has been for the good of the world, this must count as Henry's great success. The crusty loaf which the usurer Piers hurled at the beggar was allowed (so great is God's mercy) as equivalent in weight to his many deadly sins. Let us hope that the heavy cannon-balls of Henry's English broadside will stand him in equal stead. But to Henry his navy was merely a fighting force which could be used to support his schemes for winning 'castles in France'. We have seen that he did not, like his wise father and his wise daughter, encourage the exploration of distant seas, although the necessity of his friendship to Charles V would have given him a lever such as neither his predecessor nor his successors possessed.[3] Henry might have been our Henry the Navigator; he preferred unsuccessful imitations of the French campaigns of Henry V. Whether we blame Henry or Wolsey for it, Henry's useless French wars 'undid the work of Henry VII, and beat England back from the seas into the dusty vortex of European politics'.[4]

And that is only one further example of the story of arrest and frustration which we have seen forming the background to

[1] POLLARD, *England under Protector Somerset*, 1900, p. 46. For the good reputation of the English coinage at an even earlier period, see the *British Museum Guide to the Exhibition of English Art*, 1934, p. 19.
[2] CALLENDER, *The Naval Side of British History*, 1924, p. 38.
[3] See above, p. 142.   [4] CALLENDER, as above, p. 47.

the life of Thomas More. The poets flocked to Henry's court; he stopped their music, and for a generation after the execution of Surrey there is nothing worth notice, save the sombre poems in which Sackville, before turning away from poetry, lamented that eminence led only to destruction. In the ordinary course, Surrey might have lived another thirty or forty years, the centre of a circle of court poets. As it is, the history of the sonnet in England is a blank between 1547 and about 1580, and English poetry as a whole is negligible till it begins its magnificent progress again with Spenser and Sidney. Prose had a similar set-back. After the generation of Tyndale and Coverdale, Fisher and More and his school, there is no eminence till we come to Hooker and Bacon – a gap of more than a generation. Contemporaries noticed the gap, and wondered that More's example had not proved more fruitful. In the field of scholarship Henry's achievement was really remarkable. There were four great international scholars,[1] and, in England, two great patrons of learning. Of the six, Henry cold-shouldered Erasmus out of England, imprisoned Vives, decapitated More and Fisher, and frightened Wolsey to death. 'Had Erasmus, instead of being an honoured guest at Rome, at Paris, or in the States of the Empire, been beheaded by Charles V or Francis I, all learning would have felt the blow, and shrunk.'[2] In England, all learning felt the blow, and shrank. It was not till the days of Bentley that classical scholarship recovered in England the position it held in the days of Erasmus, before Henry axed it. To the Universities, Henry's spoliation meant a loss, for which his well-advertised benefactions were an inadequate compensation. In 1550 Latimer writes: 'It would pity a man's heart to hear that, that I hear of the state of Cambridge . . . I think there be at this day ten thousand students less than were within these twenty years, and fewer preachers.' As to the grammar schools, More's school of St. Antony was only one of a vast number which withered away.[3]

Historians sometimes speak of the 'material comfort' which Henry secured for his people. For the aristocracy there was, no

[1] See above, pp. 107, 217.
[2] J. S. PHILLIMORE, *The Arrest of Humanism in England* (published in the *Dublin Review*, 1913); a vital essay, to which every student of More is under a heavy debt.
[3] On this, see TAWNEY, *Religion and the Rise of Capitalism*, 1926, p. 143.

doubt, material comfort, tempered by decapitation; but all the evidence shows that financial chaos and the corruption of the coinage brought the mass of the population to a state of utter misery. But it was in the sense of beauty and the sense of freedom and justice that the set-back was most serious. When Henry came to the throne every Englishman, even the poorest, had many chances of seeing masterpieces of craftsmanship, and, if he was a craftsman, of learning from them. When Henry died, most of these things had been destroyed, and the possibility of rejoicing in works of art had become the perquisite of the aristocrat. No longer were 'the Beauties of the realm' open 'to all men and strangers passing through the same', as the leader of the Pilgrimage of Grace urged that they should remain. From Henry's revolution onwards, 'the Beauties of England' are not the Abbeys, but the country seats of the gentry, jealously surrounded by fine red brick walls.

As to freedom and justice, no one I think would deny that in Henry's reign 'the English spirit of independence burned low in its socket, and love of freedom grew cold', or that 'the finer feelings seem to have been lost in the pursuit of wealth'.[1] It was left for men who were certainly not engaged in the pursuit of wealth – Thomas More, Fisher, the Carthusians, to stand as the champions of liberty of conscience in the darkest day of English freedom. In the more remote parts of Henry's dominions, where the pursuit of wealth was least possible, in the North of England, the West of England, Wales and Ireland, the innovations of Henry were disapproved by all. A little more than a year after More's execution, in the North of England, thirty or forty thousand well-horsed warriors rose, under Robert Aske, in the 'Pilgrimage of Grace'. Wearing the badge of the 'Five Wounds', they rallied round the crimson and white standard of St. Cuthbert of Durham, 'which had always before brought home the victory'. They demanded that the rule of tyranny, spoliation and desecration should cease. The Duke of Norfolk, who commanded the King's forces, reported that he could not stand against the rebels, and that whilst he could rely on the noblemen and gentlemen, there were right few of the common soldiers in his army who did not think the cause of the

---

[1] PROF. A. F. POLLARD. See above, p. 243.

Northern men 'good and godly'. Norfolk's evidence[1] is conclusive, and is supported by the words of Henry's contemporary panegyrist, William Thomas. Henry's people, Thomas says, came so slowly to him, his enemies were so many, that he was compelled to treat with the rebels 'and promise them what they would ask'.

If Henry had kept his promise, English history would have been different. He waited till the rebels were disarmed and scattered, and then arrested and executed Aske and the other leaders. 'A king is never so powerful as when he has crushed a rebellion.' Though the free Parliament at York, which the rebels demanded, was never called, in 1539 Parliament met again, and passed the Act of Proclamations. This, subject to various provisos, gave the force of law to the proclamations of the King and Council. No proclamation was to prejudice life, liberty or property, but this safeguard did not apply to the King's doctrinal proclamations. Men might be punished with death for offence against 'any proclamation to be made by the King's Highness, his heirs or successors for and concerning any kind of heresies against Christian religion'.[2] The Act, we are told, was only passed 'with great difficulty and long debate, and with little pleasure of those who gave their consent to it'.[3]

But passed it was. Things had come to that, ten years after the 'Reformation Parliament' first met 'to reform abuses'. Heresy was punishable by death, and what heresy was, was left for the King and his successors to define by proclamation from time to time. Such was the culmination of the royal tyranny which More and his fellows had given their lives to resist. More's headless body had been mouldering in the grave for four years, and for two years the bones of the leaders of the Pilgrimage of Grace had been swinging in chains over the gates of Yorkshire towns. The tragedy of the Carthusians, Fisher and More is an incomplete thing, unless we keep also in mind the tragedy of the Pilgrimage of Grace. With More perished all that was wisest in England; with him, Fisher, and the

[1] For the full text of his letter see *The Pilgrimage of Grace*, by M. H. and R. Dodds, I, 268.
[2] 31 Henry VIII, Cap. 8. *Statutes*, 1817, vol. III, p. 726.
[3] Marillac, 5 July 1539, *L.P.*, XIV, No. 1207.

Carthusians all that was holiest. With the leaders of the Pilgrims perished the Medieval Chivalry of England.

Yet my enumeration of the things which Henry destroyed is incomplete. An excellent life of More, just published,[1] reminds us that 'Henry killed laughter'. That is true. There remained, of course, the hysterical laughter of poor Anne Boleyn in her last hours. But the Henrician tyranny is a *dull* period. How could it be otherwise? 'It was, as ye know,' said Bishop Latimer preaching before Edward VI, 'a dangerous world; for it might soon cost a man his life for a word's speaking.' Laughter and liberty go together.

Henry succeeded in establishing a dictatorship, which he maintained for the remaining years of his life. But at what cost? Whether we think of the exploration of distant seas, of English poetry, of English prose, of English scholarship, of English education, of the material prosperity of the English people (apart from a small body of profiteers), of finance, of craftsmanship, of architecture, of freedom, of justice, Henry's tyranny marks a real set-back. Everything had to pass through the bottle-neck of one man's mind, and Henry, though able, was not equal to the task. Henry's dictatorship was bound to fail in the long run, because it revolted the consciences of his subjects. The resistance to despotism which More began was bound to be carried on, from opposite sides, both by Catholic and by Puritan.

Henry failed, because the keystone of the arch he sought to construct was a son, inheriting the amazing personality and ability of his race, who in the vigour of young manhood was to take over the vast accumulation of power, civil and religious, which Wolsey had amassed, and Henry had taken from Wolsey and developed. No one else could carry on Henry's despotism; no child, no woman, no foreigner. Mary undid Henry's work, and Elizabeth neither could nor would establish such a tyranny as her father had wielded. She 'made no windows into men's souls', as Henry did. Terrible as was the religious persecution under Mary, and again under Elizabeth, both Roman Catholic and Puritan established in the end their right to exist. And Parliament, which Henry had fostered as an instrument of his

[1] CHRISTOPHER HOLLIS, *Sir Thomas More*, 1934.

despotism, Parliament, which was to him what 'the bow which he alone could bend' was to Ulysses,[1] became an instrument of freedom.

> God, moving darkly in men's brains,
> Using their passions as his tool,
> Brings freedom with a tyrant's chains
> And wisdom with the fool.[2]

Yet we must not forget those who 'shared the work with God'; those who, in the darkest hour of English liberty, dared to say 'No' to the fiat of despotism, and who nevertheless kept their loyalty unimpaired: Thomas More and the white-robed Carthusians, Robert Aske and the horsemen of the North.

Many of the protests of the men of the North have been preserved, and it is remarkable how often they echo *Utopia*, a book which these Yorkshire squires had assuredly never read. Both are protesting against the new autocracy. The protest is eternal. Only the other day a distinguished lawyer wrote:

> The life and death of Thomas More are witness to the principle of limitation of the power of King or of Parliament, and the writings and the judgments of a constellation of Catholic and non-Catholic historians and lawyers in our own time have led to a reaffirmation of the principles of Natural and Divine Law for which he lived and died.[3]

Edward Hall, who was present, records the speech in which Henry, a year before his death, finally 'set forth his mind' to Parliament. His faithful Lords and Commons had given him the remaining hospitals, and the chantries, to supply his bankrupt treasury, and so the final stage began in Henry's plunder of the Church, the sick, and the poor, against which, when it was first proposed sixteen years before, More had protested.[4] Henry thanked his subjects, and then went on to lecture them on religion: 'Of this I am sure, that Charity was never so faint amongst you, virtuous and godly living was never less used, nor God himself amongst Christians was never less reverenced, honoured, or served.'[5] Henry's words are his own final con-

---

[1] POLLARD, *Henry VIII*, p. 258.   [2] MASEFIELD, *Pompey the Great*.
[3] RICHARD O'SULLIVAN, *The Survival of Blessed Thomas More, Blackfriars*, Oct. 1934, p. 698.
[4] *The Supplication of Souls, passim.*
[5] HALL's *Henry VIII*, ed. WHIBLEY, II, pp. 355-7.

demnation of his own policy. All contemporary sources are at one as to the wretched state in which he left his realm. Protestant and Catholic agree as to its desolation, spiritual and material.[1]

A cynic might retort (most untruly, I believe) that Henry cared nothing for the spiritual or material welfare of his people, and sought nothing save his own happiness. But even here he was not successful. After he had broken with Catherine of Aragon, all his cunning diplomacy gave him little ease or security. There is something pitiful in his complaint 'of the sundry troubles of mind which had happened to him by marriages', just before he learnt that he had been betrayed by his fifth Queen. His horrible ulcer gave him such torment that one cannot but admire the vitality which enabled him to carry on. Yet even when Death came as a deliverer from agony, Henry feared Death.[2]

A thing, the medieval scholars held, is known by its contraries, and in everything Henry is the contrary of More. It is not merely that More opposed Henry's wishes in the matter of the divorce and of the unity of Christendom and of the plunder of the Church. Almost all that Henry did and was, is condemned, by anticipation, in *Utopia*. Henry would make his subjects too poor to rebel: upon the wickedness and folly of this Raphael Hythlodaye had dilated.[3] Henry plundered churches to provide jewels to wear on his own person: the Utopians, ruler and people alike, are dressed with complete simplicity,[4] whilst all the churches and public places are magnificently adorned.[5] Henry pulled down and built up recklessly: both things are avoided in Utopia.[6] Henry's corruption of the coinage had been condemned by Hythlodaye a quarter of a century before.[7] Henry's riches went in continental wars, and he never dreamt of finding homes in waste lands for his homeless subjects: the Utopians hate all warfare,[8]

---

[1] For some examples of the Protestant evidence, see above, p. 261. The Catholic evidence is everywhere: see, for example, HARPSFIELD, *Pretended Divorce*.

[2] We may discount the grim stories told by partisan hatred; but it is certain that Henry's physicians did not dare to tell him of his approaching death. He was 'loth to hear any mention of death' (FOXE, ed. TOWNSEND, v, p. 689). Earlier, Marillac, the French ambassador, notes his fear of the plague: 'he is the most timid person that could be in such a case' (6 July 1540, *L.P.*, xv, No. 848).

[3] *Utopia*, ed. LUPTON, pp. 93-4.   [4] p. 140.   [5] p. 289.   [6] p. 149.   [7] p. 88.   [8] p. 243.

and Hythlodaye denounces[1] the purposeless wars of Europe, but the Utopians hold it against the law of nature that they should be stopped from settling a starving population on empty territories. In such a case these peace-loving people are even ready to go to war.[2] But in nothing is the contrast between Henry and More so marked as in their feeling about death. Judged by Utopian standards, Henry's life was unsuccessful, More's successful: for the criterion in Utopia is, how a man dies.[3] Those who die unwillingly the Utopians bury with sorrow and silence; to those who die 'merrily and full of good hope' they erect monuments, and speak of their good deeds; but of no good deed so much as of their merry death.

§ 8 . THE FAILURE OF MORE

And so, although he failed, 'ruin' is hardly the word to use of More's end. Neither his imprisonment nor his execution were to him matters of regret. A death on the scaffold might be ruin to you or to me, but it would be no less absurd to think of More's death as betokening ruin to him, than it would be to think of the nakedness of St. Francis' dying body as a sign of the ruin of the Poverello. More knew that by his death the final seal was being placed upon his life, no less clearly than St. Francis had received it 'on the rugged rock between Tiber and Arno'.[4]

Here, as everywhere, the parallel with Socrates, and the contrast, strikes us. To More, as to Socrates, all his life had been studying nothing but dying and being dead.[5] Socrates assured his judges that his death could not be an evil – for the sign which was always vouchsafed to him when danger or evil was approaching had not been given.[6] More's assurances were more positive. He had longed for 'convenient time and space': it was granted. Latterly he had used that space to write his meditations on the Passion: when he reached the words, 'They laid hands on him', his books, papers, and all that he had in the prison were taken from him. More, like St. Francis, combines a complete personal humility with a full and grateful sense of the honour which is being conferred upon him: he

---

[1] *Utopia*, ed. LUPTON, pp. 81 etc.   [2] p. 155.   [3] pp. 276-7.
[4] DANTE, *Paradiso*, XI, 106-8.
[5] *Phaedo*, 9 (64). Compare MORE's *Works, passim*, but especially p. 77.
[6] *Apology*, 31 (40).

dares in addressing his judges to liken himself to the first Christian martyr. It was a strange coincidence that the eve of the translation of St. Thomas à Becket and the octave of St. Peter – the one day in the year most appropriate to More's death – should have fallen so near the date of his condemnation; he hoped that his execution might be on that day, and when Mr. Pope entered his cell he knew that it was to be so. His words to the woman who offered him drink on the way to death show what was in his mind: 'I will not drink now. My master had easell and gall, not wine, given him to drink.'

But, though he died as and when he wished, More's statesmanship had not compassed the ends he sought. He failed to avert the violence he feared. He opposed a revolution which had behind it Henry VIII, Machiavelli's Prince in action, as Professor A. F. Pollard calls him, and Thomas Cromwell, embodying the new commercialism. Such opposition was, to quote Professor Pollard again, as if one should try to save men's lives from the avalanche by preaching to the mountain on the text of the Sixth Commandment.

The avalanche destroyed, not only men's lives, but treasures of art which the English nation had been accumulating for eight centuries. Buildings, manuscripts, stained glass, paintings, woodwork, brasses, work of goldsmith and silversmith, were swept away. Only fragments have survived. 'Marbles which covered the dead were digged up. Inscriptions or epitaphs, especially if they began with an *Orate pro anima*, or concluded *cujus animae propitietur Deus*, for greediness of the brass, or for that they were thought to be anti-christian, pulled out from the sepulchres.'[1]

We may take the Oxford of More's day, which he loved so well and served so strenuously, as a type of what he wished for England. That Oxford belonged to a Europe still largely medieval, not yet utterly rent asunder by the sense of nationality: an Oxford where Erasmus felt at home. More's Oxford included the things we most admire in the Oxford of to-day: Cardinal College was rising (and, thanks largely to More's intercession,[2] was to continue to rise); to the east Magdalen

---

[1] WEEVER, *Funeral Monuments*, 1631.
[2] MAXWELL LYTE, *History of the University of Oxford*, 1886, p. 482.

tower was standing white from the masons' hands. But to the west, where to-day we approach Oxford amid a wilderness of 'gas-holders, coal-heaps, railway sidings, modern tombstones and obscene jerry-buildings', More saw vast churches, each as big as a cathedral, standing amid their conventual buildings – Oseney Abbey and the Houses of the Black and Grey Friars, a group far surpassing anything Oxford can show to-day, and of which nothing was spared, except only the Oseney bells.

More wished that England should be the full heir, both of the Middle Ages, and also of the new knowledge; he wished to keep all the positions that had been won, and to advance as well. But he realized that this could only be, if matters were conducted, as King Utopus had urged, 'with reason and sober modesty'. More's contemporaries agree in describing *Utopia* as 'a warning against the evils which beset states'. These evils are all forms of self-willed, individualist violence: the nationalist ambition which disregards the rights of the rest of Christendom, which is the subject of much of the First Book; commercial greed, 'My Lady Money', the thought of which underlies the whole of *Utopia*; above all, violence in matters of religion, against which King Utopus legislated, holding that 'as the worst men are the most obstinate, the best and holiest religion would be trodden underfoot and destroyed'.

More's fears came true; everywhere violence prevailed. And so grass is growing to-day on the most sacred spots in England; Glastonbury, Lindisfarne, and Whitby are desolate enough to satisfy 'even the most ferocious advocate of impartial religious toleration'.

More did not see why the new knowledge need necessarily destroy the old ideals, whether those ideals were of unity in Christendom, or of the Common Life, or of beauty in building and ritual. More's countrymen have thought differently. Not a generation has passed since More's time, without something of the legacy of the Middle Ages being wasted. Yet 'we are still living on the inheritance, without realizing what the world will be like when all is squandered'.[1]

As we stand amid the mean streets of our towns we may

---

[1] W. R. LETHABY in Crump and Jacob, *The Legacy of the Middle Ages*, 1926, p. 90.

think of the towns of Utopia, where no building was ever mean, most buildings were ancient, all were in perfect repair, and all were for the public service. Then we may remember that, often enough, we may be actually standing on the site of a most beautiful building. In More's day the vast churches of the Friars still stood round about the old towns of England, as Santa Croce, Santa Maria, and San Marco stand round about the old town of Florence to-day. In More's day these English churches were rendering their last public service. Then we may remember that in Utopia no building was ever wantonly destroyed.

The avalanche has passed. But, in *Utopia*, in his English works, and in the strangely neglected *Lives*, we may yet, if we will, listen to Sir Thomas More 'preaching to the Mountain'.

But if More had failed to avert the violence he feared, equally he had failed to ensure the unity he loved. Of his three hopes, each was signally defeated. Universal peace among Christian princes; uniformity of religion; a good conclusion to the matter of the King's marriage, which 'otherwise would be a disturbance to a great part of Christendom' – none of these things were attained.

From *Utopia* to his great speech at his trial, More's ideal is the same: peace and unity among the princes of Christendom. From this would follow a common front in defence against the Moslem hordes driving up from Asia, and threatening to swamp Germany and to dominate the Mediterranean. Chapuys tells how More complained to one of his secretaries in a very piteous tone of the blindness of Christian princes who refused to help the Emperor against so cruel and implacable an enemy as the Turk.[1] So far as loyalty to his own country allowed, More's sympathy was always passionately on the side of the Emperor, as head of a league of Christian nations, and protector of Christendom. So much was this the case that, Chapuys tells us, More was known in England as 'the father and protector of the Emperor's subjects'.[2] It was no accident that More occupied himself in the Tower by writing the long *Dialogue of Comfort against Tribulation*, supposed to be a translation of a work written by a Hungarian in Latin, on the way Christian

[1] 11 April 1531, *Spanish Calendar*, IV, ii, p. 114.   [2] 1 March 1531, the same, p. 80.

men were to behave under the tyranny of the Turk. Of course More is thinking of the troubles in England; but he is thinking in a very real way also of the harrying of the Eastern frontiers of Europe.

§ 9. MORE AND EUROPEAN HISTORY

And this is why More has been misunderstood by so many generations of English historians. His whole outlook upon English history is different from theirs; and before we judge him, we must work hard to try and see the past as he saw it. If our interest begins only with 'The Renaissance' or 'The Reformation', if we despise the Middle Ages, we shall never understand More. It may be said that no one to-day would speak of the Middle Ages as one 'long Gothic night'; but when prejudices have held sway for so long, their after-effect is enormous. And to reinforce these prejudices with pseudo-science, the Nineteenth Century added the Great Teutonic Myth. Englishmen were of pure Teutonic race, and therefore predestined to become Protestants, because the Reformation was the work of men of 'the grave and earnest Teutonic race', the race endowed with the 'deeper moral consciousness' which characterizes 'the graver Northern nations'. I was myself brought up on Kingsley and Froude, Freeman and John Richard Green, and rejoiced to think of my ancestors in Germanic forests, with souls naturally Protestant, though still heathen, each householder sacrificing for himself, and allowing no priest to come between him and his God, till Hengist and Horsa landed in Kent, clothed in little save the primitive integrity of their Liberal and Puritan principles; so that Englishmen were destined to revert to their innate Protestantism as soon as the trumpet sounded from Wittenberg. How blind of More to resist.

But if we abandon, as we must, the Teutonic racial myth, we must abandon the theories based upon it.

An understanding of Thomas More seems to me to be a corollary to an understanding of the history of England during the preceding thousand years. And that history, as I see it, is this.

---

[1] BEARD, *The Reformation*, pp. 42, 43.

It was not the Norman Conquest that made England part of continental civilization, as modern historians so often assert.[1] Thomas More, though he knew little or nothing of the details, was right when he argued at his trial that the conversion of England to Christianity had resulted in England taking her place forthwith in a European unity. Monk Wearmouth, Jarrow, and York become the centres of Western European civilization and learning. Britain had been part of the ancient Roman world, and, in spite of a century and a half of Teutonic heathendom, the earlier Christianity of Britain had been passed on to sanctuaries like Glastonbury or Iona. The mission of Augustine meant 'the return of Britain to Europe'.[2] Then, before there was any such political state as 'England', the English people, conscious of their nationality although politically divided, brought Christianity and Catholic unity into vast areas of Central Europe, under the leadership of Boniface, the man 'who had a deeper influence on the history of Europe than any other Englishman who has ever lived'.[3] And so England set to work to cement and confirm European unity by converting the Teutonic heathen around – in Friesland and Germany, and later in Norway and Sweden. For nearly five centuries from the landing of Augustine, the part of England in the European unity was twofold: to stand as a bulwark to receive the first shock of the pirate hosts of the North; but still more to carry European civilization to all those hosts of Saxons, Frisians, and Northmen, and to bring even remote Picts and Scots into the unity of the Catholic Church. English Christianity is a more venerable thing than the English state, and above all it is a European, not an insular thing. The Norman Conquest only emphasized what was already a feature of English Christianity. Two generations after the Norman Conquest, Englishmen, Normans, Flemings, combined with the Portuguese to recover Lisbon from the Moslems, and so to give Portugal that place in the expansion of Europe which in due time is marked in literature by the figure of Raphael Hythlodaye. 'We are all children of one mother,'[4] exclaimed Hervey Glanvill, who

---

[1] e.g. TREVELYAN, *History of England*, p. 324.
[2] CHRISTOPHER DAWSON, *The Making of Europe*, 1932, p. 209.   [3] The same, p. 211.
[4] *De expugnatione Lyxbonensi*, in *Itinerarium regis Ricardi*, ed. STUBBS, 1864, Rolls Series, p. clviii.

brought his East Anglian contingent to the service of the common cause; and later it is as the children of one mother that Peter Giles the Fleming, Raphael Hythlodaye the Portuguese, and Thomas More the Englishman, meet together in the garden at Antwerp, understanding each other fully, as members of a common civilization.

More was giving a true view of English history when he claimed that Englishmen, as Christians, had always been part of one great unity, and that to separate the English Church from the European fellowship, and make it subordinate to the English state, as Henry claimed to do, was a new thing, a departure from a tradition nearly a thousand years old.

We all appreciate Falkland ingeminating 'Peace, Peace', for England; there has been less sympathy for the man who ingeminates 'Peace, Peace', for Europe or the World. We have accepted as inevitable the position of the nations as 'gladiators in the European arena'; and as Henry VIII stands before us, his legs apart, his hand on his dagger, we see a fine gladiator, who has many admirers. Mr. Gilbert Chesterton has said that to the modern historian

> a statesman always meant a man who maintained the more narrow national interests of his own state against other states, as Richelieu maintained those of France, or Chatham of England, or Bismarck of Prussia. But if a man actually wanted to defend all these states . . . then that poor devil, of course, could not really be called a statesman. He was only a Crusader.[1]

The tradition of Agincourt led Henry VIII to make one fatuous attack after another upon France, till the wealth and civilization of England were squandered in expeditions to burn the houses of French peasants. For five centuries Englishmen have gloried over the butchery of Agincourt, which led to nothing save misery. How many Englishmen even to-day know anything of the marvellous adventures of St. Boniface and his companions, when all that was noblest in England flung itself abroad in a passion of organized and disciplined effort? This effort succeeded in winning for Christendom a territory in central Europe which compensated for the con-

[1] G. K. CHESTERTON, *St. Thomas Aquinas*, 1933, p. 59.

temporary loss of Spain to an alien civilization. 'That was the real occupation of Germany by the English,' a German medieval scholar said to me, at the time when the English army of occupation was in Cologne. How many Englishmen realize that these efforts of the English missionaries made possible the renaissance under Charles the Great, upon which in its turn the whole future civilization of Western Europe was based? How many who read this page will not think these sentences exaggerated? And yet they express the considered opinion of those best qualified to judge.[1] If they appear revolutionary, it is because Englishmen have persistently turned their eyes away from what is noblest in their own history. In the excellent history of England by Mr. Trevelyan, the name of Boniface does not occur.

The cleavage of Western Christendom, more than a century of Wars of Religion, the rise of a nationalism entirely self-seeking and scorning the idea of any duty to Europe as a whole – were these things in More's day so clearly inevitable as to make it folly to have looked for any other way of 'reform'? Were they 'progress', and were the humanists who sought another path 'reactionaries'? From 'Reform' as it took place many good and great things have been attained. But might they not have been attained at the price of less destruction, if Europe had followed the reform which More and Erasmus sought, through unity rather than through cleavage, through the cultivation of the humanist ideal of a European fellowship rather than through violent national sectionalism?

To say that a reformation on Erasmian rather than Lutheran lines was so impossible as to make it futile to seek it, is to beg the question. Christendom in the days of Boniface seemed in a much more desperate state than in the days of More, yet reformation was carried through, not only without loss of European unity, but with much increase of it.

In some ways the task of the statesman seemed perhaps easier in More's days than it does now; the humanists had only to teach three young men to be reasonable.

[1] Compare the verdicts pronounced independently and simultaneously by CHRISTOPHER DAWSON in *The Making of Europe*, 1932, and by that great scholar whose loss we deplore, Mr. S. J. CRAWFORD, in *Anglo-Saxon Influence on Western Christendom*, II, 1933 (a lecture delivered in 1931).

Maximilian's death in 1519 followed by Charles' election to the Empire placed the sovereignty of Western and Central Europe in the hands of three young men, who were chivalrous and impressionable, Henry and Francis and Charles: only the year before they had been treating for universal peace. If they would really act in concord, it seemed as though the Golden Age might return, and Christendom show a united face against the watchful and unwearying Turk.[1]

And yet our historians continue to admire Henry, because he helped to break such European unity as he found, although in doing it he had to break all the most beautiful things in England. But he is called 'the founder of England's religious independence'[2] because he made every man's religion depend upon the King, claiming to pronounce, *ex cathedra*, from the English throne, what every Englishman must believe on pain of death.[3]

The Greeks of the Fourth Century B.C. were ashamed of their ancestors in the Fifth Century, because, when they were threatened by an alien civilization, they had not held together, and in their narrow sectionalism had left two states, Athens and Sparta, to bear the brunt. It was far from honourable to Hellas, Plato thought, and ought to be kept in mind as a warning to statesmen, past and present.[4] Indeed it ought, and we may draw lessons from it to-day. But what Englishman ever regrets the abolition of the forty-three commanderies of the Knights of St. John? England had taken her share in the heroic defence of Rhodes. But by the time of the siege of Malta and the battle of Lepanto, the Marathon and the Salamis of our European civilization, England had deserted the common cause. Sir William Weston, the English Prior of the Knights of St. John, had won fame at the siege of Rhodes. Henry pensioned him off handsomely, but he died on the day of the dissolution of his order. 'Gold, though a great cordial, could not cure a broken heart.'

To-day, a disunited Europe is threatened, not by any alien invader, but by an even greater danger – the growth of its own materialistic knowledge and its own powers of destruction.

Let us think yet once again of that scene by the Thames side, and of More's three wishes: Universal peace among

[1] ALLEN, *Age of Erasmus*, p. 166.   [2] TREVELYAN, *History of England*, p. 326.
[3] 31 Henry VIII, cap. 8. See above, p. 381.   [4] *Laws*, 692, 693.

Christian princes; a settlement of the divisions of the Church
and a good conclusion to the question of the King's marriage,
which he foresaw must else trouble a great part of Christendom.
These were the ambitions of the statesman about to receive the
highest office in the realm. If he could attain these things, he
would be content to be 'put in a sack, and here presently cast
into the Thames'. We need not repeat the cynical old rhyme:

> The like shall never more be seen
> Till More be there again.

But assuredly the special characteristics of More as a statesman are what we most need to-day: a combination of loyalty to
his own country and loyalty to Europe. By Europe we mean,
nowadays, 'not the geographical conception, but a certain
attitude to life and to society'. The words are those of Professor
Einstein. If the 'certain attitude' seems to demand practical
definition, I do not know where, in practice, a better example
could be found than in the life and writings of More.

§ 10. 'OUR HUMAN ESTIMATION'

This is the man whom some of the wisest critics and historians of the Nineteenth Century could only see as 'an official
engaged in justifying what was convenient for the moment',
'deceiving himself', 'repeating platitudes', 'putting his principles aside',[1] a man who 'allowed his sentiments to be moulded
by the official theology of the court',[2] who 'turned his back on
the ennobling enthusiasms of his youth',[3] and became a
'merciless bigot'.[4] And so we may, from these judgments, learn
at least not to judge. We may

> learn one lesson hence
> Of many which whatever lives should teach:
> This lesson, that our human speech is naught,
> Our human testimony false, our fame
> And human estimation words and wind.

And this indeed was the moral which Sir James Mackintosh drew,
in the closing phrases of his exquisite little biography of More:

> Protestants ought to be taught humility and charity from this
> instance of the wisest and best of men falling into what they

---

[1] CREIGHTON, as above, pp. 130, 355.   [2] ACTON, as above, pp. 226, 354.
[3] LYNDSAY, as above, p. 355.   [4] FROUDE, as above, p. 354.

deem the most fatal errors. All men in the fierce contests of contending factions should, from such an example, learn the wisdom to fear lest in their most hated antagonist they may strike down a Sir Thomas More.

But other things than a warning against rash judgments can be learnt from More's life.

We can gather something from the fact that he is regarded as a hero alike by the Communist and by the Catholic. Four hundred and two years before it came into existence, he sketched out the pattern of the Communist state. Those eyes which Holbein drew, anxiously but fearlessly peering into the future, had seen far indeed. And More's political disciples are found far outside the ranks of Communists and Socialists. More's description of the commonwealth of his day as 'a conspiracy of rich men, procuring their own commodities under the name of the commonwealth' has roused the conscience of social reformers from his day to ours.

More is the hero of the Catholic, because he gave his life 'in and for the faith of the Holy Catholic Church'. He should be the hero of all men of good will, because he died for unity; died that the prayer of his Master at his first Eucharist might be fulfilled, 'That they all may be one'.

§ 11. 'A MAN UNDER AUTHORITY'

Now Communism and Catholicism have one thing in common. They compel a man to think of himself as a member of a corporate body, under the strictest discipline. Discipline is the essence of More's life. He is a hater of war, but he had the mind of the centurion in the Gospel, the one man of whom it is recorded that his spirit moved Christ to words of enthusiastic praise. More, like the centurion, knows that he is 'a man under authority', and therefore, for all his gentleness, he can never be other than stern to those who deliberately defy discipline. Very rightly Nicholas Harpsfield spoke of More as a soldier: 'it is not known that ever he was in any warlike expedition', yet, although there are many English captains renowned for their chivalry, 'they drag all behind this our worthy captain'. And it was true insight that made Ruskin[1] put Sir Thomas

[1] *Fors Clavigera*, 22; *Works*, XXVII, p. 385.

More among the fighting men distinguished by their high quality of captainship – St. Louis and Richard Lion Heart, Drake and Sir Richard Grenville. More has just that mixture of endurance and cheeriness, which those who saw it among the sick and wounded in the hospitals during the war can never forget. More does not demand martyrdom, like the Christian saints of the medieval martyrologies: he will not be bold to offer himself to death, lest God, for his presumption, might suffer him to fall. But, if God commands, he trusts that God will not fail to give him grace and strength. I am reminded of the last words of a friend, Captain Howard Lister, who in his gentleness and his sternness, his courage and his modesty, had much of the spirit of Sir Thomas More:

I only pray that I may be able to do my duty without shrinking, even if with fear.

And it is this submission to discipline which gives the special character to More's martyrdom. Martyrs have generally been individualists; despisers of all mere human authority, they have often forgotten to render Caesar his due; many martyrs have been persons not given to reverent address; 'most martyrs', says Ruskin, 'have been made away with less for their faith than for their incivility'.[1]

More is the most civil of martyrs. Discipline, subjection, order, are his ideals. He is an official of Sixteenth Century England, with very little sympathy for the pedlar who will wax a meddler in theology. Nothing is gained by making him into a Nineteenth Century Liberal, and then complaining that he wasn't. He had been the first modern to draw a picture of the corporate state with its remorseless discipline. In *Utopia* he had reserved to the individual almost nothing, save the integrity of his soul: that no man who submitted loyally to the state discipline should be forced to say he believed that which he did not believe. He was willing to be silenced – the very idea of any seditious conduct was hateful to him. But when he had withdrawn into the last inviolate sanctuary he would yield nothing. He, who had placed the authority of the state so high, had nevertheless to give his life as a witness to the fact that there are some things which the state cannot command.

_____
[1] *Fors Clavigera*, 26; *Works*, XXVII, p. 480.

It has been remarked, with some truth, that the University man is not built for martyrdom. St. Paul, although proud of his University town of Tarsus and his College days in Jerusalem, found few volunteers for martyrdom among his fellow-students. He had to ask with pain, 'Where is the wise, where is the scribe?' Henry VIII, in 1534, had a most learned bench of bishops ('scarce one dunce wore a mitre in all Henry's days'[1]), but all save one could be intimidated. Even in the London Charterhouse, the percentage of stalwarts was somewhat higher among the unlearned lay-brethren than among the more literate choir-monks. And it was among humble folk that the greatest number of the Protestant martyrs under Mary were found. A scholar sees, or should see, both sides; and ability to see both sides makes for civility, but is inconducive to martyrdom.

Now in More the power of seeing both sides is enormously developed. It makes him love the dialogue, which he some-times uses in such a way that it is difficult to say where his sympathies lie. He is always slow, on account of mere differ-ences of opinion, to condemn the consciences of other men – violence and insubordination are another matter. We have seen how Cranmer, characteristically, seized hold of this out-look of More to persuade him to bend to Henry's will. If he did not condemn the consciences of other men, that showed, said Cranmer, that More regarded his own view as 'a thing uncer-tain and doubtful'; but he knew of a certainty that he ought to obey the King. Let him take refuge in certainties. But Cran-mer's own life was to be the *reductio ad absurdum* of his own argument. What was poor Cranmer to do when the civil power reversed its policy, and when the Queen and the Parliament of England commanded him to accept the Pope's supremacy? What could he do, but make change after change, and recanta-tion after recantation? Only on the last day of his life, did he come clearly to the position of Sir Thomas More. Without necessarily blaming the consciences of other men, he found that there were certain beliefs which he himself must hold, irrespective of what the Queen and the Parliament might tell him to believe. So he renounced 'things written with his hand,

[1] FULLER, *Church History*, 1655, p. 254.

contrary to the truth which he thought in his heart'; and saying 'this hand hath offended' he held it steadfastly in the flames till it was consumed.

From the moment of his imprisonment, More refused to judge any man. His controversial work was a thing of the past, and he was concerned only with his own conduct. This makes him the great example of all those who, rather than profess to believe what they do not believe, have given their lives cheerfully for any cause. We can think of him in the great words inscribed in the Harvard War Memorial Chapel over the names of the German students of Harvard who fell in 1914-18:

> Nor is the University of Harvard unmindful of her sons who, albeit under different banners, gave their lives for their country.

It is all in the great words of Abraham Lincoln, 'With firmness in the right, as God gives us to see the right'.

The real difference lies, not between Catholic and Protestant, but between Catholic and Protestant on the one side, and on the other the tools of Henry, the Norfolks and Riches and Southwells and Paulets. The creeds of Catholic and Anabaptist had more in common with each other than with the creed of these men, which contained but one simple clause, *The wrath of the King is death*. Or, to put it in the terms of *Utopia*, the difference lies between the men who merely obey the laws of the state, and the men who have, as every citizen of Utopia was bound to have, a belief that there is an ultimate standard of right and wrong, beyond what the state may at any moment command.

§ 12. SURSUM CORDA

And here is the last and greatest parallel between More and Socrates. Socrates as depicted by Plato respects the laws of his city so much that he will not violate them by escaping from prison, even to avoid a sentence which he believes to be unjust. That is the argument of the *Crito*. Nevertheless there are things as to which Socrates cannot obey the command of his city, even though the penalty be death. That is the argument of the *Apology*:

> I should have done a horrible thing, men of Athens, if, whilst

I stood my ground with the rest, even at the risk of death, and obeyed the generals whom you chose to command me at Potidaea and Amphipolis and Delium, yet, when the god gave me a station, I were to desert my post from fear of death or any other thing.

More believed, as Socrates believed, that 'the god had given him a station'. And he strengthened himself, as Socrates had strengthened himself, with the conviction that no harm can come to a good man after death, and that the gods do not neglect him or his affairs. In *Utopia* and on the scaffold we have those two great articles of More's creed.

We are so used to pious, platitudinous, meaningless phrases about these ultimate things that it is difficult for us to understand the reality of them to More. That is what struck Erasmus and surprised him. This reality is a theme which occurs everywhere in More's writings and More's life – that others should not feel it, as he does, is with More a topic often of indignant protest, often of humorous amusement. So to Mistress Alice in the Tower:

'I pray thee, good Mistress Alice, tell me . . . is not this house as nigh heaven as mine own?'

To whom she answered, 'Tilly vally, Tilly vally.'

'How say you, Mistress Alice,' quoth he, 'is it not so?'

'Bone deus, Bone deus, man, will this gear never be left?' quoth she.

More watching Dame Alice is like Shakespeare watching Mistress Quickly by Falstaff's death-bed:

'How now, Sir John!' quoth I: 'what, man! be o' good cheer.' So a' cried out, 'God, God, God!' three or four times. Now I, to comfort him, bid him a' should not think of God; I hoped there was no need to trouble himself with any such thoughts yet.

'To look first unto God, and after God unto the King', meant everything to More. Sidney Lee dismisses the words as an empty phrase of 'conventional counsel'. Lee was one of the best of men, but he could not see that to More the words meant what he himself would have expressed as 'a guarantee of complete liberty of conscience'.

But, if there be indeed some power dwelling in the heart of

man, which may give him commands at variance with those of
the State to which he is also subject; if there be, besides the
written laws, what Antigone calls the unwritten and unfailing
laws of the gods; if man must render, not only to Caesar the
things that be Caesar's, but to God the things that be God's;
how is poor man to decide which things belong to which?
More placed the right of the State to silence the individual very
much higher, and the right of the individual to claim liberty of
conscience from the State very much lower than we in England
should place them to-day. Yet he died for the right of the
individual conscience, as against the State. Hence he has been
attacked on both sides; in his own day, and occasionally since,
because he claimed any right whatever against the all-
competent, supreme State; by the English historians in the
great Whig and Liberal tradition of the Eighteenth and Nineteenth Centuries, because he conceded to the State so much.
The problem of what is due to the individual conscience, what
to the State, is indeed an eternal one, and not a few people
have been surprised and distressed to find it emerging in
Europe to-day, as much alive as ever it was. 'Wherefore our
battle is immortal, and the gods and angels fight on our side,
and we are their possessions ... And the things that save us are
justice, self-command, and true thought, which things dwell in
the living powers of the gods.'[1] So wrote Plato, naming three
of the four Cardinal Virtues on which Utopia is founded –
Fortitude is the fourth. Plato's fine words do not solve the
problem for us; every man at need must do it for himself, for
the ability to weigh two duties, and balance them against each
other, is the measure of human worth and dignity. It rings
through the *Antigone* of Sophocles as it does through the *Apology*
of Socrates, and nowhere will it be found more clearly than in
More's writings in prison. It was as one of a mighty company
that, on Tuesday, 6 July 1535, he spoke on the scaffold his last
words:

> that they should pray for him in this world, and he would
> pray for them elsewhere, protesting that he died the King's
> good servant, but God's first.

[1] *Laws*, Book x, quoted by Ruskin, *Fors Clavigera*, Letter 76.

NOTES AND INDEX

BIBLIOGRAPHICAL NOTE

Quotations made without further detail are from the following editions:

The Life of Sir Thomas More, by William Roper, edited by E. V. Hitchcock, 1935. (First critical text with collations of manuscripts.)

The Life and Death of Sir Thomas More, by Nicholas Harpsfield, edited by E. V. Hitchcock, with historical notes by R. W. Chambers, 1932. (First edition.)

The Rastell Fragments, printed as an Appendix to Harpsfield's *Life*, 1932.

The *Paris News Letter*, describing More's death, printed as an Appendix to Harpsfield's *Life*, 1932.

Vita Thomae Mori, in the *Tres Thomae* of Thomas Stapleton, 1588. Page references are to the Cologne edition of 1612, as the most accessible; but the chapter number is also given, so that the passage can be traced in the English translation of Mgr. Philip Hallett, 1928.

The Life of Sir Thomas More, by his great-grandson [Cresacre More]. Page references are to the edition of 1726, as easily accessible. That, like other early editions, erroneously attributes the *Life* to Cresacre's brother Thomas.

The Life of Blessed Thomas More, by T. E. Bridgett, 1891. (The standard modern *Life*, which can never be superseded.)

Utopia, in Latin and English, with notes by J. H. Lupton, Oxford, 1895.

The Workes of Sir Thomas More, wrytten in the Englysh tonge, London, 1557. (Quoted as *Works*, 1557.)

The English Works of Sir Thomas More, edited by W. E. Campbell, with introductions and notes by A. W. Reed, R. W. Chambers and W. A. G. Doyle Davidson. Vol. 1, 1931, etc. *In progress*. (A reproduction of the edition of 1557, with modernized version and apparatus.)

Thomae Mori Lucubrationes, Basel, 1563.

Opus Epistolarum Des. Erasmi Roterodami, recognitum per P. S. et H. M. Allen. Oxford, 1906, etc. *In progress*. (Quoted as 'Allen' by volume and number of letter.)

The Epistles of Erasmus, arranged by F. M. Nichols, London, 1901-17. A translation, with most valuable commentary, of the letters to Dec. 1518.

Calendar of Letters and Papers, Foreign and Domestic, of the reign of Henry VIII, vols. 1-4, ed. by J. S. Brewer, vols. 5-21, ed. by J. Gairdner, 1862-1910. (Quoted as *L.P.*, by volume and number of document.)

State Papers, published under the authority of His Majesty's Commission: vol. 1, King Henry VIII. 1830. (Quoted as *State Papers*.)

A Calendar of the Correspondence of Sir Thomas More, by Elizabeth F. Rogers. In the *English Historical Review*, 1922, pp. 546-564. (Most valuable. Dr. Rogers is preparing an edition of More's correspondence.)

ADDITIONAL NOTES

pp. 60, etc. Peter Giles. Biographers of More and Erasmus have used both forms of the name, *Giles* and *Gilles*. It might have been better to have used *Gilles*. Professor Geyl writes '*Giles* sounds impossible to Dutch ears; *Gilles* on the contrary is a well-known surname'.

p. 103. The *Journal of the Court of Common Council* records that, on 13 Dec. 1509, Thomas More, Mercer, was elected one of the burgesses for the City in the forthcoming Parliament. In the notes to Harpsfield's *Life* (p. 312) we refused to regard this as referring to our Thomas More, because he is always referred to in the *Journal* and *Repertory* as Thomas More, gent., or Thomas More, jun. We were inclined to identify the burgess of Parliament with a Thomas More, Mercer, who is referred to as deceased in the *Journal* (20 Oct. 1513). But Prof. A. W. Reed has pointed out that in the Balliol MS. 354 (Richard Hill's *Commonplace Book*), folio 236 verso, 'Yong More, burges of the parlament for London', occurs against the year 1510. (See p. 156 of *Songs, Carols and other miscellaneous poems from the Balliol MS. 354*, edited by R. Dyboski, 1907, *Early English Text Society*). 'Young More' at this date always means our Thomas More. Of course, Hill's note may arise from a mistaken identification, but, in view of it, it would be interesting to establish the identity of the Thomas More who was made free of the Mercers' company 'by redemption gratis' on 21 March, 1508 (Watney, *Hospital of St. Thomas of Acon*, 1906, p. 86). It seems certain that, about this time, our Thomas More was performing services for the Mercers (Watney, *The Mercers Company*, 1914, p. 23). The matter needs, and is receiving, further attention.

pp. 121, 170, 371. Luther published his 95 Theses on the door of All Saints' Church, Wittenberg, at the anniversary festival. All Saints' day (1 Nov.) was 'the day of the year which drew the largest concourse to the church' (Lindsay, *History of the Reformation*, 1909, I, 214). It is therefore a 'memorable' date, as the authors of '1066 and all that' would say. I have accordingly allowed the traditional date, 1 November, 1517, to stand, although it is undoubtedly true that the theses were actually nailed up on the eve of All Saints' day.

INDEX

BY ELSIE V. HITCHCOCK

The references are to pages. 'M' or 'More' signifies 'Thomas More'. Head-words in square brackets do not occur in the text. Owing to limitation of space, footnotes are indexed only in cases of special importance.